Putinomics

Albrecht Rothacher

Putinomics

How the Kremlin Damages the Russian Economy

 Springer

LAKE VILLA DISTRICT LIBRARY
847.356.7711 www.lvdl.org

Albrecht Rothacher
Brussels, Belgium

ISBN 978-3-030-74076-4   ISBN 978-3-030-74077-1 (eBook)
https://doi.org/10.1007/978-3-030-74077-1

© The Editor(s) (if applicable) and The Author(s), under exclusive license to Springer Nature Switzerland AG 2021
This work is subject to copyright. All rights are solely and exclusively licensed by the Publisher, whether the whole or part of the material is concerned, specifically the rights of translation, reprinting, reuse of illustrations, recitation, broadcasting, reproduction on microfilms or in any other physical way, and transmission or information storage and retrieval, electronic adaptation, computer software, or by similar or dissimilar methodology now known or hereafter developed.
The use of general descriptive names, registered names, trademarks, service marks, etc. in this publication does not imply, even in the absence of a specific statement, that such names are exempt from the relevant protective laws and regulations and therefore free for general use.
The publisher, the authors and the editors are safe to assume that the advice and information in this book are believed to be true and accurate at the date of publication. Neither the publisher nor the authors or the editors give a warranty, expressed or implied, with respect to the material contained herein or for any errors or omissions that may have been made. The publisher remains neutral with regard to jurisdictional claims in published maps and institutional affiliations.

This Springer imprint is published by the registered company Springer Nature Switzerland AG
The registered company address is: Gewerbestrasse 11, 6330 Cham, Switzerland

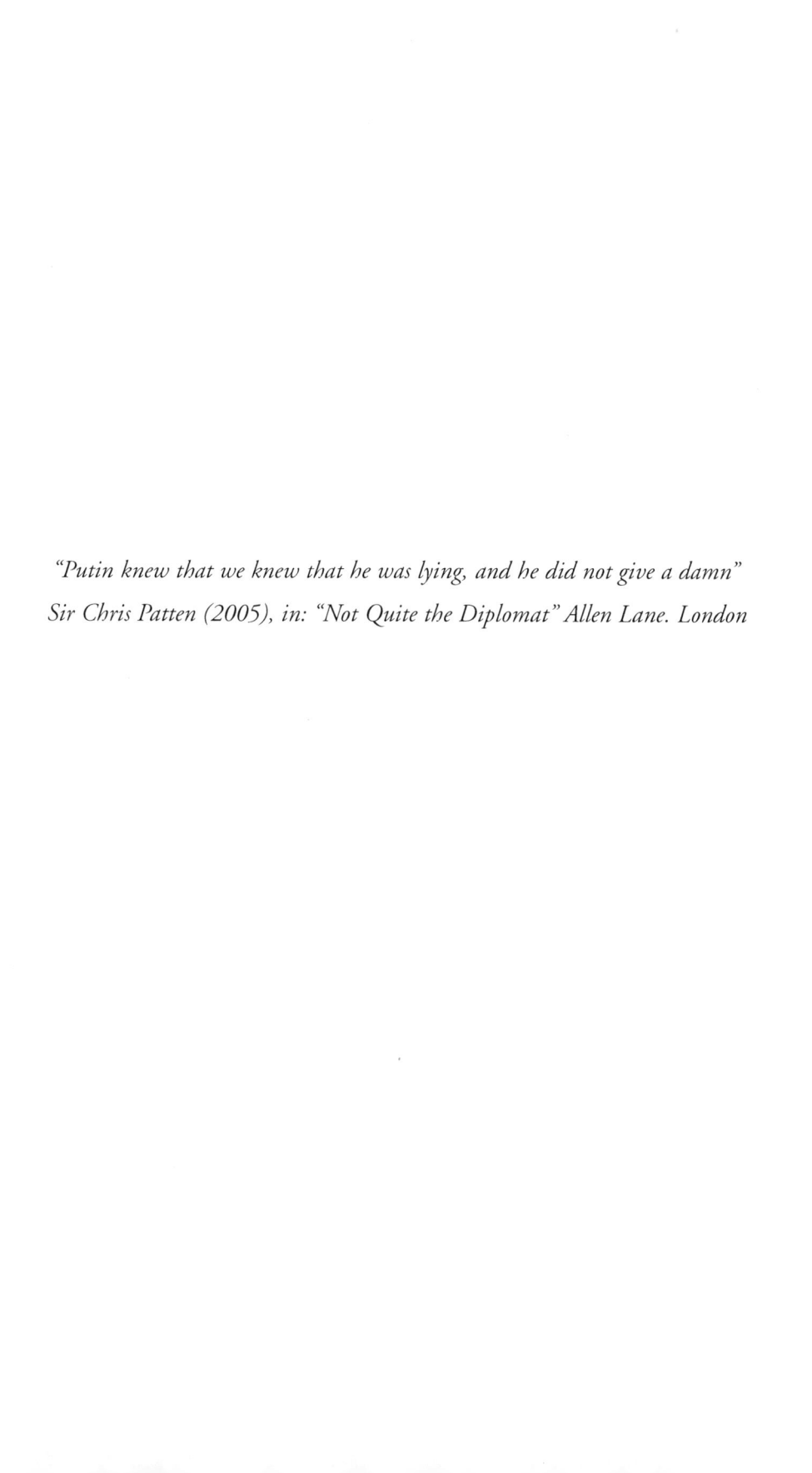

"Putin knew that we knew that he was lying, and he did not give a damn"
Sir Chris Patten (2005), in: "Not Quite the Diplomat" Allen Lane. London

Preface

Abstract The introduction usefully summarizes the results of this monograph: How the narrowly based St. Petersburg clique of former KGB officers around Putin took control of the semi-privatized energy sector, muzzled or expropriated the Yeltsin oligarchs, and since three decades have set up their own state based management and control of key sectors of the Russian economy: oil, gas, minerals, armaments, banks, aviation and railways. Their self-serving and unpredictable "rule by law" continues to encourage endemic corruption and capital flight and to discourage investments, both foreign and domestic, the development of SMEs and the urgently needed diversification of Russia's raw material based economy.

Russia is a country of surprises, positive and negative. I remember back in 1980, when flying from Niigata in Japan to Khabarovsk (Vladivostok was still a forbidden city) to take the Transib to Berlin via Moscow and Minsk—as a doctoral student I had plenty of time—a customs officer immediately fished a dissident book out of my rucksack, and judging from my East German experiences I was sure never ever to see it again. Fifteen minutes later his boss, the chief of Khabarovsk customs, came and handed the book back to me and said: "Oh, I see you read very interesting stuff. May God bless your journey!" And this was in the middle of Brezhnev's communism.

So, Russia remained a life-long intellectual and political passion. I have dealt with Russia when posted as a Counsellor at the EU Delegation to OSCE in Vienna during 2006–2010, as an exchange diplomat at the Quai d'Orsay during 2015–2017 and more recently as a principal administrator in charge of bilateral economic and trade issues with Russia at the European External Action Service in Brussels. During these years I had plenty of often fascinating exchanges with Russians in power like ministers, ambassadors, diplomats, lobbyists and spies, but surely more interestingly ones with those who were out of power and were often incredibly courageous and perceptive dissidents, scholars and journalists, and also with those who were in-between (like I would have been).

So for me, given Russia's intellectual and enormously rich literary heritage, the question of her belonging to Europe's civilization is not an issue, far from it. Rather, Russia conserves many of the traditional values which have become abused in the West. Yet the question is about governance. And there have to be very big question marks, as the reader will see.

This book is based on public sources which are duly quoted. Needless to say that my conclusions are all personal and do not represent the positions of my previous employer. Secrets are not revealed. So, there is no need for libel suits or for GRU-Speznaz operations to shorten my life expectancy.

Russia is by far the largest country on earth, which as various invaders, from Napoleon to Hitler, have shown, it is practically invincible. Yet, its population stagnates at 143 million, even after the repatriation of millions of ethnic Russians from Central Asia (often former deportees and their offspring) and after adding on some 2.5 million Crimeans forcefully in 2014. Two million of their best and brightest have left during the last 10 years. There was $350 billion in capital flight for good and bad reasons. Three million businessmen were prosecuted for shakeouts. As a result of this hostile economic environment and in spite of the great talents of Russian graduates in mathematics and in the sciences, there is little innovation and economic stagnation. The country technologically simply falls further behind the West and China.

Basically, Russia now appears a corrupt petro-state with huge demographic problems, with its working population shrinking rapidly. Deaths by accidents, violence, alcohol, drugs, abortion and transmittable diseases (from hepatitis to AIDS), with which a neglected health sector cannot cope, have taken their toll. Male live expectancy still hovers around 66. Women, who are wiser, live a decade longer. By the time Putin is likely to leave his office (one way or the other), Russia will have less inhabitants than Turkey, Nigeria or the Congo, with its GDP remaining at the level of Spain and much below Italy. So much for a presumptive world power.

A total 110 individuals (including Putin's cronies, his relatives and himself) control 35% of Russia's wealth, while 50% of Russian households have a "fortune" of $870 or lower. Again, this is not Angola or Nigeria, but happens in an East-European civilization. In short, Putin's policies have led Russia into a lower-middle-income trap, from which there is no escape, given the weakness of the manufacturing and service sector, unless competition and property protection legislation is enacted effectively, and productive FDI is genuinely encouraged. It is as simple as that.

Failing this Russia remains dependent on the unpredictable vagaries of the global commodities markets and of the fluctuations of the world oil prices in particular. At $45 per barrel Russia's budget will be ok, but below that it has a serious problem. This surely is not a sustainable policy.

As the events of the crises of 1998, 2008, 2014 and 2020 proved, such external shocks could not be absorbed by national emergency funds alone for long. And Putin's business model of gas exports to subsidize Russian wasteful heavy industry, and of its oil industry to prop up the national budget to finance his military and private pet projects, might no longer work. His decades of abusive power have left a tragedy for the more educated parts of the workforce who after all have deserved better.

German Chancellor Helmut Schmidt once famously said that the Soviet Union was Upper Volta (now called Burkina Faso) with missiles. Unfortunately, under Putin's state monopoly capitalism fundamentally very little has changed in this mismatch, although the queues for soap and sugar have disappeared. It is still a military giant and an economic dwarf with a GDP of the size of Spain. Putin will not change his ways. He will continue to reward his corrupt friends generously and punish critics and opponents mercilessly.

Is it legitimate to personalize Putin's economic policies? After all, neither the US nor the French president can do much to change the economic fundamentals of their countries. Yet from the beginning of his presidency 20 years ago, he systematically centralized his personal power and altered the course of Russia's fragile transition economy towards a model of state-controlled monopolist capitalism and for the enrichment of the small band of his trusted personal friends and of himself—often at the expense of the old oligarchs (whom he either expropriated, drove them into exile or cut them down to size), but mostly paid for by the welfare losses of the population at large—and of other bureaucratic and secret service clans which followed the Kremlin's lead with impunity.

The results of this kleptocratic mismanagement are as striking as they were predictable. The glamour and glitter of Moscow, St. Petersburg and Sochi apart, the underdevelopment and depopulation of the regions with their decrepit infrastructure and national poverty rates at 25–30% is palpable. And yet in spite of expensive protectionist policies Russia is persistently unable to diversify from its dependency on raw material extraction and to develop competitive services and industries, apart from armaments. Private entrepreneurship is systematically discouraged, denied credit from state banks, subject to arbitrary taxation, other bureaucratic harassment, and subjected to frequent arbitrary arrests. The Kremlin in general—and Putin in person—simply distrusts an emerging economically independent middle class, which he perceives as a threat to his autocratic rule. Hence the repression does not come by accident. With the lack of effective property protection capital flight has taken endemic proportions, since 2008 fluctuating between $60 billion and $150 billion per year, corresponding to 4–10% of GDP. But also people are leaving for good. 50% of the most educated and prosperous citizens and 30% of 18–24-year-olds have declared their intention to leave Russia, as they see no future, fear insecurity and the dangers from law enforcement (though many of them undoubtedly eventually will stay). In turn, the country received about 9 million mostly poorly qualified migrant workers from Central Asia and the South Caucasus. This is surely not the way to modernize a country and to diversity its economy, rather the opposite.

Basically, Putinism is about control through the state security apparatus: over the provinces, the parties, the media, the judiciary and the economy. To be fair, Russia is not China. In spite of frequent police harassment, some political opposition, critical media, NGOs and foreign thinktanks are still tolerated, provided that they don't become dangerous. The World Wide Web is freely accessible. People can travel as they like at home and abroad and courageously speak out their minds.

Putin's goal is not to present an alternative economic and political model (unlike his earlier advisers Vladimir Yakunin and Vladislav Surkov, who advocated Russia's exceptionalism and the concept of sovereign democracy to preserve its unique superior values). Rather in his foreign policies, apart from aggressively expanding Russia's influence in her "near abroad" of the old Soviet Union and the Balkans, he seeks to undermine Western democracies which he sees as a threat to his rule—as role models they had helped to overthrow Communism, had aided the colour revolutions from Georgia to Kirgizstan and to generate the Maidan revolt of 2014 against his equally corrupt but less competent puppet Yanukovych. Instabilities, which Putin like all turmoil, including the October Revolution but also democratic elections with unpredictable outcomes, instinctively abhors.

Thus like most Soviet leaders before, who learnt from their surprising success in 1917—Czarism after all had recklessly provoked and lost the

Crimean War of 1854–1855, the Russo-Japanese War of 1904–1905 and the First World War in the East (1914–1917)—Putin takes only calculated risks. He uses perceived Western weaknesses and indecision, like against his war against Georgia in 2008, the annexation of the Crimea in 2014 and the ongoing military intervention in Syria. But he conducts only limited wars which can be stopped any time at short notice, if an escalation threatens.

Putin's personal power seems unlimited being, like the old Czars, responsible only to God. In other presidential systems, like the US, the President's powers are checked by a federal system, a powerful Congress, an independent judiciary and a very free press. Putin does not have to worry about an impeachment nor about a lost election. There is a bit more analogies between Putin's Kremlin and the Elysée (as created by de Gaulle for the V. Republic). Both decide on all major policy issues, including war and peace, and the ministries are told to execute in centralist structures, with parliaments usually being weak and compliant (unless in France the President loses his majority there and has to enter into cohabitation with the opposition). Yet the analogies end here. Unlike in Russia, in France the judiciary is fiercely independent, the opposition unhindered, the press vigilant and the public does not tolerate corruption and the abuse of power. As a result, French presidents (which preside in the Elysée in royal style, bien sur) leave their office with an upper-middle-class wealth (usually a chic apartment in Paris and a modest house in the countryside) as before.

Gary Kasparov once famously wrote—with slight exaggeration: "Putin wants to rule like Joseph Stalin and live like Roman Abramovich". Indeed, the obsession with status and money of the current Russian elite is striking. Why does one need to steal $10 billion when, say, $10 million are more than sufficient for a very comfortable life at home and abroad, especially since Putin and his friends in the Kremlin live in a money-free world? When his girlfriend wants a diamond, he does not have to check his wallet or his bank account. The answer probably lies in his insecurity. As he was afraid of the oligarchs' money and power, early on he decided to give only to his close and trusted friends. Once in place, this unchecked kleptocracy took on a life of its own and into a virility contest of who owns more and whose palaces, yachts and airplanes were bigger. In the course time—20 years already and no end in sight—an element of pharaonic delusion developed, perhaps inevitably so after two decades of absolute power. One such example is Sochi at the Black Sea, where Putin had himself build 1$ billion palace. Like Peter the Great in St. Petersburg, the resort had to be built up to splendour out of almost nothing, regardless of the financial or ecological costs.

As a result, during goods years—i.e. with world oil prices above $45 per barrel, which were needed to break even the federal budget—one-third of the export revenues were pocketed by some 200 people, one-third was used to increase public wages and was eaten up by inflation, and one-third was wasted, like for the 2014 Olympics, the soccer world cup of 2018 and for military adventures. With a lower oil price there will be no alternative but a new round of collective belt-tightening, to which the Russian people are accustomed and which they usually stoically accept, but given Russia's cross-social inequalities the sacrifice will equally be distributed unevenly surely not hurting Putin's cronies.

As he is about to extent his term in office until 2036, making him more or president for life, with him a brilliant tactician but not a strategic thinker, he is unlikely to change his ways and policies which so far against all odds have put him in power and kept him there, while all other world leaders whom he met early have faded in the meantime. Thus, the long-term ruin of the Russian economy in all likeliness unfortunately is set to continue.

While in real life there are sometimes positive surprises when expectations are low, yet in Russian fairy tales there are only very few happy endings.

Brussels, Belgium
November 2020

Albrecht Rothacher

Contents

1 **From Alexander II to Gorbachev: The Economic History of Modern Russia** 1
   1.1   The Autocratic Czarist Era (1613–1914) 2
        1.1.1   A Case Study: von Wogau & Co 11
   1.2   The War Economy (1914–1917) 13
   1.3   The Civil War, War Communism and the New Economic Policies (1918–1924) 17
   1.4   The Soviet Economy (1924–1991) 20
        1.4.1   The Gulag Economy (1921–1954) 23
        1.4.2   The War Economy of WWII and Post-war Policies 28
        1.4.3   Mono-industrial Cities 31
        1.4.4   Perestroika and Its Origins 32
   1.5   The Transformation of the Soviet Economy 37
   References 40

2 **Post-Soviet Industrial Policy: From the Red Directors to the New State Oligarchs** 43
   2.1   Putin's State Monopoly Capitalism 44
   2.2   The Red Directors 47
   2.3   A Short Story of the Russian Oligarchy 49
   2.4   The Russian Crisis of 1998 51
   2.5   Putin's Start as President 52

	2.6	The Fate of Oligarchs I—Falling Out of Favour	54
		2.6.1 Vladimir Gusinsky (1952–)	56
		2.6.2 Boris Berezovsky (1946–2013)	58
		2.6.3 Mikhail Khodorkovsky (1963–)	62
	2.7	The Fate of Oligarchs II: Super-Rich, Obedient and Still Tolerated	67
		2.7.1 Roman Abramovich (1966–)	67
		2.7.2 Oleg Deripaska (1968–)	71
		2.7.3 Vladimir Potanin (1961–)	76
		2.7.4 Mikhael Fridman (1964–)	78
		2.7.5 Viktor Vekselberg (1957–)	80
		2.7.6 Yuri Luzhkov (1936–2019) and Sistema	80
	2.8	Other Fallen Oligarchs	82
		2.8.1 Yevgeny Chichvarkin	82
		2.8.2 Sergey Pugachev	83
		2.8.3 Ziyamudin and Magomed Magomedov	84
	2.9	Putin's State Monopoly Capitalism	85
		2.9.1 Gazprom First	85
		2.9.2 Russia's Energy Export Policy	87
		2.9.3 Rosneft	90
		2.9.4 Case Study: Bill Browder's Hermitage Fund	91
	2.10	Putinocrats	93
	2.11	Conclusion I: Wealth and Economic Power in Russia	96
	2.12	Conclusion II: Whither the Russian Economy?	100
	References		104
3	**Putin's Autocracy: Siloviki Rule and Their Kleptocracy**		**105**
	3.1	Putin's Political Biography: From Leningrad to Dresden	106
	3.2	In St. Petersburg	108
	3.3	In Moscow	108
	3.4	The Putin System and Its Ideology	112
	3.5	The Legal System According to Putin	116
	3.6	The KGB in Power	116
		3.6.1 Anna Politkovskaya's Testimony	122
		3.6.2 Alexander Litvinenko's Testimony	124
		3.6.3 The Case of Alexei Navalny	127
	3.7	Early Corruption: Putin in St. Petersburg	129
	3.8	Corruption in Yeltsin's Kremlin: Putin in Moscow	135
	3.9	The Tragedy of the Kursk	139

	3.10	The Case of Chechnya	140
	3.11	Putin as President: The Kleptocracy	141
		3.11.1 The Sergei Magnitzky Case	147
		3.11.2 The Case of Michael Calvey	149
	3.12	Economic Mismanagement in the Later Putin Years	150
		3.12.1 The Riches of Putinism	154
	References		155
4	**Putin's Budget Policies**		**157**
	4.1	The Figures and Prospects	158
	4.2	Budget Politics	160
	4.3	Conclusion	162
	References		162
5	**The Russian Petro-State**		**163**
	5.1	The History	163
	5.2	The Oil Industry	166
		5.2.1 The Soviet Oil Industry and Its Decline	168
		5.2.2 The Battle for the Oil Industry	171
	5.3	Putin's Power Structures in the Oil and Gas Industry	178
		5.3.1 The End of Yukos	180
		5.3.2 Rosneft's New Role	182
		5.3.3 The Crisis of 2008/2009	184
		5.3.4 The Regulatory System	186
		5.3.5 The Outlook	187
	5.4	The Gas Industry	189
	5.5	Putin's Logic	192
	5.6	Pipeline Politics	194
		5.6.1 The Nord Stream 1 and 2 Story	199
		5.6.2 Gerhard Schröder's Russian Energy Career	201
		5.6.3 Gas Pipelines in Asia	202
		5.6.4 Policy Implications	203
	References		204
6	**The Liberalization of Russia's Electricity Market**		**205**
	6.1	The Soviet Heritage	206
	6.2	The First Reforms	207
	6.3	Electricity Under Putin	208
	6.4	Conclusion	211
	Reference		212

xvi   Contents

7	**The State-Controlled Banks and the State-Owned Enterprises and Their Privileges**	213
	7.1 The Finance Sector	215
	7.2 Insurances	218
	7.3 The Stock and Bond Market	218
	7.4 The Capital Markets	219
	7.5 State-Owned Enterprises (SOEs)	219
	7.6 Public Procurement	221
	7.7 Trade Restrictions	222
	7.8 Investments	224
	References	225
8	**Russian Industry**	227
	8.1 The Development	227
	8.2 The Soviet Planning System	231
	8.3 Russian Defence Industries and Their Chinese Competitors	233
	8.4 Russia's Car Industry and Its Cooperation with European Makers	239
9	**Russia's Railways and Logistics**	245
10	**Russian Agriculture, Forestry and the Agrofood Business**	251
	10.1 The Natural Conditions	252
	10.2 The Russian Farmers	254
	10.3 After the Revolution	256
	10.4 The Holodomor	257
	10.5 The Kolkhoz and Sovkhoz Economy	258
	10.6 Soviet Agricultural Policies	264
	10.7 The Reprivatization Process of Collectivized Land—And How It Failed in the Black Earth Region	267
	10.8 The Russian Land Market	270
	10.9 Agriculture in a Market Economy of Sorts	271
	10.10 The New Agrobusiness	274
	10.11 Exports and Agricultural Protection	279
	10.12 The Agricultural Policies of the Eurasian Economic Union (EEU)	280
	10.13 The Tiraspol Kvint Distillery—A Case Study of Vicissitudes and Survival	282
	10.14 Russian Wine Production Today	291
	10.15 Forestry and Timber Exports	292

11	**Russian SMEs and Their Problems**		297
	11.1	R&D and Training	299
	11.2	Governance Problems	299
	11.3	Access to Finance	301
	11.4	SME Policies	301
	11.5	Conclusion	302
	Reference		303
12	**External Trade: The Roles of the EU, of the Eurasian Economic Union and of China**		305
	12.1	EU–Russia Trade Relations	305
	12.2	Russia and the Eurasian Economic Union (EEU)	308
	12.3	A Very Unequal Alliance	310
		12.3.1 The Politics and Economics of China–Russian Relations	310

About the Author

Albrecht Rothacher was born in 1955 in Erlangen (Germany). After military service he studied social sciences at universities in Berlin, Konstanz, Bridgeport and Yale (Connecticut), Tokyo and at the EUI in Florence. He obtained his Ph.D. at the London School of Economics. After a stint at Deutsche Bank and as a lecturer at FU Berlin he joined the diplomatic service of the European Commission with posts in Vienna, Paris, Singapore and Tokyo, last as a Minister Counsellor. He dealt with Russia professionally for many years, lastly as a principal administrator in charge of bilateral economic and trade relations at headquarters of the European External Action Service in Brussels. He published some 25 books and numerous articles notably on economic and military history and on European, Eurasian and East Asian politics.

1

From Alexander II to Gorbachev: The Economic History of Modern Russia

One of the striking features of Russia's contemporary economy, even a quarter-century after the fall of communism, is the persistence of—ever-growing—state involvement in the economy. By 2018, 80% of banks are state-controlled and so are the all-important resource sectors, their infrastructure and their exports, as well as the armaments industry as part of a tightly controlled military-industrial complex, and the railways. Even the forests remain all (bad managed) state property. Obviously, the wild privatizations and the preaching of liberal economics during the Yeltsin years have had a little lasting impact. Not just the siloviki entourage in charge of the Kremlin's economic policy, but also the public at large seems to believe firmly that the economy has to serve Russia's policies and public interests, and not the other way around. Even if there is little nostalgia to return to the organized inefficiencies, the shortages and the pilferage of state planning, competition only appears to confuse, duplicate efforts and risk investments. Hence the popularity of state and oligarchical monopolies in the key industries, even if they go at the expense of prices, services, quality and innovation with consumers ultimately paying monopoly rents as collateral damage of the system. Ultimately the population becomes a victim of its own economic illiteracy.

The question obviously arises: Is this sorry state of play only an accident of history, the heritage of seventy years of Bolshevism, or is it the consequence of a traditional Russian way of running the economy in difference to the "West" (which many Russian interlocutors suggest)? For evidence, we need to look

© The Author(s), under exclusive license to Springer Nature Switzerland AG 2021
A. Rothacher, *Putinomics*,
https://doi.org/10.1007/978-3-030-74077-1_1

at the modernizing decades of the Czarist days, until the advent of the war economy (1914–1917).

1.1 The Autocratic Czarist Era (1613–1914)

With little doubt, the co-existence of a centralized arbitrary autocracy under the Romanovs (1613–1917) with the vast majority of the people living as illiterate subsistence farmers in serfdom, from which they were only belatedly and gradually liberated in 1866 by Alexander II, with an underdeveloped urban bourgeoisie and educated middle class had lasting effects on economic and civic behaviour. People had internalized to avoid initiatives and to take decisions, to shirk responsibilities and saw virtue to live on with only a minimum effort. At the same time, a strong sense of egalitarianism was prevalent among peasants and later urban workers alike, which perceived individual efforts and differences in wealth as basically illegitimate.

In addition, there are enduring factors of geography and climate. As Trotsky puts it: "The population of this gigantic and austere plain open to Eastern winds and Asiatic migrations was condemned by nature itself to a long backwardness. The struggle with nomads lasted almost to the end of the seventeenth century, the struggle with winds bringing winter cold and summer drought continues still. Agriculture, the basis of the whole development, advanced by extensive methods. In the north they cut down and burned up the forests, in the south they ravished the virgin steppes."[1]

While the frozen Northern tundra remains impossible to cultivate, and the forest belt of the taiga, apart from slash and burn, is suitable only for hunting, fishing and forestry, further South the fertile Black earth belt made Czarist Russia in the nineteenth century—as well as Putinist Russia in 2017—the world's foremost exporter of wheat and oilseeds. Yet vast regions of the Southern steppe remain suitable for extensive pastoral uses only. In addition, long cold winters shortened the growing season. Farming techniques remained primitive well into the mid-nineteenth century with wooden ploughs, the lack of fertilizers, strip farming and under-motivated serf labour. Hence low productivity subsistence agriculture was the base reason for Russia's poverty well up to the beginning of the twentieth century.

One further handicap was that Russia's continental landmass was virtually land-locked, even after its centuries of relentless territorial expansion: The Caspian Sea, the Black Sea, the Baltic Sea and the Sea of Japan were

---

[1] Leon Trotsky. *The History of the Russian Revolution*, Vol. I, London: Penguin 1932, p. 23.

more or less inland seas whose exits were controlled by foreign powers. The Barents Sea in the North was mostly blocked by ice. In difference to the early capitalist nations of the Northern Mediterranean, the Atlantic and the North Sea, Russia did not develop through navigation, foreign commerce and banking. Rather it remained a quasi-colonial economy, exporting unprocessed raw materials and importing manufactured and luxury goods.

Most importantly, it lacked commercial law and legal codes protecting private property and inheritance and enforcing contracts. The Orthodox Church focused on spiritual values and salvation through pious works. The notion of a Protestant work ethic, valuing hard work, savings and the accumulation of capital remained utterly alien.[2]

Western ideas, whether religious, political, economic or moral, were seen with great suspicion and fought with censorship, travel restrictions and the promotion of anti-Western ideologies. Yet public attitudes with a mixture of envy, admiration and detestation remained ambivalent, almost schizophrenic, notably as Western technology and societal progress appeared as vastly superior to Russia's backwardness. Peter the Great (1682–1725) systematically invited Western engineers, counsellors and capital, especially to modernize the military in order to achieve Russia's aspirations for great power status. The urge for military reform according to Western patterns was felt even greater after the defeat in the Crimean War (1853–1856). Then French, British, Italian and Turkish forces fought victoriously. Russian deficiencies from tactics to armaments, naval power and logistics—in the absence of railways South of Moscow supplies were still relying on ox carts, trekking for weeks through the Southern steppe being unable to supply the Black Sea fleet with coal and the troops with modern weapons, ammunition, food and medical supplies, let alone lift the one-year-long siege—were striking compared with the Western expeditionary forces.[3] In the end, the lack of Russian military reserves, financial exhaustion, an overburdened transport system and with epidemics raging among the malnourished and exhausted troops with approximately 300,000 deaths on both sides forced Russia to abandon her imperial ambitions towards the Ottoman Empire.[4]

Yet progress in the West remained stronger, and the notion to catch up turned illusionary throughout the nineteenth century.[5] Some Czars like Nikolai I (1825–1855), shocked by the Decembrist coup attempt (1825) and by the Polish uprising (1831), sought to preserve social stability and

---

[2]W.E. Mosse. *An Economic History of Russia 1856–1914*. London: I.B. Tauris. 1996, p. 6.
[3]Alain Gouttman. *La Guerre de Crimée 1853–1856*. Paris: Perrin 2006 (1995) p. 84 and p. 119.
[4]Gouttman. Op. cit., p. 373.
[5]Mosse. Op. cit., p. 13.

their autocratic rule—in his case by holding back early industrialization and railway construction taking place elsewhere in Europe. His successor Alexander II (1855–1881) with the help of French capital started railway construction in earnest. In 1856, he warned the Moscow nobility that it was better to abolish serfdom from above than to wait until it was abolished from below.[6] The issue was complicated by Russia's complex agricultural geography. In the rich Black earth zone of the South, landlords were interested to keep the land for commercial operations. They did not mind freeing the farmers, who thus far had to serve as unpaid labour at least three days a week (*bartschina*) nominally with little incentive to work hard and to hire them as cheap labourers instead. In the infertile Northern woodlands, the owners did not care about their landed property, as long as they owned the serfs, whose artisanal production they exploited as cash-based rents (*obrok*).[7] After a struggle of four years with the conservative gentry, Alexander II in 1861 managed to liberate the 47 million serfs (38% of the population of the European part of Russia), which however remained largely landless, except for their huts, farmyards and a patch of land for subsistence and got rid of their unpaid labour obligations for their former owners only after long years of transition. However, they had to pay their landlords 16 2/3 times the value of their annual labour, with 80% of the sum advanced by the state. The farmers had to pay this debt back for 49 years including interest.[8] Many smallholders in fact resented their liberation, being afraid of the economic risks as independent small farmers. Clearly, nearly all of them remained very poor. Due to high birth rates, the rural population grew quickly and average farm sizes remained minimal. Lacking draft animals and capital, wives often had to pull the wooden ploughs, sowing was done by hand and harvesting with a sickle.

Yet communal farming arrangements continued, through which the village collective, to whom the farmers remained tied. The local self-government (*mir*) allocated and redistributed the land for temporary use, as it was—like in traditional Asian rice economies—also responsible for the payments of taxes. All farmers as a community were collectively responsible for paying the sum allocated to the village, with the more successful and hard-working farmers paying for the lazy and drunkards. Hence the disincentives to individual initiative, innovation and land improvement continued. Yet Alexander also introduced to beginnings of rudimentary rural education with village schools and a notion of independence for the judiciary. During the tenure of finance minister Reuter (1862–1878), railway lines, financed mostly by

---

[6]Günther Stoekl. *Russische Geschichte*. Stuttgart: Kröner. 1997, p. 537.
[7]Stoeckl. Op. cit.; p. 539.
[8]Norbert Wein. *Die Sowjetunion*. Paderborn: UTB Schöningh 1985, p. 80.

French bonds, expanded from 2,200 miles to 14,200 miles, coal production multiplied sevenfold and external trade quadrupled. Military service also was reformed. Instead of 20 years of compulsory service, the new concept was one of a relatively smaller standing army in which conscripts served six years of active service, followed by nine years in the reserve. Yet in spite of all reforms, endemic corruption remained,[9] the unavoidable collateral of autocratic regimes. With the murder of the "Tsar Liberator" Alexander II in March 1881 by terrorist bombs, all political and economic reforms came to a fatal temporary standstill.

Foreign wars, starting with those of Catherine II (1762–1796), the campaigns and defence against Napoleon, the Crimean war and finally the Russian-Turkish war of 1877 had always been financed by printing paper rubles. With national savings wasted on unproductive military expenditure, the tax burdens on the agricultural economy inevitably increased. One of the results of rural capital deprivation was the famine of 1891–1892.

In 1892, the successful railway manager Sergei Witte became Minister of Finance (and shortly Prime Minister during 1905–1906). Not only did he push for the development of railways and heavy industry, but with the Trans-Siberian railway for economic and military-strategic purposes achieved by 1905 also opened the country for foreign direct investment, like for French and Belgian capital to develop the coal mines and steel industry in the Donbas, British capital to invest into oil and gold exploration, and German interests in the electrical industry. My great-grandfather's company Briegleb, Hansen & Co in Gotha, for instance until 1913 became an important supplier of turbines for Russia's energy generation. Though many of them are still in operation like in Chelyabinsk in the Urals,[10] tempi passati. In Baku the Nobel brothers developed the oil industry, and a British, John Hughes became the steel king of Russia, both in the 1870s and 1880s. Witte, however, also took the lessons of Friedrich list of tariff protection for Russia's own infant industries to heart and thus tried to promote a textile industry which he hoped would be able to push the British out of the Chinese and Mid-Eastern markets. Yet in spite of all efforts at the beginning of WWI in Russia, all indicators of heavy industrial development still lagged behind its UK, US, German and French competitors. Pig iron, steel and coal output, for instance, stood only at quarter to the levels of Germany.

Still, between 1890 and 1900 the number of factories increased from 32,000 to 38,000, while the workforce almost doubled from 1.4 million

---

[9]Mosse. Op. cit., p. 66.
[10]U. Ellenberg, M. Siegmund. Briegleb, Hansen & Co. Eisengießerei, Maschinenfabrik & Spezialfabrik für Turbinenbau. Gotha: Urania Kultur- und Bildungsverein 2000, p. 27.

to 2.4 million people. They were concentrated mostly in St. Petersburg, Moscow, the Donbas, the Urals, parts of the Caucasus und of Poland, working mainly in textiles, metallurgy and railway works. Work conditions as elsewhere during early industrialization were tough and insecure, work hours were long, housing conditions and wages were poor and paid only irregularly. Discipline was tough and workers were continuously threatened by dismissal and unemployment, notably when overcapacities became evident in metallurgy once the rail construction programme had levelled off. State support to industry and high tariff protection was of little help. Witte had hoped that rapid industrialization would help to raise living standards quickly.[11] Instead, there was a long series of ever-increasing strikes, often instigated by revolutionary intellectuals: in the cotton mills and the metal works of St. Petersburg in 1904, the railway workshops in 1902, and the miners in the Urals in 1903. Social democratic agitation also affected foreign-owned companies. During and after 1905 mass strikes shut down half of the Russian industry. During the Russo-Japanese War strikes for an 8-hour-day and increased minimum wages spread from the giant Putilov metallurgical works nationwide. Political demands for free education, the end of the war with Japan, a Constitution, the separation of Church and State, the substitution of indirect by proportional direct taxation, etc. followed. Typically, however, the strikes were unsustainable in the long run and repressed by the military. When petitioners demonstrated in front of the Winter Palace, they were fired upon by the military with dozens of victims. The universities were closed and terrorist acts proliferated in response. Factories were typically much larger than in the West and are often located in the rural areas as single employers near the sources of raw materials. Work conditions were tough and wages were miserable as usual in the first stage of industrialization. But the fact that Russia's modernization was delayed by one generation compared to the West made them less tolerable, with more sustained and better-organized workers unrest and intellectual support.

Yet politics was not unresponsive. In 1897, a labour law limited the work hours to 10½ hours maximum, and further reduced it to 9½ h in 1905–1906. In 1903, legal responsibility for work-related accidents was introduced for employers with the obligation of free medical services, sickness pay and invalidity pensions, very much following the Bismarckian model. While the rules were strict, unfortunately, as usual, they were little respected.[12] After

---

[11] Moses. Op. cit., p. 119.
[12] Cyril Fitz Lyon and Tatiana Browning. *Les Russes avant 1917*. Paris: Editions Autrement 2003 (1993), p. 48.

1905 industrial wages increased substantially. Yet by 1910, they were still only at 50% of the UK's level.[13]

In sum, however, the two decades of the rule of Nicholas II (1868–1918) from 1894 to the beginning of WWI were an era of economic, cultural and artistic bloom based on a rapidly expanding middle class, the spread of elementary and higher education, and the mecenat of the new class of industrialists. Russia was a latecomer to industrial development. Yet with rates of 8% annual growth in industrial production after 1890, which slowed down to 6% after 1905, it seemed to catch up quickly in its more developed parts.[14]

Also, the agricultural crisis loomed largely. The overuse of land, overcropping, soil erosion and the lack of fertilizers notably in the central Russian provinces led to a famine in 1901, while wheat exports continued from the Black Sea harbours to finance industrialization, railway construction and the military. In addition, farmers—counting for 80% of the population—were burdened with high taxation and increased excise taxes on sugar, vodka and tobacco, their major cash outlays. While some farmers prospered from increased agricultural production, the majority, being mostly illiterate and without access to modern farm equipment to increase productivity, remained dirt poor. Farmsteads were typically single-room wooden structures centred around a brick oven which served for heating, cooking, baking and sleeping. Benches lined the walls. Apart from a large table and shelves for kitchen equipment, there was little furniture. Grassland and forests were in communal property. Farmers remained subject to customary law, with village courts ruling on civil law cases, while the civil law codes only applied to the urban population. As the rural population grew rapidly, the hunger for land increased correspondingly. In response, the government opened up Siberian lands, and unlike in the past, it supplied migrants with credit and equipment. During the rule of Nicholas II four million settlers moved to Siberia, whose population during these decades doubled to 10 million (out of which one million were indigenous people). This was helped not only by the constriction of the Transib but also by romantic literature on settler farmers (similar to the US West), propagating the adventure, ruggedness and freedom of these tough virgin lands.[15]

In 1860, China ceased what is today Russia's Far East: the East Coast of Manchuria from the Amur River to the Korean border. They are the last of the Unequal Treaties forced upon the decaying Manchu dynasty which Communist China still resents and considers illegitimate.

---

[13] Ibid., p. 47.
[14] Ibid., p. 10.
[15] Fitz Lyon and Browning. Op. cit., pp. 76.

After 1895 imperial ambitions in the Far East, notably in Northern China, Korea and Manchuria, including railway construction, with the Transib crossing Manchuria via Harbin to Vladivostok and the (Russian) Chinese Railway going South to Port Arthur (built during 1881–1896) increased, as did the military rivalry with Japan, which felt threatened. Obviously, heavy military expenditure, the costs for railway construction, for foreign—mostly French—loans and economic modernization and paid for by high taxation and customs duties, brought little immediate benefit to the mass of the people. If there was a development model it was based on cheap labour and low productivity, as capital and innovations remained scarce. Witte's policy was to curtail public discontent and opposition by lazy traditionalists by prolonging autocratic rule, often with the collateral damage of arbitrary bureaucratic decisions against which recourse was not possible and endemic corruption among the poorly paid officialdom.[16]

In spite of larger numbers of troops, reserves, cavalry, guns, equipment and stronger naval ships in the Russo-Japanese War of 1904–1905, incompetent and lethargic military leadership, outdated tactics and logistical difficulties gave victory at both land and sea to the Japanese. Already in Korea Russian troops were told to live off the land as supplies did not arrive. It took troops up to 40 days to move from Moscow to Mukden, as railway capacities were blocked in Siberia. As a short, glorious campaign had been expected, unlike a war of attrition which foreshadowed World War I (no lessons were learnt by neither side), there were shortages of winter clothing and food and fuses for artillery shells.[17]

Only after Russia's defeats in Port Arthur in 1905, at the sea battle near Tsushima and during the land campaign in Manchuria, did public mass strikes, notably in the Putilov arms factories, force the enactment of constitutional law and the promise of civil liberties. At the same time, Russia during 1906–1968 saw a threatening upsurge in anarchist terrorism, which cost the lives of some 6000 officials (and of 2000 executed terrorists), with numerous armed robberies bordering at a small civil war, with hundreds of millions of rubles stashed away abroad in a major capital flight.

P. A. Stolypin as the new prime minister, with overdue agrarian reforms and the methods of an autocratic state, began to address the fundamental problem of rural backwardness: to expropriate and to redistribute two-thirds of the large landholdings and communal lands, to develop agricultural cooperatives and to end three-field crop rotation. He also freed farmers from their

---

[16] Mosse. Op. cit., p. 138 and p. 277.

[17] Richard Connaughton. *Rising Sun and Stumbling Bear. Russia's war with Japan.* London: Cassell 2004, p. 67, 109, p. 233 and p. 273.

compulsory membership in the village collective (*mir*). Indeed, until 1914 three million private farms were set up as farmsteads independent from their village commune. They were often successful commercial operations mostly in the Southern steppe and in the West, run by the kulaks which Stalin would deport and murder 20 years later. By 1916, individual farmers owned 81% of cultivated land and 94% of farm animals.[18] Interesting is also the development of rural cottage industries. Between 2 and 4 million households were engaged in wood processing, making wooden tools and furniture in the idle winter months, or processed linen, jute as local raw materials or cotton transported from Central Asia. Entire villages specialized in icon making, a trade sadly and quickly terminated by the Revolution. In other villages farmers were assembled as work gangs by an elected leader, who organized seasonal winter work for them in factories, distributing wages and buying food for communal living in nearby very frugal dormitories.

Yet past railway and foreign investments started to pay off with new markets being gradually developed and as access to raw materials and energy was facilitated. Also, Stolypin's industrial policies began to work. By 1908, foreign capital started to pour into Russia's industries again. Real wages and farm incomes increased (often to be spent on liquor) with a series of good harvests and high cereal prices. Textile production and construction started an industrial boom after 1912. During the rule of Nicholas II (1894–1917) coal output quadrupled, steel and cast-iron production tripled, and cotton and oil doubled. Overall the Russian economy grew by 6–8% per year during 1890–1913. Essentially, this growth was foreign-financed and was helped greatly by foreign direct investment.[19] Substantial timber, wheat and paper exports serviced the foreign debts in part. This progress helped to feed a population between 1909 and 1914 that had grown from 157 million to 175 million.

The big magnates like Timofey Morozov, who ruled over textiles, railways and banks, were seen as fearsome, rigid, brutal, yet hardworking, hard-drinking, pious and paternalist at the same time. Some of them were barely literate but were also Maecenas of the arts, of splendid architecture, of literature and music. Their slightly unbalanced offspring sometimes even financed Lenin's Communists.[20] Religious minorities and dissident Orthodox sects were often prominent in business. After the annexation of Ukraine and Eastern Poland, a large Jewish population was incorporated. Being blocked from farming, most worked as artisans and traders. By 1903, seven million Jews lived in Western Russia, even after 1.3 million of them emigrated to the

---

[18] Fitz Lyon and Browning. Op. cit., p. 43.
[19] Ibid., p. 174.
[20] Fitz Lyon and Browning. Op. cit., p. 57.

West to escape pogroms and discrimination. While a few became very rich as bankers, railway magnates and ship owners—most obviously the Brodsky as the "kings of sugar"—with Jews being very prominent in grain milling, brewing, textiles, tobacco and leather processing. Most, however, remained poor shoemakers, tailors, furniture makers, pharmacists and peddlers.[21] For the farm economy, they played an important role as traders of cattle and cereals, as well as suppliers of agricultural tools and sometimes as usurious money lenders.

In total, there were about two million noblemen in Russia. Many of them were ennobled after reaching the rank of colonel in the army or captain in the navy—which was made hereditary after two generations—or as a decorated senior civil servant, like Lenin's father as a principal district school inspector. Most lived on their country estates with modest means—as we know from nineteenth-century literature from Turgenev to Tolstoy, but yet trying a sometimes extravagant and hospitable way of life. As a social class with no great riches available from their agricultural holdings, gradually they were bypassed by the ascent of industrialists, bankers, traders, officers and liberal professions whose ranks they sometimes joined.

As one-third of the tax revenue was spent on the military, Russia was able to expand its army to 114 infantry divisions and to supply it with 6700 artillery pieces—nominally much stronger than the German army—and to rebuild her navy entirely which had been sunk in Port Arthur and near Tsushima in 1905. Plenty of finance continued to be provided by bonds subscribed by French banks and the French bourgeoisie, fascinated by the speculative returns on Russian war bonds—not heeding the prescient warnings of the pacifist Socialist leader Jean Jaures that they would never be paid back.[22] Obviously, the spectre of a rapidly modernizing and mobile continental superpower haunted the German general staff, which saw itself sandwiched between a revanchist France and an expansionist Eastern neighbour in an unenviable two-front scenario. Russia as an emerging power was thus similarly scary to Germany, as Germany herself had been to Britain ten years earlier, as Japan had been to the US in the 1930s, or as China appears today.

---

[21] Ibid., p. 69.
[22] Max Gallo. 1917, une passion russe. Paris: XO editions. 2017, p. 23 and p. 46.

1.1.1 A Case Study: von Wogau & Co

Interesting also is the role of foreign business in the rapidly industrializing Czarist empire. For enterprising Germans Russia with its huge unified market like the US for another German family, the Rockefellers, for instance, was the land of unlimited possibilities. The most successful of them was Maximilian von Wogau (1807–1880) who in 1827 moved from Frankfurt/Main to Moscow where he started as little more than an errand boy in a German-owned shop for colonial goods. He then moved into tea trading with China, which was bartered physically at a Siberian border crossing for Russian-made textiles, and managed often personally the difficult customs clearance at Siberian border crossings. And this was done in Siberia where at the time 3 million people lived without a railway, and the transport was done by horse-drawn carriages across rivers with no bridges. In Siberia, he found his Russian partners full of patience, fatalist acceptance, bonhomie, lacking ambition and needs, enjoying whenever possible comfort, sociability and drunkenness, which allowed them to forget all sorrows, and lacking the sense for time management, for organization and property, all expressed by one word: *Nitshevo!*[23]

As a first sideline, von Wogau moved into sugar trading as Russian tea is drunk with a lot of sugar. Gradually drugstore merchandise, oils, pharmaceutical base products and textile colourants were added. This was to service the needs of the Russian economy, which until 1850 essentially consisted of the artisanal processing of agricultural products like leather, wool, furs, rape, silk, wood, fats and oil. Once industrialization set in after 1850, he moved into commodity trading: importing iron, copper, chemicals, pharmaceuticals, soda, paper, coal, metal products, building materials, cement and other semi-finished products for Russia's rapidly developing industry and construction trade, and in the process setting up a complex logistical network across the Eurasian continent. The secret of von Wogau's success, as the largest German-owned trading house and industrial-holding company, was the weakness of Russian merchants and industrialists: They remained local and regional in orientation, were unsophisticated in international dealings and financial techniques and rarely ventured commercially beyond its borders. Further, German and British traders—then as now—were more reliable to honour payments.

He set up a private family bank to give credits to his underfinanced Russian suppliers and customers, who like all Russian companies had difficulties in getting access to finance, as state-credit institutions were only set

---

[23] Erik Meyer. *Wogau & Co. Das größte deutsche Handelshaus im russischen Zarenreich.* Berlin: Pro Business. 2017, p. 52.

up in 1855 and were essentially bureaucratic institutions to serve the needs of indebted landholders. When his customers ran into financial trouble, von Wogau used debt for equity swaps through which he then owned dozens of corporate participations in iron and copper making, chemicals, cotton spinning, paper production, cement works and other building materials and sugar refining. The collection of industrial interests hence went more by chance and did not reflect a purposeful primary industrial strategy.[24] Often then Wogau's associates or family members managed a turnaround and financed much-needed expansions and modernizations. One should remember that industries outside Moscow and St. Petersburg due to the lack of infrastructure far from any railway had to operate fairly autonomously, producing their own bricks, workers housing, hospitals, canteens, food, wood, electricity, charcoal, etc.[25] much like the Soviet combines for reasons of a deficient planning economy 100 years later. There remained real continuities as well: In 1874, Wogau modernized outdated iron works in the Urals with modern sinter technologies and in 1910 build his own 175 km railway to transport the output. Forced to sell in 1916, Stalin turned the plant in 1932 into the centre of the giant Magnitogorsk metallurgical complex with coal supplied from the Stalinsk, the mining town nearby. Today, Magnitogorsk remains the world's 30th largest steel company.

During 1864–1871, a series of corporate banks were founded with a larger capital basis than the private banks hitherto: The Russian Bank for Foreign Trade, the Commerzbank of Riga, the Moscow Diskontobank etc. von Wogau took minority participation in all of them, the main purpose being to maintain influence.

All remained the property of his extended family without shares ever having been issued and sell-outs being frowned upon. During WWI, his successors survived first the scapegoating for the deficiencies in Russian arms and ammunitions supplies, then the anti-German pogroms in May 1915 and even the liquidation attempts of Wogau & Co as "hostile" German property, when they were forced to "sell" strategic assets for worthless debentures, but the Revolution they did not. The company had survived and prospered for 78 years with returns on capital averaging 7.6% annually during 1873–1913 alone and as the largest German trading house in Russia had a turnover of today's equivalent of €8 billion. Yet with Revolution 50 million gold rubles were lost. Most of the family were barely able to escape alive.[26] Obviously, the clan had overlooked the warning sign of the 1905 revolt of social unrest

---

[24] Ibid., p. 72.
[25] Ibid., p. 83.
[26] Ibid., p. 7.

(which also affected their factories), kept almost all assets in Russia and subsequently lost almost all of them, worth the equivalent of €2 billion, generated during the eight decades of the family holding's existence. Then they had been on a par with the Wallenbergs or the Nobel brothers with their oil business in Baku (whose fortunes started with supplies to the Russian army in the Crimean war 1853–1855 from their arms plant in St. Petersburg).[27]

Some property was saved in Poland, like a copper mill in Glowno, or in the Baltics, like a cement factory in Riga. A successor company engaged in diffuse unfocussed trading operations in the Baltics. Its London branch lost its money in speculative ventures in South Africa. By 1952, it was declared bankrupt. One offspring, who had converted to Communism and stayed behind, was shot by Stalin in 1938.

1.2 The War Economy (1914–1917)

None of the countries which in July 1914 stumbled into World War I was reasonably well prepared. They all expected the war to be short and victorious, over by autumn and to be fought by quick cavalry offensives similar to the Franco-German war of 1870–1871. As a consequence, British colonial troops did not have heavy artillery, the French did not have machine guns, the Russian army had no telephones and the Germans wore leather hats which only protected against sabre strikes. Further, all armies were woefully undermechanized. All had overlooked the lessons of the Russo-Japanese War which had taught the importance and temporary superiority of defensive weapon systems—compared to offensive ones—at the time, and the likeliness of trench warfare and a war of attrition. Yet as the Russian industry was booming in 1914, as we have seen, the Russian military did not face immediate shortages. Rather it faced administrative problems of logistics and inter-service coordination, like between infantry, cavalry and artillery units. Hence the alleged "shell-shortage" and the shortage of rifles were more of a political football used for intrigues between generals and for political infighting. Also, most heavy guns were used as fortress artillery in obsolete fortifications (where they were often captured in abundance by the Germans) and missed for the needs and protection of infantry.[28] The over-reliance on horses, both for the draught of guns and supplies and for the cavalry, meant that scarce railway stock had to be devoted to them and their voluminous fodder needs. All this restrained the mobility of troops and the difficulty to move reserves either

---

[27] Bengt Jangfeldt. «Die alte Liebesgöttin trifft sich mit Merkur» *Frankfurter Allgemeine* 2.12.2019.
[28] Norman Stone. *The Eastern Front 1914–1917*. London: Penguin 1998, p. 32.

to stem or to advance in case of breakthroughs. High inflation, worsened by deficit spending during the war, induced farmers to hold back food supplies to the military. By 1917, as the economic crisis increased, the supply of food and clothing to the army effectively ended.

As Russia had planned for a short war, like all other participants she just built up the stocks of armaments and ammunition instead of building factories to produce weapons. Public finances were no shape to finance this conversion, nor did the interruption of foreign trade seem to allow this, given Russia's dependence on the imports of German machinery and engineering skills.[29] As production for civilian consumption remained unhindered, the increase in military output remained largely insufficient. Certainly, also the conscription of skilled labour hurt not only agricultural output but also industrial production. In addition, large parts of the industrial workforce during the planting and harvesting season as usual absconded to their home villages to help their families out. In sum, the timeless general rule to Russian economic administration applied: "centralization brought inefficiency, decentralization brought anarchy".[30]

As a result, large and overprized orders were placed with UK and US companies for rifles and ammunition. This rapidly doubled Russia's foreign debt and used up its gold reserves (which landed in British coffers). Yet there were practical problems with supply. Not only were foreign suppliers busy with British needs but they also had to ship via Archangel and Vladivostok, with their very limited railway capacities, as the main import harbours—Odessa and Petrograd—were no longer accessible.

By 1915, public and business discontent grew after the retreat from Poland and the loss of the border provinces West of the Duna. Moscow industrialists resented that armament contracts rather went abroad and to their competitors in Petrograd. Prices for essential commodities, like sugar and cotton, in the cities increased by 50%. In turn, the government encouraged wage inflation. Fuel supply became irregular. Shortages of coal and the disruption of railway transport affected the industry. In summer 1915 already 25,000 workers went on strike at the Putilov arms factory in Petrograd and occupied their works for days. When the police reoccupied the factory about 50 strikers were killed.[31] Also hundreds of thousands of refugees fleeing the fighting and the Cossacks' scorched earth policy in Poland, and in the Baltics they had to be housed and fed.[32]

---

[29] Stone. Op. cit., p. 150.
[30] Stone. Op. cit., p. 95.
[31] Gallo. Op. cit., p. 49.
[32] Stone. Op. cit., p. 195.

Already in 1914 Russian heavy industry was organized in price and production cartels, which in order to stabilize profits fixed prices and limited the output. They were Prodameta in metallurgy, Produgol in coal mining, Prodvagon for railway equipment and Med for copper. These de facto monopolies pressured for economic concentration and for the merger and absorption of smaller firms and competitors, which enjoyed less access to resources, railway transport and skilled labour. No question that this monopolization four years later facilitated the Bolshevist takeover of Russia's heavy industry. At the same time, as in imperial Germany, with the imperatives and the constraints of war, political power gradually shifted from the imperial court to Stavka, the military supreme command, to the cartel organizations (much less to the official war industries committees) and to the reformist factions of the Duma (in charge of war credits). They would set up the provisional government in March 1917. Yet with a concerted war effort, the Russian industry gradually managed to substitute new machinery for previously imported ones and to overcome its erstwhile backwardness. The year 1916 finally saw considerable increases in the production of guns, ammunition, lorries, aircraft and ultimately tanks[33] (which like a lot of stored war material were used by the Red Army in the civil war and the Russian-Polish War of 1920–1921). As a result, during the second war winter of 1915–1916, there was less a shortage of war material, but more importantly, a shortage of officers and NCOs to train their men and to put the equipment to professional use.

As the war and its sacrifices progressed, so did the Russian war aims, wishing to set up a series of Slavic satellite states from an enlarged Poland, Bohemia and Serbia to the control of the Dardanelles. This was encouraged by the British, who wanted the oil-rich parts of the Ottoman Empire (plus the German fleet and colonies) for themselves, and by France which in the tradition of Louis XIV and Napoleon wanted the Rhine border in return, both eager and generous to avoid a feared German–Russian separate peace treaty. As wartime inflation impoverished foremost the middle classes with losses of professional employment, savings and fixed rentier incomes, political elites (notably in France) focussed on prospective reparations by the defeated side to make up for these losses. For France in particular the loss of its sizable—now technically bankrupt—Russian bond holdings accumulated since pre-war years posed a huge risk.

Already on 25 February 1917, a general strike was followed by mass demonstrations of 200,000 strikers in Petrograd, Baku and Moscow, which

---

[33]Stone. Op. cit., p. 211.

were fired on by the police.[34] By March 1917, food shortages in the cities, mostly in Petrograd, triggered the protests of housewives and urban workers, joined by idle garrison troops. Shops were looted, officers shot, notably by discontented seamen of the Northern fleet in anchored in Petrograd, Helsingfors (Helsinki) and Reval (Tallinn), and warships were taken over by their mutinous crews. Galloping inflation froze most productive economic activity. With the set-up of the provisional government by Kerensky major hostilities ceased. After V.I. Lenin's return to Petrograd in April 1917, the Bolsheviks radicalized and began to pursue an aggressive programme of urban and rural class war, with the demands for immediate peace and of all powers to the Soviets. Unending strikes by the urban workforce and railwaymen worsened the cities' precarious supply situations. While the front army did not fight and abstained from revolutionary action, units of the rear army were organized by the Soviets in a parallel command structure independent from formal authorities and allowed the Bolsheviks to stage their armed coup in November 1917. Lenin had begun to organize Communist workers militias and armed Red guards, set up from deserters and volunteers to prepare for the civil class war he had envisaged. The promise of land for all toilers and of the expropriation of all private landholdings triggered a wild demobilization of many troops who returned to their villages in order not to miss out. In the countryside, order broke down. Bands of deserters roamed as brigands, farms were burned down and manors were looted, often after wine cellars had been emptied.[35] With the armistice in Brest Litovsk in December 1917, WWI ended for Russia and in March 1918 a peace treaty was signed with the axis temporarily victorious in the East. Lenin had all secret Czarist war agreements with the allies published and de-recognized Russian war debts as illegitimate. It came as no surprise that revolutionary Russia dishonored also all its foreign pre-war debts.

It is certainly true that Russia (like Germany and Austria-Hungary one year later) was not economically "advanced" enough to withstand the strains of an enduring modern war (in the case of the axis powers also the British naval blockade). Yet, as Norman Stone puts it, the Revolution occurred in a crisis of growth, as industry and the urban proletariat expanded massively during the war. Employment in railways, mines, state factories and construction all almost doubled, as much more rural surplus labour was recruited by industry than it was drafted into the army. At the same time, rural cottage industries were absorbed by larger factories. Like in Germany the government had decided not to increase taxation but to flood the economy with

---

[34]Gallo. Op. cit., p. 56.
[35]Gallo. Op. cit., p. 114.

liquidity through deficit spending on unproductive armament. Not only were the savings of the middle classes sacrificed, but also wages became meaningless as they could not be translated into food or necessities. Obviously, the black market boomed as a barter economy emerged (which later helped the Bolsheviks to survive their politically induced economic chaos). As the cash economy vanished, farmers returned to the subsistence economy from which they had just emerged a decade earlier.[36] Their aged machinery could not be replaced. There was no access to fertilizers. Rather they began to feed their grain to their own livestock. In spite of good harvests, as a result, the urban masses remained under-supplied and hungry. The revolution could have its way. In many regions, small farmers and the rural poor took the law into their own hands, drove out the landlords (if they did not kill them outright) and ransacked their mansions.

1.3 The Civil War, War Communism and the New Economic Policies (1918–1924)

After a lull of a few months of combat fatigue, armed resistance emerged to the Soviet coup. The civil war of 1918–1920 was largely fought along railway lines. With forced conscription and subsequent mass desertions, it was a fairly extensive affair, with decisive battles initially only involving a few hundred combatants.[37] Although in the end after the fighting ended in November 1920, between 7 and 10 million Russians are believed to have lost their lives, less through actual fighting and the Red and White terror, but through malnutrition, hunger, epidemics (typhus, dysentery, the Spanish flu and infant mortality) and lack of medical services.[38]

Allied interventions, their own war-weary troops having only limited reliability, were only peripheral and temporary. The UK was more interested in oil and gas in Baku and Ashgabat, and in the port of Arkhangelsk, France in Odessa, and the Japanese and the US more extensively in the Far East. Of more importance was their economic blockade in response to the expropriations without compensation and the negation of war debt by the Bolsheviks.

The White generals Denikin, Kolchak, Judenich and Vrangel were neither politicians nor administrators nor economists. Only interested in military operations, they did not set up a civilian administration, nor did they offer

---

[36] Stone. Op. cit., p. 291.
[37] Gallo. Op. cit., p. 165.
[38] Evan Mawdsley. *The Russian Civil War*. Edinburgh: Birlinn, p. 287.

views on agrarian reform or a decentralized state structure. Their political failures, unable to offer any positive vision to a starving restless population, proved to be their undoing. In the end, it was continued Soviet control over Russia's industrial heartland centred on Moscow as its transportation and communication hub and stretching to Petrograd and the Urals,[39] which controlled the major armaments industries, railways, the mines, food production and the huge Czarist arsenals which allowed to revolution to survive all of the uncoordinated military challenges from the periphery. The permanent and growing control over 60 million inhabitants in the Russian centre allowed Trotsky to raise a conscript Red army which by the end of 1919 comprised more than three million soldiers, which was not only better equipped and fed but also thus outnumbered its White opponents on any battlefield by more than ten to one. Politically reliable Commissars were supervising the Czarist "specialist" officers. By the end of 1920, at the end of the civil war, the Red Army numbered 5.2 million men. Obviously, this war effort put a huge strain on a fragile economy. Trotsky hence began to turn armed divisions into "labour armies" charged with reconstruction. Having thus militarized society, the concept of labour conscription and to apply military solutions with tight discipline and punishments of "saboteurs" began to appeal to the Bolshevik elite to deal with the problems in industrial production, agriculture and transportation.[40]

The first economic steps of the Bolsheviks were guided by ideological blindness, ignorant even of basic economic laws and realities. Nationalized industries were supposed to be run by workers councils. Trading was only allowed by state bodies. The "bourgeoisie" was subjected to punitive taxation. The new state administration barely performed. Money was simply printed, resulting in worthless paper bills, while farmers were subjected to food requisitioning. The predictable result was a massive fall in industrial and agricultural output, and a subsistence black economy resorting to barter trade.[41] Soviet war production centred on a few key factories, who as central planning did not work, had to rely on a multitude of small artisanal workshops for essential supplies.[42] By 1921, total output had fallen to 16% of

---

[39] There are strategic lessons to be learned from this Civil War experience but also from Napoleon's march to Moscow in 1813, via the German and Allied advances in 1917–1918 up to Hitler's attack in 1941: without effective control of her landlocked industrial center region Russia cannot be defeated, strategically a very tall order indeed.

[40] Mawdsley. Op. cit., p. 230.

[41] Mawdsley. Op. cit., p. 74.

[42] Mawdsley. Op. cit., p. 187.

its level in 1912. The production of coal, steel and cotton was even more reduced.[43]

The civil war had helped Lenin to eliminate rival left parties, to consolidate the Communist dictatorship with its centre of power in the small inner Politbureau and to set up the centralized control structures, which he had propagated all along in order to create his modern electrified industrial state as a prelude to communism. Under the pretext of war needs only the state would produce, distribute and employ exclusively and alone. The aspirations of workers' soviets at the self-management of factories and of farmers promised privately owned land were brutally cast aside. The war efforts justified the (temporary?) sacrifices. Two giant bureaucracies with dictatorial powers were set up in May 1918: A Supreme Economic Council with 40 main departments which directed all nationalized industrial production, and the People's Commissariat for Supplies whose main purpose was to equip and to feed the Red Army. Requisitioning of food at the farm level was done with such brutality that—not for the last time—it drastically reduced agricultural productivity. In factories bourgeois specialists were appointed as managers in order to restart the production. It was foremost Trotsky with his experience in running the Red Army successfully who argued forcefully that military control and command structures should run the economy. Party cells reduced trade unions to docile "transmission belts" of Politbureau instructions. A Central Transport Committee after years of chaos and bottlenecks already ran the railways reasonably well. The same control methods applied to agriculture through nationwide "seed committees" however produced disaster. In January the food rations, which were already at the bare minimum in cities, were cut by one-third. Industrial output ran at one-quarter of its pre-war level. In February 1921, a fuel crisis forced the closure of the largest Petrograd industries, including the Putilov works. Instead of living in the promised workers' and farmers' paradise, the proletariat was hungry, freezing and out of work.

Workers went on strike and demanded free trade with the villages. Farmers started to resist expropriations and the conscription of their sons with partisan methods against confiscating police squats. Thousands of Kronstadt seamen, the cradle of the revolution, demanded new and free elections, freedom for political prisoners, fair trials, freedom of opinion, equal food rations and the free use of farmland. The party's reply was to declare martial law and to put down ruthlessly the counterrevolutionaries.

---

[43]Mawdsley. Op. cit., p. 288.

As the catastrophic supply situation risked becoming politically unsustainable, Lenin in 1921 undertook a major turnaround. His New Economic Policies (NEP) would abolish the arbitrary confiscations of harvests, but instead tax farmers progressively less in kind, so as to give them an incentive to produce more and to sell surpluses freely on the market. State land would be leased to private farmers and artisans, who were equally freed to produce and to sell at their own risk and gain. Given the abysmal failure of the state trading agency, internal trade would be freed. Concessions to produce privately would be distributed, also to foreign investors. This obvious relapse into capitalism was accompanied by brutal political repression of the surviving opposition, like the social democratic Mensheviks to the right, and the workers' opposition to the left of the Communist party. Very quickly the economy and food supply recovered; mostly agriculture and consumer light industry, much less the heavy industry which remained subjected to state and party intervention and control.[44] Soon the first "NEP rich" became visible.

With these discrepancies the year 1923 saw a "capitalist" crisis, for which Lenin and his people were unprepared: Food prices fell, and with growing prices for scarcer industrial goods inflation grew and reduced demand which in turn created persistent unemployment. Lenin, who had begun to see his NEP as a long-term economic policy and no longer as crisis expediency, due to his series of strokes was incapacitated to react.

1.4 The Soviet Economy (1924–1991)

After Lenin's death in January 1924, the Soviet Union has constituted a centralized greater Russian state surrounded by nominally autonomous republics and regions. Stalin's as executor of Lenin's testament first pretended to be an ardent supporter of the NEP and a great friend of the Russian peasant. This he used to eliminate Trotsky and the leftist opposition. Once this was achieved he attacked the NEP in order to purge its right-wing supporters. Economic and welfare considerations were secondary and would be adjusted to suit his power struggles, the main objective being to achieve absolute personal power, eliminate all potential opposition and establish direct rule cutting across institutions and hierarchies.

For doctrinal reasons, industrial development, especially machinery production, and electrification was pushed in the first Five-Year Plan from 1927 to 1932, as Marxism taught it as the precondition for the dominance

---

[44]Stoekl. Op. cit., p. 686.

of an urban proletariat as the necessary power base for Soviet rule and the ultimate advent of Communism. Heavy industrialization was also meant to serve the security interests of the young Soviet state against its Western enemies. In order to mobilize workers and all available resources, any other human interests could be sacrificed in a dictatorship. The plans were aided by the development of the new rich coal fields of Kuzbass South of Tomsk in Western Siberia and Karaganda in Kazakhstan. Indeed, the production of machine tools, tractors and mechanical ploughs shot up impressively. Yet steel production overall increased only by one-third. In order to enforce the plan already in 1930, a great purge of factory directors and foreign specialist managers was undertaken, who ended in front of firing squads as saboteurs. Not reaching targets by definition was never the fault of party planners but of those who had to execute them. State terror, however, did not resolve the shortage of qualified workers in the rapidly built-up huge plants. The destruction of cottage industries and artisanal production—done to eliminate the politically undesirable petit bourgeoisie—did not help to remedy the inevitable shortages caused by heavy-handed central planning. Agriculture did not just need the new mass built heavy tractors, but also the wooden carriages and snow slides which nobody built anymore. Over-ambitious plan targets meant that overcapacities were created and investment capital wasted on a massive scale, which went at the expense of domestic welfare and the potential prosperity of the agricultural sector in particular.[45]

By 1927, Stalin decided that the last independent stratum of the population had to be brought under control. The planners also wished to increase agricultural output and productivity, which in difference to an industry still lacked behind pre-war levels, in order to feed the rapidly growing industrial cities and to increase export earnings. Most small and middle farmers with their diverse production of cereals, potatoes, vegetable, fruits, honey, poultry, pork and milk aimed at self-sufficiency for their families foremost. The party's resort to confiscations of surpluses ("war communism"), like during a new food crisis in 1927, gave them little incentive to increase productivity. Although experiences with Sovkhoz state farms had not been encouraging, Stalin in 1929 decided to liquidate the kulaks—usually successful and modern middle farmers, which made up 10% of the farming population—as a "class" in order to re-instigate class warfare in the villages and to urge the remaining farmers to join kolkhoz communes "voluntarily". Most villages, however, lived as relatively harmonious communities with little inclination for class hatred. For farmers also there was no

---

[45] Stoekl. Op. cit., p. 716.

incentive to abandon their independence, won so hard by their grandfathers six decades earlier, to become landless kolkhoz labourers. Hence in winter 1929–1930, Stalin had 500,000 kulaks and their families expropriated, maltreated by urban thugs and deported to Siberian wastelands without any shelters or means for survival. Thanks to the state terror of the totalitarian system, collectivization rates shot up from barely 4% in October 1929 to 58% six months later.[46] By 1933, the figure had reached 65%. In the meantime more than 50% of farm animals—from horses to sheep—had lost their lives, because farmers either butchered them or they perished in kolkhoz herds where nobody cared professionally. The predictable result of forced collectivization and an incompetently engineered industrial agriculture was a food crisis beginning in spring 1932 and culminating in the hunger winter of 1932–1933 when 4.5 million people died. This did not prevent Stalin from exporting 1.7 million tons of confiscated wheat. During 1928–1933 the already miserable living standards in the Soviet Union fell by one-third. Stalin now sets two national priorities: heavy industry and electrification, and poured most national resources into 1500 giant projects, like the metallurgical works of Magnitogorsk and Kuznets, the Turkestan-Siberian railway, the Volga-White Sea canal, the giant Dnepr dam, constructed by armies of "voluntary" Komsomol youth or slave labour colonies. Constructed at the cost of huge human sacrifice and suffering, in financial terms their labour costs were minimal. This explains why millions of lives were wasted for projects of often very little economic value and utility. The tractor works in Stalingrad for instance (of horrific notoriety during the battle 12 years later) during their official grand opening produced just one tractor, and then for months for the lack of parts nothing.

As the myriad of external parts suppliers, private repairmen and industrial service providers needed to keep complex industrial operations going did not exist any longer, the industry had to produce it all in-house, from the construction of factory buildings and storage sheds to the design and set up of assembly lines, maintaining and operating its fleet of trucks for logistics, and the supply and running of canteens and first-aid stations for the staff. If there were unplanned breakdowns, production and deliveries would come to a stand-still. As a result, the notorious *tolkatch* made a mass appearance: handymen and black market traders who as trouble-shooters could organize the urgently needed parts and supplies extra-legally, thanks to their manyfold contacts out of nowhere to keep operations going where state planners had necessarily failed.

---

[46]Stoekl. Op. cit., p. 719.

1.4.1 The Gulag Economy (1921–1954)

To the Soviet Union's vast networks of labour camps, there were antecedents already since 1649 with forced labour brigades in Siberia (then considered as progress compared to the death penalty, corporal punishments and physical disfigurations). Peter the Great infamously built St. Petersburg on the bones of convicts and serfs (*katorga*). Fyodor Dostoevsky (as a convict in Siberia during 1860–1862 in: "House of the Death") and Anton Chekhov (on Sakhalin in 1890) have described the horrible conditions of deported slave labour impressively enough.[47] Also, the 9340 km of the Transib after 1890 were built by convict labour. Yet in Soviet Russia, there were in total 18 million—at any given time 2 million—plus 6 million doing forced labour without barbed wire around them in Kazakhstan, other parts of Central Asia and Siberia.

Already in the summer of 1918, Lenin ordered "unreliable elements" to be locked up in "concentration camps",[48] if they had not been shot already. By 1921, there were already 84 camps to rehabilitate "enemies of the people" (White Russian officers, capitalists, clergymen, aristocrats, kulaks and their families).[49] In 1929, Stalin decided to use them in his plans to speed up the forced industrialization and to use the raw materials of Siberia and the underpopulated North, with slave labour organized by the secret service, which became massively available first after the deportation of two million "kulaks" during 1930–1933, and then during the Great Terror of 1937–1938 and even more so during the war and peaked until Stalin's death in 1953. The camps were continuously fed—often overwhelmed—by deported nationalities from Karelia, the Baltics, Eastern Poland to Moldova, by Crimean Tatars, Greeks of the Pontian coast, Chechens, ethnic Germans of the Volga Republic, Koreans of the Far East, Axis prisoners of war (including Japanese), "liberated" Russian prisoners of war, and hundreds of thousands civilian deportees, including women and youngsters, from annexed or occupied Central East Europe, including East Germany and Eastern Austria (the last to return in 1955). There was never any attempt to construct individual "guilt". People were

---

[47] During the same time there had also been forced labour condition on across the Japan Sea on Sado island its gold mines with similar horrific conditions during the Meiji era in Japan. The mines can still be visited.

[48] A Spanish invention in the Cuban war in 1885, equally used by the British in the Boer war of 1900, by the Americans to intern Japanese civilians in Western desserts during 1941–1945, and perfected in SS run camps mostly in what is now Poland—both as penal labour, but also as extermination camps. All had in common that the inmates were innocent civilians, had the wrong nationality, class or religion and that the death rate usually stood at a horrific 25–30%. Also the French in the nineteenth century had their forçats in shipyards and in Guyana.

[49] Anne Applebaum. *Gulag. A History of Soviet Camps*. London: Allen Lane. 2003, p. 31.

deported by category as ethnicity, as class enemies or as potential saboteurs, with pre-established quotas to be filled by the NKWD.

Starting with the senseless construction of the White Sea Canal of 227 km by 200,000 prisoners, the Moscow-Volga canal by 170,000 labourers (of which at least 25,000 died) with the most primitive of tools, the Gulag economy quickly expanded to coal and gold mining, logging, construction of railways, motorways and housing, to collective cotton farming and factory work. Epidemics of malaria, dystrophy, pneumonia, typhus and dysentery, hunger, cold, the lack of hygiene in the mass quarters and outdoor toilets, of proper clothing and basic medication in 1941–1942 alone killed one-fourth of the Gulag population. As these death rates obviously affected productivity, more care was taken to feed at least the necessary minimum to those able to fulfil the working norms. Death rates were highest for those who had to do logging in winter as there was no mechanical equipment, in the Kolyma gold mines (producing one-third of Soviet gold and paying for Soviet technology imports) and in uranium mining without any protective equipment.[50]

Already the mass transport in unheated prison carriages, with almost no food and water, and the forced marches of the weakened prisoners took a high toll. Those who were unable to walk were simply shot by the guards.[51]

Stalin himself saw the Gulag as a commercial enterprise. It disposed of his real or imagined political enemies and should be profitable. By 1925, already the first "successful" case was shown to him with a camp financing itself through logging, road building, fish farming and a brick factory. Food was given only when planning targets were met, while the weaker and underperforming prisoners ultimately died.[52] In 1929 his five-year plan foresaw a 20% increase in industrial output which required even higher production of oil, gas, coal and wood from Siberia, Kazakhstan, and the Far North, and of gold from Kolyma to pay for machinery imports. In order to achieve this, "specialists" were needed for mining and prospecting operations, which were duly arrested during party purges beginning in 1929. Also, Stalin, like all dictators, liked the sight of mass labour working at his whim on his megalomaniac projects, like canals and railways.[53] Grand projects, like the BAM, the Baikal-Amur Magistrale, which he ordered, were started in great haste without proper prior surveying. With the mass arrests during 1933–1936 camps were overwhelmed and unprepared by the sudden arrival of 180,000 under-nourished and under-clothed prisoners, who had to live in

---

[50] Ibid., p. 118.
[51] Erwin Peter. *Von Workuta bis Astrachan*. Graz/Stuttgart: Stocker. 1988.
[52] Applebaum. Op. cit., p. 54.
[53] Ibid., p. 68.

earth dugouts or tents where the weak would simply freeze or starve to death. During 1933–1934 (the great famine) and in 1942–1943 four million victims were in the camps. The Great Terror of 1937–1938 affected more the party elite, which according to pre-set quotas for each republic was usually shot, including Yagoda as NKWD chief and many camp commanders. The purges in the camps, plus the reductions in food rations and summary executions led to the loss of specialists and reduced productivity further. But in 1939 the camps were flooded again with people deported from the Baltics, East Poland and Western Ukraine, and after 1942 also by those who had remained on the wrong side of the front during the German occupation. In 1948, a wave of re-arrests of old inmates started.

The infrastructure of Komi Republic far North East of Moscow, yet still West of the Ural was almost entirely built by prisoners, including the cities of Ukhta, Syktyvkar, Pechora, Uta, Vorkuta and Inta, again without any mechanical equipment, where in permafrost conditions roads and pipes had to be replaced and repaired each spring. The main business lines were coal mining, forestry and oil. Equally the city of Magadan at the Okhotsk Sea was built by slave labour as were cotton farms in Uzbekistan. Yet there were also prison laboratories for rocket engines, manned by German engineers captured in Peenemünde, and a certain Tupolev, who designed Soviet aircrafts, missiles and sputniks.[54]

Interesting also is the case of Norilsk in the Far North. In 1952, it was settled by 69,000 prisoners who had to mine nickel, build a nickel processing plant (now owned by the oligarch Potanin), power stations and housing for their NKWD wardens. Thousands of large and small "Camp-industrial complexes" emerged, similar to Auschwitz and Birkenau, which were built around gold, coal and nickel mines, undertook road and railway construction, built airports and apartment blocks, ran arms, metal processing and chemical factories, were canning fish, or digging peat. Logs were processed to sawmills and then to furniture making. The camps produced a wide range of products: car parts, door locks, furniture, shoes, skis, textiles, bags, fur hats, cups, lamps and even toys.

At the whim of the camp administration, the assignments of prisoners frequently changed from digging ditches, mining, carpentry, painting propaganda pictures to tending chicken and doing laundry. Obviously, the work conditions were horrible. In the Kolyma uranium mines, for instance, there was no protection against radiation.[55] In the Vorkuta coal mines during 1945 alone there were 7100 work accidents, of which 137 were deadly and 480

---

[54] Ibid., p. 119.
[55] Ibid., p. 118.

with serious injuries.[56] The reasons were shortages of lamps and electrical failures, poor organization and sloppier management than at usual Soviet workplaces, which were already bad enough.

In logging operations, three were no chain saws, no tractors, no mechanical loaders, plus a constant lack of spare parts and the breakdown of machinery, like in all other camps. Yet, with the quota unfulfilled there would be no food. Stalin decided on absurd railway projects in the tundra in 1939, like connecting the Yenissei River to the Ob River over 1300 km, with 120,000 prisoners working on it in winter in permafrost conditions and in summer in the mud. The tracks naturally remained unstable. After Stalin's death with 700 km completed, the project was abandoned.

After the war there was a new wave of repression, with the population of the camps growing to 2,560,000 people due to the re-Sovietization of the Baltics, of Moldova, Eastern Poland and Western Ukraine and re-arrests of released inmates in 1948. Yet the new inmates were tougher, they were "liberated" Russian POWs, soldiers of the Vlassov and the Polish Home Army, Ukrainian and Baltic partisans, German, Japanese and Italian POWs. They had seen death into the eye and defended themselves against the rule of the thieves and of the camp administration.[57] Apart from the prisoners, there were similar numbers of "exiles in perpetuity" (including their children), who were sent to Kolyma, Krasnoyarsk, Novosibirsk and Kazakhstan. With their *propusk* they could only move within a perimeter of 30 km of their assigned residences. Sandra Kalniete has documented the fate of her family well. Both grandfathers together with their families were deported from the Baltics. Both died in the camps. Once freed their children could marry but had to live and work in a sawmill North West of Novorijsk. Here Kalneite, foreign minister of Latvia during 2002–2004, was born in 1952.[58]

By 1952, the Interior Ministry MVD through the camps controlled 9% of all investments, which according to Stalin, who believed in the virtue of slave labour, was to double during 1951–1955. He also asked for the construction of a high-tech asbestos plant in a Gulag, which the system could not deliver. In 1950, he demanded the construction of a railway tunnel to Sakhalin and of another railway in the Arctic tundra. Tens of thousands were put to work. Yet the projects were aborted within days after his death. Within the Soviet elite slowly a consensus emerged that the camps were wasteful, corrupt and unprofitable with their primitive technologies. With continuous fights

---

[56]Ibid., p. 217.
[57]Ibid., p. 419.
[58]Sandra Kalniete. *Mit Balettschuhen im sibirischen Schnee. Die Geschichte meiner Familie.* Munich: Herwig. 2005. During 2002–4 she became Minister of Foreign Affairs in Latvia and is now an MEP.

between criminals (*blatnoy*) and the "politicals", and strikes and uprisings multiplying since 1949, they felt the use of free labour in these colonies was more productive, saving the costs of food, clothing, barracks and guards.[59] As an almost free good slave labour was frequently wasted not only on senseless projects but also offered no incentives for innovation and enhanced productivity. In the summer of 1954, the Central Committee relaxed the camp regime with early releases. By 1957, most were disbanded, with ministries taking over the camps industrial complexes like mining, machine building, forestry or road building.[60]

There are plenty of surviving eye witnesses' reports (only that they get very little public attention). One of Horst Schüler, who was deported into the Vorkuta coal mines, surrounded the city in the North.[61] Forty camps with barracks of some 2000–3000 prisoners each would supply the 17 mines with labour, making a total of 100,000 at any given time. There was a regular re-supply from the Moscow central prisons Lubjanka, Butyrka and Yaroslava with Stolypin prison carriages. Most of them, including former Soviet prisoners of war, had been sentenced to 25 years of hard labour. The winter lasted 9 months and food consisted almost exclusively of *kasha*, porridge of barley, maize and millet, salty fish, bread and watery soup. In total, the Komi Republic in the North East of Moscow had a prison population of 400,000, which developed the entire region, from coal mines to paper mills and furniture plants. Michael Reck went through 11 camps from May 1945 to December 1949,[62] mostly working in forestry and wood sawing, with the worst jobs being peat cutting. Prisoners also had to construct their own barracks, the housing of officers, roads, dams and bridges, but sometimes even to paint monumental murals and party slogans, liked by their camp hierarchy. The problems were poor accommodation and sanitary conditions, under-nutrition, sadistic guards, uncaring brigade leaders and arbitrary camp commanders engaging in unpredictable violence and killings, the lack of medical care and medication, frequent epidemics, poor or absent protective clothing and the psychological despair with all the uncertainty of releases and the fate of their unprotected families as "lost years". Tools and trucks were frequently broken or materials like cement and steel simply missing. With Russian sloppiness towards the equipment, its rough handling and poor work organization, it often implied waiting around for hours in the cold for repairs and supplies and in consequence less food for unfulfilled norms.

---

[59] Applebaum, Op. cit., p. 425.
[60] Ibid., p. 457.
[61] Horst Schüler. *Workuta*. Munich: Herbig 1993.
[62] Michael Reck. *Tagebuch aus sowjetischer Kriegsgefangenschaft*. Munich: Verlag Gieseking 1967.

There were also a lot of political agitation and re-education attempts with propaganda films, libraries, Communist newspapers, and agitprop sessions to recruit cadres for the Soviet occupation zones in Central and East Europe and for subversion in the West. In total, some 3.2 million German POWs, often captured after 8 May 1945, plus those delivered by Western allies or from "neutral" Sweden, were in the camps, plus 900,000 German and Austrian civilian deportees, some of them highly skilled engineers. In total, 1.1 million of them died. The payment was miserable, wake-ups at 5 a.m. in the morning and beatings frequent. Guards usually stole food and equipment. A lot depended on the frequently corrupt *natshalnik* as work supervisor. Yet when prisoners were caught, military justice was harsh with sentences of 10 years for stolen potatoes. Yet it has to be kept in mind that the civilian population also suffered from hunger during these post-war years, and it was often women who saved prisoners by secretly sharing their small food rations with them. In January 1956, following the visit of Chancellor Konrad Adenauer in Moscow, the last surviving Germans after at least 10 years left the camps and were replaced by Russian prisoners. The last Austrian could leave after May 1955 when the State Treaty was signed recognizing Austrian neutrality and ending Allied occupation.

The black economy in the Gulag had a long history and probably started very soon after the revolution. My late uncle, an air force mechanic at Juncker's Werke in Dessau was captured in East Germany in the last days of the war and had to cross the Soviet border for the first time after 9 May 1945. In the Czarist fortress of Kaunas he had some official "specialist" function but his real job was to repair radio sets and watches stolen by Soviet officers in great numbers in Germany and which they had broken in the meantime. Since they were in a hurry to get their loot home, this was good business for his *natshalnik* and him. As he was usually paid in rubles or sausages, after four years he was released in good health—and since money was not allowed to be transferred out of the country—bought himself a nice fur coat and a fur hat—certainly an absolute rarity for a German POW who had not collaborated with the former enemy.

1.4.2 The War Economy of WWII and Post-war Policies

Yet for the war economy and the military loss of the Western regions, the Soviet Union in 1941–1942 was better equipped to cope than Russia in 1917–1918 with similar territorial losses. With the ruthless methods of a totalitarian state and its intact apparatus behind the front lines—in difference to the disorganized chaos of the WWI—and appealing to the patriotic reflexes of self-sacrifice, 1500 of strategic factories, their equipment and workforces were shifted East, mostly into the Urals and beyond on a massive scale. Here they created the centre for Russia's post-war armament industry at a safe distance from its external borders. Also, US lend-and-lease shipments quickly made up the huge Soviet losses of equipment and ammunition during the first months of the war. Like the Nazis with their self-defeating policies of genocide and ethnic submission in the occupied territories, Stalin, as mentioned, in 1941 engaged in summary ethnic cleansing, in deporting wholesale—similar to the Koreans ("Japanese spies"), Pontian Greeks ("internationalists") and the educated Baltic classes beforehand—Crimean tartars, Kalmucks, Volga-Germans and North Caucasian populations as suspected potential German collaborators to Siberia and to Eastern Kazakhstan as usual without provisions and shelter to an all-too-certain death and year-long starvation for the survivors. Once the tide of the war had turned with the battle of Stalingrad in January 1943 in the areas liberated by the Red Army, the hunt was on for real or suspected collaborators. Merciless fighting and scorched earth policies, practised by both sides during their retreats, had created a horrific wasteland with traumatized and starving survivors in the "blood lands" between the Volga in the East and Bug and Pruth in the West. Re-construction and the re-settlement of displaced and deported people and demobilized soldiers took almost a decade. Again the Red Army confiscated generously anything remotely useful from machinery to livestock and bicycles in its occupied areas as reparations and helped itself to able-bodied deportees among men and women for forced labour purposes in reconstruction projects.

In his post-war years, Stalin stuck rigidly to his policies of heavy industrialization and collectivization regardless of the pressing needs for reconstruction and the suffering of the population. Hence after the dictator died in March 1953 and his henchman Beria arrested in July and liquidated in December, Malenkov as the new prime minister made a plea for a new course favouring the consumer industries over the heavy industry which was in line with popular expectations after Stalin's death. This was opposed by Nikita Khrushchev who was then allied with the military which feared reduced spending on armament by the "new course". In the ensuing power struggle, Malenkov duly lost his job. Khrushchev (1953–1964) as the new first secretary transmitted the image of superficial pragmatism, but in reality adhered rigidly to unreal doctrinal objectives. One of them was the creation of "agro-cities" through merged mega-kolkhozes, while reducing further the miserably small private patches of the kolkhoz workers. The stated ideological objective was to eliminate the difference between "progressive" proletarian towns and the reactionary backward countryside, by industrializing and urbanizing the latter. The gigantic Sovkhoz state farms were supposed to cultivate new crop monocultures in the semi-arid pastures of Kazakhstan, where the thin and fragile layer of topsoil (so far extensively used as pastures by nomadic herders) was quickly eroded by wind and stormy rains, and crops decimated by frequent droughts and inclement winters. Equally, he ordered union-wide agricultural miracle cures with maize production and agricultural chemicals (whose overdoses continue to pollute Uzbekistan and the left-overs of the dried-up Aral Sea. In 1957, he experimented in decentralizing Stalin's excessive centralization by creating more than 100 economic districts in charge of regional economic decisions. When they, for reasons of localized egoism, appeared to do more harm than good, already in 1960 the experiment was reversed.

After Khrushchev with his firework of incoherent initiatives was overthrown in October 1964, Leonid Brezhnev for the next 18 years established a rule of systemic inertia. In his first decade 1965–1975, the absence of disruptions allowed for 6% annual growth, at least on paper. Good harvests—like in 1970, 1973 and 1974—were followed by failures. While he continued to engage in a nuclear and conventional arms race with the US and NATO, agriculture remained a source of perennial worries, while technologically the imperceptivity of the Soviet Union steadily continued to fall behind. The urbanization rate had reached 63% in 1980, with 18 cities then having more than one million inhabitants. In the meantime, the life expectancy for men had fallen from 67 years (1964) to 62 years (1980), a unique reversal in all industrialized countries. Usually, smoking and heavy drinking and related diseases and accidents are blamed. Equally important are surely poor nutrition, polluted urban and working environments and very rudimentary health service. In order to feed their city dwellers, the Soviet Union had to import one-quarter of its food needs, mostly from the US, but also subsidized exports from an overproducing EEC disposing of its meat, butter and cereal mountains. The notion that kolkhoz farmers' private plots in 1976 produced 64% of all potatoes, 53% of vegetables, 41% of eggs, and 22% of all meat and milk marketed in the USSR, failed to make any impression on the Kremlin's ageing leadership.[63] For Brezhnev, the miracle solution was an extremely costly virgin land reclamation scheme (where already Khrushchev had failed) in putting the sparsely populated lands of Southern Siberia and Northern Kazakhstan under the plough with huge irrigation projects and giant animal

---

[63] Stoekl. Op. cit., p. 796.

holdings. In 1977, nationwide the "Ipatowo method" was made compulsory: Large mechanized teams with armadas of huge harvest and transport machinery would move out to work on the collective and state farms of an entire region that had none of equipment (but had to pay for the work). But as distances were large and the harvesting season short, many crops were left to rot on their fields.

The preferences of the old party bureaucracy and its Brezhnevite leadership, like him, most of his cronies and allies hailed from the Dnepropetrovsk Institute of Metallurgy, continued to see the production of steel, tanks and missiles as signs of progress. The armaments industry hence was allowed to absorb the best engineers, skilled workmen and resources. The consumer goods industries, however, were perceived as annoying concessions to the masses and received correspondingly less attention and favours.[64] When mines and sources of energy became increasingly exhausted in the European part of the USSR, the costly development of Siberia's riches from the frozen North down to Kazakhstan and Turkmenistan had to be undertaken.

1.4.3 Mono-industrial Cities

The most enduring Soviet industrial heritage is probably its giant mono-industrial cities (*monogorod*). Some like St. Petersburg as the centre of machinery and shipbuilding, and Moscow, where one-quarter of all engineers are employed, are more diversified due to their qualified workforce and historically evolved industrial locations. Yet most of the Russian industrial towns remain mono-industrial: Cherepovez for metal processing with coal from Vorkuta; Murmansk for fishery and fish processing; Archangelsk for wood processing; Yaroslavl, Kostroma and Ivanova, North East of Moscow for the textile industry; Tula for iron ore; Voronezh for Tupolev airplanes; Nizhy Novgorod for automobiles and the chemical industry; Stavropol for cars and Kama trucks; Volgodonsk for nuclear power plants; Novosibirsk for machinery; Tomsk, Kemerovo and Novokusnezk for heavy machinery and metal processing; Krasnoyarsk for machinery; Chita for SIL trucks; Norilsk for nickel and platinum....

Officially, there are 314 such *monogorod* company towns in Russia today (and possibly even 400), of which by 2015, 94 had been classified at risk of collapse, as their main industry fails with no other options of local employment.[65] Usually, workers stay since their skills are tied to the plant and they

---

[64] Christian Schmidt-Häuer. *Michail Gorbatschow. Moskau im Aufbruch*. Munich: Piper 1985, p. 27.
[65] *The Economist* 22.8.2015.

have nowhere else to go and would find neither work nor accommodation. So they stay unpaid for a month and try to subsist with their families, tend their chicken, grow potatoes and vegetables, go hunting or pick mushrooms and berries. Some examples from West to East: Pikalevo, East of St. Petersburg, population 22,000, one-third unemployed with the local cement plant in trouble; Voskresenks, East of Moscow, population: 90,000, the fertilizer plant had stopped operations; Tolyatti, at the Southern Volga, population 700,000, home to Avtovaz, Russia's largest car factory, suffering from the rise and fall Russian domestic car demand; Nizhi Tagil, Southern Ural, population: 450,000, job cuts in the local iron industry; Zlatoust, equally in the rust belt of Southern Ural, population: 190,000, closure of steel factory; Miass, also Southern Ural, population: 160,000, short-time work at the local UralAZ truck factory; Baikalsk, at lake Baikal, population: 15,000, closure of local pulp mill.[66] More recent examples are the city of Kuvshinova East of Moscow, with a population of 10,000, where the local paper and cardboard mill still used machinery taken from Germany as war reparations, is now 100 years old, before it collapsed,[67] or the city of Orsk in the Southern Ural, with a population of 240,000, whose machinery factory also went under, dismissing 75% of the workforce, for the lack of investment and modernization, the last dating back to 1941 when it was relocated from Ukraine to escape from the German advance.[68] This list could go on endlessly. All of the *monogorod* suffer from the fact that once they were set up further investments more or less were stopped, with their machinery and production already hopelessly out of date at the advent of Gorbachev's perestroika.

1.4.4 Perestroika and Its Origins

In the eternal debate between Stalinist central planning and more empowerment of factory directors at the plant level (like during the NEP), Brezhnev (1964–1982) typically took no decision. He rather tried to import lacking technologies and turn-key factories and order pipelines to be paid for in long-term oil and gas deals. The logic was to develop the Soviet Union's energy sources for export revenues which should pay for domestic deficiencies. Equally, he leant heavily on the Central-East European satellite regimes to pay for armaments and his costly overseas adventures from Angola to Afghanistan. Yet domestic inefficiencies and endemic corruption continued,

---

[66] Charles Clover "Russia's one-company towns face a bleak future." *Financial Times* 28.10.2009.
[67] *The Economist*, 22.8.2015.
[68] *Financial Times* 4.12.2018.

1 From Alexander II to Gorbatchev: The Economic History …   33

even when after his death in November 1982 the tough KGB disciplinarian Yuri Andropov took over for 15 months. He was not a reformer but simply tried to tighten the screws on a restive workforce, which went queuing and shopping during work time, and on the equally shirking apparatchik class. He allowed media criticism of the corrupt Brezhnev clan—including daughter Galina and son Jurij and their entourage—in order to facilitate the subsequent purges and the punishment and execution of lesser figures. By February 1984, 20% of ministers and regional party chiefs had lost their posts. In Azerbaijan, the KGB general Gaidar Aliyev was made in charge of purging the corrupt party in Baku (38 years later his even more corrupt son Ilham is still in power there). Economically he focused on tightening the work discipline, sensing that sources for external growth (like drawing on virgin lands, new oil and gas fields and mineral deposits) were getting exhausted. The stated ambition of Khrushchev and Brezhnev of catching up and bypassing the capitalist economies regardless of social, ecological or economic costs was over. Yet all campaigns for cost accounting and increased productivity remained ineffective due to the simple doctrinal fact that prices were set politically irrespective of the market realities of supply and demand. Premia for more productive work, which soon could amount to a thirteenth monthly salary, only increased wage levels and liquidity without sufficient merchandise to match. Hidden price inflation mounted in consequence. Yuri Andropov was no liberal reformer and continued the repression of dissidents, only to be followed after his death in February 1984 by equally very sick septuagenarian Konstantin Chernenko, who tried to revive Brezhnev's heritage but died one year later in March 1985. Obviously, the Soviet system was at its wit's end.

According to Robert Kaiser[69] the national economy had been one of the most paradoxical in the world. On the one hand, the USSR then had the world's second-largest industrial capacity, including nationwide railways and power plants, which it had imposed on a fairly backward country at high growth rates. Yet the Soviet economy had remained utterly uncompetitive compared to the West. A US worker produced twice the output of a Soviet one and a US farmer ten times more than his colleague from a kolkhoz. At the same time—apart from armaments, vodka and caviar—the quality of products was so poor that they could not be sold abroad. In a way, the Soviet Union had remained a developing country. It had no nationwide network of roads nor a functioning national telephone system. There was no consumer services industry. Scarcities of basic foodstuffs, like meat, fruit and vegetables

---

[69] Robert G. Kaiser. *Russia. The People and the Power*. Harmondsworth: Penguin 1977, p. 296.

and a chronic housing shortage remained, which forced one-fourth of the people to live in a single room in communal flats.[70]

The Soviet journalist Vitaly Vitaljev in the glasnost journal "Krokodil" painted a vivid picture of lawlessness in the late Brezhnev and Chernenko era.[71] The spread of privileges and nepotism among the party elite and the scarcity of attractive consumer goods fueled corruption, illegal productions and crime and prostitution. Thus the trade in smuggled or fake jeans, perfumes, sunglasses, medicines and drugs became irresistibly profitable, luring young women—unwilling to do drudgery work for long hours and miserable wages in textile mills—into prostitution, while it encouraged criminal gangs to blackmail the underground producers (*centrovik*) and restaurant "collectives" for protection money. The poorly paid militia was bribed and closed both eyes, as prostitution and organized crime were unfathomable in a Socialist state. The evidence he collected and published from Riga to Dnepropetrovsk, the City of the Brezhnev clan, Krivoj Rog and Rostov-na-Donu. He contrasts the privileged and fenced off dachas, hotels, sanatoria, hospitals, waiting lounges, drug stores and *berioska* shops (where all foreign and unavailable goods were on shelves)—a system established by Stalin—with the miserable living conditions for ordinary Soviet people, living in crowded one-room apartments in communal flats, dirty hospitals with shortages of medicine and syringes, the lack of food in shops and of urns at funerals, and finally the virtual slavery of kolkhoz workers under the *propiska* in-land pass system, who could not leave their villages unless permitted by their kolkhoz chief. While criminal gangs (unlike the high-placed Uzbek cotton mafia) were only relatively small local groups of undisciplined hooligans and violent misfits at the time, all-in-all the general erosion of legitimacy and beginnings of lawlessness in what used to be a tightly controlled and reglemented society for decades provided a fertile ground for the upsurge of organized crime during the chaotic transformation of the 1990s.

As an agricultural expert and Andropov protégé, Mikhail Gorbatchev in 1985, for the first time since Alexander II and Stolypin, a real reformer came to power. He preached *perestroika* (restructuring) and *glasnost* (openness) as his new buzzwords. The Chernobyl disaster of April 1986 dramatically underlined the need for more than cosmetic reforms. However, the inertia of the system was such, that only glasnost worked, but little was seen or felt of perestroika. Mismanagement and abuses could be criticized openly but little changed. Hence in July 1989 miners' strikes, unheard of since 1921, against

---

[70] Ibid., p. 321.

[71] Witali Witaljew. *Die rote Mafia. Recherchen im kriminellen Untergrund der UdSSR*. Düsseldorf: Econ 1990.

their horrific working conditions spread from Siberia like a bush fire to the Kuzbas and the Donbas up to Vorkuta and Karaganda. Calls for free trade unions and healthier work and living conditions could not be appeased by small wage increments. At the same time, the public re-awakening of long and brutally repressed national aspirations made the creation of the Russified Soviet man, the homo Sovieticus, a figment of propagandist imagination. First, it made an ugly appearance in the shape of Azeri pogroms against their Armenian Christian neighbours, followed by peaceful and disciplined singing revolutions in the Baltic States, where the masses demanded the reconstitution of their independence of which they had been so cruelly deprived by Stalin in 1940 and again in 1944. Gorbachev's economic and energy blockade and his limited military aggression against Lithuania, which in April 1990 declared the restoration of independence first, was met by failure.

Domestically Gorbachev continued Andropov's purges of corrupt Brezhnev people. In Uzbekistan in 1985 alone, 9000 officials were fired. In Moscow, 19 ministers were dismissed. As an agricultural apparatchik in Stavropol (the home region of his two mentors Fyodor Kulakov (1918–1978), an early agricultural reformer in the Central Committee, and of KGB chief Andropov) in 1976, he had successfully experimented with a bonus system rewarding farmers' brigades for harvest gains and saved implements, until it was squashed on instructions from Moscow.[72] On coming to power in 1984 with the help of anti-Brezhnev allies like the nationalist orthodox purist Mikhail Suslov and the corrupt reactionary governor Grigori Romanov of Leningrad, in agriculture as well as in industry he insisted on better management of existing facilities with responsible leadership and incentives rather than continuing with even more grandiose expensive new projects. With the party's preference for new investments over modernizing old ones, these were neglected and skilled labour wasted in endless repair jobs to patch up the run-down facilities with obsolete machinery. Gorbachev's reforms started by allowing joint ventures with capitalist enterprises. Another taboo was broken by allowing Soviet companies to negotiate directly with foreign traders and companies, instead of going through the Moscow foreign trade bureaucracy. His 1986–1990 five-year plan for the first time provided for the increase of consumer products and preference for domestic consumer industries. Yet the powerfully vested bureaucracies of state commissions, branch commissions and planning committees for all products continued to stifle all company initiatives. The main problem remained how to coordinate the diverse regional economic activities with central ministries ignorant about

---

[72]Schmidt-Häuer. Op. cit., p. 76.

local conditions and needs, while at the regional rayon level there was a lack of experts and competencies to decide. Ministries and state commissions continued to decide over product types and production targets. In Leningrad alone, 170 production associations in charge of the individual factories were controlled by 150 ministries and authorities. When it came to setting norms for premia companies in collusion with employees and their unions lowered standards to gain higher wages and premia for little additional effort. Yet workers for the most part continued their preference for equal pay over performance-oriented wage differentials.

In the meantime, the Soviet military was forced to withdraw from their former "allies", starting with Hungary, and even from the Baltics. German unification loomed after the popular overthrow of the Communist dictatorship in the East in 1989. Gorbachev reacted by accumulating—increasingly empty—power positions for himself, and after "controlled" elections in spring 1989 to the Congress of People's Deputies had himself appointed President of the USSR after striking the CPSU's monopoly on power off the constitution. Yet as the old planned economy collapsed, ruble inflation started spinning out of control. There was too much liquidity in the system and factory directors reacted to the fall in demand by increasing prices. Being economically illiterate they hoped that this would keep their balance sheets even. Black markets and organized crime began to flourish. The resulting chaos and disorganization even disrupted a good harvest, which subsequently was not properly stored and processed, but fell to waste. In June 1990, Boris Yeltsin, a more firebrand reformer whom Gorbachev had sacrificed earlier for political expediency, was elected President of the Russian Federation.

Yet it also must be stated that Gorbachev sent OMON troops into Vilnius in January 1991 which brutally killed 14 and injured 700 peaceful demonstrators for Lithuanian independence. He also watched cynically when in the same year in Azerbaijan hundreds of innocent Armenian were butchered by mobs and refused to give orders to the locally stationed Red Army units to intervene.

During 1985–1986 the price per barrel of oil had fallen from $25 to $12. The oil price erosion by each dollar did cost the Soviet Union $550 million per year. Possibly this was a coordinated strategy of the Reagan administration with the Saudis, to force the Soviets to ask for international credits for much-needed machinery imports and thus gain external leverage for internal reforms in Russia.[73] If this was the case, the strategy worked wonders. Gorbachev felt compelled to approach the IMF and GATT in 1986

---

[73]Maria Huber. *Moskau 11.März 1985. Die Auflösung des sowjetischen Imperiums*. Munich: DTV. 2002, p. 79.

and 1987, and started to decentralize and liberalize the Soviet Union's export trade. As of January 1987 individual ministries and large enterprises were allowed to do foreign trade on their own. Gorbachev also finished the 10-year-old doomed Soviet campaign in Afghanistan, yet in vain had hope for a peace dividend at home. His campaign against vodka similarly failed. This drink was used as a substitute for missing food, like meat and vegetables, in shops. Now there was nothing.

Gorbachev himself in August 1991 fell victim to a reactionary, if amateurish coup attempt of senior apparatchiks of the military and party apparatus. Boris Yeltsin rose to the occasion to decide the end not only of the Soviet system but also of the Soviet Union. Gorbachev, the CPSU and its misdeeds against the peoples of the Soviet Union were history, and mostly for the better and only sometimes worse, a new era had started.

1.5 The Transformation of the Soviet Economy

The transformation of the results of the October revolution and 70 years of totalitarian state socialism, which thoroughly had wiped out any significant private property and any memories of bourgeois civility, the rule of law and the spirit and practice of entrepreneurialism and systematically sanctioned all such attempts, is surely one of the most fascinating chapters of economic history. Nowhere in the former East bloc, this was painless, even though there the Socialist period that lasted "only" 40 years and in some countries like Poland, Hungary and Yugoslavia allowed earlier reforms and small businesses. There were massive industrial dislocations, job losses, the devaluation of old professional profiles with almost universal retraining needs for industrial, service, administrative and managerial jobs, and massive investment need to upgrade industry, infrastructure, energy and environmental sectors. Finally, the entire public administration, from schools to ministries, from courts to the security apparatus required thorough reforms and restructuring. Understandably, frustrations were high among the liberated peoples when instead of the expected riches of the capitalist West overnight they were faced with unemployment, legal and social insecurity, administrative incompetence, decline into poverty, as all of their countries underwent a serious economic crisis as industrial output suddenly collapsed when substandard products became unsellable with customers being deprived of purchasing power—except for imported necessities. In less than a decade during the 1990es in Central Eastern Europe, all future member states of the EU, with the help of Western funds and EU member states administrative support, in spite of lots of trial and costly errors (notably in East Germany), miraculously the transformation was more or less accomplished. In the Balkans due to prolonged governance problems and the Serbian wars, it took more time and sacrifices. But nowhere—perhaps apart from Ukraine and Central Asia—the process of transformation took such a tormented road and the privatization was done so ruthlessly for the benefit first of private and later Kremlin-linked oligarchs, the societal pain and economic depression prolonged and was so deep.

In difference to Gorbachev, already by 1986, the young reformers around Yegor Gaidar and Anatoly Chubais understood that the crisis of the Soviet economy could only be resolved by introducing a capitalist market economy.[74] In St. Petersburg, they organized summer seminars to gather congenial minds, which after Yeltsin's rise to power could supply him and his entourage and apparatchiks with the necessary ideas and know-how for reforms. As "Mc Kinsey revolutionaries" they believed in shock therapy and were animated by the Leninist belief that the suffering of the Russian people in the present was justified by its brighter future.[75] They were not interested in personal power. This they left to Yeltsin, of whose erratic moods and tactical plots they remained dependent. As "Marxism in reverse" their main interest was to transfer public property into private hands as quickly as possible.[76] How this happened and to whose benefit was relatively secondary. Thus the "red directors" became the great winners of the first round of coupon privatization of industry.[77] When coupons (actually shares of co-ownership) were distributed to their workforce, for instance, they spread the rumour that these were actually worthless, and in the canteens offered to trade them in for two bottles of vodka and packs of oranges. Most workers accepted the offer. That the new owners exploited their factories, had no funds to invest and to modernize, stashed cash abroad and did not pay their workers, did not disturb the reformers.

By 1994, the second group of entrepreneurs developed, who used legal loopholes skillfully and utilized scarce import privileges, export licenses and corrupt civil servants and judges to build up funds and riches in foreign currencies very quickly. Many of these future oligarchs were academically trained physical scientists of Jewish origin (later in case of trouble an Israeli passport would serve as life insurance of sorts and as a helpline). Typically,

---

[74] Chrystia Freeland. *Sale of the Century. The inside story of the Second Russian Revolution.* London: Abacus 2005, p. 27.
[75] Op. cit., p. 37.
[76] Op. cit., p. 52.
[77] Op. cit., p. 87.

during their Komsomol days under Gorbachev they would have founded then permissible trading cooperatives, which from very modest origins of barter trading of scarce domestic goods they would under Yeltsin branch out into much more lucrative import/export commodity trading, set up banks which the proceeds and acquire the accounts of authorities and big corporations. These funds then served to buy industry participations for their own gain.

The access to the court of Yeltsin was facilitated and controlled by Boris Berezovsky, who had published his autobiography and kept him amused by paying Yeltsin any amount of royalties. He befriended his daughter Tatiana and with his ORT TV channel provided positive political PR.[78] When in 1995 public discontent threatened Yeltsin's re-election by the sudden re-emergence of the Communists in the shape of Zyuganov, the young reformers, who feared for their capitalism, and the oligarchs, who feared for their newly gained property, concluded a Faustian pact in Davos. The oligarchs would provide loans to the illiquid state to get by election day, finance and revitalize with the help of Chubais Yeltsin's election campaign, and support the president with their media. In return, the state would hand his crown jewels, the gas, oil and metal combinates which thus far had been exempted from privatization, as collateral to the oligarchs. After the election victory of Yeltsin and the oligarchs, Yukos, Norilsk Nickel, Sidanco and Lukoil were transferred to them in faked auctions for about 2% of their later market value.[79] Red directors, foreign interests and minority shareholders were shifted aside.

The agreement of Davos did, however, not last between the oligarchs. Already in 1997, unsurprisingly they started to argue over their prey. Gusinsky, for instance, whose press and NTV television channel had supported Yeltsin, had claims for the telecom holding Sviasinvest, which was however contested by Potanin and the young reformers, who offered higher bids. Both Gusinsky and Berezovsky in revenge then started a press campaign alleging corruption of Potanin and the reformers. As a result, Berezovsky and Chubais quickly lost their government jobs.[80]

In the global financial crisis of 1998, the government became illiquid, several big banks collapsed, the ruble was massively devalued and public debt no longer honoured. The new middle classes and small businesses were hard hit. Most oligarchs however survived, thanks to their industry holdings and overseas foreign currency accounts. In any event the reputation and political credibility of the reformers were gone. Actually, they had planned a second

---

[78]Op. cit., p. 133.
[79]Op. cit., p. 172.
[80]Op. cit., p. 277.

wave of reforms aiming at strengthening proper governance and the judiciary, protecting private property and consolidated state finances. In this situation of crisis, Berezovsky in 1999 recommended an unknown tough guy, whom he had met as an energetic vice mayor of St. Petersburg before, a certain Vladimir Putin. Yeltsin, who at that time was only interested in immunity for himself and his family, appointed Putin to become his successor. Again the oligarchs' finances and media power produced the right election results.

The new president, however, showed little obedience and gratefulness and very quickly opted for a regime-run siloviki colleagues of the power apparatus. The oligarchs were told that they could keep their property only in case of political neutrality. The media oligarchs Gusinsky and Berezovsky found this unacceptable and went into their London exile. Most, however, grudgingly accepted, and when firmly told to do so, accepted to sell strategic holdings to the new state oligarchs designed by the Kremlin. Roman Abramovich for instance moved his centre of business activities and capital gradually and discretely into Switzerland, the Cote d'Azur and to London. Most oligarchs were actually traders of companies rather than managers. There was one notable exemption: Khodorkovsky. He renovated his Yukos oil conglomerate and did not heed the Kremlin's warnings to abstain from supporting the liberal opposition.[81] His subsequent martyrdom illustrated the limits of private property protection and civil liberties under Putin's new authoritarian rule.

References

1. Applebaum A (2003) Gulag. A history of the Soviet Camps. Allen Lane, London
2. Connaughton R (2004) Rising sun and stumbling bear. Russia's War with Japan. Cassell, London
3. Fitz Lyon C, Browning T (2003) Les Russes avant 1917. Editions autrement, Paris
4. Freeland C (2005) Sale of the century. The inside story of the second Russian Revolution. Abacus, London
5. Gallo M (2017) 1917, une passion russe. XO editions, Paris
6. Gouttman A (2006) La Guerre de Crimee 1853–1856. Perrin, Paris
7. Huber M (2002) Moskau, 11. März 1985. Die Auflösung des sowjetischen Imperiums. DTV, Munich
8. Kaiser RG (1977) Russia. The people and the power. Penguin, Harmondsworth

---

[81] Op. cit., p. 338.

9. Kalniete S (2005) Mit Balettschuhen im sibirischen Schnee, Die Geschichte meiner Familie. Herwig, Munich
10. Mawdsley E (1987) The Russian Civil War. Birlinn, Edinburgh
11. Mayer E (2017) Wogau & Co. Das größte deutsche Handelshaus im russischen Zarenreich. Pro Business, Berlin
12. Mosse WE (1996) An economic history of Russia 1856–1914. I.B. Tauris, London
13. Peter E (1998) Von Workuta bis Astrachan. Stocker, Graz
14. Reck M (1967) Tagebuch aus sowjetischer Kriegsgefangenschaft. Gieseking, Munich
15. Schmidt-Häuer C (1985) Michael Gorbatschow. Moskau im Aufbruch. Piper, Munich
16. Schüler H (1993) Workuta. Herbig, Munich
17. Stoekl G (1997) Russische Geschichte. Kröner, Stuttgart
18. Stone N (1998) The Eastern Front 1914–1917. Penguin, London
19. Trotsky L (1932) The history of the Russian revolution. Penguin, London
20. Wein N (1985) Die Sowjetunion. UTB Schönigh, Paderborn
21. Witaljew W (1990) Die rote Mafia. Recherchen im kriminellen Untergrund der UdSSR. Econ, Düsseldorf

2

Post-Soviet Industrial Policy: From the Red Directors to the New State Oligarchs

The reversal of the October revolution of 1917 is certainly one of the most exciting stories of contemporary history. All countries in transition after 1989 experienced cases of illegitimate and disproportionate private appropriation of people's property. However, they have often been corrected through the courts, in the event of democratic changes of power and as a result of competition in an increasingly functioning market economy. Soviet-occupied Estonia, Latvia and Lithuania after their liberation coped with this remarkably well. So, this was possible. Yet in most successor countries of the USSR, including Central Asia and parts of the South Caucasus, the public property has been used as fraudulent and unevenly transfer to a handful of well-placed politically favoured nomenclature capitalists like in Russia. For the sake of simplicity, three phases can be distinguished: In the early Yeltsin era (1991–1994), the factory grabbing of the Red Directors, who bought the shares ("vouchers") of their employees cheaply. Following the re-election of Yeltsin (1996), the acquisition of the basic industries and oil industry by the Yeltsin oligarchs with their heavily discounted debt for equity deals, and since the beginning of Putin's rule (2000–), the re-nationalization and growing economic control by the Kremlin in the form of the state oligarchs, mostly former KGB officers, the siloviki, and former senior officials of the Petersburg city administration, who were all in a personal loyalty relationship to the new head of state.

2.1 Putin's State Monopoly Capitalism

During that change, quickly some of the short-term owners were expropriated again, including a number of red directors. After Putin's arrival, it hit first the Gazprom directors (Chernomyrdin and Vyachirev). Then the politically bullying oligarchs Vladimir Gusinsky and Boris Berezovsky were eliminated as independent media moguls, and finally as a brutal deterrent: the fate of Mikhail Khodorkovsky in 2003.

In the meantime, all of the Kremlin's strategically defined industries—as well as foreign shareholdings like those held by Shell and BP—were gradually being sold to directly controlled state-owned companies such as Gazprom (gas), Rosneft (oil), Surgutneftegas, Rosoboronexport (armaments), as well as to oligarchs submissive to the Kremlin's industrial policy imperatives like Oleg Deripaska (Rusal), Alexei Mordechai (Severstal), Leonid Reyman (Telecominvest) and Valery Yashin (Svyzinvest).

Often, the staff appointed by Putin, such as Alexei Miller and Dimitri Medvedev at Gazprom, Sergei Bogdanchikov and Igor Sechin at Rosneft, Vladimir Yakunin and Alexandre Shukov at the Russian state railways, Viktor Ivanov at Aeroflot and Almaz-Antey (air defences), Alexei Kudmin at Alrosa (diamonds), were very well paid, and at the same time, often remained ministers or held functions at the Kremlin. They became millionaires quickly, and within ten years most of them turned into billionaires like the few surviving Yeltsin oligarchs.

The share of the economy controlled by the state oligopolies is now estimated at 40%. If Putin was initially concerned only with the extraction of oil and gas as basic industries, as "strategic sectors" since 2005–2006 he has gradually re-nationalized a large segment of 40 economic sectors with more than 1000 companies, covering the defence and space industry, diamond, gold, platinum, nickel, titanium, vanadium and aluminium extraction and smelting, shipbuilding, the aircraft, automobile and paper industries which to the largest extent possible should be monopolized and put under state control with the role of foreign co-owners being reduced. According to Putin's annual speeches to the oligarchs gathered, in order to restore Russia's world reputation and improved access to foreign technology, Putin called for foreign ownership, alongside local infrastructure investments, to be reduced to minority participations and also the supply of foreign technologies.

Gazprom, for instance, has been investing for years notoriously at the Kremlin's request, in an attempt to invest a lot of its cash flow into Eastern, Central and Western European gas distribution networks—from Armenia to Portugal—in an ill-conceived effort to control its pipelines to the final consumer and thus to keep out the competition, until EU regulations struck. At the same time, it has neglected the development of new gas fields.

The management practice of these former secret service officers confirms that they are well trained, tactically smart and hard negotiators having survived in the tough school of the Byzantinist branches of the Kremlin, but they were surely no trained economic managers, as they had generally no commercial or sectoral experience before being appointed to their top positions.

Intimidated by the tax police and the periodical raids by the Public Prosecutor's Office, the surviving Yeltsin oligarchs, having adhered to their original survival conditions, which were defined by Putin in July 2000 as only political abstinence and tax compliance, and which have since been gradually extended, have through "voluntary" payments generally repaid for their under-priced industrial takeovers of 1995–1996. They must continue to keep the lord of the Kremlin in good humour through de facto special taxes, like the donation of $100 million for imperial Fabergé eggs by Viktor Vekselberg, the payment for the 300th-anniversary celebrations of St Petersburg ($360 million) and the reconstruction of Sochi airport near Putin's new holiday resort for over $1.5 billion, sponsored by Oleg Deripaska. Gazprom and Potanin's Interros in 2014 had to build two new ski resorts with new runways in Krasnaya Polyana including lifts and access roads for $270 million, and certainly not because nickel or natural gas are found there.

Most of the oligarchs—Roman Abramovich, the richest among them foremost—struggled to bring their money and their centre of interest to West Europe, the Caribbean islands or to Israel as quickly and as discreetly as possible. They pretend to follow the Kremlin's strategy of restoring geopolitical influence on Russia through foreign investments abroad, even though arguably the acquisition of soccer clubs (like Chelsea), yachts and real estate from Kensington to Miami can hardly be termed as strategic. In short, the Putinist state, whose policies are not always consistent due to internal political struggles, is attempting geopolitically to re-monopolize the key companies to be controlled by a personal power cartel of the leading state cadres. The monopoly economy of Putin Inc., which accounts for 40% of the Russian economy, then becomes the instrument of the authoritarian state, the state acting as an agent of the power clique controlling the key industries. This is state monopoly capitalism in a pure vulgar Marxist–Leninist version. The imperialism theory of Lenin, many of whose statues are still around in the country, clearly described the external aggressiveness of such a system: its addiction to spheres of influence, dependent markets and exclusive sources of raw materials, and the desire to subject or to destroy economic-imperial rivals. Nobody has better predicted Russia's foreign and energy policy 100 years later. For state monopoly capitalist actors—in difference to liberal economists—the world economy is a zero-sum game. I win, you lose, or the other way round.

According to Putin, this personalized monopolistic industrial policy and the State's control of the exploitation of natural resources is about the restoration of Russia's unique influence and greatness, as explicitly stated in Putin's 1999 pronouncements reflecting the views of his candidate dissertation of 1997 at the Petersburg Mining Institute.[1] However, looking more closely at methods and results, which are often sub-optimal in economic terms and conflict with Russia's long-term interests, the effect of these industrial policies is primarily about securing personal power and wealth.

Logically, for a while there were persistent rumours, according to which, after appointing a reliable successor like Dmitry Medvedev from among his Petersburg followers, that Putin himself would take over the management of the then merged Gazprom and Rosneft giant as the world's greatest energy czar commanding the world's largest integrated energy company, and thus occupy a decent job for an ex-President, residing in style in the new Gazprom skyscraper in St. Petersburg, a tower of 400 m height and built at the cost of $2 billion.[2] As we know, this scenario has not occurred.

Those who came under the wheels in the sequence of red directors/Yeltsin oligarchs/Putin state oligarchs were the independent, struggling Russian medium-sized entrepreneurs, which remained unprotected both against the arbitrariness of oligarchs, obstructing unwanted competition, and also against the corrupt, greedy state and regional administration. At any given moment some 160,000 Russian businessmen sit in jails until they pay their ransom to get out without any conviction of course. The more successful they are, the likelier they become candidates for these criminal shakeouts. But also the Russian population as a whole suffers, which continues to be excluded and cheated from the usufructuary of the wealth they had created during the last century—and which nominally at least was the "people's property"—by the sequence of private and state oligarchs facilitated by a corrupted political leadership.

In other words: "A theft of the century" on the largest possible scale.

How was this made possible?

---

[1] Harley Balzer "Vladimir Putin on Russian Energy policy" *The National Interest*, November 2005.
[2] Erich Follath, Matthias Schepp. "Der Konzern des Zaren" *Der Spiegel* 5.3.2007.

2.2 The Red Directors

As early as 1986, a group of young reformers around Yegor Gaidar and Anatoli Chubais realized that capitalism was the only way to remedy the crisis of the Soviet economy. In St. Petersburg they invited like-minded people to seminars, which provided the necessary economic and reformist expertise after Yeltsin's and his apparatchik's seizure of power. As "McKinsey Revolutionaries", they believed in shock therapy and were inspired by a Leninist belief that the suffering of the people today is necessary for a better future. They were little interested in a personal power base or, so it seemed, in personal gain. They left this to Yeltsin and his entourage, from whose erratic moods and tactical moves they remained detached yet dependent. The main challenge was: As "Marxism in reverse" to transfer state property rights to private owners as soon as possible. To whom and how this happened was comparatively secondary to them.[3]

The red directors were the first big winners of major industrial coupon privatization. As Igor Yavlinsky, the leader of the liberal Yabloko party, rightly observed at the time, the dissolution of the Soviet Union in 1991 was not a democratic revolution as it happened in Central Eastern Europe, but—similarly to Romania in December 1989—a coup of the nomenklatura. Accordingly, it continued to control the law of action, especially when the distribution of public property is concerned.

During the first wave of privatization in 1992–1994, the share ownership of individual factories was transferred to the workforce (50%), 9% to executives and 41% to government agencies and third parties through coupons.[4] Already during perestroika, the directors had perfected the art to milk their companies for the benefit of their own (mostly foreign) accounts through their personal control or in collusion with over-charging suppliers and by intermediate buyers of their under-prized end products by strawmen or relatives. Thus, they had sufficient capital to purchase en masse cheaply the coupons of their employees, who had often not been paid for months before. Typically, the apparently worthless coupons, which had a nominal value of 10,000 rubles (EUR 30 at the time), were traded for a few bottles of vodka (for men) and tropical fruit (for ladies) in the usually empty factory shops or canteens. Later the packages of coupons acquired in each factory were bundled and re-sold with a mark-up to the corporate management (or possibly interested out-side "collectors").

---

[3] Chrystia Freeland. *Sale of the Century. The Inside Story of the Second Russian Revolution.* London: Abacus 2005, p. 52.
[4] *Financial Times* 6.8.2002.

The best-known red directors include Vagit Alekperov (Lukoil), Vladimir Bogdanov (Surgutneftegas), Alexei Mordechai (Severstal), and Viktor Chernomyrdin and his successor Rem Vjachiev (Gazprom). Until 1989, Gazprom had been part of the Soviet Ministry of the Gas Industry. Chernomyrdin was its minister (1985–1989) until he took control over his nominally state-owned gas monopoly together with all associated gas pipelines, production facilities, distribution systems and gas fields, as a chairman. Once he became Yeltsin's Prime Minister during 1992–1998, his successor and former deputy Rem Viakhirev continued as CEO. Chernomyrdin and his successor had managed in such a way that Gazprom under their helm stopped most investments, yet still wrote red figures, hardly paid taxes and they themselves became ever richer. Chernomyrdin at a formal salary of $8000/year with his two sons had reportedly diverted from the parent company $5 billion through transfer transactions with subsidiaries.[5] Putin dismissed him and Viakhirev soon after took office in 2001. He was replaced by the non-industry expert Alexei Miller, a close collaborator of his in St. Petersburg, who was also in charge of financing his election campaigns and in control of the numerous printed and electronic media owned by Gazprom.

The red directors had typically studied engineering or metallurgy and, as a party-loyal factory leader faithfully adhered to formal plan fulfilments. Yet at the same time, given the shortages, they had to operate skilfully on the black market and to get to know the right operators during the Brezhnev era and beyond.

Quickly, however, the young ideology-led reformers also had to realize that the red directors as owners performed very poorly, as they continued their decade-long recipes of survival under central planning: maximizing output while ignoring markets, customer demands, innovation and quality, and as new elements: engaging in the private diversion of profits, the non-payment of debts, salaries and bills. Moreover, as the legacy of the Soviet era, their factories were too large as effective production facilities but too small in terms of product range and marketing abilities as individual companies. As a result, from 1994 onwards, a new, younger, more entrepreneurial and much more aggressive type of ownership was encouraged.

---

[5]Chernomyrdin in 2001–2009 was appointed ambassador to the Ukraine. In a famous incident he met in Kiev with US businessmen, one of whom asked: "How would you invest 5 million US$ in the Ukraine?" Through an error in translation Chernomyrdin misunderstood and felt insulted: He did not own a mere 5 million US$, but 5 billion US$. He was also famous, when in office for sayings like: "We wanted the best, but it turned out as always".

2.3   A Short Story of the Russian Oligarchy

Next to the red directors, the second group of entrepreneurs had developed by 1994: They had used the previous "slump" economy, which was made possible by inadequate laws, import privileges, export licenses, corrupt officials, politicians and judges, and had quickly acquired ruthless wealth. These future oligarchs were often science-based academics of Jewish origin, who had set up cooperatives during the Gorbachev years and after a number of lucrative export/import deals, set up banks in which they managed the accounts of public authorities and large companies, accumulating the control of sufficient funds with a view to obtain targeted industrial stakes. Access to Yeltsin's court had been opened to them—via Chubais as an intermediary—by Boris Berezovsky, who had published the President's autobiography, held him with royalties in good humour, remained a close friend to Tatiana Diatchenko, Yeltsin's daughter, and ensured positive political coverage with his ORT TV channel. When public dissatisfaction and the strength of the communist Zyuganov seemed to pose a serious threat to Yeltsin's re-election in 1995, the young reformers in Davos concluded a Faustian pact with the oligarchs—at the time Potanin, Gusinsky, Khodorkovsky, Aven, Fridman, Smolinsky and Berezovsky—who feared for their property: The oligarchs would help the insolvent state by providing loans, finance the election of Yeltsin, dismiss Yeltsin's bodyguard, alcoholic campaign manager and drinking companion General Korsakov, co-opt and neutralize the war hero General Lebed as a potential rival, revitalize his campaign with Chubais as manager and support him with their media. In return, the State would pledge its crown jewels, which previously excluded oil and metallurgical groups from privatization to the oligarchs. Following the victory of Yeltsin and the oligarchy, Yukos (Khodorkovsky), Norilsk Nickel and Sidanco (Potanin), Sibneft (Berezovsky) and Tyumen Oil (Fridman, Vekselberg) were then transferred to the oligarchs at about 2% of their later capital value in faked auctions.[6] The aim was to create a capitalist elite loyal to Yeltsin and liberal economic order. The red directors, foreign stakeholders and minority shareholders were all to be disregarded.

However, the Davos pact of oligarchs was not to survive their election victory for long. As early as 1997, they disputed about the prey. Gusinsky, whose press and NTV had supported Yeltsin, had a claim for the telecommunications holding company Svyasinvest, which, however, with the support of the young reformers was contested by Potanin for a higher bid. Gusinsky and

---

[6]Freeland. Op. cit., p. 172 et seq.

Berezovsky then launched a denunciatory media campaign with allegations of corruption against Potanin and the reformers, a self-destructive operation as a result of which both Chubais and Berezovsky lost their government positions.[7]

Originally, the young reformers had assumed the romantic expectation that Russia's wild capitalism—this time within a short time span—would develop along the lines of American capitalism in the nineteenth century. Finally, ruthless predators such as Vanderbilt, Rockefeller, Carnegie and J.P Morgan, who originally had abused monopolies, cheated minority shareholders, suppliers as well as customers, bribed politicians and judges, but within two generations had turned into venerable institutions of the US East Coast establishment.

However, after several years of their exorbitant new wealth, the oligarchs showed little sign of a civilizing influence of the new billions. The 36 Russian billionaires on the 2004 Forbes list had possessed only a few thousand rubles back in 1985.[8] Twenty years later, Russian national income had halved. One-third of the population lived below the poverty threshold. The manipulative and often violent predators, who beheaded the magnum bottles in the bars of St. Tropez with a sword and ordered hostesses in company strength to fly to Courchevel in the French Alps, were universally disliked in Russia. According to Vladimir Potanin, who was supposed to know, the average cost of living for an individual oligarch is $2–3 million per year. Roman Abramovich is likely to have significantly increased this average. In November 2006, he spent EUR 1.5 million on a two-week cure at the Lauserhof in Tyrol, where his precious body was taken care of by a team of 30 people.[9] In general, it is assumed that he spends €100,000 a day. This means €36 million per year.

Yet, according to a World Bank study published in 2004, their operations were managed better than those that remained state-owned, regionally owned or managed by red directors.[10] However, as a business dealer by origin, the oligarchs were less efficient managers than the real entrepreneurs of smaller new businesses, whom they threatened with their financial power, their control of export transactions and of political privileges in the sectors which they dominated (metallurgy, energy, vehicle construction, media and banks). The rapid growth of oligarchic business empires was less due to the expansion of market and production shares but rather the effect of the

---

[7] Freeland. Op. cit., p. 277.
[8] Marshall I. Goldman 'Putin and the Oligarchs' *Foreign Affairs* Nov/Dec. 2004.
[9] "Luxuskur von 1.5 Millionen" *Österreich* 16.11.2006.
[10] Andrew Jack "A map of Russia's new Empires" *Financial Times* 7.4.2004, Christian Caryl "Tycoon Takeover" *Newsweek* 19.4.2004.

somewhat indiscriminate acquisition of production sites and new business lines, which favoured the control of lucrative export markets (using raw materials which at domestic prices were sold cheaply to offshore subsidiaries and then sold by them at real-world market prices) and which were privileged by central and regional authorities (with tax concessions, subsidies, special rates for electricity and rail transport). These opportunities, which distorted the development of the Russian economy—and always required generous donations (a "special tax") to officialdom in Moscow and in the other regions—were hardly accessible to the new middle class.

2.4 The Russian Crisis of 1998

As usual, international loans helped to delay the self-inflicted catastrophe caused by mismanagement. At some point, however, the harsh realities inevitably prevailed. On 17 August 1998, when official Moscow was dreaming in their dachas, the Russian state became insolvent. Due to the lack of tax payments, declared export revenues and the losses of state-owned enterprises, the government was no longer able to pay its foreign debt and interest due. The ruble had to be devalued in a crisis. Its value was slashed by a factor of more than four from 6 rubles to 28 rubles per dollar. As a result, a number of large over-indebted Russian banks could no longer settle their foreign liabilities, were besieged by panicked savers and went bankrupt. The most prominent ones were the SBS Agrobank of Alexander Smolenski (who later disappeared) and the Inkom Bank of Vladimir Vinogradov, whose collapse alone resulted in 260,000 savers losing their money, while the owners had previously moved some billions of euros abroad. They themselves in good time had moved to their overseas country estates and yachts and disappeared from public view. The Communists immediately used the crisis to agitate against Jewish bankers who allegedly had ruined Russia.[11]

However, most other oligarchs managed to save their assets in Russia through immediate export earnings. Khodorkovsky, for instance, also defrauded his domestic and foreign debtors[12] while securing the pledged securities in good time and transferring his company's value to subsidiaries. He then presented his debtors only with a shell company, his Menatep Bank.

After a few months, the Russian economy swung back, with the domestic consumer goods industry being the first to recover due to the high price

---

[11] *International Herald Tribune* 9.4.1999.
[12] *Financial Times* 16.6.2004.

of competing imports caused by the low ruble rate. The surviving oligarchs bought cheaply the devalued banking groups and companies.

As a result of the crisis, its unequal distribution of sufferings with many losers and only a few winners as the obvious scapegoats, the political reputation of reformers suffered irreparable damage. They had actually wanted to implement a second wave of economic reforms to consolidate the rule of law, property protection and orderly public finances. In addition, corruption revelations were spread in the media owned by Gusinsky and Berezovsky, according to which the purportedly innocent reformers had received up to $100,000 as an advance for never written books.

When the replacement of Sergei Stepashin, who as a Prime Minister had become deeply unpopular during the crisis, was imminent, in 1999 Berezovsky recommended to Yeltsin an unknown tough cookie who in St. Petersburg, then the crime capital of Russia, as a vice-mayor had acquired the reputation of being loyal and able to implement things.[13] It turned out to be certain that Vladimir Putin, who after his time as lieutenant colonel and head of the KGB residentura in Dresden, had ended his secret service career in 1990 and after a time at St. Petersburg university had become vice-mayor of Economic Affairs under Petersburg's first elected reform mayor Anatoly Sobchak. At the beginning of his career there, Anatoly Chubais had been his superior. Later state oligarchs were his subordinates or colleagues at the time, including Alexei Miller and Valeri Golubev (Gazprom) Igor Sechin (Rosneft), Leonid Reyman (Telecominvest) and Vladimir Kogan (Promstroibank).

After Sobchak's election loss, Putin became deputy head of the Kremlin administration in 1996 and FSB chief in 1998 until he was recommended by Berezovsky and supported by his people in the Kremlin (Boris Abramovich and Yeltsin's chief of staff Alexander Voloshin) in July 1999 as Prime Minister. Yeltsin, who was already in bad health and interested foremost in immunity for himself and his family, soon appointed Putin also as his successor. In the subsequent presidential elections, in addition to the victorious small war in Chechnya, the oligarchs' finances and media power again ensured the desired result.

2.5   Putin's Start as President

Even after his election, Putin was still profiled in the domestic and foreign media as a grey mouse and creature of the oligarchs. The Economist described him as a "puppet president" at the mercy of Berezovsky pulling the strings. He

---

[13]Elfie Siegl "Putin und die Oligarchen" *Frankfurter Allgemeine* 8.7.2000.

was strongly advised to free himself from the dictate of oligarchs. According to the Handelsblatt[14]:

> In his future handling of the oligarchs, it will be possible to assess whether Putin is following its own paths—or whether he remains only the administrator of the Yeltsin heritage and the guardian of the interests of the dubious circles around the former master of the Kremlin.

At that time, freedom of the press was primarily threatened by the control of the main television channels (ORT—Berezovsky, and NTV—Gusinsky) and of the print media by manipulative oligarchs.[15] Apart from the left-leaning newspapers Pravda and Trud, there was no significant media criticism of oligarchic acquisitions in Russia.[16] In the 1997 "oligarch war", their own media had been used recklessly to promote their own business interests and defame their political and economic opponents—as was the case during the 1996 and 2000 presidential election campaigns. Nor did they not have any scruples to publish phone calls listened in by their private security services or real or fabricated kompromat. Gusinky's Most group alone employed more than 1000 security guards. Most had learned their craft from the KGB.

However, against all expectations and in spite of Berezovsky's public outrage, Putin quickly showed himself unthankful and, with the help of his Petersburg confident and siloviki colleagues, quickly started an authoritarian regime of his own making, relying on the security apparatus instead of the quarrelsome oligarchic regime. As he had come to power rather by accident without personal power and very limited resources, he had initially relied equally on the siloviki and liberal economic circles. To the extent that he consolidated his grasp on power and organized his own political finances through direct access to Gazprom, his supporter base increasingly narrowed to the St. Petersburg siloviki scene of senior ex-KGB officers and former civil service colleagues as disciplined, loyal, power-oriented followers of his own, a very narrow recruitment base for his personal power and for Russia's political leadership to last for the next two decades at least.

In July 2000, he lectured the 21 oligarchs gathered at his request, stating that they would be able to retain their dubious property, provided that they paid their taxes correctly, that they no longer bribed civil servants and that

---

[14] "Die Zukunft der Oligarchen ist Putins Lackmustest" *Handelsblatt* 27.3.2000.
[15] *Le Monde* 25.4.1997.
[16] *The Economist* 14.11.1997.

they no longer interfered in politics. Similar warnings were sent to the provincial governors and the Kremlin administration. In the Chekist tradition, these warnings after a short break were followed up by dissuasive examples.

In February 2001, the most corrupt of all governors, Nadratshenko from the Far East federal district, who had ruled in Vladivostok with impunity in association with organized crime, was fired. From the outset, Rem Viahkirev, the powerful head of the miserably run Gazprom, was also on Putin's list of first replacements. He was the first red director to be replaced by Alexei Miller, a reliable Putin hand. Ever since then, the Kremlin directly controls Gazprom and its finances.

The chief of the Kremlin administration, Pavel Borodin, who, as a ruler of all public land, also had control over all Russia's embassies, state buildings, state dachas, yachts, hundreds of planes, car parks, palaces and hotels—which in Russia, of course, were never restituted to the heirs of the legitimate pre-revolutionary owners, and who under Yeltsin[17] acquired certain fame for corruption, was equally prominent in the firing line. Putin, who as his former deputy knew him all too well, got rid of him with an elegant trick.[18] Borodin was the subject of a US arrest warrant for money laundering. All of a sudden, he received a faked personal invitation by George W. Bush to attend his inauguration ceremony. Deeply flattered he felt safe and flew to New York, where the anonymously alerted US authorities immediately apprehended him at the airport. They were not impressed by the fake invitation. Hence it was jail time for him instead of a presidential candlelight dinner. Some FSB staffers, including Putin, who has a very dark sense of humour, were probably greatly amused. Once released without being charged, Borodin was made Secretary-General of the Russian-Belorussian Union, a purely honorary post with little access to slush funds.

2.6 The Fate of Oligarchs I—Falling Out of Favour

Vladimir Gusinsky was by far the leading candidate for oligarch cleansing. Gusinsky, allied with Mayor Lushkov in Moscow and his city syndicate Sistema, was highly indebted and fought with most of the other oligarchs. Shortly after Putin's inauguration as President, true to form he already fell in June 2000. His financing and the organization of the Russian Jewish

---

[17] *The Economist* 18.9.1999, *Süddeutsche Zeitung* 15.9.2000.
[18] *Süddeutsche Zeitung* 2.2.2001.

Congress had annoyed the Kremlin already during Yeltsin's times. The second to go was Boris Berezovsky, politically the most powerful among the oligarchs. With the pride of a kingmaker he had sovereignly ignored Putin's instructions and therefore had to go. Number 3 became Mikhail Khodorkovsky. He had become too dangerous in his independence and with his superior strategic and economic leadership talents compared to the more tactical and opportunistic oligarchic colleagues was the most convincing public challenger of the Kremlin's power, of its primitive energy nationalism, its corruption and its self-serving economic interventions. This is why he had to suffer the hardest "pour encourager les autres", that is: for general deterrence.

With periodic raids by public prosecutors and the tax police with investigations into the habitual offences (money laundering, fraud, tax evasion, forgery, currency offences, bribery, extortion and contract killings) the rest of the Yeltsin oligarchs were intimidated. At annual conferences they were summoned to the Kremlin to receive orders from the President,[19] who usually requested donations for his pet projects, ranging from the Sochi Olympics 2014 to soccer stadia for the world championship of 2018, which nobody in his right mind would refuse. On occasion he forces them to sign codes of good conduct in front of cameras running, to show to them and to the general public "who is the wolf in the forest", as the Russian saying goes.

Every year, they also have to fear whether their much needed *vertushka* direct lines to the Kremlin's special telephones will remain connected. Those who become disconnected must perceive this as a troubling sign of having fallen out of favour.

Nonetheless, second-tier oligarchs continued to be expropriated regardless if they did not sell on time at the Kremlin's command, especially in the energy and commodity sectors, where Kremlin's material interests are particularly strong. In 2007, Mikhail Guzerijev, the owner of Russneft, Russia's ninth-largest oil company, of Ingushetian origin, was singled out for special treatment because he refused to sell his company voluntarily to Gazprom. He also disturbed Kremlin's circles in bidding at the faked auctions for Yukos, and supported politicians unwanted by the Kremlin in his home province.[20]

The fact that his Russneft, with a turnover of EUR 1.9 billion, had made a profit of EUR 120 million a year and had the fastest growth of all Russian oil companies, did not impress anyone in the Kremlin. All shares were frozen in June 2007 due to alleged state aid problems and tax evasion. Guzerijev fled

---

[19] *Financial Times* 8.2.2007.
[20] *Die Presse* 14.4.2007, *Frankfurter Allgemeine* 22.6.2007; Gerald Hosp Ein harter Brocken wird weich" *Frankfurter Allgemeine* 4.8.2007.

abroad and lost most of his wealth. In the end, as the Kremlin had wished for, there was a discounted and uncontested takeover by Gazprom.

An almost similar fate awaited Vladimir Yevtushenko, who in 2000 had bought Bashneft from Ural Rachimov, the son of the governor of Bashkorstan (who then had to flee to Austria). On charges of money laundering in September 2014, Yevtushenko was put under house arrest for 3 months until he wisely sold out to Rosneft, as Igor Sechin wanted to expand his empire. Yet he could still hold on to his Moscow-based "Sistema" holdings, which owns the MTS telecom operator.[21]

Kacha Bendukidze launched his exit in time. In 1993–1994, the Georgian had cheaply acquired, restructured and merged into the largest heavy-machine group in Russia (OMZ) 20 machinery companies which had been close to bankruptcy such as Uralmash, the Ishorkije plants in St. Petersburg and the Krasnoe Sormovo shipyard in Nizhniy Novgorod.[22] With OMZ's important links to the oil and gas, metal smelting, defence, nuclear power and shipbuilding industries, Bendukidze provoked the disapproval of the Kremlin which soon became visible in the form of the usual public prosecutor's raids. He sold his nuclear interests in time to Gazprom and his OMZ stake to the Kremlin-obedient Potanin and returned to his Georgian home with his remaining billions. Then, after the Rose Revolution under President Saakashvili, he acted as an ultra-liberal Minister of Economy, putting his lessons learned the hard way in Russia to good use. In June 2004, after a radical tax cut, he took away all corruption-promoting licenses, tax concessions and subsidies. He promoted the Georgian economy in such a way that, after all the social hardship and adjustment pain caused by such reform shocks, Georgia even after the Russian military attack of 2008 is now growing as a Caucasian tiger with the least incidence of corruption.

2.6.1 Vladimir Gusinsky (1952–)

Gusinsky hails from a Jewish family of industrialists persecuted under Stalin. His grandfather was shot and grandmother was sent to the Gulag for years. As a drop-out student, he became a taxi driver and a black market dealer in Soviet times. During Perestroika, he organized theatre and concert tours and in a "cooperative" produced huge amounts of cheap copper bracelets as expensive fashion amulets. With the proceeds, he founded the Mostbank (which disappeared after the 1998 crisis). His breakthrough took place when

---

[21] *Die Presse* 15.5.2016.
[22] *The Economist* 31.7.2004.

Moscow Mayor Yuri Luzhkov transferred the settlement of the city's finances to Mostbank and awarded numerous public works contracts to Gusinsky's construction companies.

Already early on Gusinsky bought into the leading media and allowed critical reports to appear about the first Chechnya war. In 1996, he associated himself with Yeltsin in the Davos Pact and, as mentioned, actively contributed to his victory over the Communist Zyuganov. With cheap (perceived as non-repayable) Gazprom loans, he then extended his media empire to include the nationwide NTV TV network, satellite TVs, radio stations, cinemas and magazine publishing houses.[23] In total, his personal property was estimated at $1.5 billion. However, when Gusinsky made the attempt to take over the telephone company Svyazinvest vis-à-vis Potanin, and failed, he started an aggressive media campaign against the young reformers, Yeltsin and the other oligarchs. In doing so, he used the Russian Jewish Congress, which he himself had founded, led and funded in 1996, which became part of the Jewish World Congress. Yeltsin countered with the establishment of a counter-organization in the shape of the Chabad Lubavich Movement, funded by Roman Abramovich, which has since enjoyed the Kremlin's official goodwill, and asked Gazprom to have him reimburse the political loan of $211 million which had been granted to Media-Most and which Gusinsky was unable to service.

At the time, the Most group was affected by the 1998 crisis and not in the least by Gusinsky's erratic management style.[24] After Putin assumed power, his caricature as an ugly dwarf in the satirical puppet show of Kukly on NTV was as equally unwelcome as were the critical reports and background reports on the new second war in Chechnya. Having overstepped his limits, he was clearly singled out as the first victim. On 13 June 2000, Gusinsky was arrested on allegations of fraud (due to the purchase of St. Petersburg TV for only $10 million) and was sent to the notorious Butyrka prison. Here it was very quickly made clear to him who was "the wolf in the forest". After just a few days in a mass cell with killers and drug addicts infected with AIDS, he sold his media to Gazprom and fled Russia instantly after his release.

Quickly his papers and TV stations were brought into the Kremlin line. Some journalists found a temporary refuge in Berezovsky's editorial teams. Avoiding some international arrest warrants, Gusinsky, who owns 25% of the daily newspaper and the cable channel Maariv, now acts as an influential opinion-leader among the Russian-Jewish emigrants in Israel, where like in Russia, he has changed political sides on several occasions.

---

[23] *Financial Times* 22.11.2000.
[24] *Financial Times* 17.6.2000.

2.6.2 Boris Berezovsky (1946–2013)

By 2000, Berezovsky with a net worth of $3 billion was not the richest, but undoubtedly the most powerful of all oligarchs. Nor did he make a secret about it. His acknowledged, yet simple business principle as the grey eminence of the second Yeltsin presidency was: "Everyone can be bought. Everyone has his or her price".[25]

Trained as a mathematician and forestry engineer, Berezovsky earned his first money during perestroika by selling software programs to state institutions. He then managed to buy thousands of Ladas at the official low price from Avtovas and to re-sell them at the going market price. Avtovas insisted on payment only two years later, when hyperinflation had reduced the amounts to mere fractions. On the basis of these effortless proceeds, he founded the largest nationwide car trading company Logowas, which in a similar way but on a larger scale sold tens of thousands of Ladas in favour of Avtovas' directors and for his own account.

Later, through a financial subsidiary, Berezovsky sold $50 million of convertible bonds to Russian small investors, to whom he promised to repay them with 100,000 Ladas from a new factory instead of interest and repayment. As it was never built, he used these $50 million to acquire one-third of Avtovas's shares for himself. As Avtovas had financial difficulties as a result of the large thefts and withdrawals from management (and due to his own marketing practices) and could only be rescued by debt restructuring, Berezovsky had only 14,000 cars to be distributed by a lottery to his borrowers. The rest was left empty-handed. Obviously, some did not like it: In 1994, he survived a car bombing in which his driver was killed. With his funds he bought 49% of the loss-making former state television ORT with his 16,000 nationwide broadcasting stations and Moscow's TV6 channel.[26]

Chubais had introduced Berezovsky at the court of Yeltsin in order to neutralize the erratic influence of General Korsakov, the President's bodyguard and drinking mate.[27] This worked only all too well. In 1996, as a reward for his election financing and propaganda services, Berezovsky claimed a controlling share (51%) of the Sibneft group for only $100 million as well as of Aeroflot. The total value of this property at that time was estimated at $3 billion. Berezovsky's mission had been to organize an alliance of regional governors in favour of Yeltsin and to give it media support in order to undermine the Moscow-centric campaigns of Lushkov and Primakov. As he had

---

[25] *The Economist* 25.3.2000.
[26] Neil Buckley "A Shady Business" *Financial Times* 8.10.2011.
[27] *New Zürcher Zeitung* 4.11.1996.

now become more politicized and had found more enthusiasm for political intrigues than for the management of his companies, he left the management of Sibneft to his junior partner Roman Abramovich, who had already some experience in the oil trade and seemed unambitious and amenable.

In November 1996, Berezovsky was appointed Vice-President of the National Security Council and began interfering in all major government decisions, preferably through the President's daughter Tatiana Diatchenko. His influence was also attributed to the dismissals of Premiers Kirijenko and Chernomyrdin. The number of his enemies soon increased exponentially. The FSB had already begun to collect eagerly appropriate *kompromat*. The recordings of his telephone conversations with Diatchenko and Chechnyan leaders were soon published.[28]

Sent off to the functions of a CIS (Commonwealth of Independent States) Executive Secretary, he developed so much undesired energy and initiative in his attempt to revitalize most of the moribund Soviet Union that Yeltsin eventually fired him in March 1999 at the instigation of a majority of Parliament, organized by the Communists, on the grounds of "empowerment". This did not dissuade Berezovsky from the centre of power for a long. He was again helpful for Putin's selection as premier, as well as for the renewal of the coalition of governors and the organization of the Kremlin party Yedinstvo (Unity) to capture the nationalist vote for Putin in the presidential election.

Putin would certainly also have won the election, thanks to the "small, victorious" second Chechnya war, which was motivated by the bomb attacks probably organized by the FSB. Feeling as a sponsor at the winner's side, Berezovsky after the elections felt entitled to criticize publicly the war as well as Putin's attacks on regional autonomy, on Gusinsky and other businessmen. When Berezovsky, after Gusinsky's departure also ignored Putin's call for political abstinence in July 2000 and documented without fear the devastating failure of the naval leadership and of Putin himself during the tragic sinking of the Kursk submarine in August in his media, Putin felt personally provoked and threatened by the overbearing oligarch. Ten months after his assumption of power the puppet cut his strings and took on the erstwhile puppet master. According to KGB tradition, "organizational consequences" followed shortly after the warnings were ignored.

In 2000 the Economist published a pertinent profile of Berezovsky: "He can be both charming, almost hypnotically so, and terrifying. George Soros … wrote recently, that after they fell out, "his anger gave me chills. I literally felt he could kill me." Mr. Berezovsky responds with a blizzard of insults

---

[28] *Süddeutsche Zeitung* 9.2.1999, *Financial Times* 27.9.1999.

against Mr. Soros. He is a "hypocrite" for mixing business with philanthropy …".[29] Presciently this edition also showed a cartoon in which the puppet Putin cuts the strings of his puppeteer with big scissors.

When fraud and money laundering investigations in Aeroflot's foreign subsidiaries were heating up, Berezovsky allegedly diverted EUR 28 million into its own pocket (possibly up to $220 million) in its ticket sales—he transferred his Sibneft, Aeroflot and media shares to his companion Abramovich and fled into exile in London.

Here he had to witness how Abramovich sold out his erstwhile belongings to the Kremlin without a fight, handed over the media and sold Sibneft as told to Gazprom. In his exile Berezovsky had to deflect the Kremlin's extradition requests, but also had to experience not only the assassination of the two co-founders of the Liberal Party which he had financed, Vladimir Goloyev and Sergej Yshenko, but also more spectacular and cruelly had to witness the poisoning of the ex-SFB officer Litvinenko, who had started to work for him, by polonium, a radioactive substance by a slow and painful death.[30]

In 2012, Berezovsky engaged in one of the UK's most expensive court battles against his ex-partner Abramovich, claiming damages of $6.5 billion, and lost it with legal costs of £100 million. The judge called him "deliberately dishonest", an "unreliable witness", for whom "truth is transitory concept".[31] Berezovsky had claimed that he had to sell his 21.5% share in Sibneft under duress to Abramovich far below market value for a paltry $1.3 billion, while Abramovich later in 2005 re-sold 73% of Sibneft to Gazprom for $11.5 billion. Abramovich however claimed that Berezovsky never owned anything of Sibneft—in fact, there were no written records of their various deals, and only oral agreements based on "words of honour" among the oligarchs. Rather Abramovich claimed to have paid him a total of $2.3 billion for political protection (*krycha*) to purchase Sibneft cheaply in the form of various cash payments in the exclusive Logovaz Club in Moscow, the Dorchester Hotel in London, in the French Alps and other exotic and expensive places. With this Berezovsky financed his yacht, his airplanes, mansions in France and the UK, his lifestyle and his girlfriends.[32]

The verdict shattered him. He became insecure, self-doubting, anguished and felt impoverished, sold his yacht and his paintings. He was also depressed that he could not return to Russia, having been condemned in absentia to

---

[29] Charlemagne "Boris Berezovsky, puppeteer or future victim?" *The Economist* 25.3.2000.
[30] *Neue Zürcher Zeitung* 7.4.2001.
[31] *Financial Times* 25.3.2013.
[32] *New York Times* 11.11.2011, *Financial Times* 11.11.2011 and 1.9.2012.

7 years in jail for fraud, and wrote a grovelling letter of apology to Putin asking for forgiveness.[33]

Yet in a Facebook entry, he also stated, "I repent and ask for forgiveness for what led to the power of Putin".[34] In one of his last public statements he further called for the violent fall of Putin in the Guardian, because in his view peaceful methods were pointless. An association with him was considered "toxic" by the Russian opposition, as he was mired in debts and lawsuits and with his reputation and string of past misdeeds did not appear as a poster boy for a fair democracy and a clean market economy.[35] In March 2013, aged 67, he was found hanging in the locked bathroom in his estate near Ascot in Berkshire, with the coroner issuing an open verdict.

Pretty much exactly 5 years after Berezovsky's "suicide" his old business mate Nikolay Glushkov (69) was also found dead in London with traces of strangulation. They had worked together in the early stages of the wild privatizations. Glushkov was placed by Berezovsky in key positions in companies like Lada and in Aeroflot. In Lada his job had been to sell new cars much below cost to Berezovsky's marketing company which would re-sell them at multiple prices to the public. In Aeroflot he was responsible that all foreign revenues since 1996 went to a Swiss financial company that belonged to Berezovsky and him (and where most deposits subsequently disappeared).

The purpose of these operations—typical at the time—was dual: first to acquire the necessary funds by whatever means, and second to damage these state companies financially, even to drive them into bankruptcy, if possible—in order to acquire them cheaply afterwards. Often enough contract killings paved the way. In the context of Lada alone some 60 were counted.

Due to the Aeroflot affair, Glushkov spent 4 years in jail until 2004. After his release he sought political asylum in London in 2010. In a new trial in Moscow, he was condemned in absentia to a further 8 years in prison and to reimburse Aeroflot for $122 million in damages. His death, like the one of Berezovsky, in all likeliness will remain unresolved.[36] So much for perfect murders.

---

[33] *New York Times* 25.3.2013 and 26.3.2013.
[34] *Financial Times* 25.3.2013.
[35] Edward Lucas "Berezovsky's dark shadow" *European Voice* 27.3.2013.
[36] *Frankfurter Allgemeine* 15.3.2018.

2.6.3 Mikhail Khodorkovsky (1963–)

Most oligarchs felt to be dealers of companies rather than as managers of their fast, cheap and often randomly acquired enterprises. Only Khodorkovsky tried to play a special role as politically responsible entrepreneur after 2000. Motivated by a new messianic personally felt mission for political and business reform in Russia, he restructured his Yukos Group, financed the opposition and did not comply with the instructions of the new lords of the Kremlin. His following martyrdom clearly illustrates the limits of the reform process and of the democratic transformation of Russia. In the confrontation with the authoritarian intervention state, the private ownership rights of the richest man in Russia became irrelevant as did the protection of fundamental rights in the Russian Constitution.

Mikhail Khodorkovsky started as a Komsomol Secretary at the Mendeleev Institute for Chemical Engineering. In Gorbachev's perestroika in 1987, he founded a centre of youth science and technology (NTTM). Such a centre has had the privilege to exchange the almost valueless transfer rubles used to pay for the services of research institutes into ten times more profitable cash. Khodorkovsky used his money for the lucrative import of computers, the export of timber and the development of Russian accounting software. In view of the incompetence of the state banks, he founded his Menatep Bank from NTTM, which as one of the first private banks should soon act as a highly profitable financial agency for state companies and regional authorities. The Ministry of Finance alone deposited $600 million in the Menatep foreign exchange account, an amount with which the banker could successfully speculate in other foreign currencies. In 1991, Khodorkovsky became an adviser to Premier Ivan Silayev and thus had access to all privatization information.[37]

However, a first hostile attempt to take over the "Red October" confectionery producer failed. The subsequent purchase of Yukos was then made in agreement with its red directors. As part of the oligarchs' pact in 2005–2006, Khodorkovsky acquired the oil company Yukos for $309 million, which was to be valued at $35 billion in 2003 before being dismantled by the Kremlin. Unlike most oligarchs, who were mainly interested in channelling funds abroad, Khodorkovsky started to restructure Yukos with tough methods. It had not paid wages in the past 6 months prior to his acquisition and had only made losses with debts standing at $3.5 billion. Thousands of alcoholic employees and managers were dismissed. Minority shareholders

---

[37] Waleri Panjuschin. *Mikhail Khodorkovsky. Vom Yukos Chefsessel ins sibirische Arbeitslager*. Munich: Heyne Verlag 2006, p. 69.

were squeezed out from his companies and were refunded at only fractions of their entry prices. For example, the stock market values of the most valuable Yukosneftegas, Samaraneftegas and Tomskneft were devalued by 98% as a result of a mass of new share issues.[38] At the same time, Khodorkovsky, like other oligarchs, used existing tax loopholes to sell oil at reduced prices to intermediaries in tax havens and to re-sell it there at market prices for a handy profit. In the mid-90s, Khodorkovsky's reputation was understandably not the best. The Menatep Bank was considered to be so corrupt that US citizens were banned from doing business due to its suspected underworld connections. During the 1998 crisis, the US Monetary Authority repeatedly investigated the bank for money laundering.[39] Western banks had to write off half of their loans to Yukos which at the time had been skilfully emptied into a corporate shell with losses amounting to a total of $236 million.

However, with rising oil prices and a now financially healthy company, Khodorkovsky started to make a perceptible change from 2000 onwards. Instead of the usual withdrawals, the reinvestment rates of Yukos were high. Khodorkovsky started to manage the group with transparent balance sheets according to Western management principles, with significant increases in value as a result. He recruited PR consultants, listened to them, started to donate large sums to universities, hospitals and museums and, following George Soros' example, he set up the Foundation "Open Russia" to promote civil society projects and education. To this end, he cultivated US parliamentarians, Wall Street bankers and opinion leaders, who all accompanied his transformation from a sinner to a role model of Western capitalism with great public sympathy.[40] This is all the more so because, in contrast to the other oligarchs, Khodorkovsky could, if he wished so, be extremely polite, modest and attractive to large audiences. Also in his personal way of life, he did not indulge in the wasteful lifestyle of his newly super-rich co-oligarchs.[41] As a reward for those efforts, Yukos' stock market value soon multiplied to $35 billion.

With this significant market capitalization, Khodorkovsky wanted to merge his group in a friendly takeover with Abramovich's Sibneft and thus become the first Russian transnational company and later to merge into a global group, like with ExxonMobil, where Khodorkovsky and Abramovich would then have owned 30%.[42]

---

[38] Floyd Norris "Investors in Russia, Beware" *International Herald Tribune* 9.4.1999.
[39] *Wall Street Journal* 3.9.1999.
[40] *International Herald Tribune* 22.6.2004.
[41] Elke Windisch. "Wer ist Mikhail Khodorkowski?" *Der Tagesspiegel* 15.5.2005.
[42] Panjuschin. Op. cit., p. 189.

For the Kremlin this intention, as much as it was admired in the West, was an unacceptable part of the ever-increasing list of sins of the oligarch whose corporate strategies challenged the power of the state in the strategic energy sector. In addition to the planned transfer of Russian crown jewels to a US-dominated multinational group, these included:

His plan to build oil pipelines from South Siberian Angarsk to Chinese Datsin in Manchuria and to Murmansk (for export to the US) which would have undermined the state-owned Transneft oil transport monopoly and the state's export policy.

Further, he openly paid for the liberal opposition in shape of the social-liberal Yabloko and the economic liberal "Union of Right Forces", as well as even for the Communists and parts of the Kremlin Party "United Russia" through former red directors. In a reckless lobbying operation, he openly sabotaged an oil tax in the Duma normally obedient to Putin's wishes, by sponsoring to the Kremlin's fury successfully a supra-partisan opposition to the tax, rejecting all compromise proposals of the Ministry of Finance.[43] There were persistent rumours at the time that Khodorkovsky wanted to leave business by 2008, sell out to an international oil major and, as a social-liberal democrat and Russia's richest man, run for Putin's succession.[44]

Finally, in February 2003 in a prepared public presentation in Putin's presence in the Kremlin, he directly accused Putin's siloviki cronies of corruption. It concerned the excessively priced purchase of the private Savernaya Neft by the state-owned Rosneft with suspected kickbacks. In March 2003, Khodorkovsky was last summoned to the Kremlin. He informed Putin about the progress of his merger plans with Sibneft ("Yuksi") and the planned future as an international group and insisted on his right to support opposition parties of his choice as a Russian citizen. It appeared as if Putin listened with a benevolent attitude.

This impression was clearly mistaken.

The first searches and arrests started in June/July 2003. With the FSB having collected plenty of *kompromat* over the years, Pitshugin, the chief of security of Yukos, was imprisoned for an alleged contract killing the mayor of Nefteyugansk (who had protested very loudly about Yukos' non-payments to the municipal budget and its dismissals in his corporate oil town) and later sentenced to 20 years in prison. As a last warning to Khodorkovsky, his deputy, Platon Lebedev, was then arrested for economic crimes. In October, it was Khodorkovsky's turn, who—unlike Gusinsky and Berezovsky earlier—had missed all opportunities to flee abroad on time. After a steered media

---

[43] *Financial Times* 28.10.2003 and 31.7.2003.
[44] *Time* 28.7.2003.

campaign, he was sentenced to 9 years in prison (later reduced to 8) in an obvious show trial for fraud and tax evasion.[45] The main reason was the use of semi-legal intermediaries to which oil was sold at a reduced price and then re-sold at world market prices in offshore tax-havens. Given the confiscatory nature of post-Soviet gains taxes, the route was mandatory for any aspiring oligarch—otherwise, they would have remained small traders selling theatre tickets and imported tea bags.

Yukos' accounts were then frozen. In vain he had sold his assets in 2005 to the GLM holding, which was run by associates. In order to seize the alleged tax debt, the group's shares were confiscated at undervalued prices similar to those at the time of Khodorkovsky's acquisition. Yukos was cut to pieces and its choice assets were gradually moved to Rosneft, through fake auctions via shell companies, in an operation carefully designed by Igor Sechin, Putin's head of administration, who by coincidence was also the head of Rosneft.[46] Rosneft, which has hitherto been characterized by low productivity as a state-owned group, with these cheap gains in modernized processing and production capacities and new oil fields, rose from a stock market value of almost $6 billion to $90 billion.[47] As a result, a Western banking consortium also forgot its moral misgivings and financed all those purchases (all proceeds due to astronomical tax claims went to the Russian treasury) for the amount of $22 billion.[48] In order to be better prepared against claims for damages, the Kremlin wanted to see the participation of Western oil companies in the faked auctions. Thus, as useful idiots, the Italian groups Eni and Enel participated—only to see their acquired Arctic gas fields immediately go to Gazprom at the same price—since with Gazprom's pipeline monopoly they were in any event worthless without Gazprom's active participation.[49] BP also participated in one of the pseudo auctions, in which it mistakenly hoped to be able to keep its huge, expensively developed Kovytka gas field through nice gestures directed at the Kremlin.

Yukos was thus crushed by the state. At about the same time, the liberal opposition parties Yabloko and the "Union of Right Forces", both funded by Khodorkovsky, had destroyed each other. They both failed in December 2003 to enter the Duma. Khodorkovsky, who with his "Open Russia" foundation had seen himself as a philanthropist like George Soros or Bill Gates, did not have to disappear in a Gulag camp, as it was sometimes described, but

---

[45] Michael Ludwig. "Politischer Schauprozeß" *Frankfurter Allgemeine* 31.5.2005.
[46] Panjuschin. Op. cit., p. 231.
[47] *Financial Times* 3.5.2007 and 11.5.2007.
[48] *Financial Times* 21.3.2007.
[49] *Financial Times* 5.4.2007.

in an overcrowded prison in Siberian Krasnokamensk close to the Chinese border, followed by a prison in Karelia. In view of his disastrous misfortune, he wrote open letters in prison, which deal in detail and self-critically with the business practices of oligarchs and the politics of liberals in the light of his new social-democratic convictions.[50] He also described quite movingly and perceptively the sad fate of fellow inmates who being poor and undereducated were basically honest men and even more unfortunate than him.[51] The question remained of course, whether this reincarnation attempt as a new Sakharov was credible to the outside world.

While most of the main Menatep and Yukos shareholders had fled to safety in Israel, an active lobby in the West, led by former US Secretary of Foreign Trade, Stu Eizenstad had been seeking Khodorkovsky's release and his recognition as a political prisoner.[52] At the initiative of the former Lithuanian President Landsbergis, more than 100 European parliamentarians had also signed a letter to Putin. This left the addressee predictably little impressed.[53]

Before long, a further indictment was prepared with the aim of preventing his early release and bringing actions against the manipulative expropriation of his property.[54] These were allegations of money laundering by his Open Russia Foundation, which could have brought an additional 15 years to both Khodorkovsky and Lebedev. This second trial took place in 2009 and extended his combined sentence to 2014. In December 2013 after 10 years of incarceration Putin—in view of the Sochi Olympics in the following year, where he feared international boycotts would hurt his expensive $50 billion pet project—ordered his early release shortened by one year as part of an amnesty which also liberated the Pussy Riot and Greenpeace protestors.[55] Khodorkovsky was flown out to Berlin, then resided in Switzerland and since 2005 in London, where he lives with his second wife and his four children. His net worth is estimated to stand at $500 million, down from $15 billion in 2003. He has revived his Open Russia foundation and remains a vocal critic of Putin and his policies.

Originally, he was awarded $50 billion compensation by International Court of Arbitration in The Hague, which would have led to a worldwide confiscation of Russian government assets (from Aeroflot plans, to ships and Orthodox churches). Yet the appellate body squashed the award, with

---

[50] Johannes Voswinkel "Der Moral-Oligarch" *Die Zeit* 8.12.2005.
[51] *International Herald Tribune* 1.4.2012.
[52] *Frankfurter Allgemeine* 31.5.2005.
[53] *Focus* 12.7.2004.
[54] *Frankfurter Allgemeine* 6.2.2007.
[55] *Wall Street Journal* 20.12.2013; *Financial Times* 20.12.2013 and 23.12.2013.

the reasoning that Russia had only signed the European Energy Charter (which provides for investor protection) but had never ratified it.[56] Hence the Kremlin could confiscate private energy assets at will with impunity.

2.7 The Fate of Oligarchs II: Super-Rich, Obedient and Still Tolerated

2.7.1 Roman Abramovich (1966–)

Roman Abramovich, with a net worth of $19 billion the richest Russian after Khodorkovsky's expropriation, is not expected to utter any political words that could infuriate the Kremlin. Despite an informal and relaxed public appearance he leads a lifestyle of the special luxury class with three large yachts, a private Boeing, weekend palaces at the Cote d'Azur, a city residence in London and a manor with 420 ha in Surrey from where he manages his assets on a day-to-day basis.

As an orphan, the mother died during an abortion and the father in an accident at work, Abramovich grew up with relatives. Rather hard-working than gifted after finishing secondary school in Moscow, he completed an industrial institute in the North-Russian city of Uchta and did his military service as an artillery man. In the early 1990s, he tried his luck with small firms in 20 different sectors from manufacturing rubber ducks and bodyguard services to tire renewal until he had collected sufficient capital, not least by moving undocumented fuel oil from Kaliningrad (Königsberg) to the Baltics, to enter the lucrative oil export trade with its super-high margins and direct foreign exchange earnings by buying an oil export license.[57]

The breakthrough came in 1995 when Berezovsky, who preferred to manage the political landscape through his direct access to the Yeltsin family, entrusted Abramovich, who seemed amenable and easy to handle, and with his expertise in the oil sector as a junior partner, with extensive management responsibilities.

For nearly $200 million, both of them in 1996 acquired the newly vertically integrated Sibneft group, which linked the production company Nojabrskneftegas and Russia's largest and most modern refinery in Omsk, a joint company worth $15 billion by 2003. Minority shareholders and the Treasury were harmed by Sibneft through discounted oil sales to subsidiaries

---

[56] *Le Figaro* 21.2016.
[57] Dominic Midgley and Chris Hutchins. *Der Milliardär aus dem Nichts – Roman Abramowitch*. Hamburg: Murmann 2005, p. 51.

followed by expensive resales and the usual manipulation of share prices and dividends in the typical oligarchical style. The high tax savings and profits also allowed Sibneft to develop new oilfields and to invest in refineries and networks of patrol stations.

Berezovsky, who was the only oligarch to have access to Yeltsin's "President's Club", introduced Abramovich to the court, where he soon won the trust of Tatiana Diatchenko, the president's daughter, thanks to appropriate gifts, and became the treasurer of Yeltsin's private finances.[58]

In 1999, as a useful diversification, Abramovich, together with Oleg Deripaska, acquired the newly merged Russian smelters (Rusal), producing 70% of Russian production and 10% of world aluminium.

In the 2000 presidential election, Abramovich's role was to co-finance the new Kremlin party Yedinstvo (Unity). Together with Berezovsky, he strengthened their nationwide leverage by recruiting regional governors against Putin's rival Lushkov, who as the mayor of Moscow (1992–2010) controlled the capital and the surrounding region. After the victorious elections, Putin quickly rejected Berezovsky's cabinet lists. He was to be his own boss and not the oligarch's puppet. After Berezovsky had been forced into exile he sold his Sibneft, Aeroflot and ORT shares to Abramovich, hoping to retain influence from afar.

Yet the latter quickly agreed to have his newly acquired media streamlined to the Kremlin's tune.

In December 2000 Abramovich, as a candidate of the Kremlin Party, as instructed by Putin, began his campaign for the governorship of Chukotka, the north-eastern corner of Siberia with its remaining 70,000 inhabitants, which had been neglected since the perestroika. By means of a helpful investigation into corruption, the Kremlin succeeded in persuading the incumbent governor Nazorov, who was initially unwilling to do so, to stand down. So Abramovich as the only candidate won the election without much difficulty after distributing southern fruits to voters, with the minimum of an election campaign. As a governor, Abramovich started a child vacation programme to the Black Sea coast at the expense of Sibneft, built a new hospital and ensured that salaries were paid again on time. For himself the function provided a welcome immunity and for Sibneft the use of tax advantages, as the regional tax was reduced from 14.5 to 3.1% in that remote corner of Russia. Promptly, Sibneft made all of its profits in its sales subsidiary in the capital Anadyr.

In the meantime, however, the Duma closed the tax loophole and the occasional air travel from warm Western Europe to cold Anadyr turned out to be

---

[58]Midgley and Hitchins. Op. cit., p. 78.

too cumbersome, and the locals, with ever-increasing demands for support, were not very grateful. After a few years Abramovich no longer expressed an interest in a second term. Yet Putin insisted, however, wishing him to support this remote region further, including the financing of improved transport connections to Alaska. After having reportedly ploughed a total of $2.5 billion as donations and tax money into the area, by 2013 after 14 years of this bizarre political career, Abramovich finally dared to throw the towel.[59]

Like most oligarchs, Abramovich is part of the Jewish Russian minority, which, as a result of the latent anti-Semitism in the Soviet Union and its exclusion from many public and security-related leadership functions, formed informal networks. Although secularized to a large extent, after the Bolshevist eradication of entrepreneurship among the Slavs, many turned out to be the first entrepreneurs and risk-takers alongside the South Caucasian nationalities.[60] Thus, Abramovich, as the main shareholder of Omsk Bacon, found nothing wrong to benefit from the annual slaughter of 300,000 pigs. Yet he also followed Yeltsin's and later Putin's instructions to finance a Chadissic counter-organization against the Russian Jewish Congress, which founded by Gusinsky in 1996 had in their view become too powerful as an internationally well-connected lobby.[61]

Already in 1998 the Russian Court of Auditors had become interested in the privatization of Sibneft and found that when selling its first half for $100 million, the government had lost $2.7 billion at its market value of $2.8 billion at the time. In 2005, Abramovich managed to reduce a tax claim of $1 billion to $300 million. Also in search of a disappeared IMF stability loan of $4.8 billion, there were raids of the tax authorities at Sibneft and at Abramovich companies in Montreux. It was clear that the Kremlin began to collect *kompromat*. In 2002 therefore, Abramovich prudently started to sell his shareholdings in Russia: Omsk Bacon, Aeroflot (26%), Rusal (25%) and the car holding Ruspromauto (37%).

Abramovich also began to extract himself increasingly from Sibneft selling shares at the tune of $1.2 billion in 2003 to $2.5 billion (2005) and cutting investment. At the end of 2005, he sold his remaining Sibneft (72%) shares in Gasprom for $13 billion—estimated at half the market value. His remaining shares (25%) in Rusal went to Deripaska for $2 billion, who alone became the owner of the second-largest aluminium smelter in the world.

Although he still participates with $3 billion in the West Siberian steel group Evraz (40%), a candidate for a Russian or international steel merger,

---

[59] *The Siberian Times* 2.7.2013.
[60] Midgley and Hutchins. Op.cit., p. 138.
[61] Ibid., p. 145.

Abramovich has clearly moved his life and financial centre of interest to Western Europe.[62] In spite of his aversion to public attention, his wasteful lifestyle and expensive toys, from the giant yachts ($420 million), his house in the billionaires' row in Kensington Palace Garden ($163 million) to the Chelsea football club ($400 million costs) and his quest for acceptance by the British upper class, are inevitably subject to publicity. He is believed to lose interest in some of his expensive hobbies as quickly as he lost interest in his political career in Chukotka. A consistent investment strategy for his liquid billions has so far not been discernible, except for the occasional purchase of some prestige properties, like a castle called "Waldschlößchen" at lake Attersee in Upper Austria (EUR 15 million) and a business complex at the Viennese Kohlmarkt (EUR 27 million).

In March 2007, Abramovich divorced his second wife Irina before a Russian court. From an English court, the mother of his two children could have expected up to $5 billion. At the Russian court, according to a lawyer, she received "as much as Abramovich is willing to pay".[63] His readiness amounted to $300 million (2% of its assets), still sufficient for life-long shopping at Harrods. Still, Abramovich's visa for the UK (an investors visa is usually given after investing at least £2 million in the country) was not renewed by the Home Office after the assassination attempt against Sergei Skripal.[64] When he tried a Swiss residence permit in Wallis he was not welcome either. Money laundering and suspected past contacts to criminal associations were cited. So he usefully remembered his Jewish parents and got Israeli citizenship, which will allow him to travel visa-free to the UK for up to 6 months per year, with the added advantage that after their "repatriation" Jews get 10 years of tax freedom for their foreign revenues. So with a net worth of $10.5 billion, he is likely to stay the richest Israeli for a long time. The whole citizenship procedure took him only a few hours until he flew off again with his Boeing 767.[65]

Yet the attraction of "Londongrad" remains for larger and smaller oligarchs who since 2006 poured $129 billion into the UK, preferably into sparsely used real estate near Harrods, at Eaton Square, Belgrave Square—the fertilizer magnate Andrei Guryev, for instance, owns the largest house in London after Buckingham Palace, when not buying soccer clubs or newspapers (like the Evening Standard and The Independent by Alexander Lebedev), parking money while craving for acceptance and reputation. Their children frequently

---

[62] *New Europe* 4.6.2006.
[63] *Financial Times* 15.3.2007.
[64] *Financial Times* 21.5 and 22.5. 2018.
[65] *Frankfurter Allgemeine* 30.2018 and 28.9.2018.

study at UK elite institutions, forming the third-largest group of foreign-born children in UK private schools, with the added advantage of a legal shelter, as there are no extraditions to Russia,[66] plus a convenient policy of no questions asked on the origins of the money.[67]

2.7.2 Oleg Deripaska (1968–)

Deripaska grew up as a half-orphan in a Cossack village near Krasnodar in the 1970s with his grandparents and relatives. As a drop-out student in 1991, he sought out the toughest sector to earn money: the aluminium trade and bauxite smelting. In the case of aluminium, prices of $70 per ton on the Russian market and of $1600 on the world market, the miracle margins attracted any number of dubious traders. With his profits from aluminium exports Deripaska bought the vouchers of aluminium smelters, with the result that at the age of 26 he was already on the supervisory board of Sajansk Aluminum. Together with the notorious brothers, Lev and Mikhail Chernoi and their Transworld Corporation, he subsequently bought additional aluminium smelters, which he merged into Siberian Aluminum (Sibal) in 1996. At that time the fight for the aluminium smelters was conducted less with auctions than with kalashnikovs and explosives. There were more than 100 deaths in the sector during the 1990s. When the Chernoi brothers, the winners of the aluminium war, in Russia became too uncomfortable with their under-world connections and their associated contract killings, they moved to Israel. Deripaska used their absence to boot out his former mentors and partners. In 1997, he paid them out after a lengthy legal dispute.[68] He also bought other aluminium plants at favourable prices because his friend Chubais, as head of the UES United Power Plants, led them—like the NKAZ smelter in Siberian Kunerovo—to go bankrupt for unpaid electricity bills, or because their previous owners[69] were subject to criminal investigations (which were immediately discontinued after the sale).[70] Other aluminium smelters, like those of Krasnoyarsk, Bratsk and Nowokuznezk, had been acquired by Abramovich via Sibneft who brought them in 2000 into their joint venture Rusal, until he sold his shares to Deripaska after 2003. In 2007, Deripaska then merged his Rusal (66%) with Viktor Vekselberg's Sual

---

[66] *New York Times* 17.3.2018.
[67] Oliver Bullough "Forget the pledges to act—London is still a haven for dirty Russian money" *The Guardian* 30.9.2018.
[68] *Der Standard* 5.6.2007.
[69] *Financial Times* 25.7.2000.
[70] Catherine Belton Rusal's Deripaska: "I don't need to Defend myself", *Financial Times* 13.7.2007.

(23%) and Glencore's aluminium interests (12%), owned by the dubious US-Swiss investor Marc Rich (who subsequently was amnestied by Bill Clinton), and thus became Russia's aluminium monopolist.[71] He enjoys the cheapest energy prices in the world in the form of neighbouring Siberian river power plants, for which there are far and away no competing customers outside his smelters. For the products of its smelters (foils, canned sheets and materials for the construction industry), electricity prices are the single biggest cost factor ("energy in cans").

As a Russian monopolist, he only has to comply with the demands of the lords of the Kremlin. In the 1990s, it was still sufficient for him to marry the daughter of Yeltsin's chief of staff, Polona Yumasheva, whose father later married Yeltsin's daughter. Yet under the unromantic Putin he first had to pay $100 million to get rid of tax investigations. In Sochi, Putin's favourite holiday destination, he had to donate a new airport and a huge sports complex for the 2014 Winter Olympics (which had obviously little to do with his core business or corporate expertise). Deripaska's new diversification strategy, his Basic Elements conglomerate established in Krasnoyarsk in 2001, faithfully follows the Kremlin's requirements in all major business decisions, including those abroad, such as his acquisition of significant minority shareholdings in the construction companies Hochtief (10%), Strabag and the Austro-Canadian car parts supplier Magna (25% each) in spring 2007.[72]

As a holding company, in addition to the dominant aluminium sector (Rusal) with 47,000 employees and $6.7 billion turnovers (2005), there are five other sectoral shareholdings:

- Ruspromavto controls the second largest car producer Gaz and its internationally uncompetitive annual production of 55,000 Volga cars and 170,000 trucks in Nizhniy Novgorod. The aim was to use Magna's technological knowledge for modernization.
- The construction sector (Glavmostroi): Following the takeover of the construction company Rasvitije, which serves one-third of the Moscow construction market, the stakes in Hochtief (10%) and Strabag (30%) were intended to enable technological catch-up and the national infrastructure investments requested by the Kremlin, including the sports complexes for the Sochi Olympic Winter Games of February 2014 (which in the end were mostly and expensively done by Putin's childhood friend and judo buddy Arcady Rotenberg and his younger brother Boris).

---

[71] *International Herald Tribune* 10.10.2006, *Frankfurter Allgemeine* 25.9.2006.

[72] The financial crisis of 2008 forced him to divest from his credit financed participations (*Die Presse* 4.10.2008 and 10.10.2008), but he gradually bought those in Magna and Strabag back by 2014.

- Airplanes (Aviakor),
- Banks (Sojus) and
- Insurance (second largest insurance company Ingostrach).

In case of the Ilim Enterprise pulp and paper mill, Deripaska tried unsuccessfully to achieve a hostile takeover in 2002. It consisted of an attempt by bona fide judges to challenge a 1994 privatization decision to confiscate two-thirds of the shares and to have them sold to him cheaply. However, after protests by foreign minority shareholders and the workforce, he eventually lost this "forest war" in a rare defeat.[73]

His quiet acquisition style on the margins of legality resulted in Deripaska not obtaining a US visa for years. He was also disinvited from Davos—an annual "must" date for oligarchs.[74] Certainly, the Russian public prosecutor's office also periodically shows an interest in old aluminium deals and past dead owners.

2.7.2.1 An Austrian-German Connection that Did not Work Out: Deripaska, Magna, Hochtief and Strabag

Half did he pull them and half did they fall. Magna, car parts and contract producer of the Austro-Canadian Frank Stronach, faced gloomy prospects at the beginning of 2007: The certain decrease of orders by its main troubled US customers General Motors, Ford and Chrysler, the phasing out of Chrysler Voyager's production, of the Mercedes E Class and possibly also BMW's withdrawal from "car cluster" in Graz (Styria). Thus Stronach was inspired by the vision of "Jeeps for Russia" and for Euro 150 million sold Deripaska 20% of his shares in Magna, the former Steyr-Daimler Puch, with its 14,000 employees in Austria.

Strabag, Germany's and Austria's largest road construction group was attracted by the 7–8% margins available in Russia, compared to only 2–3% in central Europe. The need for new airports, railway stations, bridges, roads, tunnels and motorways in the giant region is almost insatiable. Ernst & Young estimated the demand by 2010 at EUR 260 billion. The infrastructural assets of the Soviet era were and are in a manifestly critical state after decades of neglect. Russian construction companies are technically and economically too weak for the large dimensions of the necessary expansion (EUR 23.5 billion for airports by 2010 alone), EUR 82 billion for the e-economy by

---

[73] *New York Times* 14.8.2002.
[74] *Financial Times* 24.1.2001.

2011, etc.).[75] Hans-Peter Haselsteiner's Strabag had hoped, as a result of the entry of Deripaska, mediated by the Austrian Raiffeisenbank, to expand its Russian business to EUR 1 billion per year in Moscow only.[76] Strabag's subsidiary Zöblin (Stuttgart) could be involved in industrial construction. These hopes, however, proved elusive. Deripaska was no match for the Rotenberg brothers' Putin connection in Russia's road construction market. Today the share of Russian business in Strabag's order bocks stands at barely 1% of turnover.[77] The decision to pay Euro 1.05 billion for 25% of Strabag stock was allegedly taken by Deripaska in 5 min. The sale was completed in 3 weeks.

Deripaska certainly is a difficult business partner. In the past, he has always forced his partners to give up and paid them out on his terms. From his personality structure, as the winner of the aluminium wars, he is surely the toughest among the surviving oligarchs who are not tender-minded either. He does not tolerate rivals nor external commercial interventions (apart from the Kremlin). Personal weaknesses are not evident. Nor does he waste his money on yachts and the bars of the Cote d'Azur. As the only luxury, he bought a £25 million villa in London's noble area Belgravia, "to save hotel costs". He is, however, also a major investor in the recently constructed Porto Montenegro, a luxury marina for billionaires' over-sized yachts (which have difficulties landing at ordinary marinas), located in a UNESCO protected bay near the historical town of Kotor in a rebuild former Austria-Hungarian and then Yugoslav naval base, replete with new five-star hotels and golf courses. His investor colleagues are Bernard Arnault (the owner of LVMH Moet Hennessy), Lord Jacob Rothschild, Peter Munk, the Canadian gold magnate, and the like.

Yet by April 2018 disaster struck for Deripaska. The US Treasury put him on a US sanctions list, alleging cosy deals with the Kremlin and past criminal behaviour, wanting to punish him for Russian "malign activities".[78] Starting with a visa ban to the US, all his foreign assets were to be frozen and all dollar-based business deals (which all have to be cleared by US banks) prohibited, plus the risk of extraterritorial US sanctions for his foreign business partners, unless he disinvested his majority shares and ceded effective management control within a few weeks. Deripaska reacted first by threatening to sue the US administration and engaged in very expensive lobbying

---

[75] Jens Hartmann "Rußland wird grundsaniert" *Die Welt* 5.6.2007.
[76] *Die Presse* 30.4.2007 and 12.5.2007.
[77] *Frankfurter Allgemeine* 5.10.2018.
[78] *Financial Times* 11.4.2018 and 27.4.2018, if anything the aluminium king certainly had very little influence about them.

activities in London and Washington to get off the US sanctions list. He hired Lord Gregory Baker, a well-connected Tory and former UK energy minister for climate change (sic!) as chairman of his holding company EN+, as well as Bob Dole, Republican senator of Kansas, to lobby for him. He befriended Nathaniel Rothschild and Lord Peter Mandelson, former EU Trade Commissioner, and took them and some of their friends out on his private plane for a jaunt in Siberia and to his yacht Queen K off the coast of Corfu. He also spent millions on expensive law firms to present his case at the US Treasury.[79]

Yet the US conditions were brutal: Deripaska would have to give up effective control over both his EN+ holding and over Rusal, switch his shares above 49% with the Swiss Glencore and put his own into a charitable foundation, and thus not get any dividends, with his voting rights being limited to 35%. All his followers would have to leave senior management positions. The new CEO of Rusal would Yevgeny Nikitin, an aluminium manager unconnected to his leadership crew, but most of the management positions would be occupied by Americans and Brits. In consequence, the Kremlin would lose any influence of its aluminium industry and its international operations. Also, his control of the car-maker GAZ with its joint production ventures with Volkswagen and Daimler came into the firing line. In short, this was meant to be a blueprint for other oligarchs who cooperated with the Kremlin and who were active in international business, like Fridman, Usmanov or Potanin.[80]

Obviously, this was a scheme that could have been dreamt by Sechin and his friends, only that Deripaska did not end up in a US jail and labour camp.

He complied with these provisions, resigned from the board of EN+, but apparently rescued sizable shareholdings by transferring them to his two teenage children, who obviously could not figure on any sanction list.

At the time also the supply of alumina to Europe was threatened since one of his subsidiaries owned the largest Irish smelter Aughinish near Limerick, which could no longer be supplied by, for instance, Rio Tinto, apart from many others, like huge smelters in Dunkirk and in Montenegro.[81] Prices for aluminium and alumina (a refined white powder used in aluminium production) briefly spiked in a global panic and the fear of shortages. After all Rusal with 1.4 million tons remains the EU's largest aluminium supplier: with the threatened interruption of the supply chain, the production of window frames, car parts and airplane bodies appeared in jeopardy, as were such

---

[79] Andrew Higgens and Kenneth P. Vogel. "Two Capitals, one Oligarch: How Oleg Deripaska is Trying to Escape US sanctions" *New York Times* 4.11.2018.
[80] *Frankfurter Allgemeine* 21.12.2018.
[81] *The Globe and Mail* 6.4. 2018, *Financial Times* 16.4.2018.

humble products like beverage cans. In the end, after credible disinvestment the storm passed.

2.7.3 Vladimir Potanin (1961–)

Potanin earned its first millions in the metal trade. As part of the nomenklatura, whose father was placed at the highest level in the Ministry of Foreign Trade, he is considered to be the only non-Jew in the top ranks of the first generation of oligarchs. In 1993–1994 he founded Oneximbank with Mikhail Prokhorov (1965–), which became the largest private bank in Russia and merged into Rosbank as the new main bank of his Interros group in 2002, thanks to the clearance of customs revenues with its foreign exchange income coming handy.

To the Financial Times he confessed: "Why did I become a Russian oligarch? Because the Red Directors were so unacceptably bad managers and had to be thrown out by the oligarch privatization"[82] which he had developed himself in 1996. Appointed by Yeltsin 1996–1997 as a Vice-Premier on privatization issues, he generously helped his Interros group at the time. It received 51% of Sidanco, the fourth-largest oil company for $130 million, 38% of Norilsk Nickel for $170 million and 25% of the telecommunications company Svyazinvest for $1.875 billion, a decision that triggered the self-destructive "war of the oligarchs" of 1997–1998.

The most valuable asset was the then highly indebted Norilsk Nickel, which not only served 20% of the world nickel market, but soon became one of the largest world producers of gold, platinum, cobalt, palladium and other precious metals through further acquisitions.

In 1997, Sidanco sold a 10% stake to BP for $570 million, but this stake was not a source of pleasure to BP, as it soon turned out that the majority shareholder was abusing its oil revenues as a cash cow for the more important Norilsk Nickel group. In 2001, Potanin then sold his Sidanco shares to the Alfa group of Mikhael Fridman for $1.1 billion.

In 2004, Potanin got into conflict with Kremlin when he wanted to participate in the South African Gold Fields mining group with a share of 20% and to merge the gold interests of both groups under his leadership. Thus he would have rescued the larger part of his Norilsk Nickel capital into a safe foreign country. When the usual initial investigations were launched, Potanin abandoned his plans as quickly as possible. In July 2000, he had already paid

---

[82] *Financial Times* 29.8.2000.

$140 million "voluntarily" for his discounted early purchase of Norilsk Nickel and has since funded the Kremlin party "United Russia".[83]

During 2007–2008, Potanin and his long-standing business partner Mikhail Prokhorov split and shared half of their assets of $15 billion each in the joint Interros holding. While Potanin sought recognition in international society and its business elite, inter alia as a trustee of the Guggenheim Museum (an honour requiring an annual donation of $1 million), his colleague Prokhorov made more unwelcome headlines when he was arrested in January 2007 by the French police for financing the stay of 16 call girls in his hotel.[84] Prokhorov then sold his 25% share in Norilsk Nickel to Rural's Deripaska.

Soon a complex three-way year-long fight ensued over the control of Norilsk Nickel between Deripaska and Potanin (who owned 40%), as Deripaska wanted to merge it with his Rusal, which would have created Russia's largest mining company. Yet in Potanin's view—apart from losing control—it made no sense to merge stainless steel with aluminium production. Rather Potanin preferred a merger with Metalloinvest (steel and iron ore) of Alisher Usmanov, which was not very logical either.[85]

The second fight was between Viktor Vekselberg (16%) and his allies Lev Blavatnik and Mikhael Prokhorov (17%) with Deripaska (46%) over Rusal. Once Abramovich bought a 6% stake in Norilsk Nickel and acted as an arbiter, Deripaska sold out there and got rid of his $11.4 billion debt in the process, while Vekselberg and his friends citing bad management left Rusal,[86] with Vekselberg focussing on Integrated Energy Systems, Russia's largest power supply and gas distribution company. Lev Blavatnik living in London, bought Warner Music in 2011, and Prokhorov diversified into real estate, the media, raw materials and investment banking.

In interviews, Potanin declared the fight had depressed the stock prices and long blocked management reforms needed to shake off the Soviet legacy in order to develop into a multinational enterprise, which now had recovered to a market value of $20.6 billion with $5 billion in earnings. In the future, he would focus on exploration and mining and divest the less profitable processing.[87]

---

[83] *Financial Times* 21.7.2000.
[84] "Der Milliardär als Zuhälter?" *Die Presse* 13.1.2007.
[85] *Frankfurter Allgemeine* 29.11.2011, *Financial Times* 30.3.2012.
[86] Financial Times 14.3., 15.3 and 20.3.2012.
[87] *Financial Times* 10.9.2013, *Wall Street Journal* 11.11.2013.

The fact that the mines and metallurgical complexes from Krasnoyarsk to Norilsk were all created and built with millions of victims along the resource-rich Yenissei River from the 1930s to the mid-50s by the slave workers of the Gulag, including German and other prisoners of war and deported civilians from all over Eastern Europe,[88] does not seem to concern the previous and current owners Deripaska, Potanin and Prokhorov. They have not yet come up with the idea of paying compensation to the few survivors of these hells on earth as a way of making their old age easier for their terrible past suffering, from which the current metal magnates are benefitting handsomely. The subject does not seem to be of interest to US lawyers and nor to the world public either.

2.7.4 Mikhael Fridman (1964–)

Like Abramovich, Fridman started as a peddler and window cleaner, like Gusinsky he traded with theatre tickets, and like Menatep, Oneximbank, or Mostbank, his Alfa Bank became large and rich in managing the accounts and foreign exchange holdings of Russian ministries. Today as one of the few surviving oligarch banks, it has become Russia's largest private bank, probably the reward of having been one of the few banks who back in 1998 did not rip off its customers and creditors like the others.[89]

The breakthrough took place when his partner Piotr Aven (1955–) became Russian Foreign Trade Minister in the early 1990s. Fridman quickly and unbureaucratically obtained a lucrative license for oil exports. As the largest importer of unpackaged tea, it was also beneficial for him that tariffs and taxes on imported tea bags were suddenly doubled.

During the major oligarch privatization of 1996–1997, Fridman, whose standing at Yeltsin's court was not spectacular at that time, received only a mixed bag of medium-sized companies, including cement plants, the Moscow supermarket chain Perekrystok and the Vodka-distiller Smirnov. In addition, however, together with Viktor Vekselberg and Leonid Blavatnik, he bought the fourth-largest oil company, Tyumen Oil (TNK), for almost $1 billion. The payment of most of the purchase price was postponed generously at the time and could subsequently be easily paid out of the group's profits. By 2003, TNK set up a joint venture with BP, creating the world's seventh-largest oil producer, of which Alfa group acquired control in 2008.

---

[88] Anne Applebaum. *Gulag. A History of the Soviet Camps*. New York: Random House 2003, p. 120 and p. 457.
[89] Guy Chazan and John Thurnhill "The Alpha Oligarch" *Financial Times* 6.3.2015.

Nowadays, Fridman's friendly and accessible ways make forget a number of rough oligarchic business practices of the early years. For example, in November 2002, his Alfa group chartered a rotten tanker called "Prestige", which had previously only served as a floating storage tank in the Baltic Sea, to ship Russian oil from Ventspils (Windau) in Latvia to Singapore. It soon sank off the north-west coast of Spain. The oil spill, the huge costs of which were successfully shirked by the Alfa Group, contrasted with the expected profits of paltry $400,000 for the unsafe cargo.[90]

Further, after he bought Sidanco cheaply, including its debts, he had it declared bankrupt and enjoyed the assets debt-free.

BP's experience with a common oil field equally was poor. Together with TNK, it had been developed for $500 million only to discover in 1998 that Fridman with some tricks had secured the sole control over revenues. When in 2003 BP acquired 50% of the Tyumen group for $6.15 billion, BP, which urgently needed new sources of oil, paid for its oil field for the second time.[91] With the merged Sidanco group, TNK-BP then became the third-largest oil group in Russia with five refineries and 1600 service stations. However, due to its foreign participation, the Kremlin excluded the company from developing new oilfields with "strategic" dimensions.

By 2013, Sechin's Rosneft declared its interest to buy and integrate the entire TNK-BP venture for a total price of $24 billion—an offer, which one wisely should not refuse. Fridman's share stood at $14 billion for an original investment of $1 billion 16 years earlier. The rest went to other major shareholders like Vekselberg, Blavatnik and German Khan. Fridman invested the proceeds inter alia in RWE-Dea, the previously German owner of 12 gas fields in the North Sea and a stake in Turkcell, a Turkish mobile operator.

Alfa also controls the second and third largest mobile phone companies in Russia, Vimpelcom and Megafon. When Fridman wanted to merge both, he disturbed the circles of Leonid Reyman, then immune as a Putinocrat, who as Minister for Telecommunications, combined professional and commercial interests in the sector until his dismissal in 2008.[92] The usual astronomical tax claims arrived soon. However, Fridman abstained from any regime-critical tunes. Although vice-president of the Russian Jewish Congress, whose first presidents Gusinsky and Leonid Nevshin (the first deputy vice-president

---

[90] *Streats* 22.11.2002.
[91] Robert Cottrell "One slick customer" *Financial Times* 15.3.2003.
[92] "Die nebulöse Rolle of Leonid Reiman" *Frankfurter Allgemeine* 28.7.2005, FT Investigation: "Megafon diplomacy: A disputed stake pits an oligarch against a Putin ally" *Financial Times* 24.4.2006.

having been Khodorkovsky) went to Israel in exile, he correctly supports and finances the Kremlin parties.

In November 2006, he expressed interest in entering Vodaphone—a 20% share for the price of EUR 22.4 billion—a company into which Mannesmann, which had become big and famous 30 years earlier in the steel-pipe business in Russia, had disappeared.[93] Once again, an attempt to transfer most of the capital to a safe foreign country.

2.7.5 Viktor Vekselberg (1957–)

Vekselberg, a mathematician with a doctoral degree, had joined the exiled Leonid Blavatnik, who injected US capital into the joint Renova holding. As a result of the aluminium war, Vekselberg won as the second winner after Deripaska by taking over refineries in the Urals and Eastern Siberia with their large bauxite reserves and the Irkutskenergo electricity producer. His Siberia Ural aluminium company (Sual) was merged into Deripaska's Rusal in 2003 with a share of 20% for him.

As mentioned above, Vekselberg's Renova also had a stake in TNK-BP and in the telecom operator Svyazinvest with a stake of just over a quarter.

Vekselberg made himself few friends in Switzerland, where together with the Austrians Georg Stumpf and Ronny Pecik (a native Croat), as speculators they bought the venerable but suffering arms and machinery builders Oerlikon, Sulzer, and Saurer, as well as the German company M. and W. Zahnder.

With 40,000 employees and an annual turnover of $10.5 billion, the Renova Group as a holding company has so far generated private assets of $10.7 billion for Viktor Vekselberg.

2.7.6 Yuri Luzhkov (1936–2019) and Sistema

As the mayor and king of Moscow, Lushkov has played a special role since the perestroika era as the paternalist-populist leader of the probably most corrupt European city administration (despite strong competition from Petersburg, Naples, Marseille, Liège and Cologne). As a former director-general of a chemical company, he became vice-mayor in 1987 responsible for the licensing of cooperatives strongly promoting, among other things, projects of a certain Gusinsky. As mayor (1992–2010), Lushkov blocked

---

[93] *Financial Times Deutschland* 3.11.2006.

all privatizations in the Moscow area and instead involved the municipal administration with the blessings of Yeltsin in all local companies.

One of those holding companies was practically led by his second, much younger wife Yelena Batvinova (1963–), who, estimated at $3.1 billion, until her exile to Ireland remained the sole female oligarch of Russia, presiding over a group of companies covering property interests, the construction industry and cement and plastic industries.[94] Her company obtained some undesired publicity when at the end of 2006, she dismissed her brother Viktor Batvin, who sued for the payment of a share of 25% ($500 million) instead offered 1% ($20 million). Once Lushkov was ousted in 2010, Baturina hurriedly left Russia.

Still, the largest Moscow holding company Sistema is headed by Lushkov's former follower Vladimir Yevtushenko (1948–). He is allegedly married to Batinova's sister. Sistema was originally the Science and Technology Department (MCST) of Moscow City Administration, then headed by Yevtushenko, which he transformed in 1993 into a private company with Sistema as a holding company, with all of its staff and competencies. At the time of Lushkov nothing in Moscow happened without Sistema's participation. Ikea as an ethically correct Swedish company had refused to comply and then had to experience the consequences of insisting to do business in Russia the Swedish way. Its first mega-store in Moscow was forced to close just after opening at the beginning of the 2003 Christmas season due to alleged safety defects.[95]

The purported strategy for this mixed holding with its 150,000 employees is scattered and difficult to discern: Ranging from the control of the Bank of Moscow, of 6 other local banks, via Mobile Telesystems, Rosno insurance (later sold to Allianz for $750 million), Moscow Intourist hotels, regional newspapers and TV stations, the Central Fuel Company, the Moscow refinery up to the Moscow brewery, retail interests and wood processing. The most important sector is probably telecommunications for Sistema, which is why a certain Ron Sommer (formerly CEO of Deutsche Telekom) also sits on the supervisory board, representing the Blackrock hedge fund, which has a 4.5% stake in Sistema.[96] With a turnover of $10.9 billion annual profits were estimated at around $900 million. Yevtushenko's personal wealth was estimated at $6.3 billion.

Yet in 2010 he committed a strategic mistake: Sistema for $100 million bought 49% of Russneft, then indebted at $6 billion, previously owned by

---

[94] *Die Presse* 20.1.2007.
[95] Rüdiger Jungblut. *Die 11 Geschäftsgeheimnisse von Ikea.* Frankfurt/M.: Campus 2006, p. 145.
[96] *Financial Times* 28.5.2007.

Mikhael Guzeriyev, a native of Ingushetia, and turned it impressively around. He further wanted to merge Russneft with Bashneft, the largest oil producer of Bashkirstan, which he had acquired earlier with its modern refineries, petrochemical plants and petrol station chains, into an effective profitable private operator, which would have been in fact Russia's sixth-largest oil company.[97]

By 2014, however, fortunes changed. This success and potential competition had not escaped Igor Sechin's attention, and he now wished to add Sistema's medium-sized Bashneft to his own Rosneft oil empire. When Yevtushenko refused, he was put under house arrest for a few months until he agreed to sell for $5.3 billion. That could have been the end of the story, but by 2017 Rosneft sued him for alleged asset stripping prior to the sale for an amount of $2.8 billion.[98] To add insult to injury Sechin wanted more than half of the agreed purchasing price back. In order to increase pressure, he soon introduced a second "compensation" claim, increasing the total to $5.5 billion, which would have bankrupted Sistema, whose assets had already been frozen by the courts. In the end, under duress Sistema had to settle for the bargain penalty of $1.8 billion,[99] which made Yevtushenko considerably poorer, now "only" worth $1.9 billion.

2.8 Other Fallen Oligarchs

Since the loss of power and autonomy of the old oligarchs who chose to stick to Putin's instructions of 2000: "Stay out of politics and you can keep your loot", and thus survived more or less, the rules have changed, but nobody knows to what. Yevtushenko obviously had crossed Sechin's path in the oil industry. But there were others who were struck down, who had a low profile, did their donations to the Kremlin, even cultivated Putin's and Medvedev's entourage with donations and the required favours, but to no avail. Let us look pars pro toto at three cases.

2.8.1 Yevgeny Chichvarkin

As a 22-year-old he founded Yevroset, Russia's biggest mobile phone chain. When prosecutors closed in on him in 2010 for an alleged kidnapping and

---

[97] *Frankfurter Allgemeine* 29.3.2010.
[98] "Russian brawl" *The Economist* 6.7.2017.
[99] *Frankfurter Allgemeine* 27.12.2017.

extorsion back in 2003, he had to sell out his company to Alexander Marat for $1.3 billion, who then sold it on to Vimpelcom of Mikhael Fridman. His original sin had been to have stopped the practice of paying bribes to import phones duty-free, a scheme which totalled $1 billion per year—mostly for the Ministry of the Interior which supervises the customs service. He now runs a luxury wine shop in London, appears lucky to be still alive and unlike other exiled oligarchs seems like a happy man.

2.8.2 Sergey Pugachev

Once called the "Kremlin's banker" with his successful Mezhprombank, founded in 1992, he fell from grace in 2010, when the state set out to seize his two modernized shipyards in St. Petersburg: Saverrnaya Verf and Baltisky Zavod, which were coveted by no other than Igor Sechin, then still chairing the state-controlled United Shipbuilding Corporation (USC), whose standard business methods for corporate takeovers should no longer surprise. The method was to force his bank into bankruptcy and then to seize its assets. Like most banks during the financial crisis of 2008, Mezhprombank had received some $2.1 billion as emergency liquidity support from the Central Bank, out of which by 2010 some $1 billion still remained unpaid. His shipyards, which had produced the first nuclear ice breaker in Russia for 35 years and advanced "stealth" corvettes for the Navy, were then valued at between $2.2 billion to $4.2 billion, enough in any event to repay the remaining debt. Yet the Central Bank chose to revoke the banking license, to seize the shipyards in 2012 and to put them up for a forced sale, which USC, surprise, surprise, won at discount prices of $415 million and $7.5 billion, respectively. It is clear that Pugatchev's assets simply had become too valuable to remain outside the Kremlin's direct control.

As usual, the story does not end here. In 2013, an arrest warrant was issued for Pugachev—since 2010 more or less safely in London, and in 2014 the Russian Deposit Insurance Agency tried to freeze his international assets.

In his view the new rules are the ones of a feudalistic system, in which all are the president's serfs, nobody can feel safe, or "untouchable", and businessmen are only the nominal owners of their assets. With Putin's campaign to retake state control of key parts of the economy, since like any chekist he fundamentally distrusts private entrepreneurs, the borders between big business and the Kremlin started to vanish, thus corrupting the power system entirely.[100] It is difficult to disagree with his analysis.

2.8.3 Ziyamudin and Magomed Magomedov

These two brothers from Dagestan ran different operations. The younger Ziyavudin (born in 1968) ran a construction holding, called "Summa", and was worth $1.3 billion. His older brother by one year, worth $450 million, who during 2002–2009 was an undistinguished senator for Smolensk, assisted politically. Both were arrested by the FSB in March 2018 with allegations of fraud at $37 million when constructing the soccer stadiums in St. Petersburg and Kaliningrad and the local airport there, and to have formed a "criminal association" in the process, which risks a decade in prison. The sharks quickly circled in: Sberbank claimed $58 million from Ziyamudin's gas producing company. VTB received a cereal terminal in Novorossiysk and shares in his logistics company "Transcontainer" and further was to acquire his stake in OSK, Russia's largely state-controlled cereal exporter.

They had built the oil terminal at Primosk for Transneft (in order to circumvent the Baltic terminals) and had been ready to sell their participation in this terminal as well as in Baltijsk and Novorosijsk to Transneft. Yet their arrest sabotaged the deal. The principal suspect as always: Igor Sechin, who wanted them for Rosneft. Yet the terminals still went to Transneft, whose boss since 2007, Nicolay Tovkayev, knows Putin longer than Sechin, and worked with him and Rostec chief Chemesov already in Dresden. The purchasing price of $750 million has since been frozen by the state.

Though as Dagestanis they did not belong to the inner circle of power, the two brothers seemed to have done everything right. They renovated at Medvedev's request and apparently at their own expense the Bolshoi theatre in 2009–2011 and cultivated expensively Putin's spokesman Dmitry Peskov and his former chief ideologist Vladimir Surkov. Magomed even organized a nightly ice hockey league for the political elite in Moscow at which Putin unfailingly scored most goals and always won. The origins of their fall from grace are not clear, as often: Be it the Kremlin's change of leadership in Dagestan and their own rumoured political ambitions there, the US affinity of the younger brother, who with his "Caspian Venture Capital" invested a lot into US high-tech enterprises, or the hostility of their rival Suleiman

---

[100]Catherine Belton and Neil Buckley "Business in Russia "serfs" to the state, says ex-Putin aide" *Financial Times* 9.10.2014.

Karimov.[101] As usual, the reasons are murky and part of Putin's instruments of intimidation, deterrence and of creating fear and uncertainty even in very high places.

2.9 Putin's State Monopoly Capitalism

2.9.1 Gazprom First

Gazprom was the beginning. After Putin's inauguration as President its supervisory board was the first to be cleansed.[102] In July 2000, Dimitri Medvedev replaced Chernomyrdin, who was sent off as an ambassador to Kiev,[103] as the chairman. The majority of the 11 seats were transferred from his followers to representatives of the state, including German Gref, the Minister for Economic Affairs, but also of foreign investors (then 6.4%), the honorary consul of Russia in North Rhine-Westphalia, Burckhard Bergmann, then on the board of directors of Eon Ruhrgas.[104]

Twelve months later, Rem Viahkirev was replaced as Chief Executive Officer by Alexei Miller, who had worked loyally for Putin as head of department for external economic relations in St. Petersburg. Soon Gazprom's commercial policy, with its monopoly over Russia's gas pipelines and distribution systems, had the quality of a proxy function for the Russian State. Vladimir Milov observed: "Putin effectively controls the firm and takes all key strategic decisions".[105] Thus he prevented the already planned dismantling of the monopoly into corporations conducive to competition and raised the Kremlin's shareholding to 51%.

Predictably, the Kremlin's dominance tended to perpetuate the habits and mindsets of a dinosaur-like Soviet-type business. It is animated by the effortlessly achieved demand of the global gas boom with a seemingly unending

---

[101] Friedrich Schmidt "Geschäftsrisiko Gefängnis" *Frankfurter Allgemeine* 2.1.2019.

[102] *Financial Times* 1.7.2000.

[103] Aslund reports on an interesting meeting of US businessmen with Chernomyrdin in Kiev, during which one of them asked: "Where would you invest in the Ukraine, if you had $100 million?" Chernomyrdin misunderstood the question and got very upset. After all he owned $5 billion. Such was the size of his loot. Anders Aslund. *Russia's Crony Capitalism*. New Haven: Yale University Press 2019, pp. 109.

[104] Werner Sturbeck "In Rußlands Diensten" *Frankfurter Allgemeine* 24.11.2006. His mandate lasted from 2000 to 2011. In 2010, after his retirement EON sold its remaining 3.5% share for €3.4 billion. *Financial Times* 2.12.2010.

[105] Arkady Ostrovsky "Energy of the state: How Gazprom acts as lever in Putin's power play" *Financial Times* 14.3.2006.

profit bonanza, which stimulated a wild and diffuse spread of capital investments into unrelated sectors and political pet projects of the Kremlin. With a purchase price of $100 per 1000 m^3 of captive Central Asian natural gas and a resale price of $270 to Western customers, which was maintained for almost a decade, profits from pipeline transport should not be too difficult to achieve. Yet 40% of Gazprom's workforce continued to work in peripheral unrelated areas such as porcelain factories, chicken farms and the management of Black Sea resorts. In 2004 alone without significant productivity improvements, the personnel costs of the 400,000 employees with their 16 monthly salaries increased by 30%.

There is little doubt that Medvedev-Miller management had stopped the practice of openly looting company capital. Chernomyrdin is said to have diverted $5 billion through, for example, his two sons and the Stroitransgas gas subsidiary. Yet Gazprom further diversified into non-core sectors, like the leading media group, as the new majority owner of the Siberian Coal and Energy Company (SUEK) with 77 coal mines and 27 coal-fired power plants, into Moscow's Mosenergo power plants, and started as an oil producer with the purchase of the Sibneft.

Further, it gave priority to investing abroad in distribution networks up to the final consumers in order to dominate export markets and postponed the development of new gas fields, despite declining yields in its three largest fields. It also did not renew the third of its 463,000 km of pipelines and half of all pumping stations whose lifetime had expired. Due to insufficient pipeline capacity, 50 billion m^3 of gas is lost or flared each year in Russia. At the politically set internal prices, which are as low as $45 per 1000 m^3, Gazprom can only earn money on exports. Hence it neglects the sales networks in Russia itself and promotes heating with coal rather than with gas.[106]

Curious intermediary companies stayed in business as settlement offices for dependent customers and export sales. They remain completely non-transparent with an often obscure ownership. As middlemen economically they are entirely superfluous. Yet they continue to be used by all sides in the gas trade in the former Soviet space as a lucrative source of discrete political funding and private rent acquisition.

One of them, RosUkrEnergo, is in charge of all-natural gas supplies from Gazprom to Ukraine and remained the main source of political corruption and financing of Russian agents. Thus, Yulia Timoshenko, as Prime Minister (2005, 2007–2010), imposed direct price negotiations and open

---

[106] *Die Presse* 10.2.2007.

tariffs bypassing RosUkrEnergo (which were soon reversed after her forced departure by Yushchenko in 2005).[107] Gazprom officially holds 50% stake in RosUkrEnergo, headquartered in the Swiss town of Zug. The other half was owned until 2007 by the Austrian Raiffeisen International for an alleged strawman of unknown identity.[108] Gazprom interests were represented by Konstantin Chnichenko, an ex-KGB officer from St. Petersburg, how it might be different? A similarly obscure intermediate company which is selling Turkmen gas exports through the only available Gazprom distribution network is EuralTransGas, based in Budapest, in which the notorious Kremlin godfather Mogilevich is still involved. Why these expensive and entirely redundant intermediaries are tolerated is difficult to comprehend, as their parasitic role only reduces the net profits of Gazprom, unless of course the generous feeding of these obscure intermediate layers is intended….

2.9.2 Russia's Energy Export Policy

The subordination of business interests to the strategic imperatives of Russian energy policy is a purposefully designed policy of the Kremlin. As natural gas, unlike oil, is much more dependent on pipelines because of the costs and risks of gas liquefaction, Gazprom since years invests into complementary bypasses for its export pipeline network. In addition to the dated Soyuz and Yamal East-West main lines, Nord Stream 1 (followed by Nord Stream 2 along the same route, and doubling capacity at completion foreseen during 2021) has been built through the Baltic Sea from Viipuri/Wyborg in Karelia, landing near Greifswald to supply Central Europe. Further "Turkstream" (originally called "Blue Stream"), was built across the Black Sea to supply Turkey and the Balkans directly. The intention is clearly to cut out both Ukraine and Belarus/Poland as gas transit countries, regardless of the immense construction costs (for each of the Nord Streams €10 billion) involved.

This openly undermined the EU's past energy policy intention to source part of its gas directly from Central Asia and Iran, independently of Russia, through a planned "Nabucco" pipeline projected from Azerbaijan via Georgia and Turkey up to Baumgarten in Austria. Russia's successful counterstrategy also applies to the sources. Russia's dispute over the sea borders of the Caspian Sea has since blocked the construction of trans-Caspian pipelines, running

---

[107] Dimitri Popov and Ilia Milstein. *Yulia Timoshenko. Die Zukunft der Ukraine nach der orangenen Revolution.* Cologne: Dumont 2006, p. 351.
[108] Andreas Bornefeld www.netstudien.de/Russland/wjachirew.htm.

from Kazakhstan and Turkmenistan to Azerbaijan. Following the unresolved death of Turkmen dictator Nijazov ("Turkmenbashi") in December 2006, his successor Berdymuhammedov accepted the expansion of the gas pipelines that will bring his gas—the fifth-largest reserves in the world—to the North along the East Caspian coast into the Gazprom grid. In impoverished Armenia, Gazprom controlled the pipeline construction with Iran through the purchase of ArmRosGas. Immediately it reduced the diameter of the pipelines to 70 cm so that only Armenia's domestic needs are covered and nothing is left for export to third countries and for the potential supply of Iranian gas to Nabucco.[109]

Similarly, Transneft is seeking to divert its main oil pipelines from Druzhba, which passes through Belarus and Poland to the refinery of Schwedt, to a new oil terminal in Primorsk on the Gulf of Finland for direct exports by tanker. The connecting pipelines in the Baltic, to Ventspils (Windau) in Latvia and to the Mazuzeikai refinery (Lithuania) have already been shut down by Transneft.

One may harbour strong reservations about Russia's energy policy, which typically cuts off gas/oil pipelines for repairs before starting price negotiations with dependent customers in January, when the winter is coldest and demand at its highest (e.g. Belarus in 2007 and Ukraine in 2006) or, as in the case of Georgia and Lithuania in 2006, the gas/oil pipelines conveniently explode by accident in the border area.

In its most important EU gas market, Gazprom expressed its interest to purchase all major distributors: Whether Centrica in the UK, RWE or Eon Ruhrgas. Here Gazprom also spends a lot for positive publicity: a US advertising company has been contracted for $11 billion for better PR and the German soccer club Schalke 04, for instance, is sponsored with EUR150 million until at least 2022.

Yet political reservations—and last but not the least the EU's competition rules in the energy sector—have prevented major strategic acquisitions. To date, Gazprom only co-owns Wingas, a BASF subsidiary operating a 2500 km distribution network in Central Germany, the Hungarian Foldgas, the Belorussian Beltransgaz[110] and regional networks in Bulgaria, and up to 50% of the leading gas companies in the Baltics and of the Italian Eni.[111] To the same end, Gasprom acquired Borsod Chemie in Hungary and Pennine Natural Gas, a smaller gas distributor in England. All these investments,

---

[109] *New Europe* 12.11.2006.
[110] *Frankfurter Allgemeine* 16.11.2006.
[111] Albrecht Rothacher. *Im wilden Osten. Hinter den Kulissen des Umbruchs in Osteuropa.* Hamburg: Krämer Verlag 2002, pp. 54 and 74.

together with long-term supply contracts, were expected to increase Russia's share of the EU gas market from earlier 25 to 33% by 2010.[112] This is a proportion entailing considerable dependence, which after the failure of Nabucco does require alternative LNG based suppliers. In the past, Putin also raised the idea of a global gas producer cartel with countries like Algeria, Kazakhstan, Turkmenistan, Iran, Venezuela and Qatar, in analogy to the OPEC. But since gas markets—in difference to globally traded oil—are too regionalized, nothing ever came out of it. Besides, also in relation to OPEC, Russia is not renowned as a team player. When the cartel cuts production to increase prices, Russia usually increases production to benefit.

For its own oil and gas fields, Putin has issued a clear line with the liquidation of Yukos: No control by foreigners or private groups, including Lukoil. Thus the owners of the production and liquefaction project Sakhalin II Shell (55%), Mitsui (25%) and Mitsubishi (20%) were first forced out in 2006, following a rather transparent campaign of alleged environmental damage (suddenly the Kremlin discovered its heart for grey whales and the Sakhalin salmon!) shortly before completion, to transfer 50% and one share to Gazprom for $7.45 billion. This, according to Putin, resolved the environmental problems of the project instantly.[113] Sakhalin II is considered to be one of the most complex production projects by far. From an offshore extraction platform (which has to be protected against massive ice floes during the frequent winter storms), gas is to be extracted in the Northern coastal waters and then transported through a pipeline to Yushno-Sakhalinsk in the South of the island, liquified there and shipped to mostly Japanese power plants. In its expropriation strategy, the Kremlin cares little about the fact that Gazprom has no experience of gas liquefaction.

Next was TNK-BP with its Arctic Kovytka gas field. The fact that half of that undertaking was Russian, owned by the oligarchs Vekselberg, Blavatnik and Fridman, and that 11% of the shares in the gas field were held by the regional government of Irkutsk and 26% by Potanin's Interros, was not an obstacle to the Kremlin's transfer campaign. The consortium was accused of producing too little gas in breach of its contract. As was the case earlier at Sakhalin II, it was threatened with the cancellation of licenses and with penalties. Unfortunately, the consortium could not supply more than 2.5 billion m^3 for the regional Siberian market, as Gazprom, as the gas pipeline monopolist, persistently had refused to build the major pipeline needed for export

---

[112] "Special report. Gazprom in Europe" *Financial Times* 21.12.2006.
[113] *Frankfurter Allgemeine* 12.12.2006, *Handelsblatt* 22.12.2006.

to China. TNK-BP then had little choice but to transfer their shares of the unusable gas field to Gazprom at the bargain price of EUR 670 million.[114]

For the development of the vast Shtokman gas field, which is situated in 350 m depth in the Barents Sea 500 km out in the Arctic Sea, as the only foreigner to date, the French Total is allowed to operate as a subordinate partner—next to Chinese minority interests—supplying 25% of the infrastructure and technical services. Total remains a supplier of the technologies still not mastered by its Russian partner Novatec and by Gazprom.

2.9.3 Rosneft

Rosneft was originally a small, poorly managed state company left over in the booming, widely privatized Russian oil industry. It assembled the scattered legacy of the remaining state-run oil facilities, for which nobody cared to bid even the usual heavily discounted prices. Between 2000 and 2004, its production grew by just 3%, while Abramovich's Sibneft, for instance, increased output by 26%.

As the oil industry's ugly duckling Rosneft's hour came by winning the choice pieces of Khodorkovsky's Yukos empire at discount prices, thus moving to the first place in sector (up from 8th place) in Russia ahead of Lukoil.

After years of mismanagement, Rosneft had been rehabilitated by Sergey Bagdanchikov, an oil manager from Sakhalin who had been CEO since 1998. The supervisory board was chaired by Igor Sechin, originally Putin's right-hand man in St Petersburg and at the time vice-president of the Kremlin's Administration. As a leading member of the Chekhist group in the Kremlin, he ensured that Rosneft and not Gazprom won the largest chunk of the Yukos heritage.[115]

Similarly to Gazprom, Rosneft uses its revenues to buy the assets of competitors. Accordingly, new investments, business development and the elimination of refinery shortages are less evident. This is nothing new for a state-owned group. As mentioned, Rosneft together with Gazprom took over the assets of Yukos worth $45 billion in 2003. In 2012, it acquired TNK-BP for $28 billion, and with a little more muscular help also Bashneft from Yevtushenko's Sistema for an agreed price $5.3 billion in 2014, which Sechin in a later court case, having had Yevtushenko re-arrested, managed to cut by

---

[114] *Frankfurter Allgemeine* 2.6.2007, *Die Presse* 23.6.2007.
[115] *Frankfurter Allgemeine* 15.7.2006.

half. There were also dubious sales of major Rosneft shareholdings to anonymous shell companies and Chinese traders in 2017 which were subsequently repurchased. Due to its high capital expenditure on acquisitions for Sechin's empire-building and not always very productive investments, one of them being a $14 billion project in Venezuela's oil industry of all places, Rosneft is over-indebted with a very small cash flow. As a result, the world's largest oil company is valued at only $68 billion (2018), with the much smaller Exxon being five times more valuable, just to put things into perspective.

Not by accident Sechin resides in the old USSR Ministry of the Oil Industry not far from the Kremlin, where all major deals have to be agreed on with Putin.[116] In September 2017, ex-Chancellor Schröder—not known to be an energy expert—was appointed as Rosneft's chairman of the board as a well-paid pliant figurehead.

2.9.4 Case Study: Bill Browder's Hermitage Fund

There were also audacious foreign portfolio investors, who wanted to join the bonanza. One of them was Bill Browder, whose grandfather had been head of the US Communist Party (not that this helped much), and who had already made some lucrative, if somewhat, exotic deals during the privatization phase in Poland. As an investment banker working for Salomon Brothers in the wild early 1990s, he was offered 51% of the Russian fishing fleet of 100 vessels worth $1 billion for the price of $2.5 million, for instance.[117]

He neatly describes his subsequent experiences with the coupon privatization: Each of Russia's then 150 million citizens received a coupon with a nominal value of some $20 which could be traded for a part of 30% of shares of all Russian state enterprises, which were thus valued at merely $10 billion. As there were no restrictions on trading coupons, a vivid and unregulated market soon sprung up spontaneously. In villages or factories they were traded in for a bottle of vodka or for food, resold in regional towns in packs for $12 each, then bundled in packets of 1000 or 2000 each and traded in Moscow at $18 each. Bigger traders then assembled stacks of 25,000 and sold them for the nominal value of $20. All transactions at the Moscow coupon exchange were cash only. Each trader had to provide for his own security and for his suitcases of cash and coupons. For the Salomon Brothers Browder bought $25 million worth of coupons.

---

[116] Aslund. Op. cit., pp. 121.
[117] Bill Bowder. *Red Notice*. Munich: Hanser 2017, p. 70.

These coupons then had to be traded for shares at "coupon auctions". They were organized in very obscure locations, in perfectly untransparent conditions with confusing rules to deter participation and to allow insiders to get the largest numbers of shares for the smallest number of coupons possible. This reduced the effective sales price of the already massively undervalued Russian companies even further. When "The Economist" in May 1994 made this public, suddenly there was a massive surge of interest by Western investors, hedge managers and speculators.[118] Share prices quickly shot up, and Browder's $25 million investment was soon worth $125 million.

The result of the unregulated coupon privatization was, however, that instead of 150 million Russians enjoying the modest fruits of their life-long labours, 22 oligarchs soon owned 39% of the Russian economy, and the rest of the people during the transition crisis lost their lower-middle- or working-class way of life and became very poor.

Browder now set up his own investment fund, called Hermitage Capital, and based on his Russian expertise collected money from rich individuals, notably from Edmond Safra, the billionaire owner of a bank in New York.[119] For an investor then as of now it was difficult to collect reliable business and financial information on Russian enterprises. Since a Soviet-inherited paranoia little is public, what is public is usually not accurate. Yet he decides to buy 4% of Potanin's Sidanco.

Potanin in response quickly decides to issue plenty of cheap new shares, which would have devalued Browder's holdings by 2/3. After Browder told this story to the press, actually to Chrystia Freeland[120] of the Financial Times, he needed bodyguards. Yet after he formally complained with the Russian Stock Market Supervision, which acted professionally and was not bought by oligarchs, Potanin stopped the emission.[121] By 1997, his Fund was worth $1 billion.

Yet late in 1998, the Asian crisis hit. International and Russian capital fled the country. Once the IMF sent $22.6 billion in support of the economy, the oligarchs snatched the funds, exchanged their rubles for US$ and stashed them abroad. With the stock market collapsing and the ruble down, his fund within a few weeks was $900 million poorer.

As the country's international reputation was ruined, the oligarchs did no longer expect any Wall Street money. So they abandoned their good

---

[118] Ibid., p. 81.
[119] In 1998, he was murdered by a domestic helper in his apartment in Monaco.
[120] Since 2015 she became subsequently Minister of International Trade, Foreign Minister and now Deputy Prime Minister of Canada.
[121] Ibid., p. 141.

behaviour, emptied listed corporations by splitting off productive assets, stole by selling products cheaply to associated companies, overcharged for services supplied by subsidiaries, watered down minority shareholdings, the whole menu. According to Browder, Khodorkovsky with his Menatep/Yukos had been one of the worst offenders.[122]

2.10 Putinocrats

The basic pattern of Russian industrial policy in the Putin era is relatively simple:

Restoring state control over commodities and other strategic industries. Wherever possible, they are organized as monopolies or duopolies. They are led by followers from a small circle around the president with very similar biographies (KGB career, law studies and administrative careers in St. Petersburg). The small number of oligarchs is made compliant by constant investigative pressure. The role of foreign capital is limited to marginal minority shareholdings and forcible technology transfers through compulsory joint ventures in key sectors, including in manufacturing. In turn, the Russian state and private sectors expand abroad in areas of interest on orders of the Kremlin.[123]

This foreign strategy is willingly followed by the oligarchs, allowing them to move their assets abroad in a legal and patriotic way approved by the Kremlin. For example, Norilsk Nickel purchased the US Stillwater mines, the Canadian LionOre, and the OM Group in Cleveland. Abramovich's Evraz Holding bought Oregon Steel and Vitcovice Steel in Ostrava (Ostrau) in Moravia. The merger of all internal airlines into AirUnion, ordered by Putin, absorbed the Hungarian airline Malev as well, while Aeroflot, whose chairman of the supervisory board is vice-premier Sergey Ivanov, as an international airline, was attempting to acquire Alitalia, an ever-elusive target for anyone (and for profit-making). Alekperov's Lukoil for $3 billion purchased three refineries in the Ukraine, Bulgaria and Romania, plus 2000 petrol stations, like Conoco's "Jet" network in Belgium, Finland and Eastern Europe.[124] Fridman's Alfa Group purchased Turkcell for $2.5 billion. The state-owned Vneshtorgbank participated in 5.4% of the European defence

---

[122] By some strange coincidence, after having both clashed with the Putin system and having economically been destroyed by it, both are now human rights activists in London. On Browder's further fate and the one of his attorney Magnitzky, please see Chap. 3.

[123] *Der Standard* 31.5.2006.

[124] Rothacher. Op. cit., p. 504; Stefan Wagstyl "Lukoil extends its reach across Europe" *Financial Times* 24.1.2007.

and aviation group EADS. Deripaska's German-Austrian investments in construction and passenger cars and parts have been already mentioned. However, according to capital market statistics, the main destinations of Russian investment remain the Bahamas, the Virgin Islands and Cyprus.[125] This is where many times more money is laundered.

As the largest coup ever, at the end of 2006, Alexey Mordachov's Severstal tried, encouraged by the Kremlin, to take over the Luxembourg-Lorrain Acelor (formerly: ARBED and Ucilor) which however failed, as the Indian Lakshimi Mittal with EUR 26.9 billion won the race[126] making him now by far the largest steel producer in the world. Severstal succeeded with the acquisition of the relatively modest Rouge Industries in Detroit for $300 million.

Interventions by the Kremlin also seek consolidation and forced modernizations with domestic or with foreign help, provided the Russian partner remains in charge. Thus Sergei Chemezov—he did not originate from Petersburg but lived in the same compound as Putin in Dresden—as the Director-General of the lucrative arms export monopoly Rosoboronexport (main customers: China, India, Vietnam, Algeria, Iran) received the order to take over and to rehabilitate the ailing Lada producer Avtovaz with its sales problems, strike threats and growing debt.[127] According to Putin's intention, Deripaska is to carry out the same miracle with the help of Magna at the Volga producer Gaz.

Over Alrosa, the world's second-largest diamond producer in Siberia, government control has been strengthened. The shares of the regional government of Yakutia have been taken over, and former finance minister Alexei Kudrin was inthronized as head of the board.[128] He then strengthened the company's grip in Africa gaining mining rights in Congo and Angola, where De Beers, the world leader, had gone out of favour.

In return, Western mining companies face difficulties even outside the energy sector in Russia. For example, Peter Hambro Mining, which is

---

[125] Pars pro toto it is very instructive to read the corporate brochure of one of the leading law firms Antis Triantafyllides & Sons LLC (www.triantafyllides.com) which serves Russian corporate interests foremost and which is owned at 13% by EU Health Commissioner Stella Kyriakides. The law firm successfully defended Russian oligarchs like Rybolovlev, Suleiman Karimov and Vladimir Potanin in Cypriote courts. It also mediates Cypriotic and hence EU citizenship to "high-net-worth-individuals", and organizes Cypriote shell companies to allow Russian investors to re-invest in Russia after having laundered their capital. An example given for the purchase of a luxury hotel in Moscow for US $160 million shows the process very openly.

[126] *Financial Times* 27.5.2006, 31.5.2006, 16.6.2006 and 21.11.2006.

[127] *Der Standard* 2.6.2007, *Financial Times* 19.4.2007.

[128] *Financial Times* 16.12.2006.

searching for gold along the Amur River, is gradually losing its licenses on account of alleged breaches of environmental rules.[129]

In the summer of 2007, under Putin's instructions, state umbrella companies were formed in the aircraft and nuclear energy sectors for the "consolidation" of all public and private companies manufacturing in these branches. Thus, vice-PM Sergey Ivanov manages the new holding for aircraft manufacturing and ex-Premier Sergey Kiriyenko supervises AtomEnergoProm, which now controls the whole chain from uranium extraction to the construction, exportation and operation of nuclear power plants, and to build 26 new nuclear power plants in the country during 12 years. In 2013, Russia's largest deal for nuclear plant exports was concluded with Turkey for US$20 billion. In 2018, after a groundbreaking ceremony by Putin and Erdogan work started on the first of four reactors in Akkuyu at the Southern coast, opposite Cyprus, in an earthquake-prone zone. By 2023, the first is expected to be operational and to ruin the local tourism industry successfully.

Thus the "Kremlin Inc." is increasingly similar to a network of state-controlled business groups whose strategic decisions are closely controlled and guided by the Kremlin directly and whose operational control on the supervisory board is exercised by Putin's ministers and by personal trustees on the board of directors. Having set up this structure, Putin, as a President, purposefully allowed for a degree of duality to divide and rule and thus to remain the supreme arbiter by promoting at least two rival groups in key positions, the Chekists around Ivanov and his aeronautics industry and Sechin at the helms of Rosneft, and the systemic "liberals" around Medvedev at Gazprom, for instance.[130]

There are also other Putinists who have also become economically powerful and rich under him: The banker Sergey Pugatshev (Mezhprombank) and Vladimir Kogan, who dominates the Petersburg financial market, Vladimir Yakunin, the former chief of Russian railways, and former telecoms minister and oligarch Leonid Reyman, all of whom had randomly crossed Putin's paths in Petersburg.

---

[129] *Financial Times* 1.12.2006 and 15.12.2006.

[130] Interview: "Steeled to succeed—Ivanov sets out his tough vision for Russia's future" *Financial Times* 19.4.2007.

2.11 Conclusion I: Wealth and Economic Power in Russia

All subsequent quantifications have to be taken with many grains of salt. There are too many hidden assets. There are difficulties in the valuation of often very transparent corporate and ownership structures and naturally also strong variations in the value of commodity producers depending on world market fluctuations, and surely also the strong ruble/US$ exchange rate variations. On top of it, some oligarchs (like a certain Donald Trump) love to inflate publicly the estimates of their assets, like a symbol of virility, while others do the opposite to stay happily out of the limelight and out of trouble (applying to both *siloviki* greed and to US sanctions). Sometimes believed assets, like Berezovsky's $3 billion, disappeared in the hot air, Khodorkovsky's $15 billion got stolen by the state, as did the $12 billions of Sergey Pugatchev, ex-boss of Mejprombank, with shipyards in St. Petersburg and Rosneft shares[131] and Yevtchuchenko's $2.4 billion (gotten under mayor Luzhkov's rule over Moscow) which largely vanished after subsequent shakeouts.

With these caveats in mind (and I am not Forbes), based on published sources let's roughly compare the old and new oligarchs:

Suleiman Kerimov, a Dagestani, who had invested in Western banks, lost a lot during 2008, but later bought Urankali (fertilizers), Vnukovo Airlines, NaftaMoskwa, an oil trader, sizable Gazprom shares and controls Fedprombank: $21 billion (2012)[132]

Mikhael Fridman, Bank Alfa, Vimpelcom, Turkcell: from $21 billion (2008) down to $17.6 billion (2015)[133]

Lev Blavatnik, Warner Music: $16 billion (2014)[134]

Viktor Vekselberg, Integrated Energy Systems: $15.1 billion (2014)[135]

Leonid Mikhelson: Novatec (second largest gas company): $14.4 billion (2016)[136]

---

[131] Isabelle Lassere "L'oligarch russe Pougatchev defie Poutine" *Le Figaro* 8.11.2016.
[132] Catherine Belton "The Secret Oligarch" *Financial Times* 11.2.2012.
[133] *Die Presse* 4.10.2008 and *Financial Times* 6.3.2017.
[134] *New York Times* 1.1.2014.
[135] *New York Times* 1.1.2014.
[136] *Die Welt* 26.11.2016.

Vladimir Potanin, Norilsk Nickel, Oneximbank: from $19.3 billion (2008)[137] down to $14.3 billion (2013)[138]

Alisher Usmanov, an ethnic Uzbek, owner of MegaFon, and Kommersant newspaper, formerly also of Arsenal and Mail.ru, a Facebook copy: from $19 billion (2012)[139] down to $12.5 billion (2018)[140]

Mikhael Prokhorov: $10.9 billion (2014)[141]

German Khan: Alfa Bank: $10.5 billion (2014)[142]

Oleg Deripaska, Basic Elements, EN+ (waterpower): $6 billion (2017)[143]

Piotr Aven: Alfa Bank: $5.5 billion (2008).[144]

And now the Putin oligarchs:

Gennady Timchenko, Stroytrantransgaz, Gunvor, which sells Rosneft oil abroad, shares in Novotec: estimated between $11.9 billion and 15.8 billion (both 2015)[145]

Arkandy Rotenberg, construction of motorways (Mostrotest) and pipelines for Gazprom: $4 billion (2015)[146]

Boris Rotenberg (brother of A.), shares in SMP Bank and Gazprom: $1.7 billion (2015)[147]

Aras Agalarov, shopping malls: $2 billion (2015)[148]

Yuri Kovalchuk, Bank Rossiya, Gazprombank, Sogaz Insurance, Gazfund (pension fund), Sibur (chemicals) 20 TV channels and telecom: $1.4 billion (2015)[149]

Dmitry Pumyansky, steel pipe-producer TMK: $1 billion (2015)[150]

Nicolai Shamalov, medical supplier: $0.5 billion (2015).[151]

---

[137] *Die Presse* 4.10.2008.
[138] *Wall Street Journal* 11.11.2013.
[139] *The Times* 18.11.2012. The *FT* on 17.11.2012 believed that he was worth $18 billion.
[140] *Frankfurter Allgemeine* 23.10.2018.
[141] *Die Presse* 18.4.2014.
[142] *New York Times* 1.1.2014.
[143] *Financial Times* 24.10.2017.
[144] *Die Presse* 8.11.2008.
[145] The first estimate: *Financial Times* 12.6.2015, the second: *The Times* 26.7.2015, which illustrates the variations and margins of error.
[146] *The Times* 26.7.2015. His Italian luxury villa was confiscated as the result of EU sanctions.
[147] Ibid.
[148] *Financial Times* 12.6.2015.
[149] *The Times* 26.7.2015.
[150] *Financial Times* 12.6.2015.
[151] *The Times* 26.7.2015.

There are also other Putinist oligarchs, like Jevgeny Prigoshin, "Putin's cook". In fact, he is one of the Russia's largest caterers, supplies the military and serves probably better food when Putin visits his luxury restaurants in St. Petersburg and Moscow. He is also suspected of running troll factories and of owning the Wagner mercenary troop, founded by KGB colonel Utkin and active with thousands of former military men in Syria, Libya, the Central African Republic and Mozambique. The Wagner business model is very simple: Protection of corrupt dictators in exchange for raw material concessions.[152] Their operations are elegantly deniable, but surely are unthinkable without top-level approval.

Then there are simple monopolists, like the "fertilizer king" Dmitry Rybolovlev, who owns Urankali and the potash mines of Berezniki (build by slave labour), but lives in a better place in Monaco and bought the most expensive penthouse at New York's Central Park for $88 million. Or Ivan Savvidis, the "tobacco king", a Russian-Georgian of Caucasian Greek origin, worth $1.9 billion who also owns the Greek soccer club PAOK F.L.

The official annual salary lists (2014) of the leading Putinocrats at the helm of SOEs cannot match the above fortunes, but certainly outrank their counterparts among most Wall Street bankers and US CEOs by a fair margin—while they remain utterly unrelated to actual performance:

Alexei Miller (Gazprom): $27 million
Andrei Kostin (head of the VTB Kremlin self-service bank): $21 million
Oleg Sechin (Rosneft): $17.5 million[153]
Vladimir Yakunin (when he was still at Russian Railways): $15 million
German Gref (Sberbank): $13.5 million.[154]

They were all are recruited from a very narrow, non-meritocratic circle of perhaps some 40 individuals out of a population of 140 million, and constitute now a new elite of boyars, with their children and nephews

---

[152] *BBC News* 4.11.2019; *TRT World* 10.1.2020.

[153] Note that his Rosneft shares, his yacht and his villa have an estimated value of some $100 million each. Bundeszentrale für politische Bildung: "*Der Fall Uljukajew. Dokumentation*" 5.2.2018. Even if he saved every *kopek* at his steep salary this would take him 17 years….

[154] *Die Welt* 26.11.2016. When I served at Deutsche Bank as a young professional back in 1982–1984 the iron rule in German banking and industry was that top executive salaries should only be a multiple by 100 of the lowest worker or clerk's job (after all they also had a multiple of responsibilities and stress), in order to keep corporate cohesion. So if the lowest pay was DM 1000 per month, the CEO would get 100,000 per month, i.e. DM 1.2 million per year (which would be €600.000 today). Everybody had enough and was content. This system, with investment banking and Anglo-US share incentives, has gone out of window, rather for the worse of the German economy and social cohesion. But the post-Soviet system of systemic corporate plunder is surely an upshot beyond good and evil.

already occupying top management positions in their mid-30s in SCOs and SOEs.[155] Yet even among this small circle of power, there remains a balance of competing vested interests—like most famously between Gazprom and Rosneft—with battles about power, money and privileges, but surely not about ideology. One may even assume that Putin's quasi-Czarist informal style of rule is likely to outlive his very long term in office.[156]

Even amongst the privileged new aspiring oligarchs, there are occasional victims. Thus Ziavodin Magomedov (worth one-time $1.2 billion) running the conglomerate Summa was arrested for fraud and criminal association, similar like his Dagestani compatriot Vladimir Evtukhenkov, who arrested in 2014 had to transfer his assets to Sechin's Rosneft in 2016. This time Rosneft wanted his 25% share in the oil terminal of Novorossiysk at the Black Sea at a cheaper price. Both were seen as close to Medvedev, who could not protect them any longer.[157]

From the data above it would seem prima vista that Timshenko apart, most of the new state oligarchs, would have a long way to go to catch up with the 11 surviving old oligarchs. After all the Russian economy is stagnating, the workforce shrinking by 700,000 people (−1%) each year and domestic purchasing power and GDP (currently at the size of Spain) correspondingly declining, and the number of external shocks to commodity prices accelerating: 1998, 2008, 2014, and now 2020. It is getting more difficult to make a billion. Yet the Putin system has a solution: You force the old oligarchs to make donations and you have your cronies, like Gennady Timshenko and the Rotenbergs overcharge massively at construction projects from the Sochi Olympics of 2014 to the stadiums for the soccer WM in 2018—usually by a factor of three, like with their motorway and pipeline constructions (as clearly evident from international price comparisons).[158]

Yet the appearances above are deceiving since with people trained by the KGB, nothing is probably real—maybe even for the sake of it—hidden via series of shell firms, straw men, whether it is Putin's cellist friend, his cook or his butcher, laundered through Cyprus, Panama and a multitude of Crown's

---

[155] Curiously the Putinists' offspring and Putin's distant cousins, unlike their fathers don't go for graduate degrees and, unlike the old oligarchs' children, don't bother to study abroad. With a cheap quick early degree they want to make money quickly and rise effortlessly to positions of Vice-Presidents of SOE's. This is neither an aristocratic nor a bourgeois meritocratic concept…. But they are all worth around more or less $500 million each befitting a new pseudo-aristocracy similar to the Chinese princelings Aslund. Op.cit., p. 148.
[156] Andrew S. Weiss "Russia's oligarchy, alive and well" *New York Times* 1.1.2014.
[157] Pierre Avril "Russie: l'arrestation de l'oligarche Magomedov fragilise Dmitri Medvedev" *Le Figaro* 4.4.2018.
[158] Aslund. Op. cit., p. 113.

territories in the Caribbean, but for what purpose? Perhaps the search for economic rationality is not the right approach.

Gazprom and Rosneft apart, there are two major cash dispensers one for the Kremlin:

One is Vnesheconombank (VEB), the former USSR Foreign Trade Bank and foreign debt agency, which fully covered by state guarantees and with $60 billion in assets, was linked to the SVR, the foreign intelligence service, and has been turned by Putin into a National Development Bank, but de facto works as a slush fund for his pet projects and distributor for state aid. In 2014, it had to be bailed out after billions of losses, though it had always received plenty of funds from the National Welfare Fund (fed by oil export revenue) for its re-capitalization.[159]

The second is Bank Rossiya, Putin's crony bank, led since 1991 by Yuri Kovalchuk, as the spider in the net of Putin's financial and media empire, controlling large financial and media assets of Gazprom, the Gazprombank, its Sogaz insurance, the pension fund Gazfond, and Sibor, a big chemical group, plus 20 TV channels. There is a puzzle: Until 2007 Bank Rossiya had $60 billion in assets, but in 2014 there were only $10 billion left.[160] So there were transfers to some 30 offshore havens through shell companies from the Virgin Islands to Panama.

2.12 Conclusion II: Whither the Russian Economy?

Although the capital destruction undertaken by the red directors, the abuses by the oligarchs and the bloody warfare of the mafiotic distribution struggles of the late 1980s and 90s have largely been contained under Putin, the political economy of Russia, with its state-capitalist monopolizations, remains a far cry from comprehensive market economy structures, the rule of law with effective property rights, and a sustainable transformation. With every year of Putin's rule, Russia moved further away from this ideal to which Russia at least in theory and in public declarations—in the WTO, for instance, where she is a member—subscribes. The usually high liquidity of the Russian state, of most of the oligarchs and of the exporting primary industries must not obscure the fact that this bogus bloom was solely due to the booming demand for energy and raw materials from China, India, Europe and Southeast Asia

---

[159]Ibid., pp. 125.
[160]Ibid., p. 145.

during the exceptionally long growth period of 2000–2008. Demand for Russian raw materials regularly contracted in any international crisis, like during 1998, 2008, 2014 and 2020. Russian "growth" patterns, hovering at around 1.5% per year during the 2010s, have nothing to do with a sustainable recovery, the purchasing power of its people, business rehabilitation and competitiveness. On the contrary, the near-effortless inflow of foreign exchange, the low employment-intensive nature of resource extraction, and the highly unequal distribution of petrodollars and natural gas euros distort economic structures as a very serious case of "Dutch disease". They increase the ruble rate, favour luxury and other imports, harm productive industries, services and agriculture, which led to speculation through frivolous lending by highly liquid state banks and continue to finance uncompetitive loss-makers, and favour an inflated unproductive service sector consisting of security services, luxury restaurants and night-club landscapes in the glittering centres of Moscow, St. Petersburg and Sochi.

Martin Wolf called Putin's Russia a "centralized and corrupt petro state".[161] The permanent controls and economic interventions of the Putin network in the Kremlin and its dependent followers in the seats of state and corporate power have in effect abolished the separation of powers, made political and personal arbitrariness and the pursuit of personal political rents a national business model for a very small, privileged elite. Without legal certainty for ownership titles, business licenses and legitimate profits, both legal and illegal capital flight abroad takes place on a scale between $16 billion and $50 billion per year. By favouring a comprador capitalism, which operates on the basis of maximizing short-term exploitative profits at the expense of long-term business development, corporate restructuring, innovation, transparency and modernization and the search for business and market transparency, which had started timidly prior to the 1998 crisis, all these private sector efforts were brought to a halt or rather reversed.

For Russia's economic partners, therefore, both the productive engagement in Russia itself as FDI and portfolio investments and the targeted foreign investments by Russia should be accompanied by sound reservations. The complaints are varied[162]: Large companies are instrumentalized for policy objectives. State institutions and courts are devalued by corruption and political arbitrariness. There is a low level of protection towards intellectual or economic property held by others. Foreign partners are seen more as useful idiots to supply missing technology and capital. If they start earning serious money in Russia, they are robbed, extorted or expropriated by the state. The

---

[161] Martin Wolf "How Russia slipped on the road to Yeltsin's new era" *Financial Times* 25.4.2007.
[162] Michael Ludwig "Die Russen kommen" *Frankfurter Allgemeine* 22.11.2006.

close interdependence between the state and the economy also leads to the discouragement of the most interesting innovative sectors and developments outside the state's control. Corporate governance remains opaque. The quality of management is often poor. Last but not the least, the most unscrupulous of the old oligarchs have prevailed. The reformed Khodorkovsky was sacrificed. The Deripaskas and Potanins won.

After his inauguration as President "under Putin" in 2008, Medvedev spoke of guaranteed property rights and that the state's share of the economy should not be further increased. However, Putin, as prime minister (2008–2012), remained responsible for economic agendas. His siloviki friends continued to be strategically commanding on all boards of directors of the state-controlled groups of companies. With Putin back in formal command, there no such talk any further.

It is justified, as Putin on occasion does, to compare his state capitalist development model with the successful post-war development of Japan and Singapore and the oligarch system with the Korean Chaebol groups?[163] Yet in spite of superficial similarities, the differences are huge. The Chaebol (as well as Japan's pre-war Zaibatsu[164]) are family-owned holding companies which had been founded by their frugal owners in decade-long efforts, developed and survived through murderous competition against similar groups in most sectors of heavy industry, consumer goods and industrial services on domestic and export markets. They are not, as in Russia, the randomly purchased conglomerates of politically privileged knights of fortune. In addition, the export success of Japanese and Korean quality producers is mainly based on the existence of free competition in the internal market, the professional meritocracy of business cultures and the Confucian work ethic, a dedication to detail, quality, knowledge and innovation by the workforce and its management. An initial mercantilist foreign trade policy was certainly helpful as long as their industries as latecomers in development were not yet fully internationally competitive, but this protectionism was not decisive and was eliminated after tough negotiations with the US and the EU, once it no longer served its purpose. In Singapore, which as a-city state is much more dependent on the international environment, with a more statist economic structure, the government and the publicly managed companies are even more exemplary in terms of strict professionalism, adherence to the law, non-corruptibility and enthusiasm for innovation. Its attractiveness for

---

[163]Robert Cortrell "Russia's rising Tycoons" *Financial Times* 6.8.2002.

[164]The Japanese post-war successor keiretsu conglomerates followed a similar pattern, only that they were management controlled and no longer family owned, after the US occupant had expropriated them in 1945.

high-quality foreign investment, from petrochemicals to the financial sector and biotechnology, is undeniable and evident in its results for an affluent sustainable economy in what only 60 years ago seemed like an impoverished harbour town in the third world—and like Japan and South Korea developed without any significant domestic raw materials.

There is no question that Putin and his narrow circle of friends still have not understood these miracles of development, or simply they don't want to. Neither the red directors from the Gorbachev era, the oligarchs of Yeltsin, nor Putin's state oligarchs are guided by ideas of functioning market economy, innovative competition, productive investments and mass welfare. Most of them favour politically protected capital outflows and the construction of passing new corporate empires with the associated status symbols, and at the same time disregard professional management, for which most of them as former traders (in case of oligarchs) or former secret service officers (in case of Putinocrats) are utterly unqualified. Putin more than once stated doctrinally that conglomerates are needed for the transition to a high growth economy like Korea and China with a lot of state financing since private companies were unwilling to take the risk.[165] If you deny property protection to private companies, the owner-founders will no longer look for their children as future successors and think in generations (as they tend both in the West and in Asia), but grab short-term profits, get out in time and enjoy. There is no point for a gifted young Russian entrepreneurial inventor to develop something in Moscow when he is sure that once successful, he will be locked up, shaken out and the fruits of his labour would be stolen by some FSB thugs. So he leaves for Berlin, Vienna, London or New York in time with his gifted friends.

It is as simple as that.

In spite of all the glitter of Moscow and St. Petersburg, Putin's state monopoly capitalism has led Russia into a lasting lower-middle-income trap, stagnating at best since 2008. Once this business model solely based on oil, gas and commodity exports runs out, it is the road to the Third World similar to where his failed predecessors from Brezhnev to Yeltsin almost ended. The country continues to pay a very high price for direct unhindered access by the ruling elite to the profits and resources of the most profitable basic industries in the name of a supposed national interest. As these are the fruits of the hard (often slave) labour of the Russian people over the past 100 years, they certainly have deserved a better future.

---

[165] Catherine Belton "Putin stands by state capitalism" *Financial Times* 31.1.2012.

References

1. Applebaum A (2003) Gulag. A history of the Soviet camps. Random House, New York
2. Aslund A (2019) Russia's crony capitalism. Yale University Press, New Haven
3. Browder B (2017) Red notice. Hanser, Munich
4. Freeland C (2005) Sale of the century. The inside story of the second Russian revolution. Abacus, London
5. Jungblut R (2006) Die 11 Geschäftsgeheimnisse von IKEA. Campus, Frankfurt/Main
6. Panjuschin V (2006) Mikhail Khodorkovsky. Vom Yukos Chefsessel ins sibirische Arbeitslager. Heyne, Munich
7. Popov D, Milstein I (2006) Julia Timoschenko. Die Zukunft der Ukraine nach der orangenen Revolution. Dumont, Cologne
8. Midgley D, Hutchins C (2005) Der Milliardär aus dem Nichts. Roman Abramowitsch. Murmann, Hamburg
9. Rothacher A (2002) Im wilden Osten. Hinter den Kulissen des Umbruchs in Osteuropa. Krämer, Hamburg

3

Putin's Autocracy: Siloviki Rule and Their Kleptocracy

After the erratic shifts of his predecessor Yeltsin in the crisis-ridden 1990s since the advent of Putin in 1999–2000 for better or rather for worse, Russian domestic and foreign policies have become more predictable. His domestic policies quickly reasserted centralized Kremlin rule, put a clique of security service (*siloviki*) acquaintances from St. Petersburg into power, suppressed the opposition, press freedom, regional self-government, the embryonic civic society and an independent judiciary, and moved the economic system from oligarchical capitalism back to state monopoly capitalism.

In foreign policies, Putin's Russia pursued the collection of ex-Soviet soil in her near abroad by reasserting her zones of influence in Central Asia, Iran, the South Caucasus, in East Europe, on the Balkans, in Syria and in Libya. Wherever the US, already under Obama, withdrew, Putin advanced to fill the vacuum. In global politics in a quasi-alliance with China he followed strategic objectives of multipolarity, based on the modernization of its nuclear forces and its still sizable conventional army for limited territorial wars (like in the Second Chechen War of 1999–2000, the war against Georgia 2008, the military aggression against Ukraine since 2014 and the armed intervention in Syria since 2015), but to a lesser extent of its navy. This policy was foremost directed against the perceived growth of Western influence by trying to destabilize potential US allies (Georgia, Ukraine, Moldova and Azerbaijan) in its backyard, by pushing arms exports to China, India, Vietnam, Iran, Turkey, the Mid East and Africa, and by so far unsuccessfully trying to neutralize Europe in exploiting the EU's foreign policy divisions.

3.1 Putin's Political Biography: From Leningrad to Dresden

Though his grandfather served (and survived) as Lenin's and Stalin's cook, Putin's background is clearly working class. His father during the war first served in the Baltic submarine fleet and then in a partisan group of the MKWD behind the German lines near Leningrad, where he was seriously wounded. After the war as a disabled war veteran and party activist, he worked in a railway carriage factory, and Putin's mother as a cleaning lady and shop attendant. Because of the universal housing shortage in Soviet towns, he grew up in a communal flat with a shared kitchen and toilet, and one room for his family only. Born in 1952 in Leningrad, memories and vestiges of the war and the blockade of 1941–1944 were still fresh.

Growing up in a grimy industrial suburb young Putin started out as a juvenile delinquent and after a first clash with the law and his father he disciplined himself as a pupil and as a relatively successful judoka.[1] Early on he read spy novels and studied German to prepare himself for a KGB career. Trying to volunteer at age 16 at the Leningrad directorate, he was told that the institution recruited only university graduates who had studied law and foreign languages as career officers. He duly enrolled in the law department of Leningrad State University. Living with his parents he is believed to have had only sports as a pastime and did physical work in logging and construction as vacation jobs. After graduation in 1975, he joined the Leningrad KGB where he was assigned to do counterintelligence work and to monitor dissidents. After some foreign intelligence training in Moscow, he returned to Leningrad again, this time to monitor foreigners and trying to recruit them. Personal assessments report him as good at observation and analysis, but as poor in communication and interpersonal skills.

After ten years with the KGB ranked as a major he was finally sent abroad to Dresden, a second-rate appointment in the East German province compared to more glamorous Western capitals, especially as his reporting to Moscow was still subject to approval and scrutiny by his line managers in Karlshorst (Berlin). His cover was the position of a director of the German-Soviet friendship society. As a deputy chief of the local *residentura,* he had a mixed portfolio of tasks like counterintelligence, industrial espionage in Saxony's industry, especially in the electronics sector ("Robotron", the leading GDR maker), and the recruitment of foreign visitors (preferably from Siemens) and of Stasi officers, one of which was a certain Matthias Warnig

---

[1] Peter Truscott. *Putin's Progress*. London: Pocket Books 2005, p. 30.

(now head of the Nord Stream 2 consortium). Life in the small Soviet colony of Dresden went calmly. Putin was able to devote himself to family life with two young daughters, developed a propensity for the good Radeberger Pils and was routinely promoted to Lieutenant Colonel in 1987. Putin is reported to have developed a certain respect for German culture and discipline.[2] He saw that the East German system was rotten, yet was shocked how quickly it collapsed. During the democratic revolution of 1989, his office had to destroy its confidential files. To his dismay there was no support from the local Soviet garrison when they were besieged by a crowd, which he successfully distracted. He was not converted to become a democrat, neither then nor later.

Catherine Belton alleges that Putin's professional life in Dresden was not only about drinking beer and recruiting a few engineers, but that he in fact also directed the terrorist left-wing "Red Army faction" (RAF) gang operating murderously in West Germany from the 1970s to the early 1990s from there.[3] The alleged intention was to destabilize the West. It is a fact that the Stasi of General Mielke helped to fly its members out from East Berlin's airport Schönefeld to Palestinian training camps and infiltrated them back into West Germany. It also provided those terrorists, who wanted to get out, with a new identity and let them live and work undisturbed in the GDR. The KGB must have known about this. Yet it is very unlikely that as disciplined professionals they trusted these fanatical sectarian freelancers. Their most prominent murder during his term of office was the one of Alfred Herrhausen, head of Deutsche Bank in 1989. But it was precisely Herrhausen, who had organized a banking consortium to finance the huge West German pipeline deals with the Soviet Union and had met Gorbatchev in person in Moscow. It is simply absurd to believe that a little KGB lieutenant colonel for no rhyme and reason would plot his assassination. Besides, there were 13 more district KGB *residentura* in East Germany, and headquarters were in Karlshorst in East Berlin. Why should it be Dresden? Not all unproven stories about Putin make sense.

---

[2] Ibid., p. 56.
[3] Catherine Belton. *Putin's People: How the KGB took back Russia and then took on the West*. London: William Collins. 2020.

3.2 In St. Petersburg

After German reunification, he returned to Russia in January 1990. In Leningrad, he obtained the post of Vice-rector in charge of foreign relations and foreign students at his alma mater, the Leningrad State University, a post which was traditionally reserved for the KGB. Although Putin made no secret of his sympathies for the coup plotters of 1991 and of his good relations with KGB general Krychkov, one of the failed plotters,[4] St. Petersburg's reformist mayor Sobchak then appointed him as one of his deputies in charge of foreign relations, including of attracting foreign investment.[5] Like many politicians during these turbulent times, he obviously found it useful to have good KGB contacts with its still intact structures close at hand. While Sobchak enjoyed the limelight raising democratic toasts at receptions, Putin performed as an effective backstage manager in city hall. In this function, he obviously could not overlook rampant corruption nor avoid dealings with the powerful local mafia. Promoted first deputy mayor in 1994 Putin was made in charge of Sobchak's re-election campaign against his challenger Yakovlev, himself a deputy mayor as well. With a poor track record of his corrupt administration, the deteriorating public infrastructure and a too laid-back campaign organized by Putin (who at the time preferred to finish his doctorate on resource politics), Sobchak lost to Yakovlev, whom Putin considered a traitor, and with Putin's helping hand had to flee to Paris to avoid corruption charges.[6]

3.3 In Moscow

After a brief hiatus, his St. Petersburg connections ("*blat*") helped Putin to secure a job as deputy head of the Kremlin's mega-rich Property Administration, run by the notoriously corrupt Pavel Borodin who controlled the vehicle fleet and the property of the central administration, including the rich possessions expropriated from the outlawed CPSU. Again like in St. Petersburg before, the corruption and bribery around him did not disturb him in the least.

In 1998, Putin moved on to become deputy head of management in the presidential administration, where he was in charge of dealing with Russia's 89 governors. He must have disliked what he saw so intensely that as a

---

[4]Truscott. Op. cit., p. 66.
[5]Ibid., p. 68.
[6]Ibid., p. 77.

President three years later as one of the first measures he dismissed most of them, appointed seven regional general governors, abolished direct elections and replaced the local chiefs by Kremlin-controlled appointees. In his new function, most importantly Putin got access to Yeltsin's "family" then dominated by Yeltsin's daughter Tatiana Dyashenko and the oligarch Berezovsky. As a courtier Putin's work style was one of understated loyal competence and discretion. Yet he ensured that his role did not go unnoticed.[7]

As a reward in July 1998, he was appointed head of the FSB. In this function Putin again faithfully executed orders. He was not interested to investigate corruption in high places and made sure that cases close to the Kremlin and the Central Bank, where billions of dollars of international monetary support had been pilfered during the 1998 crisis, were stopped.[8] He dissolved the two FSB units dealing with top-level corruption. He also used his time to dismiss or retire some old and tired generals as well as personal enemies and to place trusted friends among his former colleagues into strategic positions, including his friend Dmitri Patrushev at the head of the FSB who was to become his chosen successor.

In gratitude, he was soon appointed by Yeltsin head of the Security Council, and after a few months in the job in August 1999 already was promoted Prime Minister and anointed as Yeltsin's future successor, after Yeltsin had fired Sergei Stepanshin, equally a former FSB head, after only three months in office. The deal over Yeltsin's succession was clear: Putin would protect the "family's interests" with the help of his FSB colleagues, including a pledge for immunity, watertight amnesties and generous state pensions, and be appointed.

One major problem was Putin's low name recognition, as he had never played a public role and his low popularity compared to rivals like Moscow's mayor Yuri Luzhkov and ex-PM Primakov. Hence the "invasion" of a few villages in Dagestan by Shamil Basaev (a Chechen former KGB informer) and a vicious bomb series in Russian cities, which were blamed without evidence on the universally disliked Chechens, came just about at the right moment to trigger a well-prepared, this time victorious second Chechen war and to present Putin as a hard man for law and order.[9]

Prior to the December 1999 parliamentary elections, Berezovsky's media did a hatchet job on Putin's major competitors Primakov, Luzhkov and Yakovlev and their "Fatherland–All Russia" party, flooding them with real or fabricated claims of corruption and debauchery. As a result, Putin's synthetic

---

[7] Ibid., p. 88.
[8] Ibid., p. 92.
[9] Ibid., p. 101.

"Unity" party grew from 4% in the early polls to a score of 24% on election day, while "All Russia" got only 13%. Like during Yeltsin's 1996 election, the usual fraud helped to produce the desired result.

Gusinsky, the media oligarch allied with Luzhkov and Primakov, was the first to incur Putin's wrath. As described before, he was soon dispossessed and forced into exile. Dyachenko and Borodin were equally quickly cleared out of the Kremlin. After facing a hostile press during the sinking of the Kursk Putin also took on his erstwhile promoter Berezovsky with fraud charges over Aeroflot, documenting the theft of foreign ticket sales of his airline. In good old KGB tradition, *kompromat* material collected on everyone in time came handy.

In May 2000, Putin, reviving a Czarist tradition, appointed plenipotentiaries in seven federal districts to supervise the 89 governors and to force regional legislation into compliance with federal law. Putin also began removing corrupt or disobedient governors by decree or forced them into resignation by unending allegations of corruption, thus ending for instance the tenure of his enemy Yakovlev in St. Petersburg in 2003. By appointing Miller and Medvedev in control of Gasprom and dismissing the corrupt pair Vyakhirev and Chernomyrdim from its helm, the Kremlin opened direct access to this major cash cow and instrument for its foreign energy policies. By March 2001, Putin had placed his *siloviki* followers in charge of all power ministries: Defense, Interior and the Security Council, and in March 2003 regrouped most of the former KGB functions, including border guards and communication services back under FSB auspices. The FSB also temporarily acquired control of all military operations in Chechnya. The period of the Yeltsin era was definitely over when the former KGB had been demoralized, underpaid, lacking purpose and officers left in droves to join private security firms, the mafia or the services of the oligarchs.[10]

In the Duma "Unity" and "All Fatherland" merged after Luzhkov and Primakov had found it advisable to reconcile with Putin. A socialist party was split off from the Communists. Also, a new green party ("Life") was created by the Kremlin, and individual deputies were encouraged by not too subtle means to defect to "Unity". This was hardly necessary as Zhirinovsky with his ultra-right-wing "Liberal Democrats" could always be relied upon to vote with the Kremlin given the right incentives, monetary or otherwise.[11] The Duma elections of December 2003 brought "Unity" with some 37% of the popular vote two-thirds of the seats. As a result of these majorities, parliamentary debates soon became rather perfunctory, with the Kremlin's drafts

---

[10] Ibid., p. 220.
[11] Ibid., p. 225.

for the budget and bills usually passing unchallenged. A tax reform, based on Estonia' successful model, produced a flat 13% income tax. Corporate taxation was cut from 35 to 24%, and urban and agricultural land became tradable again for the first time since the October Revolution.[12] During Yeltsin's era Communist resistance had prevented these much-needed reforms, which are essential for a functioning market economy and rural development. With the low rates tax compliance improved perceptively: Promptly the tax revenue doubled.

Meanwhile, by 2000 the Russian economy was fueled by a global energy and raw materials boom. Average incomes in Moscow increased to $630 per month and nationwide to $385. In 1992, the figure had been $70. With unpaid pensions old ladies then had to sell pickled cucumbers, mushrooms and their knitwear by the roadside to survive. Out of 145 million Russians, 25 million by 2006 had an average EU middle-class income. But 30 million continued to live below the poverty line.[13]

At the time, given Russia's shortage of capital Putin still claimed to favour foreign direct investments. During a foreign visit, for instance, he declared himself disappointed by the relatively low level of German investment in Russia.[14] This may have been due to the fact that Germany does not have international energy companies of the size of Shell or BP (whose investments have since been expropriated by the Kremlin via Gazprom). Interested companies, like Siemens in the case of Siloviye Machinery, like many other foreign investors had been frustrated with the Kremlin's definition of a large number of strategic industries in which foreign investment was undesirable.

In the Kremlin Inc., excessive bureaucracy and low labour efficiency than as now discouraged productive foreign investments, as does endemic corruption, which according to Roland Haug had increased tenfold from already high levels since Putin took over.[15] In addition, physical safety had not been fully restored with at least 80 contract killings per year during his first decade in power. The main thrust of the oil and gas boom was to boost the state-bureaucratic power cartel.[16] Since Putin's second term of office (2012–), there has been a notable absence of any significant reforms, and the only certainty for planning for large companies is to maintain close relationships with the circles of power close to current top of the Kremlin and to invite them to sit numerously and well remunerated on the boards of directors,

---

[12] Ibid., p. 210.
[13] Roland Haug. *Kreml AG*. Stuttgart/Leipzig : .Hohenheim Verlag 2007, p. 165.
[14] Ibid., p. 162.
[15] Ibid., p. 173.
[16] Ibid., p. 178.

even though they are already well served by the rich assets of the Kremlin's property administration.

3.4 The Putin System and Its Ideology

In Putin's state-centred development philosophy, the consolidation of state power has always been more important than democracy. He has also been strongly reluctant to make campaign promises since his St. Petersburg's failed campaign for governor Sobchak. During his own presidential election campaign of 2000, he consistently rejected to participate in any substantive debate, as well as to make programmatic statements.[17] For Putin, personal freedom is only possible in a strong state that is able to defend the individual effectively.[18]

Similarly, for him, foreign policy should be guided by national interests, including economic interests. In this realist worldview, Russia has zones of vital interests and should remain a respected "great power".[19] His first encounters with Bill Clinton and Tony Blair were positive. After the chaos of the Yeltsin years, the West saw him as an earnest reformer and modernizer.[20] Yet his brutal conduct of the second war in Chechnya with the total destruction of Grozny and his continued exports of arms and nuclear technology to Iran alienated much of this initial goodwill. In addition, the incoming Bush administration perceived Russia as a spent force and felt no need to invest in good relations.[21] Yet following the Ljubljana summit of June 2001 and the US war against the Taliban, a temporary rapprochement ensued which was ended however with NATO's Eastern enlargement of May 2004 and the unprovoked US invasion of Iraq.[22] Russia had a big economic stake in Saddam's regime and was furious to be sidelined and to have its oil concessions and commercial debts negated. Putin felt that his support for the US over Afghanistan had been unrewarded. Subsequently, the Shanghai Cooperation Organization (SCO) was revived. Yet neither Russia nor China had an interest in a full anti-US alliance.[23] They were united in more limited

---

[17] Truscott. Op. cit., p. 344. In this he was similar to Charles de Gaulle, who equally refused to campaign and declared, he himself was to programme.
[18] Ibid., p. 126.
[19] Ibid., p. 127.
[20] Ibid., p. 251.
[21] Ibid., p. 271.
[22] Ibid., p. 295.
[23] Ibid., p. 274.

common objectives, like to keep the US out of Central Asia and to oppose the US missile defence.[24]

As an underpinning for this foreign ambitions and to preserve his personal rule, Putin has recentralized power and put civil society back under state control. Informal elite networks have come to supersede formal institutions. Public criticism is unwanted. In Russia's authoritarian tradition "legal nihilism" is reasserted: Law is used as an instrument of rule. Laws are drafted so vaguely and all-encompassing that they render any conduct liable to punishment almost at any time: As a result, citizens usually ignore laws as long as they believe they remain undetected and unpunished.[25]

This may be interpreted as a legacy of Byzantine traditions when power was sacral and its criticism unthinkable. Until 1905, Czars were almighty and responsible for their actions only to God. Although the democratic constitution of 1993 was modelled along with French centralized patterns of presidential powers while sticking to a formal division of powers and guaranteed fundamental freedoms, under Putin actual constitutional and administrative practice further eroded the division of powers. In line with the ideology of Russia's "special way" (*Sonderweg*) Putin favours a strong state, based on centralism and strong security services including the military.[26] Political competition and free media are seen as incompatible with economic and societal consolidation. His democratic declarations rather appear as half-hearted and contradictory. Chaos and the dissolution of the state are feared.[27] State power and great power aspirations for him clearly take precedence over the development of democracy. Hence any criticism of Russian policies and the spectre of colour revolutions in Russia and its vicinity are forcefully opposed.

Boris Yeltsin in contrast had been a skilled architect of compromises and had allowed the creation of regional power centres and of the oligarchs controlling large parts of the economy. Still during 1998–1999 when Sergei Primakov (with a Communist heritage) was a strong Prime Minister, with a parliamentary majority he could match the president, similarly to French Prime Ministers during the rare periods of "cohabitation", when the opposition had a parliamentary majority.

Putin would have none of this parliamentarization. He reasserted the "verticality of power" (*Machtvertikale*), i.e. the strict chain of command from the Kremlin to all state organs already in 2000, first by striking a lightning attack

---

[24] Ibid., p. 274.
[25] Margareta Mommsen and Angelika Nussberger. *Das System Putin*. Munich: C.H. Beck 2007, p. 15.
[26] Ibid., p. 20.
[27] Ibid., p. 26.

against the governors. Similar to the military districts, as mentioned before, he set up seven general governorships, whose incumbents (former generals mostly) were to supervise them. The federal council, Russia's second chamber, was stripped of its vetoing power. Later in 2004 the governors also lost their seats there.

They were compensated with seats in the new merely ceremonial state chamber instead.[28] Later their direct election was abolished and replaced by appointments by the Kremlin. Typically, the new governors had no local roots and were unable to develop a regional power base. For the loss of regional democracy and power, governors were granted the possibility of four terms of office (up from a maximum of two terms previously), hence enough time to become prosperous in office.

Russia's first chamber, the Duma, since 1999 was increasingly controlled by the presidential administration, which could manipulate factions and deputies almost at will.[29] Synthetic pro-Kremlin parties, first "Unity. Bear", then "United Russia", were set up. "Independent" deputies elected mostly from single-seat constituencies were recruited. During the 2003 election "United Russia" gained 37% of the vote, but soon due to recruitment drives among deputies with 310 (out of 450) seats, it enjoyed a majority of two-thirds. This helped to pass, as mentioned, necessary laws on the private ownership of land and modern tax laws which due to Communist resistance had been blocked in the past. If needed, also the left-wing "Rodina" (founded to capture Communist votes) and Zhirinovsky's right-wing populist "Liberal Democrats" could be bought in for support. Only the Communists remained a serious opposition. The Kremlin's disregard for the Duma was evidenced during ministerial appointments: No parliamentarians were ever considered.[30] As an innovation yet another consultative body, a "Societal Chamber" was set up with 126 appointees, prominent faces from the worlds of sports, religion, the economy, science and culture, again as a purely consultative organ without germane political or controlling functions.[31] Resembling a Soviet popular front, it was soon used by the people to address petitions, reviving this tradition of authoritarian Czarist and Communist times.

Free mass media were quickly identified by Putin as enemies of the state.[32] He used the unpopularity of the oligarchs to expropriate the media empires

---

[28] If there is any similarity with the EU's Committee of Regions (ECR) it is purely accidental.

[29] Ibid., p. 39.

[30] Ibid., p. 41.

[31] Again there is no intended similarity to the EU's Social and Economic Committee (ECSC). It is equally only consultative like the ECR, but it does not contain any sportsmen, clergy, scientists or artists!.

[32] Ibid., p. 47.

3 Putin's Autocracy: Siloviki Rule and Their Kleptocracy

of Gusinsky and Berezovsky first. By 2003, state control over all TV stations was re-established.[33] Only the internet and print media with small print runs limited to the big cities or some remote regions without national distribution still offer some freedom of opinion (which is significantly more than China!). Still also for them there are taboo subjects, like government corruption, social mass protests, past military violence in Chechnya, and failures in combating terrorism. In 2006, the definition of banned "extremism" was widened to include any criticism of officials.

In order to prevent any colour revolution in Russia, state youth organizations, called "*Nashi*" ("Ours") and "Young Guard", the party youth of "United Russia", were set up. "United Russia" during 2006 also began to conclude formal alliances with all sorts of societal organizations: women, sports and youth clubs, welfare and professional associations, trade unions etc. The party remained an electoral machine void of any programme except for unconditional Kremlin support. Again the similarities with Communist popular front strategies were striking.[34] The re-introduction of the Soviet hymn and compulsory patriotic and military education in schools moved in the same direction.

Yet Putin's inner power circle of around 12/15 men was and remains not monolithic and is far from friction-free. Competing informal networks of power holders already existed in Soviet times. During Yeltsin's second term some of the oligarchs joined his "family" as the second group of influence. After all, regular business lobbies did not exist. Once Putin was appointed and elected as President, he was first fenced in by two Yeltsin "family" members with strong links to the oligarchs: Mikhail Kasyanov as Prime Minster and Alexander Voloshin as head of the presidential administration. He freed himself gradually by systematically appointing his own people from St. Petersburg into key positions. Among them was a minority faction of "systemic liberal" lawyers and economists, like Dimitri Medvedev, Dimitri Kozak (in charge of the Caucasus), Alexei Kudmin (MoF) and German Gref (MoE), and the majority of "*siloviki*" appointments of former senior KGB officers, like Igor Sechin, Victor and Sergei Ivanov and Nikolai Patrushev. Up to 2003, the co-habitation of Yeltsin's "family" and the St. Petersburgers continued. They fell out over the Yukos affair, whereupon both Voloshin and Kasyanov lost power and their positions. Russia subsequently transited from oligarchical capitalism to state capitalism in consequence.[35] Since then there is a continuous struggle for power and the spoils of their control over

---

[33] Ibid., p. 48.
[34] Ibid., p. 57.
[35] Ibid., p. 68.

a growing chunk of Russia's industry (Rosneft, Gazprom, Rosoboroexport, Almas Antey, Aeroflot, Russian railways etc.) between the two factions and within several *siloviki* strands, with Putin purposefully acting as an aloof ultimate and unpredictable arbiter.[36]

3.5 The Legal System According to Putin

Law in Russia has always been an instrument of power, with a correspondingly low public standing of judges. Salaries are low and corruption high. There are few acquittals.[37] In political trials, the sentences are dictated by phone ("telephone justice") by the Kremlin, much like by party secretaries before and not dissimilar to the way in which the Central Committee had scripted the show trials during the Stalin days when legal forms were mere rituals to execute mass terror.

Today judges are constantly threatened by disciplinary procedures should they display too much independence. In any event, the procurator, a unique Russian institution created originally as the "eyes of the Czar" to watch over prosecutors and judges, can revoke any judgement anytime and ask for a retrial. He can also declare his competence to investigate exclusively certain highly political cases. This was done by Prosecutor-General Ustinov for the Kursk, Yukos and Beslan cases, and by his successor Tshaika for the murders of Politkovskaya and Litvinenko and for Yukos II. Clearly, his findings and decisions are political in nature.[38] All famous trials of the first Putin term, like the ones against Gusinsky and Khodorkovsky, and the lenient sentence for the rapist-murderer Colonel Budanov, etc. confirm a picture of top-level political interventions to secure a wanted outcome of the trials.[39]

3.6 The KGB in Power

Did the assumption of power by Putin and his St. Petersburg KGB colleagues imply a takeover of the country by former secret service officers? In the often violent chaos of the 1990s, KGB men had made themselves indispensable in the anarchy of democratic change as rival oligarchs and Mafiosi fought over economic power and privileges.

---

[36] Ibid., p. 78.
[37] Ibid., p. 94.
[38] Ibid., p. 117.
[39] Ibid., p. 125.

The qualification of KGB agents, originally semi-literate butchers in the service of the Revolution and of Stalin's terror, did not come by accident. It was during Chelepin's tenure as KGB chief (1958–1961) that the organization gradually changed from a brutal instrument of torture and executions towards elite political police.[40] The transformation of the chekist from mass murderer into a more or less respectable civil servant took some effort. By 1987, for instance, 88% of KGB officers, like Putin, were university graduates already. At the same time, the memory of Stalin's terror was repressed. Originally, the subsidiary-armed arm of the party, since the 1960s CPSU and KGB functions became intertwined with a mixed "party-chekist oligarchy" emerging at the top,[41] notably so since Yuri Andropov's arrival at the helm of the KGB in 1967 and of him joining the politburo in 1973. Since 1978, the KGB formally received equal status to the party. Both were declared as subordinate only to the politburo. As the economic crisis, the demoralization of the population and the corruption of the party apparatus spread, it was only the KGB that could bypass the disinformation monopoly of the regime and produce realist internal assessments of the Soviet Union's economic and social crisis. At the time through its control of foreign trade institutions, it could place sufficient capital abroad. Under Yuri Andropov as Secretary-General (1982–1983) selected intellectuals were allowed to reflect on reforms and *perestroika* to overcome the stagnation, corruption and technological backwardness of the Brezhnev era.[42] Andropov's anti-corruption drive ended the great Uzbek cotton swindle. He also began a campaign against alcoholism. Yet his term, due to sickness, was too short-lived to start structural reforms. However, he promoted future *glasnost* and *perestroika* reformers like Gorbachev (who like himself also came from Stavropol), Ligatchev and Yakovlev, only to be succeeded by another conservative apparatchik, Konstantin Chernenko, who died in March 1985 already.

Gorbachev's subsequent *glasnost*, was essentially an attempt to preserve the CPSU's hold to power by regaining legitimacy and opinion leadership, to sell Communist reforms as freedom, to get Western financial and technological support—and to purge Brezhnev's corrupt supporters from the party apparatus.[43] As the Soviet Union's crisis deepened, Gorbachev had to rely more and more on the KGB, giving it a large measure of discretion to fight against sabotage and economic crimes and granting it extensive privileges in foreign

---

[40] Thierry Wolton. *Le KGB au pouvoir. Le système Poutine*. Paris: Buchet Chastel. 2008, p. 19.
[41] Ibid., p. 21.
[42] Ibid., p. 25.
[43] Ibid., p. 31.

trade and technology acquisition.[44] During 1986–1988 private artisans and service providers were allowed, followed by the liberation of all state companies from the diktat of the plans, and the authorization of "cooperatives" in the fields of banking, foreign trade and joint ventures with foreign capital. These opportunities were mainly used by Komsomol officials and KGB officers, notably those of its sixth department, having contacts with capitalist companies. This came handy in terms of knowledge of business practices, foreign trade opportunities and access to capital, as they already maintained a large number of more or less phoney corporations abroad for purposes of economic espionage and technology acquisition.[45] As a result, early in the 1990s in Russia, a sort of "komsomol-chekist capitalism" emerged, based on the limited pool of early beneficiaries of systemic change. The most prominent of the first type was Mikhail Khodorkovsky of Yukos, and of the second Vladimir Potanin, owner of Norilsk Nickel, whose father had been a senior official in the Foreign Trade Ministry. One could add here a third category, the class of "red directors", which equally benefited in the first stage of transition.

The KGB also attempted to organize *perestroika* type reforms and the removal of ossified party cliques by infiltrating dissident groups and setting up popular fronts, both in Eastern Europe and in the Soviet republics.[46] Yet except for Romania, where the KGB agent Iliescu had *conducator* Ceausescu and his wife shot after a palace coup and engineered riots, elsewhere revolutionary events overtook prescribed plans as movements radicalized beyond the KGB's manipulative control. Embattled within the Soviet Union, with ethnic riots in the Caucasus and in Moldova, and with movements for re-establishing independence gathering irresistible strength in the Baltics, Gorbachev leant more and more on the KGB and representatives from the military-industrial complex for support. He appointed hard-line men, like Vice President Yanayev, PM Pavlov, Interior Minister Pugo, KGB chief Krytshov and Defense Minister Yasov, all of which became later coup leaders against him, and ordered *speznaz* crackdowns in the Baltics with heavy bloodshed in Lithuania.

Gorbachev waited out the August 1991 coup in his Crimean vacation home, knowing about it well in advance and waiting how things would turn out. Once it failed, he took his distance—like from the military crackdowns he had ordered in the dissident republics.[47] The coup had been badly

---

[44] Ibid., p. 34.
[45] Ibid., p. 40.
[46] Ibid., p. 46.
[47] Ibid., p. 51.

prepared. Too few troops had been mobilized. Planned arrests had not been made, and lines of communications had not been cut. Yeltsin could move freely from his *dacha* into the centre of Moscow to turn the tide unhindered. After their failure the punishments meted out on the coup leaders were symbolic given the magnitude of their crime. There was a series of mysterious suicides, defenestrations mostly, among people involved in the planning, but the incompetent ringleaders were soon amnestied. In Wolton's view, the failure of the reactionary putsch was wanted by too many mid-level chekists and apparatchiks who were already benefiting handsomely from the transformation and disliked the prospect of losing their recent gains.[48] With the Soviet Union unravelling Gorbachev was forced to resign in December 1991. The KGB, however, survived due to series of reorganizations—most importantly the split-off of its foreign intelligence service as SVR—and renamings. Its apparatus of repression, good contacts and expertise abroad, ideological pragmatism and interest in self-enrichment remained intact.[49] Useful in this early stage of Russian capitalism were networks of shell firms set up in Cyprus, in Southern Europe and in various tax heavens which could be used to shift metals, oil and weapons abroad and to benefit handsomely with little effort from the big gap between domestic and world prices.[50]

Around Yeltsin there were no born democrats. He and his advisors were all products of Soviet education, who practised their new liberal orthodox beliefs with the rigidity of recent converts. Local and cultural difficulties, the giant size of the combinates, the need to convert the military-industrial complex, the lack of infrastructure and regulatory institutions did not count. The coupon privatization was abused by the red directors to acquire their own factories. Disagreements were settled violently. Reportedly some 350,000 people were murdered during the first half of the 1990s. The aluminium war at Krasnoyarsk alone did cost 140 lives.[51] In some of these murders current and former KGB agents were involved. Some of the poisons used, like radioactive cadmium, came from KGB laboratories.[52] Among Russia's 800,000 private security staff one-third consisted of former chekists.

KGB access to Yeltsin's family was facilitated by the rapid promotion of Korsakov, who as a KGB major acted as Yeltsin's bodyguard and favourite drinking buddy, to general and commander over the 40,000 Kremlin troops. This position allowed him access and control over lucrative arms exports via

---

[48] Ibid., p. 57.
[49] Ibid., p. 60.
[50] Ibid., p. 68.
[51] Ibid., p. 79.
[52] Ibid., p. 93.

Rosovooron as well. Yeltsin's purge of CPSU cadres did not pertain to former KGB officers. As he was interested to centralize all security structures in the Kremlin, he appointed senior KGB officers, like Primakov, Stepanshin and last but not least Putin to the position of Prime Minister as well. As Putin then joked, there was no need for a coup by the FSB, since they were already in power.[53]

Putin in Yeltsin's eyes had recommended himself for the job by having been an eager civil servant, obedient and without too many initiatives of his own even in the most senior positions. Equally his previous KGB career had been an average, even without any outstanding achievements. Subsequent to his days in St. Petersburg's city hall (1991–1996) all investigations of corruption regarding the administration's external trade (of which he was in charge) were squashed. A Duma deputy, who showed too much interest, was poisoned, and a prosecutor dismissed.[54] After Sobchak's departure, the city's finances (for which Putin also was responsible) were $600 million in the red and St. Petersburg close to bankruptcy.[55] As FSB chief Putin aided Sobchak's flight to France, thus helping to protect himself as well. When Sobchak returned feeling safe after Putin's assumption of the presidency, he conveniently soon died of a heart attack.

Already prior to the first Chechen war the Kremlin had ordered commandos to destabilize Chechnya into the breakaway province, and at the same time tolerated large scale arms smuggling which increased the Chechen threat.[56] The start of the second Chechen war and the bombs not too subtly planted in Moscow helped to push Putin's and popularity ratings from a hopeless rate of 2% approval to more than 50%, thus easily surpassing his earlier much more powerful rivals Luzhkov and Primakov, who had enjoyed the support of Gusinsky's media.

Yet even after his victory, unresolved mysteries continue to haunt the Chechen insurrection and its associated terrorism. Thus in 2002, the entire terror team aiming to strike at Dubrovka theatre was able to assemble and store weapons in the heart of Moscow unhindered, with only the ringleader escaping, and everybody else being shot or killed by poison gas. Prior to Putin's re-election in 2004 yet another unclaimed bomb exploded in Moscow. This time in the Moscow metro with 40 people killed. Wolton observes

---

[53] Ibid., p. 119.
[54] Ibid., p. 134.
[55] Ibid., p. 135.
[56] Ibid., p. 88.

that chekists with their bureaucratic mindset always proceed with the same pattern.[57]

Their assumption of power since 2000 produced evident consequences for Russia's politics, legal order and economy. Not only were all public honours for the KGB's and its predecessors past dirty work, including the Day of the Chekist (20.12. [1917]), reintroduced. Their organs were again empowered to search residences and to arrest people for preventive purposes. The *propiska* residence obligations, abolished in 1993, were reintroduced as *registratura*. Patriotic and compulsory military education is re-taught in schools. A Kremlin-sponsored youth movement imitates the *komsomol*. Nationalist propaganda is publicly financed, praising the superiority of Russia, its Orthodox Church, Slavic culture and Soviet glory in WWII.[58] An extremism law, amended in July 2007, threatens jail terms of up to 6 years for the defamation of a state representative. Since 2004, NGOs have been attacked as fifth columns of the West. The FSB has now infiltrated all institutions of the state: justice, diplomacy, army, tax administration etc.[59] After 2000, a large-scale purge had occurred, with 85% of public prosecutors, 70% of the regional police and FSB chiefs losing their jobs, to be replaced by followers of the president and his circle. The formal institutions of democracy: parliament, the judiciary, elections and media have since turned into empty Potemkin villages. In the economy, Putin's men now control all the major state holdings, oil, gas, transportation, mass media and armament industries, including those companies effectively re-nationalized from disobedient oligarchs (Gusinsky, Berezovsky, Khodorkovsky). About two-dozen Putin followers (and some of their children) thus control companies accounting for 35% of Russia's GDP and a total market value of $350 billion.[60] The surviving oligarchs (Potanin, Fridman, Deripaska, Abramovich etc.) have to pay close attention to heed the Kremlin's wishes in any respect at short notice. SME development and genuine entrepreneurialism, however, remain discouraged with extensive needs for expensive permits and continuous inspections by officials eager to line their pockets. Weaknesses in industrial manufacturing outside the armaments sector, and of public transport and social infrastructure, in which the *siloviki* are disinterested, continue to weaken Russia's competitiveness.

The strengthening of Russia's international role thus appears to have been achieved almost exclusively by external factors: the growth of energy and raw

---

[57] Ibid., p. 152.
[58] Ibid., p. 203.
[59] Ibid., p. 154.
[60] Ibid., p. 192.

material prices due to Chinese and Indian demand, and by the weakening of the US, as they got tied down in the quagmires of self-inflicted Mid-Eastern wars. Putin essentially wants the re-establishment of a bipolar world, where only the US and Russia count, with her "near abroad", the former Soviet space and her new allies forming her exclusive zone of influence, foremost established by the use of her energy weapons, limited military operations and the techniques of destabilization and disinformation.[61] Multilateral fora will only be used to force the despised West into concessions and to heed the Russian agenda. Yet, in Wolton's conclusion, the West (and probably Asia as well) should not be overawed by Russia's aggressive performance. Her internal weaknesses in terms of energy development, social disequilibria, rapid demographic shrinkage, lack of entrepreneurialism and legal safeguards, and her technological and industrial backwardness will safely implode the rise to great power status before long again. If anything, then Putin's authoritarian rule, its attempts to emulate the Chinese model notwithstanding, has made long-term prospects in Russia worse, rather than better.

3.6.1 Anna Politkovskaya's Testimony

The author, shot in 2006 by an unknown contract killer, presumably one of Kadyrov's death commandos, minces no words towards Putin's regime. She calls it despotic, revengeful, unresponsive to criticism and riddled by corruption and organized crime. Putin himself always behaves like the KGB lieutenant colonel, the highest rank to which he rose during his undistinguished career of 17 years with the service.[62] Yet the Russian people remain collectively disinterested in civic affairs and thus tolerate his rule.

She spells out his government's arbitrary policies and their nefarious effects on ordinary people: The army's hostility against the mothers of soldiers, its heartlessness towards the hazing of recruits, the victims of wars and to the relatives of fallen soldiers, the treatment of war crimes in Chechnya, human fates after the transformation: portraits of the *nouveau riche*, those destroyed by alcoholism, of officers in poverty, the fights between criminal oligarchs in Yekaterinburg—supported by corrupt justice and police, the disregard of natural parks by oligarchic developers and the collusion of courts and authorities, police brutality and poison gas use during the liberation of the hostages in Dubrovka opera, the incompetence of the security forces during the Breslan school massacre, and finally, a portrayal of Putin's rule, which is

---

[61] Ibid., p. 260.
[62] Anna Politkovskaia. *La Russie selon Poutine*. Paris. Gallimard 2005, p. 7

unfavourably seen as despotic, based on a cynical view of people, with the attitudes of an eternal chekhist.[63]

As Politkovskaya does not pull her punches and names the people whose misdeeds she has investigated in her articles, her enemies are not limited to the Kremlin alone. They also include military officers and Chechen warlords operating there, gangsters and local oligarchs in Yekaterinburg, and developers and police officers in Moscow. Anyone among them might have decided to hire her so far unknown assassin. Many have been killed in Russia for even lesser motives.

There was no shortage of war crimes committed by all sides in Chechnya. Politkovskaya documents the case of Colonel Yuri Budanov, who kidnapped, raped and murdered an 18-year-old Chechen girl and then had her corpse buried in a forest. Intoxicated he had earlier ordered an artillery attack on a peaceful Chechen village and savagely beaten up a lieutenant who had objected to the order. After some attempts by the military hierarchy to hush up his crimes or to acquit him on grounds of temporary insanity, he was finally demoted and sentenced to 10 years in the penal colony. He remains the only Russian officer condemned so far.

Usually, it is the Chechen civilians who were at the wrong place at the wrong time to be captured as terror suspects, first tortured in dug-out pits ("*zindan*") in the open, and later transported to FSB torture centres. If their families do not manage to find their whereabouts and pay ransom in time, provided that the victims survive their ordeal, there will be a secret trial, based on forced confessions, false witnesses and fabricated evidence (weapons or drugs "found" in their possession). Inevitably, there are convictions with a lengthy dispatch to a penal colony, where they will be murdered before long.[64]

Politkovskaya also describes rising of a gangster, a certain Pavel Fedulev, from small-time alcohol smuggler to business tycoon in Yekaterinburg, a large industrial town in Western Siberia. As he bought himself into companies with credits, he subsequently killed his partners and creditors, while working closely with parts of the local police and justice. In the end, in bloody battles, he managed to take over the giant Uralmach metal combine, as well Uralkhimmach, Uraltelekom and three hydrolysis plants. His closest allies, the local police commander, a certain Ovchinnikov, was promoted by Putin to vice minister of the Interior, and the corrupt chief of the regional district

---

[63] Ibid., p. 339.
[64] Ibid., p. 47.

court had his term extended,[65] thus disproving the regime's claims to crack down on organized crime and corruption.

She also painstakingly documents the administration's failure to deal professionally with the hostage dramas at the Moscow Dubrovka Opera in October 2002, and with the Breslan school siege of September 2004. Each time the liquidation of all hostage-takers took precedent over the lives of the hostages. Negotiations were refused by the Kremlin. In Moscow, a secret poison gas was used, which killed the 40 terrorists but also 90 hostages (which due to the lack of information on the composition of the gas could not be treated adequately in the hospitals[66]). In Breslan the use of massive fire power triggered an implosion which killed some 300 children. After the drama, independent investigations were suppressed and media criticism silenced.[67]

According to Politkovskaya Putin's rule represented Neo-Sovietism with a new secret service nomenclature attempting to centralize power and to enrich themselves from the new hybrid capitalism, while trying to suppress all independent rivals to their claims, like the middle classes, small and medium enterprises, and regional and local autonomy.[68] Unfortunately, it is difficult to disagree with her findings, for which this conscientious writer paid so dearly.

3.6.2 Alexander Litvinenko's Testimony

Litvinenko, a former FSB lieutenant colonel, was murdered publicly in London by polonium poisoning in November 2006, with a radioactive trail of the assassin leading back to a secret state laboratory. If anything, then the often-shocking claims of Russian state terrorism made by the author have become more credible by his violent end, which according to the dying victim must have been ordered by Putin himself, a horrific death reserved for traitors.

Litvinenko's break with the FSB, according to his own account, occurred in 1998 when he was ordered to assassinate the oligarch Berezovsky. Instead, he warned his victim, was subsequently jailed for 9 months and with his family (and Berezovsky's help) escaped to London. He gives a detailed account of how the FSB in 1994 and 1999 organized bombing campaigns in Russian cities and blamed them on the Chechens in order to generate the pretexts and the public mood for Russia's two wars against this small breakaway

---

[65] Ibid., p. 218.
[66] Ibid., p. 281.
[67] Ibid., p. 365.
[68] Ibid., p. 139 and p. 368.

republic. Litvinenko also describes incidents of extrajudicial killings, of organized crime groups merging with FSB units, and of systematic attempts of the FSB and other Russian secret services to destabilize the country and to discredit Yeltsin's early liberal reforms in order to permit the ascendance of Putin and his FSB colleagues to power by 1999–2000. Notably, Chechnya had become a training ground for FSB operatives to learn their trade and to engage in kidnappings, torture and murder.

Obviously, some of his claims are more plausible than others. For instance, a stated master plan for national destabilization seems far-fetched, when it is criminal gangs who kill manager-owners of energy and metal plants, secret service assassins liquidate underworld bosses, and various secret service branches fight each other and the police when trying to take over lucrative businesses and smuggling rings during the chaotic Yeltsin years.

During 1991, the KGB was split into four structures: the SVR for external intelligence, FAPSI as the Federal Agency for Communications and Information, the Federal Border service and the president's security service, consisting of his bodyguard department and an ultra-secret Department for Special Programmes. Through a series of re-organizations and re-namings the reformed KGB, however, essentially succeeded to preserve its functions, archives and most of its personnel. Freed from CPSU control and ideology, its successor organization sets out to exploit their networks and personnel resources in the wild new economy. Through one of their senior operatives, General Korsakov as Yeltsin's bodyguard and drinking mate, they controlled access to the president. Others like Sobchak, the mayor of St. Petersburg, were controlled by a deputy, in his case by a certain V. Putin. Once Yeltsin had been trapped by the FSB into the first (1994–1996) and then the second Chechen war, he in Litvinenko's view was forced to resign before the end of his term and to hand over power to the FSB in return for its guarantee of immunity.[69]

Already in November 1994, an FSB captain is said to have been killed by his own bomb at a Moscow railroad bridge. But most bombs, including those left in buses, are claimed to have been planted by a gang of secret service sponsored assassins headed by an FSB agent called Maxim Lazovsky.[70] They were quickly blamed on Chechen terrorists with few attempts to prove it or to catch them. Within Russia then an FSB branch named Office for the Analysis of Criminal Organizations (*Vympel*) began its operations. According to Litvinenko its tasks essentially consisted of the elimination of underworld

---

[69] Alexander Litvinenko. *Blowing up Russia. The Secret Plot to Bring Back KGB Terror*. London: Gibson Square. 2007, p. 3.
[70] Ibid., p. 21.

bosses, political opponents and unwanted witnesses with the help of contract killers, and, after a while, of the contract killers themselves. Thus Lazovsky's group was duly liquidated during 1996, as was the Moscow police chief investigating the case.[71]

Once Putin moved from the post of FSB chief to become Prime Minister in 1999, he was succeeded by his loyal follower Nicolai Patrushev, who according to Litvinenko was responsible for the bombing campaign of 1999.[72] Things went wrong in the provincial town of Ryazan. Sacks containing hexagon and detonators were discovered by residents and defused by the local police. This was first hailed officially as heroism preventing a Chechen terrorist act. Once, however, FSB agents were caught as perpetrators, Patrushev called it an anti-terrorist exercise and claimed the hexagen to consist of sugar, and the detonators to be dummies. Yet Litvinenko proves these assertions to be patient lies and the conduct of the entire "exercise" to be contrary to all standard regulations.[73] Other bombs of the same design had earlier gone off in Moscow, Volgadonsk and in Buinaksk (Dagestan), killing 301 people and injuring thousands in their sleep. Later the Chechens captured an FSB First Lieutenant who confessed to the Buinaksk bombings (as well to know of FSB murders of Red Cross people in Chechnya), for whatever such confessions in captivity may be worth. Litvinenko also reproduces the testimony of a businessman who claims to have been duped into renting the storerooms in Moscow and Volgodonsk to a KGB agent, which were later used for placing the bombs. After the second bomb went off, he alerted the police to the other places, thus preventing their explosion, and went into hiding. Subsequently, the FSB with forgeries tried to link him to the Wahhabite terrorist group Hattab.[74]

At the same time, in August 1999, the Chechen terrorist Shamil Basaev undertook a senseless invasion of neighbouring Dagestan under the watchful eyes of the Russian military which did nothing to deter his gang. As Basaev had been the commander of the sizable contingent of Chechen mercenaries in the Russian sponsored war against Georgia in Abkhazia in 1991–1993 and had been trained by the military secret service GRU for the purpose, he in Litvinenko's view was an FSB agent provocateur, aiming to discredit the rule of Chechnya's legitimate president Aslan Mashadov. With the bombings and the "invasion" he was tasked to prepare Russian public opinion for the

---

[71] Ibid., p. 43.
[72] Ibid., p. 51.
[73] Ibid., p. 80.
[74] Ibid., p. 270.

planned second "short successful war" which Putin needed for his presidential campaign to act as a tough law and order man.

Litvinenko also claims that the FSB systematically scouted the penal colonies for violent criminals of North Caucasian descent and let them off in Chechnya with orders to abduct and kill Russians, foreigners[75] and moderate Chechen politicians.[76] Later the FSB relentlessly foiled all of Mashadov's and the Chechen leadership's attempts to negotiate for a peaceful end to the second war, as Putin, Patrushev and Sergey Ivanov (a former FSB general serving as defence minister) had decided that the war during election time would provide the right cover for the FSB to seize power.[77]

Litvinenko also provides evidence for several crime groups in other parts of Russia (Far East, Samara etc.) being infiltrated by the FSB and the GRU, whose leaders were usually liquidated and their business lines (contract killing, blackmail, smuggling of arms and narcotics) taken over by the local secret service. They usually made sure that the killers themselves were later killed and there were no witnesses, no police investigations and no court cases.[78] The FSB also became party during violent fights over control of several privatized state companies, like in the oil and aluminium industry and the Volga Automobile plant in the mid-1990s. He alleges links to people like Korsakov, and the connivance of Patrushev.[79]

Frequently Litvinenko's fact-filled accounts read like a fast-paced detective story. If some of his claims seem occasionally far-fetched or as pure assertions, his horrific death proves that his revelations must have struck a raw nerve in the FSB's hierarchy and within the Russian president himself.

3.6.3 The Case of Alexei Navalny

Navalny as a trained lawyer began as a shareholder activist investigating and exposing corruption at state-run corporations, of which there was no shortage of material. He later exposed political corruption and obscene richness in very popular videos distributed on the net by his "foundation against corruption", like of the clan of general prosecutor Yuri Chaika, of Yevgeni Prigoshin ("Putin's cook") and of Dmitri Medvedev's foreign residences and vineyards in Tuscany, the latter viewed by 35 million people. During the Moscow mayor's election in 2013, Navalny scored a surprise success and with 27% of the

---

[75] Ibid., p. 117.
[76] Ibid., p. 219.
[77] Ibid., p. 150.
[78] Ibid., p. 186.
[79] Ibid., p. 191 and p. 222.

votes ranked second. The Kremlin decided that this would never happen again and started an unending series of lawsuits against him, his brother and his followers, with the result that a trifle conviction banned him from running in an election ever again. Until his assassination by Chechen contract killers in February 2015 Boris Nemzov had been viewed as the leading light among Russia's fractious opposition movement. Nemzov had been governor of Nizhniy Novgorod (1991–1997) and Deputy Prime Minister (1997–1998) and was shot on a Moskva bridge in a high-security area near the Kremlin. After his death it was Navalny's turn, who does not profess a clear-cut political programme but endorses a blend of occasionally nationalist and social-democratic slogans. During local elections, he advocates a policy of "voting smart": to rally behind a reasonably acceptable leading opposition candidate of whichever party to beat the Kremlin's nominee. As this proved successful in quite a few smaller towns, the FSB closed in on him. During a tour of Siberia he had been filming local trouble spots, like the neglected city of Akademgodorok, the Soviet-designed "science city" of Novosibirsk, Russia's third-largest town, with its defective housing, lack of warm water, absence of jobs and development, but plentiful of corruption and pollution—obviously Silicon Valley it was not—in order to give nation-wide publicity to the causes of the local opposition candidates. On the flight to Tomsk, he was then poisoned with Novichok, the same substance which had been applied by GRU operatives to the retired defector Sergei Skripal and his daughter in May 2018 in Salisbury. As a military toxin Novichok is not available to free-lancers at a local pharmacy. As compared to anonymous and more effective shootings and other "accidents", poisoning is meant to terrify and intimidate by leaving traces, the usual Kremlin fairy tales of disinformation notwithstanding. As Andrei Soldatov rightly pointed out, the Kremlin lives in its own paranoid reality of threats and foreign conspiracies and has tightened control over its own security apparatus through regular purges, that a decision to take out the leading opposition leader could only be taken at its top.[80] Comatose Navalny was flown out to Berlin where in the leading Charite hospital he was brought back to life and cured after five months. Instead of choosing to remain in exile, he fearlessly decided to return home and prepared his return by publishing a documentary video on Putin's opulent and tasteless palace near Sochi at the Black Sea, which immediately attracted 65 million viewers. Upon arrival, Navalny was immediately arrested and in a pre-cooked trial sentenced to 3½ years in a labour camp for the violation of the probation rules of a 2014 judgement—which having been treated abroad he patiently

---

[80] Jutta Sommerbauer. "Der Kreml hat zum ersten Mal Angst" *Die Presse* 26.9.2020.

could not have followed. Some 40,000 people protested in around 90 cities against this travesty of justice, most numerously in Moscow, Vladivostok, Irkutsk and Novosibirsk, though the protest was harshly suppressed by riot police with numerous arrests. The purpose of this sentencing—with more to follow—is clearly to decapitate once again the opposition movement by isolating Navalny from external communication and to destroy his network of followers.[81]

3.7 Early Corruption: Putin in St. Petersburg

For a long time, there was this myth that Putin only watched corruption, but that he did not enrich himself.[82] The thorough research work done by the late Karen Dawisha has debunked this entirely.

Putin had joined the KGB in 1975. As one of his early mates, he met Sergey Ivanov, later his Defence Minister and head of his presidential administration. As mentioned before, during 1985–1990 he was posted in Dresden. Officially his job was to recruit Western visitors to gain access to Western military technology as industrial espionage. But there was an interesting and lucrative sideline in which the KGB in East Germany engaged: namely to travel to West Berlin without any border checks and to purchase all those goods urgently needed at home and to smuggle them out under diplomatic cover with a neat mark-up.[83]

One of the main partners in Dresden was Matthias Warnig, a Stasi officer, who also worked for the KGB and who was subsequently sent to Düsseldorf—equally on industrial espionage business. Warnig, though not a banker by training, in 1991 opened the Dresdner Bank branch in Petersburg to cooperate with Putin on various privatization deals and now is managing director of the $10 billion Nord Stream 2 project. He also sits on the board of Rusal, Transneft, Gazprom Schweiz AG, Rosneft, Verbundgas and the VTB Bank.[84] Clearly, Putin does not forget his friends. Basically, according to Dawisha, already in Dresden Putin created an inner circle of five close

---

[81] Jutta Sommerbauer. "Die Brutalisierung des Putin Systems" *Die Presse* 30.8.2020; "Gerichtsfarce rund um Navalny" *Die Presse* 19.1.2021; "Der Kreml setzt auf Repression" *Die Presse* 3.2.2021. Stefan Schnell "Proteste gegen das System Putin" *Kleine Zeitung* 24.1.2021. Manfred Sapper. "Der Fall Nawalny: Das Gift und die Lüge" *Die Presse* 20.8.2020. Klaus-Pater Schwarz. "Der KGB bereitet der Nowitschok-Demokratur von Putin den Boden" *Die Presse* 9.9.2020.
[82] Prescott, Op.cit., p. 72.
[83] Karen Dawisha. *Putin's Kleptocracy. Who owns Russia?* New York. Simon & Schuster. 2014, p. 48.
[84] Ibid., p. 56. I have met the man in Brussels during a nice Gazprom reception in Brussels in the summer of 2019. He was not a demon, but a friendly, slightly overweight person, who struggled to speak good English to his audience.

associates, including Warnig, who was subsequently appointed to very senior political and economic positions.

Back in St. Petersburg in 1990, Putin at his university witnessed how both the KGB and the mafia made a head start in spontaneous privatizations. Here he could rely on old KGB acquaintances from the 1980s, like Nikolai Patrushev (later FSB chief and since 2008 head of the Security Council) and Sergey Ivanov (later chief of staff of his presidential administration) from common university and KGB training days. There was no shortage of dubious privatization deals from which he received commissions—usually he directed them to the mayor's slush fund to which he had access. Failing this, the investor would be threatened by a security company, called "Baltic Escort", not run by pretty girls, but by former KGB officers and led by a certain Roman Tsepov, who was also Putin's bodyguard and in charge of collecting the tributes due to him. This role he continued also in the Kremlin, collecting cash also from candidates for governor and other senior posts in return for nominations, presidential visits and public praise. In 2004, he was poisoned, probably because he overstepped his limits or simply because he knew too much.[85]

Putin started his political career as an advisor to mayor Anatoly Sobchak and by 1990 became one of his deputies. During 1991–1996 he was the chairman of the city's committee for foreign liaison (KSV), in charge of licensing thousands of foreign investments in Petersburg and of Russian investments going abroad through Petersburg, a town through which 20% of all Russian trade must pass. With a capital participation of the KSV, and contributions to Sobchak's slush fund, things were made much easier.[86] A lot of this trade concerned illegal raw material exports, stolen cars, arms, or funds from fictitious real estate transactions.[87] Already then Putin assembled his future Kremlin team around him: Dmitri Medvedev, Igor Sechin, Alexey Kudnin, German Gref, Alexey Miller, Viktor Zubkov.

Dawisha identified several major vehicles of early enrichment for Putin and his friends:

The Ozero Dacha cooperative,
Petromed, a medical supplier,
Bank Rossiya,
Gunvor, a commodity trader,
the Petersburg Fuel Company (PTK), and
the "Twentieth Century Fund".

---

[85] Ibid., p. 79.
[86] Ibid., p. 83.
[87] Ibid., p. 83.

3 Putin's Autocracy: Siloviki Rule and Their Kleptocracy 131

The Ozero cooperative was set up in 1996 by Putin and 7 of his friends. They included Vladimir Yakunin, later head of Russian Railways, Yuri Kovalchik (head of Bank Rossiya), and the Fursenko brothers (one of them, Andrey later became minister of science and education). It acquired ground around the Lake Komsolskoye in the North East of St. Petersburg, had all existing small houses razed in 1992 and set up a gated community with residences for all eight members and a joint account. This joint account had the beauty that Putin could withdraw any amount without any trace and without being seen bribed, while his friends were doing lucrative businesses with his licences and kept on feeding their joint account. Putin himself bought 6800 m^2 of land and built a 2-storey mansion in the summer of 1996, which he could not have afforded from his salary, and probably also from the Mayor's contingency fund bought a house in Spain.[88]

Petromed was an import company supplying medical equipment to state hospitals, set up by Putin and his friends in 1992. It later financed the construction of Putin's palace at Sochi, which reportedly did cost $1 billion.

Bank Rossiya was set up in Leningrad in June 1990, and as a "crony bank" was controlled by five members of the Ozero cooperative. It became a prime vehicle for the new companies approved by Putin, and continued as a personal banker for senior officials, including Putin.[89] At the same time, it maintained links to Petersburg's leading Tambov-Malyshev crime syndicate, which at the time controlled fuel trading and the Kirishi refinery in Petersburg. In 2005, Bank Rossiya could purchase SOGAZ, one of the largest insurance companies and owned by Gazprom, with an estimated value of $2 billion for the bargain price of $50 million. By 2014, it had become the 17th largest bank in Russia with $10 billion in assets, until US and EU sanctions struck.

Gunvor, a global commodity trader, in which Putin reportedly is a major shareholder (with up to 50% of shares), remains controlled by Gennady Timshenko,[90] the sponsor of Putin's judo club and considered the treasurer of Putin's private fortunes. In the early 1990s, one ton of oil could be bought in from Rosneft at the domestic price of $1 (the price of a cigarette pack) and resold abroad at the world market price of $100. Little wonder that only organized crime and old KGB hands—or traders protected by both for a hefty share—could survive in this lucrative business. Gunvor in any event since 2003 is the world's third-largest oil trader and with oil bought from Rosneft

---

[88] Ibid., p. 94.
[89] Ibid., p. 64.
[90] Ibid., p. 6 and p. 68.

ships one-third of Russian sea-borne oil exports. Annual revenues stand at $70 billion per year.[91]

The Petersburg Fuel Company was also controlled by Ozero members. Licensed by Putin in 1994, it promptly got the exclusive right to supply the city's entire fleet with gasoline. At the same time, it had to find working arrangements with the Tambov syndicate which dominated the local fuel industry and the petrol stations.[92]

City funds of at least $28 million were given as a loan to a dubious "Twentieth Century Fund" at favourable rates and never paid back. As a vehicle to transfer money abroad it ended up in Finland and in Spain for the construction of vacation homes for Sobchak and Putin as well as for a hotel for "veterans" in Spain. These veterans turned out to be senior city officials and their families.[93]

Sobchak as a mayor helped himself also an apartment renovated at city expenses on Vasilyevsky Island and generously distributed others to Putin and his colleagues.[94]

As mentioned before, in the early days of transition only KGB cadres posted abroad had experience of foreign trade operations with their front companies. Once the CPSU was dissolved in 1991 the party's rich assets abroad were also taken over by KGB people. Within Russia the party's property, office buildings, vacation homes, printing houses and schools were equally snatched. Major black market operations only worked with KGB protection—and this did not come for free. It was only after the oligarchs set up their own security services that the KGB people lost their monopoly.[95]

Putin's speciality was giving licenses for exports, as 20% of Russian foreign trade went through St. Petersburg's harbour, and for real estate purchases. Typically money laundered abroad would flow back and be invested in Russian real estate to appear legitimate. Putin usually took a commission of 25%, sometimes up to 50%, but prudently never pocketed it directly but deposited it into the mayor's slush fund (to which he had access anyway).[96]

One case which nearly went wrong was a deal in which he provided dubious partners with raw materials worth $1 billion at heavily discounted prices which they would barter abroad for foodstuff to alleviate the massive food shortages in St. Petersburg. However, the companies all vanished after

---

[91] Ibid., p. 113.
[92] Ibid., p. 143.
[93] Ibid., p. 146.
[94] Ibid., p. 117.
[95] Ibid., p. 25.
[96] Ibid., p. 125.

putting the proceeds of the sales into offshore accounts and the promised food never arrived.[97] The case against Putin lingered on for years until it was closed forever once he became President.

Friends of Putin also benefitted early on. His Azeri university mate Ilham Rahimov dealt with raw earth metals. Putin signed with him contracts at much below market rates and expedited the export licenses overruling the objections of a Moscow ministry. The result: fat effortless profits for his crony.

A certain Dimitri Medvedev, then a lowly legal adviser in Putin's office, already in 1994 owned 10% of Ilim Pulp Enterprises in Karelia, then and now Russia's and Europe's largest producer of pulp and paper. From 1994 to 1998 he worked as Ilim's legal director and through a holding called Fintsel expanded his stock to 20%, worth $80 million in 1999[98] already.

Putin's loyalty to his handful of Petersburg friends is legendary and lasting.

A certain Strzelkovki, also formerly a lieutenant colonel in the Leningrad KGB, ran the travel agency of the St. Petersburg city administration. Thus qualified, Putin in 1999 appointed him as minister for sports and tourism. He later also headed the State tourism Committee. After gentle pressure from the Kremlin in 2008 he was appointed CEO of Norilsk Nickel, the world's largest producer of nickel and palladium, a private company after all. Vladimir Potanin supported his appointment against the objections of Oleg Deripaska, who not without reason cited his lack of managerial and industry experience. Without hopefully doing much harm he departed with a golden handshake of $100 million in 2012.[99]

The Rotenberg brothers Boris and Arkandy are old childhood friends and judo partners from his rough Leningrad days. Both now are middlemen in pipeline sales to Gazprom and Transneft (who both could do perfectly well without them) and have a de facto and very expensive monopoly on pipeline construction, drilling operations and an increasing role in road construction.[100] Alexey Navalny estimated in 2010 that as a result, Transneft's construction costs for the Siberian ESPO pipeline were inflated by $4 billion,[101] obviously at a loss to the state. And Bill Browder, whose Hermitage Fund had invested $3.5 billion into Gazprom, observed that the Gazprom sponsored building projects for the Sochi Olympics at $7 billion had been vastly overpriced by the Rotenbergs. This amounted to "only" 15% of the Sochi budget but was already more than the Vancouver Winter Olympics had

---

[97] Ibid., p. 107.
[98] Ibid., p. 83.
[99] Ibid., p. 72.
[100] Ibid., p. 93.
[101] Ibid., p. 57.

costed in total. This time also at the expense of shareholders and Browder's clients.

Then there is Putin's doctoral supervisor Vladimir Litvinenko of the Petersburg Mining Institute. Predictably, there are charges of plagiarism with whole sections lifted from obscure US journals. This typically happens when you ghost-write someone else's dissertation and could not care less. Yet the good professor was rewarded for his labours by receiving 10% of PhosAgro (formerly part of Yukos), worth $523 million in 2004, surely the world's best honorarium! Hopefully, the research assistant, who had to do the work, also got his million.

In sum, the early friends of Putin by 2013 according to Forbes were worth between $1 billion (Viktor Ivanov) and $10.2 billion (Roman Abramovich, albeit a later friend). The annual salaries for his cronies appointed as SOE top managers ranged between $4 million and $25 million.

But Putin also cared for friends in need. After Sobchak, his former boss, lost his elections in 1996 and was prosecuted on corruption charges, Putin got him out of his hospital bed and with the help of his KGB friends on to a private plane to Paris, and as a Prime Minister squashed the case.[102] This touching loyalty commended him strongly to the Yeltsin family, which had even more skeletons in the cupboard. Once Putin became President, Sobchak felt safe again to return, but soon died conveniently of a heart attack while visiting Kaliningrad (Königsberg).

When Putin went to Moscow after Sobchak's defeat in 1996 and was made in charge of the Main Control Department where he had access to all of the numerous files implicating him, not only did the files disappear but also those who had investigated him. He took some of his cronies along and placed them strategically, like Igor Sechin (in 2012 to become head of Rosneft, the world's largest oil company) and Sergei Chemezov, a friend from Dresden (who after 2004 as head of Rosoboroneksport would control all of Russia's armaments exports). Others he left behind in Petersburg, in order to keep the situation under control with his KGB friends surveying his enemy Vladimir Yakovlev as the new mayor.[103]

The Putin system is very transparent. It supports his friends with cash and privileges, provides them with exclusive state and SOE contracts, protects them in court, supports them in their raids against competitors, be they foreign or domestic, and criminalizes their opponents. In return for these lavish privileges, they have to remain loyal, discreet, pay tribute and support him politically without fail. As a secret service man sceptical to paranoia, he

---

[102]Ibid. p 121.
[103]Ibid., p. 94.

only trusts a handful of old friends from school, university, the KGB and his Petersburg city administration. At this time he became the champion of his old colleagues who as KGB cadres felt shifted aside by the liberal reformers like Anatoly Chubais, who was Yeltsin's chief of staff. Instead of surviving as mercenaries in private security companies, there was now the promise to be back in business and in power.[104]

At the same time, the critics of his Petersburg years were brutally silenced. They were fired, threatened, put in jail or killed in various ways: poisoned, shot, beaten to death, killed "by Mercedes" in engineered traffic accidents, or died very suddenly for other unexplained reasons. In short, Putin remains merciless in his vengefulness.[105] Once in Moscow after 1996, he would expand his Petersburg leadership style—which was and remains not much different from Don Corleone—to the national level.

3.8 Corruption in Yeltsin's Kremlin: Putin in Moscow

In St. Petersburg Putin had become head of the local "Our home is Russia" party, the first of the many synthetic "parties of power" which the Kremlin would set up and had worked for Yeltsin's re-election during 1995–1996. In Moscow he wanted again a key post behind the scenes as an expert in controlling businesses, allowing him to select the businessmen who would become and stay rich, and the others who became targets.

Yet his first job was to be appointed deputy head of Presidential Property Department, run by the brazenly corrupt Pavel Borodin. What in other countries would seem like glorified facility management was different in the Kremlin. Yet the Presidential Administration, on instructions of Yeltsin, had taken over the rich possessions of the banned CPSU, property which the party had mostly stolen since 1917. Abroad alone 715 properties—mostly registered in the name of front companies—were counted in 78 countries. Since 1997 every year some 2000 nice apartments, for instance, were distributed to the friends of Yeltsin and Borodin, who pocketed the commission and shared it with Yeltsin and friends.

Finally, Switzerland brought corruption charges against Borodin, after he had demanded and received kickbacks of a paltry $30 million over renovation works at the Kremlin by a Swiss company. As described earlier, he was arrested

---

[104] Ibid., p. 166.
[105] Ibid., p. 158.

in the US in 2001. Released on a bond of 5 million Swiss francs, in 2002 the case was closed and the bond returned. During 2000–2011 he served as the state secretary of the Union of Russia and Belarus, a job which was not too stressful but offered less side income.

After his re-election in 1996 Yeltsin's ship started sinking. His drinking got stronger and more obvious and his behaviour more erratic while his physical and mental condition visibly weakened also in public. As corruption grew, with ratings down, more and more of his advisors and erstwhile allies defected to the opposition. This was the right moment for Putin as a loyal factotum to work his way gradually into the embattled "family", the inner circle around Yeltsin with Tatyana Diatchenko and Berezovsky in command. Mainly he worked through the two successive chiefs of the presidential administration, Valentin Yumashev and Alexander Voloshin (who stayed on in 2000 when Putin became President).

Concurrently to his job as Borodin's deputy soon he was also made head of the Main Control Department (GKU). Its task was to oversee the implementation of federal laws, executive orders, and presidential instructions, and since 1996 also the control of regional administrations. As mentioned above, he now had access to all the files collected against him, which to no one's surprise quickly disappeared.[106]

During two months in the summer of 1998, he was promoted first deputy chief of staff in charge of re-asserting control over Russia's regions. In a period shorter than most traineeships he obviously could not achieve much, but quickly became convinced that vertical chain of command, which had been destroyed—as governors pretty much did what they liked regardless of Moscow's wishes—had to be urgently re-established over regional semi-independence.

Finally in autumn of 1998, Putin reached his first dream job: Head of the FSB and concurrently secretary of the Security Council. One of his first measures was to disband the two directorates investigating economic crimes and corruption by the oligarchs and officialdom. Quickly also he forcefully retired old generals and his enemies from the service and promoted his friends into key positions. At the same time, he instructed the FSB to produce the usual *kompromat* against prosecutor Skuratov, who was investigating the "Family" too eagerly, forcing him to resign.

In August 1998 the Asian financial crisis belatedly started hitting Russia and first hurt the exposed commodity exporters harder than almost anyone else. Then the government defaulted on domestic bonds. Pushed by a sudden

---

[106]Note that this is not a Russian specialty. It also happens in high places in Western European politics.

capital flight of $25 billion the rouble dropped 64% in value, with inflation shooting up to 41%. In despair, Yeltsin appointed Yevgeny Primakov as the Prime Minister who was popular among Communists and nationalists, but not among oligarchs. Quickly he announced he would fight corruption as his priority, also the one within the "family". Berezovsky and Putin felt threatened and began to act as allies.[107]

The idea of a second, this time victorious, little war against the Chechen Republic emerged. A bombing on the crowded market of Vladikavkaz on 19 March 1999—the first bombing since the end of the first Chechen war in 1996—conveniently derailed the talks foreseen between Primakov and the Chechen leadership. Interior minister Stepashin advocated a limited, low-risk operation of troops occupying the largely Russian settled Northern plains up to the river Terek, but not beyond, leaving Grozny and the mountains to the Chechens. Putin in the Security Council argued for a hard line of an all-out war, however.

In May 1999, the impeachment proceeding was getting on steam in the Duma while Yeltsin was in the hospital. Rumours of a state of emergency emerged. Yet Yeltsin narrowly survived the vote, while Primakov was dismissed and replaced by Stepashin as Yeltsin's fifth PM in eight years. Then the threat of an electoral alliance (OVR) of Luzhkov, Primakov and Yakovlev jointly with Stepashin emerged. Its likely victory would spell the end of oligarchic rule and of Putin's career.[108]

Having gained the family's confidence due to his proven loyalty to Sobchak even after his fall and after having promised immunity to all, Putin in August 1999 was appointed Prime Minister and soon after was designated successor to Yeltsin. Putin quickly appointed Nikolai Patrushev, a KGB friend from St. Petersburg, as his successor at the FSB, a function in which Patrushev remained until 2008, when he became secretary of Security Council (like Putin before as well).[109]

As aptly described by Litvinenko above, in August/September 1999 a few hundred Chechen militants, led by the former KGB informer Shamil Basayev crossed into neighbouring Dagestan and occupied and plundered a few villages. This may have been instigated by Berezovsky's money after a meeting between Voloshin and Basayev at the French Riviera, promising

---

[107] Ibid., p. 186.
[108] Ibid., p. 194.
[109] One son, Dimitri, since 2018 is Minister for Agriculture, his second son, Andrei, deputy CEO of Gazprom Neft.

him power in Chechnya in return for a small war with "fireworks at the border".[110]

MVD troops at the Dagestani border were withdrawn in time for his raid. Subsequently, Russian bombers destroyed the villages entirely while allowing Basayev and his people to escape.

In the meantime, with Berezovsky's money and his ORT channel endless stories were spun about Primakov's failing health, Luzhkov's corruption, and Putin's youth versus Yeltsin's feebleness. As of August, the Russian air force started bombing Chechnya and from 31 August to 16 September 1990, a series of five bombs went off mostly in apartment blocks in Moscow and Volgodonsk which killed 301 residents in their sleep and wounded 2000 others. The campaign came to a sudden end when an FSB team placing another bomb of the same make in yet another apartment block in Ryazan was caught red-handed. The terror was nonetheless blamed on the hated Chechens, even though Alexander Lebed (1950–2002), an Afghan war hero, who finished the Moldovan-Transnistrian civil war in 1992 and negotiated the end of the first Chechen war in 1996, publicly stated terror against civilians went against the Chechen honour code. They would only pick senior military targets.[111] For the conduct of the war, Yeltsin gave his PM a free hand. After a long-prepared ground offensive half of Chechens became refugees and Grozny was bombed to rubble, the first European town since WWII.

Vladislav Surkov, the ideological hawk and mastermind in Kremlin until he was fired—not for the first time—in February 2020, as an electoral strategy recommended of a combination of "party of war" with a strong response to the "Chechen" terror, yet at the same time calming the people and to prevent a mass panic after the bombings. This cynical strategy worked. While he did not participate in any campaign activities and gave no interviews, Putin was constantly in the media and nightly on TV, while Luzhkov in his mayor's office had been unable to react. The oligarch dominated TV channels continued to do their best to destroy Luzhkov's and Primakov's reputation. As a result, Putin's ratings went up from 2% in August to 45% in November 1999.

Still the Duma Elections of December 1999 and the Presidential Elections of March 2000—like in 1996—Were Marked by Massive Fraud.

---

[110] Ibid., p. 200.

[111] Ibid., p. 219. Popular among the army and the general public this charismatic general died in 2002 in a helicopter crash as the governor of Krasnoyarsk after having defeated the local gangsters as well.

Governors, mayors and other power holders got the message: Either to support the Kremlin and become a compliant puppet or be doomed.[112] As a result, Putin got the support of 50 governors out of 89. In Dagestan, Tatarstan, Ingushetia, in most army barracks and many villages his score was close to 99%.[113]

As from Day 1, Putin reasserted central control by strengthening his presidential powers, went against corrupt regional elites, and against too independent oligarchs, starting with Gusinsky who had backed the wrong side during the presidential campaign. As promised he granted an amnesty to Yeltsin, while dismissing his daughter Tatyana Diatchenko very quickly. His friends, as should be expected, all got senior posts around him and in the ministries. German Gref, Sergey Ivanov and Victor Ivanov becoming senior members in the Presidential Administration, with Sergey Ivanov, as an old KGB hand, also running the Security Council as its secretary. Aleksey Kudrin got the Ministry of Finance and Leonid Reyman the Ministry of Communications. Patrushev stayed at the FSB.

Following the outlines of the military districts per Ukase 7 super federal districts (5 of them run by generals) were created in Czarist tradition to rule over the 89 governors, to coordinate all federal services in the region and to assure compliance with federal legislation. There is one notable exception: Chechnya was handed over to Akmad Kadyrov, a mufti who had defected to the Russians in 2000, as a personal fiefdom. After he was assassinated in 2004 his son Ramzan (1976–) has inherited the republic, where he can do whatever he pleases, introduce the sharia, and organize death squads and torture, provided that he suppresses any separatism. In return, Russian money has rebuilt Grozny into a replica of a glittering Mid-Eastern oil town, replete with a megalomaniac mosque, named after Kadyrov's father.

3.9 The Tragedy of the Kursk[114]

Shortly after Putin assumed power and while vacationing in Sochi the Kursk, one of Russia's most modern nuclear submarines sank in the Barents Sea in August 2000. The facts are straightforward and tragic enough. There was an explosion of fuel in a defective torpedo which triggered a subsequent

---

[112] Ibid., p. 224.
[113] Ibid., p. 245.
[114] Based on: Robert Moore. *A Time to Die. The Untold Story of the Kursk Tragedy.* New York: Crown Publishers. 2003.

explosion of the front section of the giant submarine and sank it. Military secrecy, a defective emergency exit and a delayed rescue operation with decayed inadequate Russian equipment prevented the timely rescue of the 23 initially surviving crew members in the undestroyed rear part of the submarine. Three to four days later they were however killed by carbon dioxide poisoning and fire in the submerged wreckage. UK and Norwegian rescue teams were authorized too late and informed misleadingly by the Russian admiralty preventing them to arrive in time and rescue the sailors alive. During the drama, President Putin continued vacationing and devoid of showing any empathy with the trapped victims remained seemingly unconcerned, he trusted the lies spread by his admirals, who were more interested to keep military secrets than save the lives of the sailors. Their families were similarly misinformed, and after a media outcry, were bought off with generous allowances and dispersed across Russia with offers of apartments. Although the naval commanders who had lied to their president and were responsible for the botched rescue were later dismissed from active service, most were able to continue politico-military careers subsequently in high places.

Having unexpectedly been frozen out of power and out of the Kremlin, Berezovsky and his media reported Putin's callous and inept handling of the Kursk tragedy very vividly and tried to organize some resistance against the quickly emerging autocracy. The reaction of the angry new president did not take very long, with Berezovsky having to take a flight to London very quickly. Another mighty oligarch had been speedily dispossessed and eliminated. His successor Abramovich did learn this lesson very quickly, Khodorkovsky did not.

3.10 The Case of Chechnya[115]

In March 2018, Putin purged the entire leadership of Dagestan, yet let Kadyrov in Chechnya continue his fight against armed insurrections. His "Chechen Khananate" or "Kadyrov's caliphate" as an almost private state could engage in any human rights violations in pretending to fight armed revolts and almost conduct a semi-independent foreign policy in the Mid-East. Within the republic no opposition is tolerated. Like Putin Kadyrov gets 100% of the votes. After some 140,000 Chechens fled the country after the second war, there is still a security apparatus of some 30,000 men engaged in a civil war, including meting out collective punishments like burning down

---

[115] Uwe Halbach. "Chechnya's Status within the Russian Federation" *SWP Research Paper* 2/May 2018. Berlin.

rebel villages. Kadyrov also maintains death squads against his enemies at home, in Russia and abroad. This comes handy when the murder of Kremlin critics like Anna Politkovskaya (2006) and of Boris Nemtsov (2015) can be blamed on Chechen killers.

3.11 Putin as President: The Kleptocracy

Transparency International estimates the total amount of bribery in Russia to stand at $300 billion, equal to the GDP of Denmark, or equal also to the budget for Russia's so-called national priority projects in health, education and agriculture. Somehow correspondingly the capital flight since 2005 amounts to $335 billion, equivalent to 5% of Russia's GDP. Putin's narrow circle of friends now are all billionaires. The state usually absorbs all of their business risks, while it privatizes the benefits to those closest to the president.

As the centre of the "vertical of power" the Kremlin shadows and supervises all ministries, the courts, the two parliaments, the regional governments, the media as well as the parties and most social movements. With the division of powers suspended, the access to riches is unhindered without any effective checks by the clique in charge of the Kremlin. In fact, while respecting a few legal niceties, the country and its riches have become a self-service shop for them. The Russian term "*bespredel*" implies the limitless and total lack of accountability on part of the elites behind the façade of restoring Russia's greatness.[116]

Once in power and having disposed of the three leading oligarchs, Putin started asking the survivors—who were after all not part of his original circle of friends—for "donations" to his various expensive private and public projects, which they better did not refuse. At the same time, he periodically charges them with tax evasion (like Vagit Alekperov of Autovaz) or asks them to pay up ex-post for underpaying the original purchase price (like Vladimir Potanin for Norilsk Nickel). The sums in question as a rule are not astronomical or ruining (unless the Kremlin wants the owner to sell out quickly and cheaply) but they come unpredictably and relentless.

More down the pecking order, every year some 110,000 smaller businessmen—the more successful they are, the more they are at risk—without political protection are arrested on tax or other charges, by the militia and

---

[116]Dawisha. Op. cit., p. 3.

the prosecutors taking a clue from above—or simply because the competition wants to get rid of them—until they submit to the blackmail and pay up to the corrupt officials and judges or get out of business.[117]

The story of Gazprom has been told before. Very quickly this reliable cash cow came under full Kremlin control, with Alexei Miller and Dmitri Medvedev at the helms, and its board stuffed with 11 Putin cronies (not that any one of them having had any energy experience) out of a total of 18, who directs this "worst managed company in the world" (Barron's).[118] Earlier parasitic intermediary gas trading companies like Itera were eliminated but quickly replaced by others like RusUkrEnergo and Eural Trans Gaz, run by similarly shady characters, like Dmitry Firtach and Semyon Mogilevich.[119]

At the same time, Gazprom maintains dozens of subsidiaries in Cyprus, the Virgin Islands, Switzerland and the Cayman Islands, and this surely not for the purpose of selling gas there.

Putin personally (actually like French presidents as well) appoints the senior executives of all major SOEs, like Gazprom, Transneft, United Aircraft, Russian Railways, Almaz-Antey, United Shipbuilding, Aeroflot, Alrosa etc. But unlike French presidents he wants absolute compliance with his future wishes and contributions in return.

Putin like Stalin (or Tito) has 26 exclusive fully staffed and well-guarded presidential residences (in order not to use ordinary hotel rooms) built, renovated or expanded with federal funds, plus five yachts (one, the Olympia, as a $50 million gift of the oligarchs in 2002, organized by Abramovich, another one donated by Unicom, a subsidiary of Sivcomflot, a SOE, which had been KGB controlled during Soviet times and is now headed by a Putin crony)[120] and apparently 58 planes at his disposal. Keen spotters have calculated the worth of his various wrist watches at $700,000—six times his annual salary.[121] Like with many African presidents meetings with Putin cost $5 million to $10 million for businessmen to solve problems. As a sort of tax harvesting, known from ancient Roman times, mayors and governors have to pay insiders in the Kremlin to get and maintain their jobs, and of course, need to recoup their costly investment with bribes in their functions.

From the beginning, Putin and his siloviki friends wanted an authoritarian system, rather than a democracy which after a lost election would

---

[117] Ibid., p. 318.
[118] Ibid., p. 331.
[119] Ibid., p. 328.
[120] Ibid., p. 102.
[121] Ibid., p. 10. Also President Sarkozy, a man of a similar size, was an avid watch collector, his collection however was worth only a fraction, and in effect his almost only possession after he left office, except for a stamp collection.

force them to render their power and privileges and to make them accountable. Democratic rituals and a legalistic system were and are simply seen as a legitimizing decoration for their political and material ambitions. Once again, their modus operandi is very simple: "For my friends anything, for my enemies the law". Obviously, as not all friends of Putin are also friends amongst each other, all of them have a vested interest to vouchsafe their gains and to move most of them off-shore to a safe heaven, just in case...

Basically, as Dawisha puts it, Putin runs a "protection racket" with a complex internal system, with subgroups balanced against each other and with a code of behaviour which punishes disloyalty "while allowing access to economic predation on a world historic scale for the inner core of his elite".[122] This sums it up neatly.

Building on Karen Dawisha's painstaking research Anders Aslund has followed this up to the present.[123] He confirms that after 1998–1999, driven by high oil and raw material prices and some important reforms during 2000–2003 notably the tax reform and establishing a market for land), the Russian economy grew admirably at an annual rate of 8% until the crisis of 2008 when it became evident that virtuous fiscal conservatism with balanced budgets, strong foreign currency reserves and emergency state funds were not sufficient to absorb an external shock for a country so dependent on world energy and raw material prices. Since then however with growth rates at barely 1.5% per year more than a decade of stagnation followed as the negative effects of Putin's rule kicked in: Energy rents permitted a ruthless crony system, a kleptocracy African style. With little legal property protection, both legitimate and illegitimate capital flees abroad, preferably to tax havens also for laundering purposes, at annual double-digit $ billion numbers. This persistent capital flight severely reduces productive investments in industry, services and infrastructure. As the authoritarian rule consolidated, since 1999 the state sector expanded notably in the banking and energy sector at the expense of more efficient private competitors, conveniently giving more space and opportunities for enrichment for the friends of Putin, but at the expense of the national economy and people's welfare. More and more, as he extended his term of office until 2036 (when Putin will be 83), he will appear like a second Leonid Brezhnev (1964–1982), whose decrepit rule was saved and prolonged by the development of the new huge West Siberian oil and gas fields.

The criteria for belonging to Putin's small long-standing coterie of friends remained the same: trust, obedience and secrecy. Merit, effectiveness and

---

[122] Ibid., p. 38.
[123] Anders Aslund. *Russia's Crony Capitalism*. New Haven: Yale University Press 2019.

ideology were secondary. This narrow circle continues to consist of three overlapping circles (with almost no outside recruitment, except for PM Mikhael Mishistin,[124] replacing Medvedev in January 2020): the senior FSB comrades from Petersburg, who assures his unlimited powers; his cronies, usually from his Kremlin administration, who run the state-controlled sector, and assure his cash flow; and the Petersburg businessmen who for a handy commission benefit from no-bid state and SOE contracts. Though Putin values order and stability above all and abhors disorder (like demonstrations and free elections) and revolutions (including those of 1917, which are not celebrated in Putin's Russia, let alone the colour revolutions of 2003–2005, or the Arab spring of 2010), still he fuels fights between the two major factions, the "systemic liberals", like Andrei Kudmin, who won on macroeconomic stability and the tax reform, and the "statitist" siloviki, who won on everything else.[125]

One spectacular duel between the two main factions became public, when Economics Minister Alexei Ulyukaev in November 2016 became the victim of a sting operation framed by Rosneft boss Sechin. Ulyukaev, an economist and a survivor of the original Gaidar reformers, had been vice president of the Central Bank (2004–2013) and since 2013 Minister of Economic Development, was considered an experienced reliable professional and was not part of Putin's inner circle. In February 2016, with Putin's blessings, it was agreed to privatize Bashneft, which was owned 50% by the federal government and 25% by the Republic of Bashkirstan in West Siberia. Bashneft with huge reserves, 175 pumping stations, 3 refineries and 600 petrol stations, was well run and had increased its output by 40% during 2009–2014. In short, it was considered the jewel of the state-owned Russian oil industry. Its sale would bring much welcome revenue to the federal budget. NKK and Lukoil were interested. Initially, Rosneft declared itself disinterested. Being a SOE logically it could not participate in a "privatization", it declared. By July it changed its mind, but Ulyukaev remained opposed at least for a while. Later the council of ministers decided unanimously to permit its participation in the auction, which Rosneft duly won, buying 50% of Bashneft for 330 million rubles.

In November 2016. Ulyukaev visited Rosneft's headquarters and was given by Sechin an attache case, which he did not open, expecting Sechin's usual gifts of expensive wine and sausages. As he left the building he was arrested,

---

[124] Mishistin, an economist and hockey playing friend of Putin, was a surprise appointment with a reputation as competent director of the Federal Tax Service (2010–2020), professionalizing this endemically corrupt institution. During 1999–2004 he was a deputy tax minister, a function, in which he did not get any poorer: Andrew Roth "Putin critics ask how his PM choice acquired expensive properties" *The Guardian* 16.1.2020.

[125] Aslund. Op. cit., p. 9.

the bag opened and $2 million found in cash. Sechin declared he had been blackmailed by the minister to give his agreement for the deal, a decision which however had been taken months earlier. Ulyukaev who maintained—quite plausibly—his innocence, was sentenced to 8 years of hard labour. Sechin, who was summoned as a witness at the trial, did not bother to show up, presumably because he knew the judgement in advance. It was clearly a political fight won by Sechin as the master of the siloviki over the liberal clan.[126]

Like all secret service officers, Putin is obsessed with detail[127] and impresses his counterparts and the general public, when his meetings are televised, with its mastery. He clearly micromanages and makes the decisions while ministers, top officials or the heads of SOEs debrief him in short, crisp bilateral talks. He is entirely disinterested in the Council of Ministers chaired by the Prime Minister. As such his top-down modus operandi—like in any presidential system—is similar to the Elysée in which the President usually uses the short weekly ministers' meetings to announce his already pre-cooked decisions without any debate. Putin, however, takes the weekly meetings of Security Council, which he presides and which is stacked with siloviki generals, more seriously.[128]

And like in all presidential systems, it is the administration which drafted the laws and decrees on instructions of the Kremlin, and certainly no longer the Duma, let alone the Federal Council.[129]

This centralism is claimed to be justified by the Russian tradition of strong central authority, unrestrained neither by law nor by parliament, as practised by Nicolas I (1825–1881), with the Russian Orthodox Church always having been supportive of the state. Yet this argument overlooks that there have also been strong liberal traditions in Russia's history, like during the reign of Alexander II (1855–1881) or during the time of Pyotr Stolypin (1906–1911).

Putin's workday starts by going through two thick intelligence folders: one on the home front, the domestic political situation monitored by FSB, and the second on foreign intelligence by the SVR. He reads no economic reports. This daily intake feeds his natural inclination to believe in conspiracy theories and the evil intentions of others. Obviously, there are also other services, like

---

[126] "Arrestation du ministre Oulioukaiev: l'ombre de Setchine" *Le courrier de Russie* 25.11.2016.

[127] During the weekly bilateral EU-Russia consultations at the OSCE in Vienna sometime during 2008 the Russian ambassador, a very impressive and educated gentleman, once showed us proudly the copy of two pages of handwritten instructions he claimed to have been written by Putin himself. No other head of an OECD member state—not even from San Marino or Monaco—would have done such thing.

[128] Aslund. Op. cit., p. 34.

[129] Ibid., p. 49.

military intelligence by the GRU, which is also in charge of strong-armed operations abroad by former *speznaz* officers, who usually are more brutal than intelligent and leave too many traces, like most spectacularly in the Litvinenko and Skripal cases. There is also the FSO—the federal protection service—in charge of his personal safety. Like all good autocrats Putin makes sure that there remains a healthy rivalry among all these services.

In the meantime, after having dissolved the FSB anti-corruption units back in 1999 to protect the Yeltsin family, himself and his Petersburg cronies, Putin had recreated a similar service in the FSB under the command of the reliable General Sergei Korolev. In a span of one year, he arrested the governors of Komi, Sakhalin and Kirov, the federal customs chief, several senior interior ministry officials, 17 vice governors and 22 mayors. They also carried out an internal purge in the FSB's economic security department and even locked up 12 officials from the Petersburg city administration[130] (probably protegés of the wrong mayor). Clearly these unfortunates must have run afoul of the Kremlin or the FSB senior hierarchy, or failed to share their spoils properly. The message is clear as in case of Ulyukaev: Nobody, even in high ranks can feel safe and nobody is untouchable. In Communist China the same system applies, only more brutally with firing squads at the end. Russia after all is more civilized.

In 2006, in response to his paranoia about a US-sponsored NGO-driven colour revolution in Russia, Putin created a National Guard of 400,000 men as paramilitary force, comprising former Interior Ministry and OMON troops under the command of Viktor Zolotov, his former bodyguard. Its purpose is to "fight terrorism", read: to intimidate and to control domestic opposition.

A preferred object of state intimidation are also private entrepreneurs, even when they are absolutely apolitical: First, their economic independence and the fact that they employ people outside of state control, makes them suspect.

Second, most officialdom, like Putin and his siloviki friends, who were socialized during Soviet days and who never did any productive work, deeply believe that all—or most—businessmen are exploitative crooks. If he was honest he would sit on his tractor or sweat in a steel mill. Third, the object is financially very tempting for a shakeout. Hence the more successful they are, the more they are at risk.

As a result, there was a continuous mass arrests of business people on flimsy grounds, be they violations of tax codes (most popular), environmental or labour standards, whatever comes handy. In 2010 alone, 400,000

---

[130] "Le FSB passe à l'attaque contre les responsables politiques" *Le courrier de Russie* 26.11.2016.

businessmen were arrested to shake them down; 146,000 received prison sentences.[131] The rest paid their ransom—which does not come cheap and is a function of their estimated wealth—and could go home shaken and considerably poorer. At any given moment some 120,000 businessmen sit in Russian jails, mostly entirely innocent. This is the Putin way to promote small and medium-sized enterprises and to diversify and to develop the Russian economy.

3.11.1 The Sergei Magnitzky Case

Bill Browder's Hermitage Fund was also a (very small) minority shareholder of the mighty Gazprom. Thanks to the brazen thefts of Chernomyrdin and Rem Vyahkirev the purchase of its massively undervalued shares looked like a good deal. But when the thefts and misappropriations continued—through the ominous intermediate dealers and the theft of Sibneftegaz through Vyahkirev and his son at a sale price of 0.5% of its value in 1998, further depressing Gazprom's share value Browder once again decided to go public. In a skilful PR operation, he fed his documentation of corporate corruption and mismanagement in subsequent pieces to the Wall Street Journal, the Financial Times, the New York Times, Business Week and the Washington Post. With sufficient material, 500 articles would appear in Russian and 275 in the English language press after October 2000. This gave Putin a good reason to fire Vyahkirev and to replace him with Miller, who promised to recover the stolen assets. Gazprom's share price then multiplied by 100.[132]

Subsequently, Browder led similar campaigns against the state electricity supplier UES with its underpriced share sales to the oligarchs, and against Sberbank, whose shares were to be sold to insider friends. Putin stopped both and even issued a law against abusive share emissions.

At the time they both had identical interests, Putin wanted to break the power of the oligarchs, the gangsters and governors—for himself, and Browder wanted better shareholder value for his investors. Then his adversaries believed that he was in fact "Putin's man", since he dared to take on the richest oligarchs publicly with his anti-corruption campaign. So for a while at least to his own surprise, Browder seemed untouchable.[133]

As a fruit of his labours by 2005, his Fund was worth $4.5 billion. From hunter, however, he turned into prey. Putin's people in the FSB—in fact it

---

[131] Aslund. Op. cit., p. 60.
[132] Browder. Op. cit., p. 175.
[133] Ibid., p. 179.

was its Department K in charge of industrial counterespionage[134]—wanted it, kicked Browder unceremoniously out of the country, cancelled his visa and closed in. Having got the message he had to sell the Fund's assets quickly and discreetly before they lost their value. In this he succeeded before his offices in Moscow were spectacularly raided and materials confiscated as usual.[135]

Then a curious thing happened. He noticed that his Moscow company had been reregistered to a new owner. This is possible without the consent or even knowledge of the legitimate owner by paying hefty bribes to corrupt officials and judges with the protection of organized crime. The new "owner" can now engage in new commitments or dispose of the company's assets as he pleases.[136] As the raiders received backdated tax requests over $973 million, they quickly acknowledged them, but absurdly they also received a tax refund over $230 million of real paid taxes by Browder's company. In the safety of his London exile, Browder then engaged the best tax attorney in Moscow, 35-year-old Sergei Magnitzky, to recuperate the refund.[137] While Browder's collaborators could narrowly escape from Russia, his attorney was arrested and kept in the notorious Butyrka prison for 358 days, and after getting sick and being deprived of medical help, in November 2009 was beaten to death by prison wardens. Bowden's media campaign to liberate him had not impressed the Kremlin's power holders by one bit. Browder then mobilized not only the media, but also the US Congress for a bi-partisan reaction, a move which the Kremlin and the crooks of the FSB surely had not expected. With the help of senators Cardin (Democrat) and McCain (Republican) a bipartisan list of potential sanctions against the identified culprits was drafted in the first version of the Magnitsky Act. When the Russian Interior Ministry responded by distributing medals of merit to all culprits concerned, the US Congress woke up: This was obviously not an individual case of transgression, but a publicly endorsed case of systemic state criminality.[138] Subsequently, the list of culprits amongst the friends of Putin with asset freezes and visa bans was widened considerably and adopted in July 2012. And in the Kremlin elite's angry outcry the Senators by accident discovered that they had a powerful weapon at hand: to deny the friends of Putin the use and enjoyment of the fruits of their loot abroad. No Russian lobby in Washington was able to resist this. The Obama administration being

---

[134] Ibid., p. 220.
[135] Ibid., p. 214.
[136] Ibid., p. 229.
[137] Ibid., p. 251.
[138] Ibid., p. 347.

very hesitant, to say the least, was overruled. In the end, the Kremlin retaliated by banning the adoption of Russian orphans by US foster parents, the inhumanity of which speaks for itself, and Browder himself was sentenced to 9 years in absentia for tax fraud (what else could it be), with Interpol at Russia's request duly issuing a "Red Alert" for him.[139]

In sum, the motives of the mid-level (Lieutenant-Colonel) FSB crooks are understandable. After all they invested at least $100 million in bribes to steal the Hermitage Fund only to discover that it was only an empty shell as its assets had already been sold. So the tax fraud had to serve to recover their losses and to still make a profit. Yet there are still three puzzling elements in this tragic case.

First, why would a government want to protect three mid-level criminals in its own ranks who want to steal $230 million of its tax money (even if some of it is likely to be shared like in any syndicate with higher up)?

Second, why does Putin for such a trivial amount accept such a massive international reputational damage, which deters all future significant portfolio investment in Russia, when the country already suffers from decade-long capital outflows and a growing shortage of productive investment?

And thirdly, why would a promising young lawyer and family father sacrifice his life to have tax money rescued to a regime which is just about to torture him to death?

Again, as Churchill once said, Russia is a riddle, wrapped in a mystery inside an enigma.

3.11.2 The Case of Michael Calvey

The American Michael Calvey since 1994 ran a $3 billion investment fund, called Fond Baring Vostek. Unlike Browder he kept out of politics, did not undertake public shareholder-value anti-corruption campaigns, and did not invest in strategic industries like Gazprom, UES and Sberbank, but rather in young and IT enterprises, like new innovative supermarkets, online businesses like Ozon, an online bank and the internet company Yandex. Yet in February 2019 his fund was raided by the FSB. He was put under house arrest and 5 of his partners and colleagues put in jail. They were charged with fraud which could put them behind bars for up to 10 years.

The background was a shareholder dispute over the control and recapitalization of Vostochny Bank with minority shareholder Artem Avetisyan, an oligarch with personal connections to Putin and the FSB. Calvey alleged

---

[139] Ibid., p. 378.

that after an earlier merger of Vostochny Bank with Avetisyan's Junastrum Bank, Avetisyan had transferred valid assets out of the common bank and had replaced them with foul ones, while the latter countercharged with allegations of a €33 million theft by Baring Vostok. Normally shareholder disputes of this sort are settled by arbitration, at the time ongoing in London. Yet, Avetisyan opted for a quicker method known as "*raiderstvo*" by calling his FSB friends to settle the matter in his sense, aided by a corrupt judiciary. True enough, soon a court in Blagoveshchensk, 5000 miles East of Moscow awarded control of the bank to Avetisyan.[140]

Obviously, the system is tolerated, if not encouraged by the Kremlin, which does not like to see foreign funds investing uncontrolled in the country, and does not care whether a $3 billion fund is being ruined, nor for the long-term consequences of deterring FDI in Russia (whose economy would need this urgently) even further. The main message from the Kremlin as the principle of Putin's rule is once again enforced: No businessman whether foreign or domestic should ever feel safe.

The same actually applies to China, and they have a nice proverb for it: "Kill a chicken to scare the monkeys".

3.12 Economic Mismanagement in the Later Putin Years

As mentioned, during Putin's first term (2000–2004) the fruits of earlier reforms were harvested, boosted by high oil prices. Suddenly salaries were paid in time and pensions were increased. The good times lasted until 2008, which Putin used to consolidate his power. While he eliminated oligarchs, governors and communists as rivals, the rest of the society was still quite free, with the private sector accounting for 70% of GDP. Under PM Mikhael Kasyanov in the year 2003 200 taxes were replaced by a flat corporate tax of 13%, and progressive income taxes made to peak at 30%. Also, different employment funds were consolidated into a single social tax, and thereby reduced from 39.5 to 26% in the mid-2000s. In 2003, even the tax policy was abolished—temporarily—the main culprit to extort money, as the biggest single complaint of Russian businessmen, only—this being Russia—to re-emerge later under a new guise.

---

[140] "Schockstarre nach Verhaftung" *Frankfurter Allgemeine* 20.2.2019; "Putins Botschaft an die Investoren" *Frankfurter Allgemeine* 28.3.2019; Max Seddon "Calvey fraud case casts pall over Putin summit" *Financial Times* 7.6.2019.

Previously Primakov, though an old Communist and Prime Minister in the late Yeltsin years, had cut state subsidies, sliced pensions by half and insisted on cash payment of taxes, and slashed government expenditure by 17% of GDP in three years, which then went down from 48% of GDP (1997)—reflecting EU levels—to 31% of GDP (2000), reflecting US levels, where they remained.[141] So reform was possible in adversity. In the following, in retrospect rare golden decade in Russian economic history (comparable only to 1906–1914) monthly average wage income rose from $79 (2000) to $946 in 2013, only to fall to $550 in 2015–2016.

Yet this first and only decade of growth was essentially wasted, as nonetheless tax distortions and legal uncertainties continued, and a dysfunctional government-supported inefficient SOEs with arbitrary decisions. During 2006–2007 "national champions" were created on the model of the national monopolies Rosneft and Gazprom: United Aircraft Corporation, United Shipbuilding Corporation, Rosatom (the Atomic Energy Industry Complex), and Rostec, assembling 700 armament makers. The appointed executives unsurprisingly were all old friends of Putin.[142]

By 2006, Putin already started an industrial policy based on state interventions, centralized micro-management, state-directed investments with assorted subsidies, price and trade regulations, and protectionism with higher import tariffs and export taxes to aid autarchy and import substitution.

During his third informal term (2008–2012), with Medvedev formally in the presidency, the Kremlin's interventions reached a new dimension. Russia's GDP had risen from $200 billion (1999) to $1900 billion (2008), becoming the world's sixth-largest economy. Gazprom after the demise of the red directors by 2008 had become the world's most valuable company worth a market capitalization of $369 billion, with its CEO Miller predicting oil prices going up to $250 per barrel. In this perceived bonanza asset stripping and the crony capitalism of the friends of Putin stopped to know any bounds. The main actors were: Gennady Timchenko as the main trader of Russian oil, Arkandy Rotenberg as Gazprom's main subcontractor, and Yuri Kovalchuk, being in charge of Bank Rossiya. Boris Nemtsov, a former deputy Prime Minister, murdered in Moscow in March 2015, estimated their loot during 2004–2007 at $60 billion alone. Subsequently, as evident during the Hermitage affair, Gazprom's stock market value eroded to merely $46 billion by 2017, simply because the wealth of its assets became increasingly obscure with its profits being siphoned off.

---

[141] Aslund. Op. cit., p. 77.
[142] Ibid., p. 29.

As mentioned before, Russia's export dependency makes the country extremely vulnerable to external shocks, reinforced by the poor state of public and corporate governance. With SOEs dominating the economy there are simply no quickly reacting private enterprises and a mass of entrepreneurial SMEs which could absorb the crisis and redress it in due time. Ample foreign currency reserves and a state emergency fund are fine and fair, but as a statist approach simply not sufficient. This was already proven four times during Putin's rule and shortly before: In 1998, when the Asian financial crisis knocked out most Russian private banks and middle-income Russians, once again lost most of their savings, as the government defaulted on domestic bonds; in 2008 when the US sub-prime crisis struck; in 2014 when the oil price halved; and in 2020 when the Chinese-made corona virus infected the world economy and Russia engaged in an oil price war with Saudi Arabia (in vain attempting to squeeze out US fracking competitors from the market), which it could not win.

Russia again remains utterly dependent on the whims of global energy markets which she even as one of the largest—but unreliable, distrusted and isolated—player cannot control. When prices are high, oil and gas account two-thirds of exports, 50% of state revenues and 20% of GDP. Since two decades there is a lot of discussions but little effective action about diversifying the economy to allow more manufacturing and service jobs.

By 2017, foreign currency reserves stood at $420 billion (2017). The sovereign wealth funds: the Stabilization Fund and the National Welfare Fund, like in Norway, were meant for long-term investments and as a buffer against lower oil prices. Yet inevitably they turned into a slush fund for dubious Kremlin investments, like the re-capitalization of the ever loss-making state-owned VEB Bank.[143] Sitting smug on their $600 billion international currency and gold reserves, after the default of the Leman Brothers during the US subprime crisis, the Kremlin reacted with a big stimulus package. The budget went down from +4.1% of GDP (2000) to −6% (2001). $50 billion of the money went to bail out companies, as did $104 billion from the Reserve Fund, and $200 billion of Russia's currency reserves, while still keeping the ruble overvalued.

As a result, Russia's GDP crashed by −7.8% in 2009, more than any other G20 country. According to the IMF some $120 billion had fled the country, including its capital injection. The Russian government's support was mostly given to big state or oligarch companies, defined as "strategic", meaning in fact the least efficient and most unprofitable.[144]

---

[143] Ibid.; p. 86.
[144] Ibid., p. 87.

As stated before, the re-nationalization started with the seizure of Yukos in 2003. Sometimes SOEs purchased private companies. Sometimes they raided them with the help of law enforcement agencies, which typically would send a huge unpayable tax bill in advance.[145] There was cheap and plentiful funding by state banks and the unique right to buy given to SOEs. Yet there are no reliable Russian statistics on the current size of the state sector. They vary between 46% of GDP and 70% of GDP (2016–2017), the first being the more realistic, according to Åslund.[146] In Russia under Putin monopolistic or duopolistic state structures dominate the energy, rail transport, banking and armaments sectors, while mining, telecom, metal processing, retail, agriculture and services are mostly private. Put simply the state sector mostly covers declining industries, which by Putin's cronies are particularly badly run, since siloviki apparatchiks don't automatically turn into good corporate managers and as rent-seekers are little interested in investment, competition, innovation and entrepreneurship—as such quite similar to the worst oligarchs they had replaced—while the private sector continues to dominate the more dynamic branches of the economy to the extent that entrepreneurs have not yet fled the country.

Apart from commodities and arms, Russia is competitive only in nuclear reactors, steam boilers, rail freight wagons and steam turbines, which are mostly exported to former Soviet republics.[147] This sad picture is quite different to the wide-ranging export profile of the Korean chaebol and the Japanese keiretsu, which are the supposed role model for Russian industrial policies!

In 2009, Russia's accession to the WTO had been completed after almost two decades of negotiations with all partners, including the EU. Yet in the meantime, Putin had lost interest to comply with the agreed free trading non-discriminatory erga omnes rules applying to all WTO members. He rather wanted a customs union with Soviet ex-republics, which after some trial and error turned out to be the Eurasian Economic Union with currently five member states (apart from Russia: Belarus, Armenia, Kazakhstan and Kirgizstan).

---

[145] Ibid., p. 97.
[146] Ibid., p. 98.
[147] Ibid., p. 186.

3.12.1 The Riches of Putinism

It was only after 2004 that Putin and his cronies became really rich, with Gazprom being the main source. As a result, in Russia 110 billionaires (including Putin's cronies) control 35% of national wealth, while 50% of Russian households enjoyed a "wealth" of $870 or below.[148] Again this is a civilized European country, not a Third World petro-state, like Angola, Nigeria or Saudi Arabia. Obviously, it is also not a functional state. Reportedly Putin's share of all crony deals was 50%, the logic being, why should he allow them to get rich without any inhibitions and get nothing for himself.

But where did the money go? The Panama papers, for instance, mention Igor Putin, a cousin, Putin's butcher Petr Kolbin and his cellist friend Sergei Roldugin with $2 billion, for instance, of which he appeared genuinely unaware of.[149] This is small fry and clearly they are strawmen. The money flows firstly via Cyprus, the Channel Islands, Malta, Bermuda and the Isle of Man into some twenty to thirty shell companies in the Caribbean, the Virgin Islands and Cayman Islands mostly. Once laundered it is invested in anonymous limited liability companies in Delaware, Nevada, Wyoming and South Dakota—using the "attorney-client privilege" for subsequent purchases for real estate in Miami, Palm Beach, L.A. and New York, including the Trump properties which are to the taste of Arab sheiks and Russian oligarchs, and in the UK. Financially, of course, these investments are dead weight and only incur maintenance costs.

Basically, we witness a purposefully designed neofeudal, patrimonial and plutocratic system, in which democracy, the division of powers, the rule of law and property rights have been demolished. It is easy to argue for more productive investments, to restore local self-government, to implement a stronger anti-monopoly policy and to shift military expenditure more productively to health, education and infrastructure. Yet this is not Kremlin policy.

According to rough estimates to maintain client regimes in Belarus, Transnistria, Abkhazia, Southern Ossetia, the Crimea and the Donbas amounts to at least to some $4 billion per year. Add on the military expenditure of 2% of GDP per year. So in total, some 4% of GDP are wasted unproductively in a country with the economic size equivalent to the GDP of Spain and which has serious demographic and competitive problems which remain unaddressed.

---

[148] Dawisha. Op. cit., p. 321.
[149] Ibid., p. 198.

In the end in an autocratic rule in place since 2010, it all boils down to something very banal, which we know since Czarist history: The character of the ruler himself. George Bush apparently has seen into his eyes and saw his soul.[150] Yet Putin is a judoka and not a chess player, hence a risk-taker. A chess player carefully reflects every move according to pre-thought strategy, but a judoka uses the right moment to distract his opponent, to catch him off-guard, to throw him off balance and then to squeeze him mercilessly until he throws the towel. The rules are win or lose. "Win-win" or compromises are not foreseen. No wonder that this is Putin's favourite sport.

References

1. Aslund A (2019) Russia's crony capitalism. Yale University Press, New Haven
2. Belton C (2020) Putin's people. How the KGB took back Russia and then took on the West. William Collins. London
3. Dawisha K (2014) Putin's Cleptocracy. Who owns Russia? Simon & Schuster. New York
4. Haug R (2007) Kreml AG. Hohenheim, Stuttgart/Leipzig
5. Litvinenko A (2007) Blowing up Russia. The Secret Plot to bring back KGB Terror. Gibson Square, London
6. Mommsen M, Nussberger A (2007) Das System Putin. CH Beck, Munich
7. Moore M (2003) A time to die. The Untold Story of the Kursk Tragedy. Crown Publishers, New York
8. Politkovskaya A (2005) La Russie selon Poutine. Gallimard, Paris
9. Rothacher A (2008) Stalins langer Schatten. Medwedjews Rußland und der postsowjetische Raum. Ares, Graz
10. Truscott P (2005) Putin's progress. Pocket Books, London
11. Wolton T (2008) Le KGB au pouvoir. Le systeme Poutine. Buchet Chastel, Paris

---

[150]One of my senior colleagues met Putin in Moscow, when the EU and Russia were still talking at top level. He observed that his eyes were "shifty" and judged him emotionally unstable.

4

Putin's Budget Policies

Russian public budgets are generally credited to be on the prudent, conservative side—compared to the US, Japanese and Eurozone recklessness—often being balanced, with little public debt, external indebtedness in manageable proportions and—having learned the lessons of the 1998 default and the 2008–2009 and 2014–2015 recessions—with sovereign funds and foreign exchange reserves ready for a rainy day.

Yet realities are not quite as rosy. State revenues have declined over the past 10 years, reflecting declining oil prices (which only during 2008 and 2011–2014 stood at or above $100/barrel) and de facto economic stagnation with growth rates remaining persistently at around 1.5% p.a. since the recession of 2014–2015, with little prospects of improvements. With inflation rates of 16% (2015) to 4% (2018), real incomes and savings have declined, offering no room for revenue growth.

Prior to the presidential elections of March 2018, expenditure for politically less sensitive policy fields like education, health, infrastructure and economic subsidies was cut. Military procurement decisions were delayed until the oil price had recovered somewhat in 2017. Yet the urgently needed pension reform was delayed until after the election, as the Kremlin understood well the power and potential fury of pensioners.[1]

---

[1] Like in Japan or Germany pensioners in Russia in great numbers vote regularly (unlike youngsters) for the parties in power, provided that their pensions and health expenditures are paid generously and promptly. They cannot improve their lot through additional qualifications, job changes, search for promotions or do harder work (except for moonlighting jobs which are frequent in Russia's informal

As arbitrage for shrinking expenditure is politically charged, budget decisions have been centralized and are taken by the Kremlin. While influential MPs may lobby for their special interests, the Duma since years approves the Kremlin drafts unchanged with little debate. Also, there are no legal checks against any spending decisions decided by the Kremlin. The budgets for regional administrations are similarly largely centrally decided.

With Russia's commodity-based economic structure and her external dependency on the oil price, budgetary policies must remain flexible to react to unforeseen shocks and sudden downturns, particularly since the reserve funds, which proved so valuable in the crisis of 2009 are nearly exhausted. The Kremlin has reacted with discretionary vagueness in budget positions and transparency by drawing on the resources of state-controlled enterprises which receive instructions to fulfil certain public tasks either at home or abroad.

4.1 The Figures and Prospects

In a formal sense, Russia's state quota is relatively low at 35.2% of GDP, consolidating overlapping public expenditure. In principle, the federal budget spends 17.8% of GDP, the regions and municipalities 11.7%, and social insurance 11.6%. In total, consolidated public spending stood at Euro 485 billion in 2017. If we, however, add on the turnover of state-controlled enterprises the state quota is increased by another 29–30% of GDP, clearly making Russia the most state-dominated developed country.[2]

During the period of high oil prices (i.e. 2008 and 2011–2014) revenues from gas and oil counted for 50% of the federal budget and for roughly 30% of the consolidated budget. In 2018, their share in the much-reduced federal budget (reduced by one-third compared to its peak in 2007) stood at 33%, and in the consolidated budget (which shrunk by one-fifth compared to 2007) at 17.5%. This is not quite the dimension of Saudi Arabia, the UAR and Iraq, where oil finances 80% of the budget, but Russia's dependence as a rentier state is obvious. Also, it should be kept in mind that the gas export revenues are basically used to cross-subsidize cheap gas prices for Russian consumers and industry. As the Russian saying goes: Oil is for exports and gas is for heating. The Russian oil and gas exporters are cushioned by the

---

sector), but mostly depend on politically set transfer incomes. They also have time at their hands, are quickly mobilized and keenly aware of their interests—which hence get preferential treatment at the expense of future generations.

[2]In the EU the state quota varies between 38% (Ireland) and 58% (Finland and France).

effects of lower oil prices by the fact that usually the ruble devalues at the same time. Their production and transmission costs are denominated in ruble and their export earnings are paid in a re-valued US$. Hence, they are expected to continue their extra-budgetary political roles.

Regional budgets are financed mostly by income and corporate gains taxes, which equally shrunk during the recessions and the subsequent stagnation. Yet they have to comply with statutory expenses, like the salaries for public employees, which Putin had massively increased in 2012. Given the vast discrepancies of economic performance and income levels between Russian regions, their public indebtedness varies greatly between Chukotka, Chita, Aga Buryatia, Saratov, Karelia, Pskov and Smolensk on the one hand, where public debt exceeds 100% of annual revenue (with a corresponding debt servicing burden at relatively high interest rates), and the more frugal and resource-rich regions of the North (Nenets), West Siberia (Tyumen, Khant-Mansysk) and Sakhalin on the other, where debts stand at less than 10% (2015).[3] These debts are mostly (i.e. at 93%) financed by the state-owned Sberbank and the VTB and rely on state guarantees.

The indebtedness of the Russian state itself stands at a virtuous 13.8% of GDP. Again, the picture is far from complete, as state-controlled enterprises are indebted at 102% of GDP. Most of the debt is owed by state-owned banks who also had to take over private competitors with their large portfolios of non-performing loans. These fiscal risks are currently unquantifiable.

Thanks to Western sanctions Russia's total external debt—public and private—were reduced to US$ 530 billion with her foreign currency reserves standing at US$ 450 billion (2018), enough to pay 19 months of imports.

The vagaries of the oil price apart, the prospect of enduring economic stagnation caused by the lack of economic reforms and industrial competitiveness and the rapid decline of the population at working age (from 84.2 million (2017) to 77.9 million (2024)) is likely to create a fiscal gap of structurally growing expenditures—notably for pensions and health—and shrinking revenues. Russia's long-term annual fiscal gap is estimated to reach 13.6% of GDP after 2050, and is thus higher than those of currently highly indebted countries like Greece, Belgium, Japan and the US (10% each).[4] As a result, the World Bank estimates that Russia's public debt could reach 116% by 2050 in the best scenario (depending on demography, productivity and the oil price) and 250% in the worst. The alternative would be to ask citizens to pay higher taxes every year, to reduce military expenditure, foreign wars and support to client regimes, and to work longer years.

---

[3] Alexander Libman «Russische Regionen» SWP Studie, Berlin November 2016, p. 15.
[4] Janis Kluge «Rußlands Staatshaushalt unter Druck» SWP Studie, Berlin July 2018, p. 13.

Again, according to the World Bank, oil production will shrink from 548 million tons (2016) to 436 million tons (2050), which is more or less expert consensus given the exhaustion of older developed fields in Western Siberia and the Urals and the difficulties and costs to access less productive new fields further afield and in the Arctic waters.

After the fiscal disasters of the 1990s, the pride of the Finance Ministry had been the reserves accumulated during the 2000s, with Norway, the UAR and Saudi Arabia as role models. Helas, tempi passati. One of the two funds was entirely used up to cover running budget deficits. The other as "welfare fund" supposed to finance future pensions was mostly spent on the Sochi 2014 Winter Olympics, other infrastructure and risky state company deals, with little liquidity left. The rules of fiscal frugality introduced by Alexei Kudrin in 2004 fell regularly victim to the Kremlin's two ruling factions—one pushing for social spending—meaning pensions mostly—for popular appeasement, the other for military expenditure and short victorious foreign wars.

4.2 Budget Politics

In 2014, Putin announced a moratorium on tax increases, lasting until his re-election in 2018. In the meantime, the Finance Ministry tried to combat the receding flow of revenues with little dirty tricks, like using funds paid and earmarked to build up a capital stock for future pensions to be paid out for current pensions. Or to "privatize" shares of Rosneft and Bashneft to ultimately another state-owned holding called Rosimushchestvo and to spend the proceeds. Also, the taxes on oil extraction and gasoline were increased.

On the savings side, the 2018–2020 budget plan heroically foresaw cuts among the two largest spenders: social and military at around—17% each. Both legitimize Putin's rule but contribute little to sustainable economic development. Pensions count for 80% of the social spending and reflect popular expectations and experiences with the Soviet "welfare state": the tacit trade off of transfer payments and basic care in return for political abstinence. Yet all of these transfers were hardly able to affect Russia's official poverty rate, which remained high at 14% (2018),[5] affecting 20 million people, mostly large families and singles with an income of 157 Euro per month or less. Although the basic pension stands at only 129 Euro per month, most pensioners are much better off. With a share of 22% of the total population,

---

[5] World Bank. "Preserving Stability, Doubling Growth, Halving Poverty—How?" Russia economic report, November 2018, p. 27.

they account only for 12% of the poor,[6] unsurprisingly given their electoral importance. In 2016, contributions to pension funds were at 4.8% of GDP, while expenditures amounted to 7.0%. The resulting gap to be financed from the budget is set to raise to 3.3% of GDP by 2024.

Official defence expenditure shows a lot of variation over the years. In 2011, it stood at 2.5% of GDP. It peaked in 2016 with 4.4% of GDP, and since went down to 3.1% (2017), amounting to 43.3 billion Euro, with further cuts planned towards 2.6% by 2020. Yet, SIPRI estimates that in 2017, a further 1% of GDP of military expenditure (13.8 billion Euro) was covered in the health, education and social (military pensions) budgets. After the war against Georgia of 2008 in 2010, a 10-year military modernization programme was decided, with a total of 472 billion Euro (representing 41% of the Russian GDP of 2010) to be spent on modern hardware until 2020. In 2012 also, salaries were increased to attract quality professional soldiers. The follow-up programme (2018–2027) foresees military expenditures at a total of 288 billion Euro—nominally on a par of those of its predecessor programme. Yet in real terms—net of inflation—it is only half of it, reflecting 20.6% of the GDP of 2017.[7]

There are necessarily only very imprecise estimates for the costs of the wars in Syria, which is being run on the cheap—i.e. destocking old bombs—at 3 billion Euros for the two years October 2015–September 2017, and in the Donbas—military expenditure only—at 800 million Euro for March–December 2015 and at 1 billion US$ for the year 2015. These expenses, if true, are relatively minor compared to total military spending in 2017 which amounted to 43.3 billion Euros.

Decisions on military spending are taken in camera by a military-industrial commission composed of men with overlapping memberships in the military, the security apparatus, presidential administration and the state's arms industry (with its 2 million workers and rare export competitiveness in India, China, Vietnam, Indonesia and even Turkey). A lead character is defence minister Sergei Shoigu.

Note that not only all military expenditure but also large chunks of "federal affairs" and economic spending of the federal budget are the subject of secrecy laws and off-limits to public and Court of Auditors' scrutiny. Like in the Elysee[8] there is also a confidential presidential reserve for discretionary spending. More important are the funds of state-owned and publicly controlled companies. Partly they have to deliver their dividends formally to

---

[6]Kluge. Op. cit., p. 20.
[7]Kluge, Op. cit., p. 26.
[8]This is used i.e. for secret service operations which are none of Parliament's business.

the federal budget. At the same time, their Kremlin-appointed management has to spend and invest at their master's will (like for instance infamously Gazprom Media buying up the media landscape). This applies to Aeroflot, Russian Mail, Russian Railways, Moscow Metro, Mosfilm, the armaments holding Rostec, 70% of the banks, Transneft, Gasprom, Rosneft etc. As Gazprom and Rosneft have to deliver most of their profits to the state holding Rosneftegas, controlled by Igor Setchin, he in turn has a shadow budget of 8.2 billion Euros (2016) at his disposal. According to a public speech by Putin this was spent to finance vaguely termed research for airplane, turbine, shipbuilding and power station development[9] for unspecified results and returns, whether military, dual-use, civilian, whatever.

4.3 Conclusion

Even with a worsening global economic outlook and economic growth barely above 1.3% for Russia in 2019, a Corona-induced fall of −6 to −7% in 2020, and a very uncertain outlook for 2021, there are little prospects for an immediate financial and fiscal collapse. Yet contrary to popular fama, Russian public finances are remarkably unsolid and unsustainable on the long run. It is striking that the Kremlin, largely insulated from public pressures and any effective opposition, seems to be aware of the implications—made crystal clear by Alexey Kudrin's discarded reform proposals—yet proceeds fairly undisturbed on its path towards an inevitable fiscal crash in the mid to long term (2025+). As Putin has had his presidential term extended by a more or less faked referendum in 2020–2036, he in difference to democratic incumbents, who are more concerned about the short-term outlook to the next election day, should be more interested in the long term, yet does not seem to care. In this unfortunately the Russians are not alone.

References

1. Kluge J (2018) Rußlands Staatshaushalt unter Druck. SWP, Berlin
2. Libman J (2016) Russische Regionen. SWP, Berlin
3. World Bank (2018) Preserving Stability, Doubling Growth, Halving Poverty—how?. Washington D.C, WB

---

[9] Kluge, Op. cit., p. 40.

5

The Russian Petro-State

5.1 The History

The foundations for Russia's oil industry were laid when Russia in 1813 captured Baku from the Persians. Robert Nobel, who arrived in 1873, then organized the shipment of kerosene to Moscow and St. Petersburg with a mix of tank ships, pipelines and railroad cars, while John D. Rockefeller's Standard Oil with high tariffs was squeezed out of the market. Yet Rothschild could build the Transcaucasian Railway from Baku to Batumi (purchased in 1911 by Shell) to facilitate exports via the Black Sea.[1] As a result by 1897, Russia and the USA accounted for 95% of the world's oil production. Early on the oil fields became a hotbed of Communist agitation. First strikes occurred in Batumi in 1901, followed by some in Baku in 1903. In 1905, two-thirds of oil wells were destroyed. 1918 nationalized by the Bolsheviks, they were successively occupied by the Turks and by the British in support of an independent Azeri state. Yet when the Bolsheviks retook them in 1920, oil production had collapsed. Lenin's NEP in 1921 allowed the return of foreigners. Once the production recovered by 1930, most were expulsed by Stalin. Obviously a recurrent pattern: witness the expropriation of Shell and Exxon Mobil on Sakhalin in 2006! By 1940, 75% of Soviet oil exports went to Germany, while in Italy, their import share stood at 48%. Obviously, ideology was not a problem for both sides. Once the Baku yields

---

[1] Marshall Goldman. *Oilopoly. Putin, Power and the Rise of the New Russia.* Oxford: One World 2008, p. 20.

began to decline, luckily oil was discovered in Tatarstan in 1929 in fields between the Volga and the Southern Urals. Due to the shortage of drilling equipment, they were developed only after WWII. During the Cold War, the West employed an embargo of advanced technologies, which delayed but did not prevent the development of the Western Siberian fields until 1968, which had been discovered in 1953. Unsurprisingly inefficiencies and waste proliferated also in energy production. Steel pipes were of poor quality, shallow holes were drilled in large numbers, too much water was injected, and natural gas as a side product usually just flared off, since the Ministry of the Petroleum Industry was not in charge of gas and, hence, did not care.[2] The Soviet Union used its oil exports mainly as a source of revenue to pay for food imports. By 1975, it had become the world's oil largest exporter, but remained uninterested to cooperate neither with the OPEC cartel nor with the "seven sisters", the then still mighty Western oil companies. Then, as now, it acted as a spoiler, expanding production when others cut back.

The collapse of the Soviet Union was followed by one of the world's greatest national depressions. The Soviet oil industry was one of the main victims, as its output dropped by half. Today, again together with Saudi Arabia, it has become the world's largest producer, counting for 13% of the world's and 22% of non-OPEC oil production. Indifference to the Soviet Union, Russia is more dependent on oil export revenues than in the Soviet days when its oil and gas were mainly bartered to East European satellite countries in return for their manufactured products. For the Kremlin, they have become the centre for power and wealth.

Yet indifference to the cliché of inherited wealth of Soviet oil as a "comfortable system of rents", also the Russian oil industry needs constant renewal and reinvestment, even more so than elsewhere given the fields' harsh natural conditions.[3] With the breakup of the Soviet system, the industry managed to escape partially from the state. In fact, the 1990s as the decade of the weakness of the state has allowed the Russian oil industry to restructure, to privatize and to modernize without the bureaucratic hindrances of today. Yet the sector proved too strategic. State control was reimposed in the 2000s with the semi-nationalization of Yukos and reinforced by the crash and recession of 2008. Ever since, a period of constant struggle between state and industry over resources, strategic orientations and profits followed.

It is a curious statistical fact of Russian oil and gas production, that they stand equal at 500mt per year. While Russia exports 3/4 of its oil, it exports

---

[2] Ibid., p. 42.
[3] Thane Gustafson. *Wheel of fortune. The battle for oil and power in Russia.* Cambridge, Mass: Harvard University Press. 2012, p. 2.

only 1/3 of its gas, of which most is consumed domestically at artificially low prices for industry and consumers. In a nutshell, gas exports are used to cross-subsidize the energy-intensive domestic industry and people's electricity and heating bills, the oil export revenue is used to fill not only the Kremlin's coffers to the extent of up to 41% (2011) of the federal budget, financing pensions, salaries but also foreign wars (from Ukraine, Georgia to Syria), prestige projects and white elephants from the Sochi Olympics, soccer stadia for the EM 2018, the futuristic reconstruction of Grozny and the Kerch Bridge, the modernization and re-nuclearization of the military and last but not least funding for the many siloviki friends of the Kremlin. As a rule of the thumb at $80 to the barrel, the Kremlin is flush with cash, at $40 per barrel, it can barely break even, and at $10 per barrel as during most of the Yeltsin years it faces bankruptcy. In other words, in the absence of an internationally competitive manufacturing industry, Russia has become a petrostate depending on the whims and vagaries of world prices, possibly even less cushioned than Saudi Arabia, Oman or the UAE. Yet with oil prices above $60 per barrel for most of the 2010s, the Kremlin elites felt that enough wealth had filtered down to raise most citizens income levels and consumption, leaving the more serious problems of a decaying physical (roads, ports, airports) and social infrastructure (education and hospitals) aside, so as to become "cocksure and complacent".[4]

What happened during the 2008–2009 crisis was that the state took money and resources away from the only cash-rich segment of the economy and transferred them via state-mandated investment, welfare and subsidy programmes back to the rest of the economy. As Gustafson rightly points out, this inevitably led to waste and corruption and induced a long-term dependence on energy (and notably oil) rents, as special interests groups congregated around these honey pots and as an ageing population was in need of stable rents. No other than Putin already in 2001 in his second "State of the Federation" speech warned of the consumptive seduction of oil and raw material exports and the dangers of rent seeking. Rather the Russian oil industry focused during the following decade to compete for the control of assets and rents rather than to work for the modernization of the industry. Equally the fiscal system remained exploitative, constrained reinvestment and stifled innovation. In the global oil, business Russia's rent-oriented managerial class missed out on the ongoing technological and managerial revolution.[5] Russia is not the only victim of the "Dutch disease" of boom and bust tied

---

[4]Ibid., p. 4.
[5]Ibid., p. 5.

to world commodity prices, triggering high inflation and wild currency fluctuations. This basically makes its non-oil and non-gas exports uncompetitive and non-renumerative, and, in any event, too unpredictable for its returns to invest.

As Gustafson rightly insists, the Soviet Union was not a petro-state. Rather it was an inefficient industrial and technological power, servicing the needs of its military-industrial machine. With the collapse of the Russian economy, being uncompetitive in manufactured products on the world market, after 1990 natural resources, mainly oil and gas were left to prop up the budget and urban consumption.[6] In difference to petro-states in the 3rd world, like Angola, Nigeria or Venezuela, Russia has a professional administration and a home-grown oil industry, which is backed by a large number of well-educated engineers and technologists. After 2000, it also adopted frugal fiscal policies, paid back its foreign debt and, as described in the previous chapter, accumulated sovereign wealth funds for a rainy day, sufficient to the extent that this does not turn into a rainy season.

5.2 The Oil Industry

Russia inherited from the Soviet Union a handful of giant Western Siberian oil fields, which accounted for most of the production. They were, however, damaged by political pressures to maximize output and the lack of modernizing investment. After a peak in 1987 with 570 million tons, production almost halved until 1996 when it bottomed at 301 million tons. It was then mostly refined into fuel oil, diesel and low octane gasoline, to be burnt in one of the most wasteful energy economies. Exports went only to satellite countries to prop up their economies. With the collapse of the Soviet empire, oil exports quickly became the major source of cash and government revenue, thus, fuelling the economic recovery under Putin after 2000. Yet the exploitation of the old fields is not going to last. New oil fields to be developed will be deeper, higher in pressure, geographically more complex, higher in Sulphur content and more remote. For this technological challenge, the industry is only partly prepared, and certainly not for Arctic offshore projects.[7]

Russian operators are typically large entities in remote areas, where they control their oil fields, build housing and facilities, their feeder pipelines and increasingly also refineries and gas stations. This "gigantism" has squeezed out

---

[6]Ibid., p. 6.
[7]Ibid., p. 10.

innovative independent service companies, including foreign ones, which had been instrumental in the turnaround of the Russian oil industry after 1990.

Russian oil men had been isolated from the global economy and their Anglophone traders and lawyers. They were petroleum engineers or geologists. The operation of foreign companies on Russian soil, their foreign capitalist ways and the need to buy foreign equipment was unsurprisingly seen with suspicion and resentment. Clearly, they wanted to retain ownership and control of the major assets. Getting rich quickly was resented by the blend of a Marxist heritage and of traditional Russian values. Russian "oil generals", who ran the oil fields and the refineries, were paternalist in their orientation. They felt responsible for their workers, their housing, heating, electricity, clinics and schools in their oil towns, which, in Western business ideology, were unproductive assets to be axed at the first round of cost-cutting. Like in the rest of the Russian economy, informal networks of mutual trust—a heritage of the Soviet era—given the defects of the legal system play an important role in survival, protection, information and scarce goods. For Western thinking, this is the source of corruption and collusion.

Curiously the oil industry was sold to the oligarchs under Yeltsin—except for the pipeline system. Yet the gas industry and parts of the electricity generation remained state property. Post-Yeltsin, obviously as the fate of Mikhail Khodorkovsky, showed, despite all new legal codes protecting private property, the state, backed up by FSB structures, retains the ultimate control over this strategic sector. Once the leading privatized oil companies like Yukos (owned by Khodorkovsky), Sibneft (owned by Roman Abramovich) and Lukoil by 2003/4 had achieved the recovery of the Russian oil industry by applying modern management and technologies, the state with tough new tax laws and with the help of state-owned Rosneft proceeded to recover the oil rents and to destroy Yukos, pretending to prevent foreign takeovers.[8] Rising world oil prices and growing oil output had made the lure of these in 1996 cheaply acquired companies simply irresistible. They were no longer seen not only as necessary for the national economic survival of the revived Greater Russia but also as key to personal power and wealth. Nobody shed tears for the dispossessed oligarchs. Yet with taxes as high at 90%, the industry understandably held back new investments, as it requires more and more capital to develop the more difficult fields. While some new fields went on stream, the old oil fields in Western Siberia appeared to be heading for terminal decline. On top of normal taxes Russian oil and gas companies have to pay informal taxes in the form of bribes or social contributions to their localities. Also,

---

[8] Ibid., p. 18.

their production costs are higher since purchase of equipment and services is done through non-transparent processes of interrelated companies.[9] Hence, by blocking the modernization of the oil industry and plundering it by far the biggest cash cow the Kremlin in the long-run risks to cut off its main revenues and to destabilize the country during the Yeltsin years.

5.2.1 The Soviet Oil Industry and Its Decline

As mentioned earlier, Russia's oil industry was born around 1900 in Baku. In the 1940 and 1950s, it migrated to the Lower Volga Urals (Tatarstan and Bashkirstan). When the giant oil fields in the Arctic swamps of the River Ob Basin were discovered, it moved to Western Siberia, to the fields North of its oil capital Tyumen in the 1970 and 1980s. Production and transportation of the crude oil were under the control of the Ministry of Oil in Moscow. Refining belonged to the Ministry of Oil Refining and Petrochemicals. Domestic distribution was done by the monopoly of Transneft products and exports by an agency of the Ministry of Foreign Affairs. Export proceeds all landed in the USSR Bank for Foreign Trade (Vnestorgbank), of which the upstream producers saw very little. Central planners in Moscow dictated the production targets and allocated supplies and manpower. Yet the coordination with suppliers on the spot (like electricity, housing, road building, other services and parts) was done by the regional apparatus of the Communist Party. The regional party secretary also had to mediate between Moscow's demands for more oil and the oil men lobbying for lower targets. Successful engineers would be promoted to political managers. They lived in a non-economic world of administratively set targets. Huge company towns would be built into the tundra. As outsourcing to service companies was not done, the production companies had to do all of this works in-house and employed tens of thousands of workers for the purpose. Costs played no role. When fields were young and world oil prices high (as between 1973 and 1980), this could be ignored. But when in the early 1980s, world oil prices and Soviet output fell, the Soviet government had to increase investments to offset the revenue loss. Oil fields became smaller and more costly to develop.

Working and housing conditions were incredibly tough. The Ob Basin in summer turned into a lake and in winter, it was deep frozen. Drilling equipment was usually substandard. Yet there was pressure for ever more drilling and water flooding to extract the oil, while little care was spent on

---

[9] Ibid., p. 25.

well maintenance, which as a result aged prematurely. Falsified data to cheat the hierarchy were also a common problem.[10]

Gorbachev's reforms in 1987 freed enterprises from administrative control, yet they failed to set up a functional price system based on supply and demand. Company directors competed for workers and scarce supplies. The West Siberian oil industry was particularly hard hit, as workers left and the supply of spare parts collapsed. The domestic oil price remained frozen while production costs went up. Debts and non-payments spread in the industry. When in 1988 Gorbachev allowed "cooperatives" to engage in foreign trade, refined oil found its way by rail or tanker across the borders benefitting from the huge differential between domestic and global prices. Well-connected foreign trade officials and refinery operators were best placed to benefit. Also, crude oil (officially belonging to the state) was bartered for food and necessities, creating a market for independent traders of all shades. Further, joint ventures with foreign oil service companies were allowed and were permitted to export as well. Now also the crude oil producers could get into the export business. The first hundreds of millions of oil money were stashed in foreign bank accounts.

Gorbachev in the meantime cut and merged most ministries and destroyed the Communist party apparatus, which in the regions still had held the economy together. The war between Armenia and Azerbaijan also cut off the supplies of oil equipment from Baku. In 1986, world oil prices collapsed, and by 1989, the Soviet Union faced bankruptcy. Fearing that the country would face an oil shortage, a 40% export tax was slapped on exports. Oil producers reacted by cutting down production and exports, which made Russia's financial crisis only worse.[11]

After Yeltsin's election in June 1991, six months later, the Soviet Union was dissolved. The former Soviet ministries were merged with the second-rated ministries of the Russian Federation. Many of the more dynamic officials left to strike luck with the new opportunities. Others benefitted by staying inside. YegorGaidar as Prime Minister in January 1992 started his shock therapy with the decontrol of prices (again except for those for energy). State spending was cut, privatization started, and with imperfect markets inflation shot up. As costs went up and sales prices—with output only partially paid— remained frozen the situation of the energy sector worsened rapidly further. Salaries and suppliers could no longer be paid. Debts kept piling up. Access to hard currency through exports became a matter of survival. Officially oil exports were still tightly controlled by the state. Yet more and more ways were

---

[10] Ibid., p. 40.
[11] Ibid., p. 48.

found around it, even though this was understandably most difficult for the upstream producers of raw oil.[12] In West Siberia, the public industry association broke up, and seven production areas declared themselves independent or even private under the command of their previous director generals. They felt encouraged by Yeltsin's calls for regional empowerment and decentralization. Tyumen's governor declared his province the rightful owner of all of its mineral wealth, but so did some of its component regional okrugs in the Far North, which were helped by local geologists stranded there. Yet beyond mere survival, the main challenge for the industry was to keep up the repair of old oil wells—there were plenty of crews in the field—and to drill for new wells to keep up for fresh supplies. All this began to slide dramatically after 1990.

Meanwhile in Moscow, the largely defunct oil ministry tried to create a national oil company called "Rozneftegaz", which would sensibly merge all 51 companies active as upstream producers, refiners and distributors and be run as their joint property. But since it smelled like the capitalist resurrection of a Soviet fossil, the project was shot down, as the spirit of independence among the oil generals had already become too great.

In difference to oil, the gas market with its Gazprom monopoly was never broken up. With Russia controlling 40% of world reserves, it was simply too important. As a source of primary energy, the share of domestic gas consumption during the Yeltsin years (1990–2000) had increased from 43 to 52%. In difference to oil, gas is easy to produce but difficult to transport and it has to reach consumers by pipe mostly. As a sector by necessity, it is more centralized and mainly an issue of transportation and distribution. In Soviet days, big trunk pipelines were built to major consumers like large energy consuming factories and power plants, mainly leading from West Siberia to Western Russia and East Europe. Exports were handled on the basis of long-term contracts by the Ministry of Foreign Trade.[13] The old gas ministry led by its ex-minister Viktor Chernomyrdin (vice minister during 1982–85, and minister until 1989) retained control over Gazprom's transport monopoly and even managed to get the lucrative export monopoly in 1991. With little difficulty, Putin then after 2000 reasserted direct Kremlin control of the gas sector.

---

[12] Ibid., p. 54.
[13] Ibid., p. 58.

5.2.2 The Battle for the Oil Industry

Assets soon were massively stripped and tunnelled to newly sprung up private structures, banks, cooperatives, joint ventures and also to organized crime, which was present also in the oil cities of Tyumen province, pushing aside the legitimate businessmen. While the big oil companies with their huge infrastructure were beyond the gangsters' reach, they attempted to control the markets, the hotels, the airports, the train stations of the oil towns and the barter trade with oil, between them, bloody gang wars ensued. Still the oil companies had to come to a modus Vivendi with them since public authorities, including the police and the FSB were of no help.[14]

The first vertically integrated private oil company (assembling downstream production from wells, refining, distribution to consumers and exports) with the help of the reformers in Moscow was Lukoil of VagitAlekperov, a freshly appointed deputy minister for the oil production. In November 1992, Yeltsin permitted the creation three such integrated private oil companies, next to Lukoilthey were Yukos and Surgutneftegaz, in which the state would hold shares of 45% for the next 3 years at least. The three companies, however, did not cover the Russian oil industry in total. All those disparate sites and processing facilities left out were assembled in a "temporary" state holding called Rosneft. In the absence of proper enforceable statutes and shareholder rights, all four companies had enormous problems to assert control over their unruly independent-minded subsidiaries, whose Soviet-era oil generals had their own business ideas on how to make money.[15]

While the 50,000 km of Russia's impressive oil pipeline system were and are still owned by the state-owned Transneft (originally the transport department of the Oil Ministry), which controls and monitors the flows closely, there were plenty of other ways to let refined products leave the country by rail, truck or river tanker. Formally export licenses had to be granted, sometimes in return for political favours like the "Century" group back in 1991 for one million tons in exchange for supporting the Yeltsin camp during the failed coup attempt.[16] But this was peanuts compared with Gaidar's estimate that about half of West Siberian production, that is, 150 million tons, during 1991 had left the country illegally. This was not without risks, as criminal gangs were involved and insisted on steep commissions.

By 1992, with the Alfa Group, led by Mikhael Fridmann, the first future oligarch moved into the oil-exporting business. He had first started with sugar

---

[14]Ibid., p. 67.
[15]Ibid., p. 78.
[16]Ibid., p. 81.

and tea imports, and then made lots of money in buying Russian foreign debt at deep discounts abroad and later redeeming it at par at the Russian treasury. The battle for exports was fought in Moscow ministries and with politicians for licenses, export terminals, access to pipelines and customs posts. No one was really interested in the domestic market, as most private, agricultural or industrial customers could not pay. The only place where there was cash, the gasoline stations, was largely controlled by organized crime, which, however, as mentioned, was equally mostly interested in export smuggling where hard currency could be gained. One of those small traders was a certain Roman Abramovich, then aged 25, later owner of Sibneft, who, in 1992, organized diesel tank trucks to move from Ukta refinery to Baltic ports. One year later, however, he had forged close links with West Siberia's upstream producer Noiabriskneftegaz and became one of West Siberia's leading crude oil exporters.

Infamously in 1995, Vladimir Potanin conceived the "loans for shares" scheme. The state offered oil (and other) assets as collateral for loans since almost no one was paying taxes anymore (in fact only an estimated 3 million out of 70 million Russian employees did so, least of them the oligarchs) in order to finance Yeltsin's re-election campaign of 1996. As the state duly defaulted, during rigged auctions Khodorkovsky with his Menatep Bank acquired Yukos for a mere $309 million (soon worth $1,5 bio). Mickael Fridman with his Alfa bank got hold of Tyumen Oil, Beresovski together with Alexander Smolensky through front companies purchased Sibneft for mere $100 million in return for supporting Yeltsin's campaign with his ORT television. Potanin with his Oneksim Bank bought Norilsk Nickel for $170 million (profits in 2000: $1,5 bio) and the oil company Sidanko for $130 million. Not that anyone of them had had any previous experience in the oil or energy industry.[17]

As Russia had no tax system at the time to speak of, its budget mainly relied on oil export revenues (as it still largely does now). At the time at least for official exports a system of "tax farming" applied: Favoritetraders, so-called "spetsy", bought cheaply oil from producers, sold it at much higher world market prices, pocketed their commissions for themselves and friends in high places and left a smaller share for the budget. By 1994, 93% of official oil exports were handled by these spetsy, that is: 83 million tons per year.[18] With Russia essentially bankrupt and depending on IMF credits for survival, under IMF pressure and with the support of the oil generals, Anatoli Chubais, as Deputy Prime Minister and last remaining radical reformer in government,

---

[17] Goldman. Op. cit.; p. 65.
[18] Gustafson. Op. cit., p. 91.

in 1994/95, persuaded Yeltsin to abolish the export licensing system and with them the corrupt spetsy.

In the meantime; however, the four big oil companies had their own spetsy as exports traders. Lukoil, the largest, as its own subsidiary, Yukos, Rosneft and Surgutneftegaz, had theirs as intermediaries. Sometimes, however, a cash-rich trader, like Alfa, became more powerful and took over the producer, like Tyumen Oil Company and Sidanco. Also, other well-connected financial groups took over weaker over-indebted oil companies.

In 1996, Russia produced only half as much crude oil as it did in its Soviet-era peak one decade earlier. Oil investment had become less than one-third of what it had been back then. Yet by the end of that year, the decline of oil output had bottomed out. The two best-performing companies, Lukoil (run by VagitAlekperov) and Surgutneftegaz (Vladimir Bogdanov), had been successful in controlling their subsidiaries, in limiting debt and thus avoided becoming easy targets for takeover like the rest of the financially weaker oil companies. All other "oil generals" had been pushed aside, were co-opted, or worse, sometimes were killed. Over them, the vultures of the newly established financial conglomerates were circling, like Alfa (Mikhael Fridman), Oneksimbank (Vladimir Potanin) and Metatep (Mikhael Khodorkovsky), controlled by future oligarchs who had made a lot of money as spetsy exporters of oil and other commodities. By 1995, there were the three majors (Lukoil, Surgutneftegaz and Yukos), the state-owned Rosneft, three regional oil companies Tatneft, Bashneft and Komitec, plus six medium-sized oil producers: Sidanco, Eastern Oil Company, Slavneft, Onako, Sibneft and TNK. As mentioned, one by one, like Yukos by Khodorkovsky, mostly during the "loans for shares" scheme during 1995/1996, they were swallowed by the new oligarchs, who by 2002 controlled half of Russia's oil production, while Tatneft and Bashneft became the family property of the presidents of Tatarstan and Bashkortostan, respectively.[19] Although widely unpopular as the new super-rich, the new oligarchs, foremost Khodorkovsky, changed the management culture of their companies very quickly for the better. They cut costs, hired Western advisors, established control over oil and cash flows and introduced new technologies to maximize output from the wells. First privatization vouchers nominally amounting to 10.000 rubles, then worth $20, distributed to employees and to the population at large were repurchased often at steep discounts, like for one bottle of vodka. Then it, in the mid-1990s, was the hour of the banks on which the indebted oil companies had become dependent. Thus, Vladimir Potanin tried gradually to take over

---

[19] Ibid., p. 100.

Surgutneftegaz with his Oneksimbank. Mikhael Khodorkovsky by the end of 1995 with his Menatep Bank acquired Yukos, got rid of the gangsters at its Samara refineries (where 50 people got killed in the process) and also cut off the "social" payments to Samara city, on which this corporate town had been fully dependent for public housing and schools.[20]

At the time with the weakness and disorganization of the central government, it appeared as if—apart from Rosneft—the sector had been effectively privatized. Government ownership of the oil in the ground and of the pipelines and its control over export quotas, over domestic distribution and its regulation of field development plans seemed to exist on paper only. Once the Kremlin reasserted its power after 2000, these, however, became essential policy tools that threatened ownership rights effectively.[21]

In the 1990s, the sector also became open to foreign participation. Western technologies and transparent management techniques replaced Soviet practices, which had wasted a lot of oil and flared gas thoughtlessly and systematically concealed mistakes, theft and wastage of manpower, money and resources. The new joint ventures used the capital and management of smaller Western oil companies and worked with Russian crews, standard equipment and local tools. Old oil fields could be rehabilitated. Clearly, in these joint ventures with their export privileges, a clash of business cultures was foreseeable and duly happened.[22] Western managers cut costs, were economical with time, insisted on quality execution and transparent data transfers and open communication. Traditional Soviet managers did not care about the cash flow and disliked controls, which exposed mistakes and incompetence and threatened internal theft and fraud.[23] The bigger Western companies by 1990 set up office in Moscow and were looking after bigger fish, wishing to add large strategic projects to their portfolio of reserves. These once mighty "Seven sisters"[24] of the 1970s had in the meantime seen most of their oil fields in the Third World and their production nationalized, and new fields were getting more difficult to acquire and more expensive to explore lying in more inhospitable regions and geologies and ever deeper waters. Russia looked promising but proved to be no exception. Talks with suspicious Russian officials could last for one decade. Also, state oil companies like Statoil (Norway), Eni (Italy), Petrobras (Brazil) and Petronas (Malaysia) became active. In the end, Chevron went for the giant Tengiz oilfield, Conoco for the Polar

---

[20] Ibid., p. 141.
[21] Ibid., p. 97.
[22] Ibid., p. 160.
[23] Ibid., p. 165.
[24] Five of them American, plus BP and Royal Dutch Shell.

Lights project in Komi Republic in Northwestern Russia, Exxon and Shell for consortia for oil and LNG on Sakhalin and Arco bought a big chunk of Lukoil. The companies during the Yeltsin years befriended powerful regional governors who felt abandoned by Moscow in their peripheral empires. Yet a Russian partner was indispensable to take care of Russian predatory officialdom, kleptocratic national and regional politics, the police, the courts, the taxmen and the mafia (which usually left foreigners in peace). When shell teamed up only with Mitsui and Mitsubishi on Sakhalin 2, after the gas fields and LNG terminals were built, unprotected they were duly taken over by Gazprom. Most projects involving foreigners were initially designed as "production sharing agreements", which reduces the investors risk and his initial tax bill. At the start, all oil produced is owned by the investor until his costs are recovered. Once this has happened, the revenues are split between the investor and the host government. With oil prices being at the low in the 1990s, Russia, however, needed cash quicker and deals tended to unravel, equally as Russian partners turned out to be unreliable, legal titles meant little, tax regulations and properties changed almost daily and regional political allies disappeared or changed sides. With the Asian economic crisis of 1998, Urals crude traded at around US $9 per barrel. In consequence, Russia defaulted on her foreign debts of US $40 billion and massively devalued the rubble. This restored the export competitiveness of Russian oil and gas and led to the turnaround ("the oil miracle")[25] after 1999, aided by the recovery of oil prices to US $51 per barrel by 2005 when the growth of Russian oil production, which also recovered after 1999 began to level off. With low domestic demand, most of the increased quantities were exported contributing in no small way to the moderation of the growth of world oil prices.

With plenty of money around in the oil industry, the oligarchs in charge, like Khodorkovsky, turned from millionaires into multibillionaires. But oil revenue also filled the state's coffers and allowed Putin to rebuild its security and repressive system permitting him to reclaim state control over this clearly vital strategic sector. By 2005, oil and gas exports accounted for 59% of Russia's exports of US $244 billion, and oil and gas revenues for 37% of the Russian budget receipts.

Most of the new oil did not come from new discoveries, but rather from rehabilitated old fields with the help of US fracking technology. These so-called "brownfields" had suffered from neglect, too much-outdated water flooding (to force up the oil) and weak and defective pumps and poor

---

[25] Ibid., p. 184.

well management in the late Soviet era. Most were located in West Siberia where the infrastructure, roads, pipelines and settlements were already in place. Interestingly, but unsurprisingly, the private companies, Yukos, Sibneft, Surgutneftegaz and Lukoil, did best, almost doubling output between 1999 and 2005, while the production of the state-owned companies Rosneft, Slavneft, Tatneft and Bashneft stagnated.[26] The latter two are located in Tatarstan and Bashkortostan, two Muslim regions along the Central Volga and the Southern Ural and were then controlled by the families of the powerful governors.

Mikhael Khodorkovsky's Yukos reacted to the crisis of 1998, when his Menatep bank went belly up, transferring its assets to Yukos and other financial vehicles.[27] As Yukos' cash flow dried up, he radically cut costs, reduced wages, paying them months late, outsourced staff and did not pay taxes including to the corporate towns, which depended on them. After the murder of the mayor of Nefteingansk, who had opposed Yukos' strategies and tactics in 1998, the company found it advisable to retract from the planned mass dismissals (an anathema since Soviet days). It also hired the world's leading oil service companies Schlumberger and Halliburton in 1999 for a quick improvement of productivity and began to engage aggressively in "tax optimization", that is: finding and exploiting loopholes in the fast changing tax legislation (which would eventually bring about Khodorkovsky's and Yukos' undoing). Khodorkovsky and his partners with US help also turned the corporate culture, its reporting and accounting systems, around. Soviet survival techniques consisted of concealing true production figures, hiding mistakes and avoiding blame from political masters. In post-Soviet times, the tradition continued by doctoring payrolls, rigging tenders, overstating payments and oil disappearing as "technical losses" to be used for the private gain of management or as underreporting for tax purposes.[28] All communication was now computerized and centralized. Khodorkovsky also had a parallel internal security system installed, which monitored all reporting and fired hundreds of fraudulent employees, in other words, management by terror ("*raznos*"). Even when hugely profitable again Yukos continued to refuse to pay for "social projects" like kindergartens, schools and hospitals in its corporate towns. Workers also feared its effective methods to empty the local oil fields would accelerate the end of their jobs and livelihoods. With its foreign and robust ways Yukos, the most modern and productive oil company in Russia then, was surely not the most popular employer. Its

---

[26] Ibid., p. 195.
[27] Goldman. Op. cit., p. 76.
[28] Gustafson. Op. cit., p. 212.

enormous profits created envy and greed. It broke too many unspoken rules of the Russian way of doing business and alienated too many powerful people both in Moscow and in the oil towns of the provinces.

Its competitor Sibneft was set up in 1995 by Boris Berezovski, then the main financer and political schemer at Boris Yeltsin's court, by merging the Noiabrskneftegaz fields with Russia's then most modern refinery at Omsk. Neither he nor his erstwhile sidekick and later owner Roman Abramovich, unlike Khodorkovsky cared much about oil, the company or its management, which they left to a professional manager, named Evgenii Shvidler. He avoided Western management imports, yet also in 1999 hired Schlumberger to improve extraction technology, followed in 2002, by a contract with Halliburton. With its new greenfield developments, Sibneft had fewer problems with Soviet management traditions than Yukos, which did brownfield rehabilitation. Yet, in the end, Sibneft's more adaptive, less abrasive style did not help either. While Yukos was dismantled and its components swallowed by Rosneft in 2005 and its owner (with assets worth US $8 billion then Russia's richest man) expropriated and jailed for 9 years of hard labour in Siberia, after the fall from grace and the exile of Beresovski,[29] Abramovich (who had purchased Beresovski's shares in 2001 for US $1,3 billion) in 2005 as well was forced to sell out to Gazprom. Both companies, thus, were effectively renationalized.

Surgutneftegaz did it differently and survived. Located with its fields at the middle Ob river basin its manager was former oil general, Vladimir Bogdanov, who did not believe in fancy expensive foreign ways, but rather ran the company Soviet style, which meant simply to drill more as they had always done. He did not buy other companies but expanded production by adding effectively new wells using cheap old-style pumps without resorting to fracking. Foreign techniques and software were only purchased cautiously and applied selectively. Unlike the others, he also paid his taxes, bills and wages correctly and in time.

Lukoil, the fourth largest private oil company and owned by VagitAlekperov, tried all of the above. First, they tried to diversify away from West Siberia and develop new fields, like offshore in the Caspian Sea or in Northwest Russia. Then Lukoil reverted to West Siberia and had to use US fracking techniques and stronger pumps in their brownfields. Then, belatedly also the management techniques seen in Yukos and Sibneft were introduced. Similarly, like Bogdanov, Alekperov, both former Soviet officials, never challenged

---

[29] Beresovsky died in March 2013 on his estate in Surrey by hanging, a case of unexplained "suicide".

the primacy of Russian state interests in the sector. Hence, their companies survived.

By 2000, oil prices had recovered from $15 per barrel (1995) to $33, due to Chinese and Indian demand. After a decade of asset stripping oligarchs began now to invest in much-needed exploration, equipment and development.[30]

5.3 Putin's Power Structures in the Oil and Gas Industry

When Putin arrived in Moscow in 1996 to work in senior posts in the Yeltsin administration, he was a stranger to the capital. Gradually he brought friends and colleagues from the St. Petersburg mayoralty in, who since 1992 served with him under the reformist mayor Anatoli Sobchak (until he lost his elections in 1996), but comrades among former KGB officers, as well as academics from St. Petersburg universities and institutes. Apart from the shared local origin and the personal loyalty to Putin, they were a diverse lot divided into many quarrelling clans, which allowed the president his favourite tactics of divide and role. Roughly they were sorted into "liberals", lawyers (like Dmitri Medvedev) and economists, who had accepted the market economy in principle and who quickly moved into financial and economic management positions, and in those of the security apparatus (*siloviki*), former KGB, police and military officers, who disliked the chaotic privatization and the oligarchs and worked to re-establish effective structures of central control. Both groups for Putin formed a reliable network to consolidate his personal power, to recapture political and economic control and rents and to rebuild centralized state structures with orders emanating from the Kremlin. In the new system of patrimonial rule, their services were richly rewarded.

By 2000, the oil sector was almost entirely in private hands. Also, the gas sector seemed equally to slip out of state control. After his presidential election in March 2000 with the able help of his Petersburg network Putin first cut the power of the regional governors and then moved to re-establish state control over the oil and gas industry and to capture the rising global energy prices for the state, for his friends and for himself.

---

[30] Goldman. Op. cit., p. 79.

Putin's first encounter with the oil sector happened as Deputy Mayor of St. Petersburg when he was made in charge of the ports. With business associates at the time, he planned a pipeline from Kirishi refinery to the port of Petersburg to give the city an oil terminal. Thus, far its port had mainly been a naval harbour. Russian oil was exported via the terminals in Porvoo (Finland), Talinn (Estonia), Ventspils (Latvia) and Klaipeda (Lithuania), which all charged hefty transit fees and export taxes, amounting to $10/12 per ton.[31] Although the project failed due to the lack of funds, Putin at the time appreciated the work of colleagues like Igor Sechin, Aleksei Miller, Vladimir Yakunin and AlekseiKudrin and reverted back to the subject immediately once he had become Prime Minister in August 1999. He also quickly moved to strengthen Gazprom's pipeline and export monopoly, first as a cash cow for the Kremlin, his pet projects and friends, to stop the flow of money abroad and to give tax and credit incentives to Gazprom to diversify into petrochemicals and fertilizer production, in order to increase value-added in Russia, a precursor of his industrial policies to come.

Also, the tax system for the sector had to be developed. In Soviet times, the state simply ordered the sales price for producers low and the purchase prices for consumers higher and pocketed the difference. During the Yeltsin years, the tax system was developed in a haphazard fashion with almost daily or weekly changes applicable ex-post. Rules were often vague, with oil majors exploiting the many loopholes to stash underreported profits abroad. At the time enforcement was arbitrary and draconic with hooded tax policemen and OMON troops raiding headquarters at gun point, confiscating PCs and documents, freezing bank accounts and export licenses and arresting staffers. After the theatrical show in front of cameras, the final tax bill would be politically negotiated with the Kremlin. Taxation would remain one of Putin's instruments of choice to intimidate oligarchs and force compliance with his plans. Yet his Finance Minister Kudrin managed to capture most of the exploding oil export revenues for the state. From US $5,6 bio (1999), they went up to $83 billion (2005).[32] The unsuspected windfall profits generated from the global oil price bonanza allowed salaries and pensions to be paid in time, the military to be modernized….. In fact, the revenues paid by the oligarchs gave the state the resources and emboldened the security apparatus (police, the FSB and the prosecutors and the courts) to take them on. Unlike Yeltsin in 1995, Putin did no longer need their money and support to win elections.

---

[31] Gustafson, Op. cit., p. 244.
[32] Ibid., p. 264.

First, Putin eliminated the two media oligarchs Vladimir Gusinsky and Boris Beresovsky who had criticized his conduct of war in Chechnya. In 2001, he fired Rem Viakhirev as the head of Gazprom whose clan together with one of his godfathers ex-PM Chernomyrdin had sponged the enterprise with a myriad of friendly subsidiaries whom they controlled. He was replaced by one Putin's men, Alexei Miller, who subsequently purged Gazprom of all the cronies of the previous regime and installed his own people instead, thus, re-establishing the Kremlin's control over its monopoly and designing it the role of a privileged national energy champion. For Russia's oil pipeline state monopoly Transneft, Putin appointed Semiyon Vainshtok. Now the state could re-establish control over almost all oil exports. In 2005, Putin ordered Gazprom to buy 10,7% of Rosneft's shares. With state controlling shares above 50%, the company was effectively renationalized.[33]

5.3.1 The End of Yukos

In October 2003, Mikhael Khodorkovsky, Russia's richest man, was arrested in his private plane at a Siberian airport. He was seen as a threat to the Kremlin and to its perception of Russia's national economic security interests and had to pay the price. Yukos had not behaved much differently than most of the other Russian oil majors (Sibneft, Lukoil and TNK): Like them, it practised aggressively "tax optimization",[34] mistreated minority shareholders (like during the collapse of Menatep Bank in 1998), hoarded licenses without exploiting them, tried its own independent export policy and negotiated about foreign capital participation without asking the Kremlin for permission.[35] In early 2003, Khodorkovsky announced merger plans for Yukos and Sibneft. Sibneft was now owned by Roman Abramovich, who was eager to cash in and get his riches and himself out of the country. Then Yukos was valued US $31,2 billion and Sibneft was US $13,3 billion. This would have created by far the largest company in Russia and one of the world's largest oil firms. Khodorkovsky became increasingly outspoken and publicly critical of Russian officialdom and policymakers.

In 2002, Khodorkovsky negotiated with the Chinese Sinopec and the CNPC the construction of an oil pipeline from his Siberian Talakan-Field

---

[33] Goldman; Op. cit., p. 83.
[34] Within Russia, there exists a multitude of "inland offshores» like tax havens in remote regions from Ingushetia to Chukotka, or through investments in technology parks. Then the corporate income tax can fall from 24% to around 9%. These perfectly legal loopholes were then retroactively declared illegal.
[35] Gustafson. Op. cit., p. 281.

across the Chinese border. This would have threatened Transneft's pipeline monopoly. Putin was opposed and insisted rather on longer stretch to be built not by Yukos but by Transneft to the Pacific port of Nakhodka, bypassing China and allowing exports to all of East Asia. In a fateful meeting in the Kremlin Putin and the oligarch clashed publicly. With a carefully prepared slide show, Khodorkovsky then accused the Energy Ministry and Putin's crony Sergei Bogdanchikov, the boss of his state-owned competitor Rosneft, openly and publicly of corruption.[36]

All Russian oligarchs had their deputies in the Duma and some parties were openly for sale. But the more Yukos became under pressure from the Kremlin, the more aggressively and openly did Khodorkovsky lobby against tax and environmental legislation, which the oil industry disliked. In a fit of Cesarean delusion Khodorkovsky announced, he would set up a rival political centre with the Yabloko party and go into politics by 2008, when Putin's second term would end. His financing of critical NGOs did not go unnoticed either. As political pressure from the Kremlin built up incessantly and fearing confiscation, in despair in 2002, he entered into merger talks with Chevron and ExxonMobil hoping that foreign capital participation in what would be the world largest combined oil company would protect him and his company.

As the general procurator Vladimir Ustinov, a siloviki who had already claimed the scalps of Gusinsky, Beresovski and Viakhirev, closed in on him and on Yukos with a series of raids, arrests and interrogations during the summer of 2003, Khodorkovsky's public defences became increasingly strident and aggressive.[37] This did not rescue him. Neither did his resignation as CEO in November 2002.

Yukos' assets—worth about $22 billion—were now seized with ever-increasing claims of unpaid taxes, in total amounting to some unlikely $26 billion, plus penalties. After the company was declared bankrupt, they were sold via front companies to Rosneft, which took over Yukos assets and the remaining technical staff and workforce. Five years of Russia's most modern oil company were over. In order to heed appearances of a proper auction, TNK-BP (which feared the seizure of BP's holdings) submitted a pseudo-bid.

Khodorkovsky after his arrest in 2003 was sentenced to jail terms until 2014 but was "pardoned" by Putin at the end of 2013. By 2006, the prosecutions were abruptly stopped, and after some purges, the balance between rival siloviki factions re-established Khodorkovsky now resides in London. Of his erstwhile fortune of US $15 billion, an estimated $500 million have

---

[36] Goldman. Op. cit., p. 114.
[37] Gustafson. Op. cit., S. 304.

survived abroad. He sets up a "Free Russia Foundation", a think tank that is understandably very critical of Kremlin policies.

In the meantime Berezovsky transferred Rusal, Sibneft and ORT to his junior partner Roman Abramovich, erroneously believing to maintain control. Sibneft, however, on Kremlin's orders was quickly sold to Gazprom, which, thus, cheaply acquired a foothold in the oil sector. The share of state control of the oil industry, thus, rose to 30%. Later also Surguzneftegaz came under state control. Derispaka, who like Abramovich as an oligarch wisely heeded the Kremlin's wishes, on Putin's orders took over Rusneft, the 7th largest oil company, from Mikhael Gutsiev.

5.3.2 Rosneft's New Role

As Thune Gustafson explains, it was more the weakness of the Russian state than by conscious design that Russia privatized most of her oil industries.[38] This actually went against the tide of nationalizing oil companies in most producer countries. Private oil companies by 1970 controlled 85% of the world's proven reserves; in 2012 barely 10%, while the share of national oil companies went up to over 75%. No wonder that the Western oil firms saw in the opening of Russia a bonanza to replenish their reserves and to guarantee their future survival, a hope which never materialized.

Yet typically Russia permitted foreign operators only in very difficult fields like offshore Sakhalin or Shtokman in the Barents Sea. Often they were plundered by a flood of taxes, like Conoco, which thereby lost $600 million in the Timen Pechora fields in the Nemets region of Northern Russia, before leaving. Their activities were seen with a mixture of paranoia and xenophobia. Typical was Putin's criticism of the TNK-BP production sharing agreement as a "colonial treaty".[39]

Rosneft, as mentioned, was the erstwhile state holding of unwanted leftovers of the Soviet oil empire scattered nation-wide with vanishing oil and cash flows in its subsidiaries. Some were in war torn Chechnya, which utterly destroyed, needed to be expensively rebuilt under army protection after 2000. Headquartered in the former Soviet Ministry of Oil in the 1990s Rosneft was scavenged for still useful fields and facilities. Today, it is Russia's largest oil company and privileged by the Kremlin as a national champion. In 2002/2003, Igor Sechin, then Putin's chief assistant and since 2012 chairman of Rosneft, led the campaign against Khodorkovsky and made sure Yukos'

---

[38] Ibid., p. 319.
[39] Goldman. Op. cit., p. 86.

assets were merged into Rosneft. This tripled the size of the company and brought new technologies and management techniques. Sechin and Sergei Bogdanchikov, Rosneft's boss at the time, also had to make sure that Rosneft remained independent and would not be swallowed by Gazprom altogether, as originally planned by Putin. Gazprom that was run by Alexei Miller with the support of PM Fradkov and its board chairman Medvedev (and was thus seen as controlled by the Petersburg business elite) wanted to swallow Rosneft (thanks to Sechin seen as Siloviki company), in order to expand its pipeline bound business—following the old Soviet trunk lines from Western Siberia to its West Russian and East European customers—by expanding nation-wide and globally, expanding into the oil business and thereby multiplying its stock value (and making many influential Russians very rich overnight in the process). To Putin, the idea was sold as creating a single national diversified giant energy champion, which would cover electricity, oil, refining, gas and LNG,[40] instead of having two of them.

In the end, parts of Gazprom's senior management got cold feet: It needed its funds more urgently to repair and upgrade its deteriorating pipeline system and to develop the Yamal LNG project instead. It also feared the legal risks in US courts and elsewhere by absorbing Rosneft, which just had swallowed Yukos. Instead Gazprom—thanks to high oil prices now flush with cash—bought out Abramovich and took over Sibneft instead. The month-long resistance in 2005 by Bogdanchikov, Sechin and their allies had been successful in the end. Instead of becoming the oil subsidiary of giant Gazprom, Rosneft remained a major independent player. Until 2009, Bogdanchikov worked successfully to integrate Yukos operations into those of Rosneft and to develop new oil fields like the giant field of Vardar discovered in 1988, which quickly produced a rapidly growing output and confirmed its status as Russia's largest and—unlike most state-owned enterprises (SOE)—then professionally well-run company, without the usual corrupt contracts, nepotistic careers and political contracts. By 2009, however, Sechin was made Vice-Minister of Energy and as a "state oligarch" could directly rule into the company, pushing Bogdanchikov aside. In spite of its heavy debt and tax burdens, Rosneft now expanded following Putin's political imperatives into the Arctic offshore, into West Siberian brownfields, into its Venezuelan mis-adventure and into the Gulf of Mexico, which in spite of strategic alliances with ExxonMobil, ENI, Statoil and GE is testing its managerial and technological capabilities.

---

[40] Putin's quote: Gustafson. Op. cit., p. 346.

5.3.3 The Crisis of 2008/2009

Thanks to rising oil prices and to her growing—largely exported—oil production volumes, the Russian economy in the early Putin years recovered nicely at growth rates of 7% per year. Through production and export taxes the state's oil revenues grew from US $36 billion (2000) per year to $173 billion (2007), accounting then for 37% of the federal budget alone. For every $1 increase in the world price for barrel, the Russian treasury effortlessly earned $1,9 billion per year[41] (and lost more or less the same in case of the reverse!). Wages, bills and pensions were paid of time, Moscow and St. Petersburg became shiny seats of corporate headquarters and of consumption, as the middle classes started to buy modern appliances, Western cars and status symbols, and the state could afford to modernize the military and to rebuild Grozny, which it had bombed to rubble.

Heading the lessons of 1998 and aware of their overdependence on international oil and commodity prices, the Kremlin—and Finance Minister Alexei Kudrin in particular—pursued a policy of fiscal and monetary prudence: The budget was in surplus, foreign debt greatly reduced, a sovereign wealth fund valued at $180 bio set up, with the Central Bank's foreign reserves amounting to $500 billion. This was a far cry to the fiscal recklessness erstwhile pursued by the Asian "tigers" like Korea, Indonesia, Thailand, Malaysia and Philippines, which had triggered the crisis of 1998. Yet with the housing and retail sectors booming, demand overwhelmed productive capacities, wages outpaced productivity gains. Inflation reached 14%, with a strong rubble sucking in imports and discouraging export: clear signs of the in-famous "Dutch disease"[42] affecting exporting nations of raw materials subjected to cyclical swings.

Like in Korea in 1998 and Spain in 2008, fiscal prudence did not help in Russia either, when the private sector, whose export earnings had been taxed away, engaged in massive borrowing. Fuelled also by a spending boom by consumers and speculators operating with borrowed money, foreign debt went up from US $106 billion (2005) to $275 billion (2007). Times were good as long as external finance flowed as short-term funds ("hot money"), attracted by high-interest rates and an appreciating rubble. Yet starting in 2017, when the US collateralized mortgage bubble began to deflate, funds predictably were pulled back. Worse, since 2004, oil output had begun to slow down, in spite of more money invested into the sector. It grew only 2% per year during 2005–2007, and by the end of 2008 even declined. The trick

---

[41] Ibid., p. 360.
[42] Ibid., p. 361.

of reviving old brownfields and opening a few new fields seemed no longer to work. World oil prices in July 2008 reached their historical peak with US $147 per barrel, but along with the banking crisis and recession soon fell to US $37 by December. Russia's third crash after 1989/90 and 1998 followed, though the Kremlin had thought it had learned the lessons and prepared for it, hitting the over-indebted private sector hard. Also, the tax bills accumulated during the oil price boom now hit the oil companies, short of revenues, hard who had to respond by cutting down on spending, maintenance and investment—which was certain to show effects.[43]

Russia applied expropriating taxes of 65% on the exports of Urals crude, on top of a production tax of 22%, thus a total of 87% applicable to a threshold of above US $25 per barrel. Though the system was easy to manage, it surely had started to discourage new investment massively. At the same time, the tax had the intention to keep domestic fuel prices low by punishing exports. This predictably encouraged waste ("over-consumption") and inefficiencies at home. Yet input costs for pipes, rigs, electricity and labour in line with price inflation had grown strongly during the decade, while the tax bill remained prohibitive. Little capital was left to invest into new field development, and economic incentives existed only if the global oil price stayed above $65 per barrel.

In 2008, the tax for exported crude oil was raised to 73%, and the export tax for refined light fuel (gasoline, diesel and jet fuel) remained at 65% and for fuel oil lowered to 38%. This obviously was intended to encourage domestic processing. Yet qualities of the refined products were often so poor that exported crude oil fetched better prices abroad than the processed ones.[44] Still, the higher global oil prices went, the more interesting due to increased tax savings, which turned processed exports. Even Putin had to admit: Oil exporters did not, as intended by the Kremlin, invest into new refineries but as classical rent-seekers rather distributed larger dividends to themselves.[45] In 2011, he changed the export tax regime again: now crude oil was least taxed at 60%, refined products at 66% and gasoline at 90%, making sure that it would stay within the country. The tax incentive scheme to promote higher value added had failed even with the Kremlin and crony affiliated oil majors. The tax changes after all were no small technical matter: Oil taxes remain by far the single largest contributor to the Russian budget.

---

[43] Ibid., p. 364.
[44] Ibid., P. 372.
[45] Ibid., p. 378.

5.3.4 The Regulatory System

After the disappearance of the Soviet Ministry of Oil a multitude of regulatory agencies, commissions, committees and institutes were created, with overlapping, frequently changing and purposefully confusing and competing competencies with often far-reaching powers to investigate and to prosecute: One more classical Russian textbook case of a weak state with divided ministries (the Ministries of Natural Resources, of Energy and of Economic Development), but with sometimes powerful officials with wide discretionary powers, breading inefficiency and corruption. This officialdom regulates the industry tightly: it issues licenses for exploration, production and exports, commands geological surveys, registers reserves, controls tenders and auctions, access to pipelines and sets transportation tariffs.[46] Other government agencies control environmental issues, labour conditions, safety, competition etc. During the first decade of Putin's rule Russia's bureaucracy expanded to 1,7 million people by 2010, half of the federal officials mostly working in regional offices. In the absence of the Communist Party, which during Soviet days, had supervised the administration and settled its conflicts, Putin made the FSB in charge. In particular, the seven new federal districts set up by Putin in 2000 to control the governors play an important role in the energy sector. They are essentially manned by the FSB, as men of the security apparatus have no checks and balances, and over the years have become used to look after their own private interests, including monetary ones. In practice, this means constant state intervention in the nominally private oil industry. In two infamous cases, the Ministry of Natural Resources (Minprirody) harassed Shell in its Sakhalin 2 LNG project and BP in its Kovykta gas development in Irkutsk oblast near Lake Baikal until the first ceded the majority holding to Gazprom and the second abandoned the project altogether. But also state actors like Gazprom and Rusneft are affected by month-long licensing procedures, inner-administrative turf battles and obstructionism. Decisions are arbitrary, unpredictable or simply inconclusive, in any event blocking initiatives and create needless delays and costs, which only large companies can absorb, having the manpower to cultivate the bureaucracy and to handle its burdensome reporting requirements and inspections.

Gustafson is right to conclude that the Russian state's approach to its energy industry is fundamentally mistaken.[47] It is based on the assumption that its resources and rents are limitless and control needs to be re-established for the common (and personal) good. However, resources are depleting and

---

[46] Ibid., p. 385.
[47] Ibid., p. 409.

rents are in decline. Public policies and their implementation in an atmosphere of mistrust, conflict and extortion only worsen the situation of the sector. As a result of the continuous current flow of rents, both the industry and the government have no interest to move out of the Soviet era comfort zone, like going into the Arctic offshore, doing East Siberian exploration, or to engage in enhanced recovery in West Siberia. Hence, Russia's oil industry is ill-prepared for the next generation of oil extraction with its higher costs, tougher conditions and reduced rents. On top of this are governance-induced handicaps with their weak protection of property rights of investors and an extortionate tax regime, which leaves them very few incentives to undertake long-term risks. Furthermore, there is the intense dislike of foreigners in this strategic sector and of their managerial skills and technological and financial resources which unsurprisingly remain underutilized.

5.3.5 The Outlook

From its Soviet peak in 1987 with 570 million tons annually, as described previously, Russia's production declined by—47% through 1996. It then recovered during the 2000s until reaching 505 million tons in 2010, yet far off the Russian share of previous Soviet peak output. While global production grew during these decades, Russia's global share dropped from 19% in the late 1990s to 12% in 2010. Efforts to discover and to develop new fields had fallen off in Russia after 1991, adding only 38 million tons to new production per year.[48] Except for the Vankor field, discoveries had been much smaller than in the past. Yet Russian oil, thanks to the infrastructure built up in the past remains competitive and this in spite of the distance of the fields to major terminals and high transportation tariffs. Since the second half of the 2000s diminishing returns are visible on investment as well as a declining effectiveness of hydraulic fracturing in the brownfields, while unit costs went up for labour, steel, electricity, other inputs and for increasing tariff rates. In short, the Soviet legacy in the sector, after a short revival, is being run down.

Small independent oil and oil service companies, which played a big role to increase productivity notable of brownfields elsewhere, in Russia were usually swallowed by the larger companies or fell victim to official predators and harassment. Yet in the mature fields of the Volga Urals in Tatarstan and Bashkorstan, they were successful in stabilizing output. But as Russian law decrees that old fields cannot be sold, but must be returned to the state for

---

[48] Ibid., p. 454.

new auctions, large companies have no incentives to have them reutilized by smaller more innovative companies.

Russia's future potential lies in the offshore of East Siberia and the Russian Far East: smaller, scattered sites—requiring expensive feeder pipelines—in complex geology, with plenty of old volcanoes, lacking infrastructure or often being of poor quality. These need more lead time and require higher costs given their remoteness and the extreme cold. At minus 30 to 40 degrees in winter, special steel equipment is needed, as everything else begins to crack and to fall apart. Hence, East Siberia will be no comparison to the bonanza of West Siberia, and with its high up-front costs discourages smaller operators but induces the powers of the central state to force its dependent oil majors into action. One such example is the construction of the lengthy East Siberian Pipeline (EPSO) East of the Amur to Kozmino at the Pacific coast in Primorye for exports to East Asia. This was done for strategic reasons at Kremlin orders at the expense of the oil companies, who like Yukos earlier would have preferred a much shorter, more economical line straight across the border to their Chinese customers.

The "bluefields" offshore are Russia's last energy frontiers. Already in the rough waters off Sakhalin,[49] Russia needed Western and Japanese expertise. The Arctic waters are reserved for the state companies Rosneft and Gazprom, which for the lack of skill and expertise to drill in deep-water offshore amidst drifting icebergs do very little, and even less so after 2014 when a Western ban on the supply of respective technologies available only in the US, Canada, Norway, the EU and Japan went into force after Putin's annexation of the Crimea.

The Kremlin's policies in the first decade of 2000 were successful in capturing the windfalls of globally rising oil prices for the federal budget and for their own needs. Through renationalization, a host of regulations and permanent policy interventions they re-established tight control over the sector. Yet expropriative taxation, especially of export earnings, and wasteful political projects reduced the companies' profits for reinvestment, modernization and new developments. With oil and gas counting for 30% of Russia's GDP, these are fairly reckless policies in the long term. Hence, once West Siberian brownfields have peaked again—this time for good—production levels are bound to decrease. Thus, Russia will be ever more dependent at the whims of global energy markets for the export revenues it so desperately needs.

---

[49] Between 1905 and 1945 the South ("Karafuto") was developed and settled by the Japanese. Prior to that, it was a Czarist penal colony where prisoners were left to rot. See: Anton Chekhov: "A Journey to Sakhalin".

There are little provisions for an alternative energy future. Inefficient Soviet era factories and power plants remain in operation with one of the highest energy intensities in the world. There is no role foreseen for alternative energies, except for nuclear power, which again is a Soviet heritage. In the oil market, Russia is a price taker, as there is little effective coordination with OPEC. On the gas market, its leverage in Eastern Europe from Finland via Slovakia to Bulgaria has been gradually eroding, where Gazprom used to hold 100% of the pipeline-bound market shares. With plenty of LNG from Algeria, potentially from Cyprus and the US on the market, the Baltic Sea pipelines North Stream 1 and 2 will not make a big difference.

Putin's visions for oil are very simple: There is plenty of it in Russia. One only needs to find it. Oil companies need to finance the state budget, not the shareholders. Large state-owned companies are preferable. They should export refined oil and petrochemicals, not crude oil. They should also serve regional development objectives internally and geopolitical interests abroad.[50]

Yet this wonderfully multifunctional cash cow, for the lack of feed, risks to milked to death. High taxes trigger a downward spiral for production as investment will remain discouraged. Globally, Russia will remain highly vulnerable to the shift from high-price scenarios to lower price realities. As needs for welfare and security expenditure will remain high under Putin's rule, taxes will stay as high as they are. But with reduced oil revenues, the government's reserve funds will face depletion before long, while inflation will eat up people's savings. The weakness of Russia's neglected manufacturing base—evident by non-investment through record capital flight—will not be able to increase export earnings. Surely the miracle of Putin's first decade in power during 2000–2011of doubling Russian oil production and the quadrupling of global oil prices will not repeat itself. It is simply impossible.

5.4 The Gas Industry

The transformation of the Russian gas industry was relatively straightforward: Viktor Chernomyrdin as the Minister for the Gas Industry in 1989 transferred all its properties into the Gazprom monopoly as a state-owned enterprise (SOE) and made himself the CEO. When Yeltsin in December 1992 made him Prime Minister (until March 1998), his former deputy minister Rem Vyakhirev took over as CEO. The company paid little taxes or

---

[50]Gustafson. Op. cit, p. 493.

dividends (by 1994 33% of shares were sold to the public), but the management was busy distributing assets to relatives, friends and mistresses. The most valuable parts went to a company called Itera headquartered in Jacksonville, Florida.[51] In 1995/1996, for instance, Gazprom had an estimated $2 billion of earnings but paid only $3, 5 million dividends to the state.

Gazprom as the Kremlin's cash cow under Putin first took over Media Most of the exiled Gusinsky and, as mentioned before, Sibneft from Abramovich. In May 2001, Chernomyrdin and Vyakhirev were replaced by Putin's confidants from St. Petersburg, Dimitri Medvedev and Alexei Miller. The asset stripping was stopped, with Gazprom now serving the Kremlin's interests, both political and economic. Itera as the corrupt middleman lost its contracts, was brought under Gazprom control and was forced to hand its gas holdings to Novatec. In difference to Gusinsky, Khodorkovsy and Berezovsky, who by the Kremlin were considered semi-criminal upstarts, Chernomyrdin and Vyakhirev as members of the old nomenclature could keep their ill-gotten gains and remain unpunished.[52]

Gazprom's business model is relatively simple: to buy Central Asian gas cheaply (which remains largely captive to Gazprom's pipeline monopoly as it needs to transit through Russia), produce its own gas and sell it expensively mostly in Europe but also in Asia, and with the proceeds subsidize, the gas prices for Russian industry and consumers (a scheme that like in Soviet days does not encourage energy efficiency!). At the same time, the Friends of Putin (FOP) are in control, with slush funds for special projects and a very comfortable life for all of the Kremlin's friends. Equally, Gazprom is a powerful foreign policy instrument to reward friends or punish dissidents among the dependent countries of Russia's near abroad. When the former apparatchiks Leonid Kravchuk (1991–94) and Leonid Kutchma (1994–2005) were in power, Gazprom sold its gas at $15 per 1000 cubic meters to the Ukraine when it sold it for $150 in the West to its East European customers. When the more independent-minded Viktor Yushchenko (2005–2010) was elected, relations cooled, with Gazprom tripling gas prices for the Ukraine-towards international levels while reducing flows. Subsequently, the Russian side alleged that the Ukrainians illegally took out gas meant for transit to their East European customers (Slovakia and Bulgaria foremost). The situation was again complicated by the fact that Gazprom and Naftogas (the Ukrainian gas supply company) then did not negotiate directly, but used dubious subsidiaries like RusUkrEnergo (on the Russian side) and UkrGaz-Energo (on the Ukrainian side) instead, who took their very generous cuts

---

[51] Goldman, Op. cit., p. 61.
[52] Ibid., p. 100.

each. When Yulia Timoshenko as the Prime Minister (1999–2001 and 2007–2010) tried to cut out these dubious middlemen,[53] they had their revenge by organizing her imprisonment for 3 years. About 60% of the gas flowing through and into the Ukraine originates in Turkmenistan. Typically, it is purchased by Gazprom at a bargain price and resold at prices three times higher. But unsurprisingly also in the transactions between the Turkmens and Gazprom dubious middlemen are involved, one being the oligarch Dimytro Firtash together with the gangster SemionMogilevich, who first controlled Itera, later renamed EuralTrans Gas.[54] Not by accident and thanks to the Rotenberg brothers, childhood friends of Putin, whose building company has a monopoly on pipeline construction, Gazprom pipelines cost three times more than elsewhere. In any event, Gazprom managed to ruin the skyline of St. Petersburg with a skyscraper of the height of 396 m.

There were, however, also foreign minority shareholders in Gazprom who were unhappy about the pilferage and unproductive political investments Gazprom had to undertake, which reduced its profitability, cash flow, future investments and dividends. When Bill Browder, the US general manager of the $4 billion Heritage Capital Fund, the largest foreign portfolio investor in Russia, in 2006 publicly criticized the political appointments of incompetent senior managers and Gazprom's policies, including its continued asset stripping and the cross-subsidization of domestic industry, whose wasteful practices continued with no incentives for conservation due to artificially low prices for domestic gas, his visa was cancelled and he was unceremoniously booted out of the country. His fund and his remaining staff were harassed with ever-increasing tax bills and raids by the tax police. As described previously, in the end, his lawyer, SergejMagnitzki, who had tried to expose the profiteers of the raid on Heritage, was killed in a Moscow prison by FSB thugs.[55] US Congress responded to Browder's incessant and admirably skilful lobbying by adopting the so-called "Magnitzki Act", which put the culprits and other Kremlin-linked profiteers on a sanction list with extra-territorial application, freezing their assets abroad and blocking any of their overseas business ventures.

Also German Gref, former Minister of Economic Development and a well-reputed economic reformer, in 2007, criticized that Gazprom wasted its resources on noncore stuff, like media, ski resorts and hotels for the Sochi

---

[53] Dmitri Popov, Ilya Milstein. *Julia Timoschenko. Die Zukunft der Ukraine nach der Orangenen Revolution.* Cologne: Dumont 2006, pp. 108.
[54] Goldman. Op. cit., p. 147.
[55] Bill Browder. *Red Notice. Wie ich Putins Staatsfeind Nr. 1 wurde.* Munich: Hanser 2014, pp. 167.

Olympics,[56] while neglecting the modernization of pipelines, pumps and compressors[57] (which led to no negative consequences for him, not that his critique brought changes for the better either). In fact, cheap domestic gas was used at 50% for electricity generation and thus subsidized excess consumption by both industry and households. There is still a lot of flaring of about 20 million cubic meters per year[58] as Gazprom as a monopolist is often not interested to build pipelines to new oil field run by private competitors. When TNK-BP offered to build their own pipeline to use this by-product from oil production, it was flatly refused. Losses during transport through leaky pipelines could amount to up to 50 billion cubic meters. In total, losses due to flaring and leaks in 2004 were estimated as the equivalent of one-third of Russian gas exports.[59] So much for Gazprom's contribution to energy preservation, resource economics and to "climate change" for whatever it is worth.

5.5 Putin's Logic

Like any self-respecting senior Russian politician, Putin in 1997 at a mature age of 45 handed in a doctoral dissertation at the University of St. Petersburg. Naturally he—like certain German, Austrian and East European politicians and similar fraudsters, some of them still in power—did not spend his time in university libraries, but had a cut and paste job done by a senior academic, plagiarizing inter alia 16 pages from "Strategic Planning and Policies" by William Richard King and David I. Cleland (Van Nostrand Reinhold, 1978).[60] More interesting are the conclusions of his dissertation, entitled "Natural Resources and Strategic Planning of the Russian Economy" of this untrained economist, which must have found his approval. He argues for national champions that serve the state's interests, for Russia to retake control of FDI in the country via tax and environmental audits, for low energy prices to subsidize the national economy, to use energy exports as a foreign policy weapon with Russia controlling 27.5% of the world's natural gas reserves being the largest supplier and to remove non-compliant oligarchs—with the

---

[56]In fact, Potanin (Norislk Nickel) and Deripaska (Rusal) had to do the same.
[57]Goldman. Op. cit; p. 182.
[58]Still not as bad as Nigeria!
[59]Goldman. Op. cit; p. 197.
[60]He is not the only senior politician who has done this. The practise is also common in other title conscious countries, like in Germany, Austria, Romania, the Ukraine …. But the exposure of fraud frequently but not always ends their careers.

purge already starting in June 2000[61]! Very early in his presidency, Putin exercised hands-on control over both Gazprom and Rosneft, and like any good secret service officer was obsessed with detail. By 2012, the protectionist policies and the promotion of state-owned enterprises were equally already in full swing, once most private banks did not survive the financial crisis of 1998, which had started in Asia. As the spoils are large, there were many predators also among the Kremlin's siloviki. Hence, the fights between Gazprom (Miller) and Rosneft (Bogdanichikov and later Sechin) were and remain legendary,[62] with Putin remaining the sole unpredictable arbiter. And should the siloviki start to make peace among each other, there is still the cohort of his technocratic cronies from St. Petersburg....

In blatant disregard for any conflict of interest, senior government officials also occupy executive corporate functions, like Viktor Sechin both in the Kremlin and at Rosneft. There are also privileged special investment vehicles like the $3,6 billion Finansgroup run by Oleg Svartsman, which was established to manage the private finances of senior FSB and SVR officers.

Finally, there is the issue of gas pipelines as a tool of foreign policy influence: on Central Asian suppliers, like Turkmenistan, or Kazakhstan (also via Transneft for oil) who as land-locked countries are dependent on Russian transit, second, on those countries dependent 100% on Russian supplied gas, like Ukraine, Belarus, Moldova, Armenia, but also Finland, the Baltics and Slovakia, with sizable dependency ratios of 66–75% equally for Austria, Hungary and the Czech Republic. The Gazprom strategy in these countries is also to get control over domestic distribution networks with the objective to exclude other suppliers and to establish monopoly rents and control over key customers.[63] Under political pressure and as a swap of debt (i.e. unpaid bills) for equity, Moldova and Armenia handed a controlling share of their domestic networks to Gazprom. The same was tried with more arm twisting in the Ukraine and in Belarus. Thus, Beltransgaz, the Belorussian gas transit and distribution company, was bought. In the end, Russia tried to raise gas prices for all, friend or foe alike, even for nominally allied Armenia and Belarus. They were all considered abroad for once.[64]

In the EU, the same strategy was attempted for even more lucrative markets, but failed due to the EU's "unbundling" energy directive, which forced pipeline operators to give fair access also to other suppliers. Hence,

---

[61] Goldman. Op. cit., pp. 99.
[62] Ibid., p. 192.
[63] Ibid., p. 152.
[64] Dmitri Trenin "Energy geopolitics in Russia-EU relations" in: Katinka Barysch. *Pipelines, Politics and Power*. London: Centre for European Policy Reform 2008, 15–24, p. 18.

Gazprom's attempts to monopolize parts of the EU's gas market fell victim to the EU's vigilant competition policies and were subsequently discontinued.

Russia is also active in Western petrol distribution and retail. LUKoil (owned by VagitAlekperov) in 2000 bought 3.000 filling stations in the US from Getty Oil and Mobil, and later purchased the "Jetts gas" petrol station chains in Belgium, the Czech Republic, Slovakia, Poland, Hungary and Finland from Conoco. From a competition point of view, these operations appear unproblematic.

5.6 Pipeline Politics

Having lost their Russian bonds and having been expropriated by the Bolsheviks, the Western allies boycotted Soviet oil sales after 1921. But two other international pariahs, Germany and Italy, were eager customers, ideological disagreements notwithstanding. In 1924, with Mussolini's Italy, a trade and navigation agreement was concluded, and by 1930, the Soviet Union supplied 30% of the Italian oil market. With Germany in 1922, a Russian–German Trade Joint Stock Company was founded, and 3 years later, 27 German banks set up a "KreditkonsortiumRußland" to finance Otto Wolf's metalworking plants to supply steel tubes to build the Baku-Batumi, and the Grozny-Tuapsepipelines in the Caucasus. In August 1939, a new trade agreement was concluded between Hitler's Germany and the Soviet Union, providing a German RM 200 Million loan for the Soviets to buy German goods, including military equipment in return for the supply of raw materials, including 900.000 tons of urgently needed petrol for the war preparations. In fact, in the battle for Leningrad in 1942, German troops captured boxes of brand-new Carl Zeiss sniper scopes from the Soviets. It made them think…

After the war, it was again the Italians who broke the ice among Western allies, in the shape of AGIP (today: ENI) the state oil company, led by Enrico Mattei, who as a former resistance fighter had strong pro-Soviet sympathies (and was killed in 1962 in a mysterious airline accident over Milan).[65] He concluded a series of barter agreements, in which Soviet oil was traded for Italian synthetic rubber (1958), for steel pipes and pipeline equipment (1960) and for cars, petrochemicals and other equipment (1963).

By the time the Soviets were moving the more cumbersome rail transport of oil to their Central Eastern European satellites and annexed territories to a

---

[65] Alexei Grivach, Konstantin Simonov. *The Grand Gas Game. A 50-year-old Rivalry between the USA and Europe.* Moscow 2019, p. 17.

more rational system of pipeline supply, like the Northern Druzhba ("Friendship") ending in Rostock and the Southern Druzhba ending in Croatia. This followed the logic of the Comecon business model: cheap energy and raw materials in return for industrial products, food and spare parts from Central East Europe for the Soviet armaments industry. Similarly for gas, a pipeline (Brastvo—"Brotherhood") was constructed from the Urengoy field in West Siberia to Uzgorod in Western Ukraine leading into Slovakia. In 1968, this line was extended to Baumgarten in Eastern Austria, where an old gas field was located. Then a first contract had been signed with the Austrian state-owned OeMV, which supplied Thyssen pipes for the gas imports. The Soviet invasion of the CSSR and the crushing of the Prague spring in August 1968 did not disrupt the deal. In 1969, Italy and the Soviet Union signed a 20-year agreement. Italy would grant $200 million loans for which the Soviets would purchase Italian steel pipes and equipment to build the Trans-Austrian pipeline from Baumgarten to Tarviso (Tarvis) in Northern Friuli, which was finished in 1974.

In 1971, Finland and the USSR signed a pipeline agreement: Leningrad-Wyborg (Viipuri)-Imatra-Lappeenranta, to be built by Soviet engineers. Yet for the Urengoy-Uzgorod gas pipeline Germany became the largest partner. Ruhrgas AG was offered 5 billion cubic meters per year, with Mannesmann supplying the seamless tubes, financed by a consortium led by Deutsche Bank, to be paid for—like in the old days—by future gas supplies. In 1970, the West German—USSR agreement was signed. Thyssen and Mannesmann[66] were to supply 12 million pipes, worth 1.2 billion DM in return for 52 billion cubic meters of gas, worth 2.5 billion DM over the next 20 years. A German bank consortium, led by Deutsche Bank, granted a 10-year loan for the project costs at 6% interest, with 50% guaranteed by Hermes, the German state export insurance. In 1972, a further agreement for a 1.2 billion DM loan for the purchase of German pipes and equipment was signed, running for 12 years at 6% interest, in return for Russian gas supplies for the next 20 years, totalling 12 billion cubic meters. Similar agreements were concluded until 1978 providing for increased gas supplies until 2000, which was to be the end of the Soviet Union.

During Leonid Brezhnevs slightly alcoholic visit to Bonn in May 1973,[67] a 10-year agreement on industrial and technical cooperation was signed by him and Chancellor Willy Brandt, including the joint construction of nuclear

---

[66] The first recently tried to rebrand it as an elevator servicing company and the second has disappeared within Vodaphone. So much for the past glory of the German steel industry.

[67] He smashed a gift Mercedes in the process but got a new one with no difficulty.

power plants. Salzgitter and Mannesmann shipped some 600.000 large diameter pipes every year, accounting for 60% of Mannesmann's production capacity. In total, during 1973–1983, 6 million tons of large German steel pipes were delivered, plus compressor stations and equipment for trunk lines. A total of 7.3 billion DM of credits were given by German banks and 73 billion cubic meters of Soviet gas received in return. Clearly, both sides had a clear interest in the continuation of détente. As more and more pipelines were constructed, the Soyuz ("Union") pipeline covering 2750 km from Orenburg to Uzhgorod at the West Ukrainian border—using components also from Italsider, Sumitomo and even US equipment for its 22 compressor stations—also Eastern Europe became better supplied with demand picking up.[68]

With oil prices going up from $1,8 per barrel (1974) to $11,6 per barrel (1978), gas consumption increased notably in Germany, France, Austria and in Italy. This coincided with the opening of more and more West Siberian gas fields, which increased domestic consumption and availabilities for exports. At the same time, the Soviet Union was given a lifeline by the huge inflow of petro-dollars, which allowed Brezhnev and his septuagenarian cronies to do strictly nothing to reform the decrepit Soviet economic system. In 1979, they committed a policy mistake, which the Soviet Union (and Russia today) very rarely did, that is: taking an incalculable foreign military risk by invading Afghanistan, where an incompetent sectarian Communist regime was threatened by US and Pakistani backed Islamic insurgents. The USA led by Ronald Reagan responded by sanctions banning high tech exports and grain to the Soviet Union—apart from boycotting the Moscow Olympics of 1980. Europeans were not particularly impressed. Chancellor Helmut Schmidt went to Moscow and signed a deal providing new energy loans of 10 billion DM for the next decade at 7.75% interest again for German steel pipes and equipment. There were similar offers from France (Credit Lyonnais), the Netherlands (ABN), Belgium (SocietéGenerale), the Italian government and the Japanese Eximbank. The Soviets responded by importing grain from Argentina and replacing Caterpillar excavators with those from Komatsu and Kato for pipe laying. GE turbines were replaced by those from Rolls Royce.[69] At the time competition was keen for the "project of the century", the gas pipeline Urengoy in Northwest Siberia to Uzhgorod, billed at $15 billion, with 4500 km, which is then the largest pipeline project ever undertaken. There were multi-billion tenders for compressor units, air cooling systems, fittings and control systems. Soviet-made equipment was simply not good

---

[68] Grivach, Simonov. Op. cit., p. 37.
[69] Ibid., p. 73.

enough for this export-oriented project. For quick repairs also inventories of spare parts had to be set up along the line. When in December 1981, martial law was declared in Poland, again the Reagan administration tried to disrupt the supply for the pipeline construction and embargoed US supplies, also from European license holders. And again the Europeans (unlike today) effectively resisted the extraterritorial application of the US sanctions: Germany under Helmut Schmidt, France under Francois Mitterrand and even the UK under Margaret Thatcher, who while being ok with sanctions against the Poland's martial law regime of General Jaruzelski, at the time argued to defend "thousands of jobs in Scotland" (by the supplier John Browne) and that existing contracts needed to be honoured. In the end, also the US dropped the US grain embargo in order to support US farm interests. Helmut Schmidt had argued publicly, that Soviet oil and gas revenues would help to sell and to pay for US grain.[70] At a G 7 summit in June 1982, Ronald Reagan, supported only by Pierre Trudeau of Canada, found himself isolated against the Europeans and Japan. The US sanctions did not delay the pipeline project, 4450 km were built in only 18 months crossing the Urals and countless rivers with Siberian climates going down to—40/50° in winter and criticized by US media like the new York Times and the Wall Street Journal, but only hurt US business interests.[71] US admonitions to buy newly discovered Norwegian gas instead could not make up the shortfall from Soviet gas. After Brezhnev's death on 10th November 1982, President Reagan after 143 days of its existence decided to lift the sanctions also against the pipeline. Once it was constructed, the share of Soviet gas in Germany and Austria doubled to 60/70% (2016).

The lifeline of a gas pipeline, its pumping units, coolers and compressor station are normally assumed to be 33 years, provided that it is well maintained. So, in the Russian view, the transit gas pipeline through the Ukraine is nearing its physical end. Due to the endless disputes with Ukraine, they cut the gas off in November 2006, claiming that the continued limited supplies for re-export, supplying Southeast Europe and the European part of Turkey were stolen by the Ukrainians.[72]

In September 2005, Putin and Chancellor Schröder in one of his last days in office approved the Nord Stream 1 route of a gas pipeline from Viipuri (Wyborg) in Karelia across the Baltic Sea to Greifswald. The outgoing chancellor granted German government guarantees at the range of 1 billion Euro to support a German banking consortium to finance a chunk of the project.

---

[70] Ibid., p. 87.
[71] Ibid., p. 142.
[72] Ibid., p. 166.

The purpose of the North Stream pipelines is clearly to bypass any transit country, that is: the Ukraine, Belarus and Poland. Whatever Russia would save in terms of transit fees was now ploughed at the range of 10 billion Euro into expensive deep sea pipe laying. Soon a parallel pipeline was to follow, North Stream 2 which in spite of new extraterritorial sanctions by US Congress (angry about alleged Russian meddling in the US presidential campaign of 2016 and interested in US LNG exports from fracking) is likely to reach completion during 2021. Surely the upkeep and renovation of the existing continental pipelines would have made more economic sense, but this was not on Putin's cards.

At the same time, Russia also managed to sabotage the EU's plan to get Central and Azeri gas directly with a pipeline project of 3500 km called "Nabocco" named after Verdi, which would have supplied Caspian—and possibly even Iranian gas—via Georgia and Turkey into Southern Europe up to Hungary and Austria. Yet Russia managed to abort this by constructing its Turkstream (originally called "Bluestream") pipeline directly from Tuapseacross the Black Sea to Samsun in Northern Turkey (and further on to Ankara and Istambul) thus, making Nabocco economically unviable. In the end, the quantities available from Azerbaijan, as the only reliable supplier, were not sufficient to make the project economically viable. Construction costs were steep with € 15 billion for the 3900 km needed from the Shah Deniz 2 field, 50 km South of Baku in the Caspian Sea towards Southeast Europe. As neither the Azeris nor the Turkmen were ready to enter into long-term contracts, with Turkey requesting ever higher transit fees, among the six consortium members, first the Hungarian MOL and the German RWE bolted, with rest then understandably seeing little future and purpose.[73] The opera was then discretely removed from the EU's foreign policy repertoire. With less fanfare in 2020 a "Southern Gas Corridor" is being built from Azerbaijan via Georgia, Turkey and Greece to Southern Italy.

Pipelines have been crisscrossing the Soviet empire, mostly from a North-Eastern to Western directions with a wide range of trunk lines. Just to avoid confusion: there are two major oil pipelines: Drushba, with a Southern link ending in Prague and in Croatia, and a Northern one ending in Danzig, Rostock and Leipzig. The second are the Baltic oil pipelines, originally mostly serving the terminals in Ventspils (Latvia) and Butinge (Lithuania). But in the early 2000s, the flows have been redirected to Primorskand Ust-Luganear St. Petersburg, in order to cut the Baltics out of the transit business.

---

[73] *Frankfurter Allgemeine* 14.5.2012; *Financial Times* 1.2.2012.

And there are three major gas pipelines: Yamal, crossing Belarus and Poland; Brotherhood crossing the Ukraine; and finally Soyuz, which transports Central Asian gas. The purpose of Putin's expensive Nord Stream projects—with both pipes having a capacity of 55 bcm—is, as mentioned before, precisely to cut the Ukraine, the Belarussians and the Poles out of the transit business. Since total gas demand in the EU is—with all uncertainties of energy predictions—hardly expected to increase, the volumes will mostly be simply rerouted. The official justification being that the old Brotherhood pipeline after 36 years of operations and poor maintenance by 2020 is at the end of its life cycle and needs to be replaced.[74] The reader is free to believe this or not.

5.6.1 The Nord Stream 1 and 2 Story

When Putin came to power, as mentioned before, he sacked all of Gazprom's senior management and replaced the board with his cronies from the ex-KGB, preferably from St. Petersburg. Matthias Warnig as a local Stasi officer was an old friend and colleague from his days as KGB station chief in Dresden (where they worked together to recruit West Germans—scientists were mostly in demand—for the KGB). Later they continued to work together in St. Petersburg, where Putin as deputy mayor procured all the necessary licences to let Warnig open and lead the Dresdner Bank branch in the town. Here Warnig allegedly organized and financed the Yukos breakup and takeover in 2006.[75]

With the 2005 Russian–Ukranian gas supply and transmission disputes, Putin became obsessive over cutting the Ukraine out of the transit business. He appointed Warnig to head NS1 and appointed Schröder, whose job next to get Germany joining the deal was to procure Finnish, Swedish and Danish acceptance of pipeline routing through the Baltics. Schröder then—always according to the Danish investigative journalist Hoevgaard—picked his address book from his chancellor days (1998–2005) and after wining and dining them in 2007 recruited his political friends Göran Persson (Swedish Prime Minister during 1996–2006) for an annual salary of SKr 1 million to lobby his successor Frederik Reinfeldt (who was originally opposed to NS1) and Paavo Lipponen (Finnish Prime Minister during 1995–2003) for a salary of € 1,5 million per year to get the necessary national permits for their territorial waters.

---

[74] Givach, Simonov. Op. cit, p. 9.
[75] For details see: Jens Hoevgaard. *Gier, Gas und Geld*. Munich: Europaverlag 2019.

With Denmark, the story was more complicated. Originally NS1 had been supposed to run South of Bornholm in international waters, where, however, huge German ammo stock son the sea bottom, dumped by the Soviets at the end of WWII, proved an obstacle. Further, South sea border remains disputed between Denmark and Poland, hence, no go for Gazprom. It was decided to reroute the pipeline North of Bornholm, requiring Danish approval. Denmark's sizable food exports (beer and pork mainly) to Russia had been embargoed in 2002 as PM Anders Fogh Rasmussen had refused to extradite a Chechen leader to Russia. Thus, a discrete deal of "food for pipelines" was struck with Schröder as the intermediary, and after 46 years of no direct high-level contacts in 2009 a short-lived thaw set in Danish-Russian relations, with pork and beer again being able to ship to Russia (until in 2014 falling victim to the countersanctions again).

Schröder with Warnig at the coffers of NS1, however, also silenced other critics. Ornithologists of the University of Gotland suddenly received a research grant of 5 SKr million from Gazprom to investigate a rare duck species, and the local harbour was given SKr 50 million for renovation works and a museum. Other harbours were encouraged in their hopes for pipeline laying and servicing businesses.

In early 2020 US Congress slapped extraterritorial sanctions on EU companies working on the project, be in finance, pipe laying or as customers, like the German E.ON, Wintershall or the Austrian ÖMV. The Democrats were still angry at Hillary Clinton's alleged (but entirely unproven) defeat by a Russian complot favouring Donald Trump, and the Republicans wanted to sell more expensive LNG gas from fracking to Europe (conveniently overlooking the fact that the European North does not have sufficient LNG terminals—only Southern Europe has). Nonetheless, LNG exports to the EU have nearly doubled since 2017 to 123 bcm in 2019, thus, putting into doubt the Russian business model.[76] US sanctions in late 2019 interrupted the construction work for NS2, as most of the European joint venture partners for fear of their exposed US business interests opted out. By 2021, it is up to Russia to complete the last 120 kilometres more or less on her own.

In September 2019 also the European Court of Justice struck. At the request of Poland, it decided that Gazprom would have to grant other competitors 50% to its on-shore OPAL pipeline, which runs West of the Oder and connects Greifswald with the Central and Western European gas networks. The problem is that 100% of the gas landed in Greifswald is Gazprom owned and that there are no competitors around to supply the 50%

---

[76] *The Economist* 25. 1.2020.

required by EU energy law. Either Gazprom would have to leave half of its NS1 and NS2 capacities empty, meaning that Putin and Miller had sunk $11 billion worth of steel pipes uselessly into the Baltic Sea, or Gazprom would have to allow other Russian and foreign suppliers access to NS1 and NS 2 and thus end its export monopoly once and for all. Thus, a judgement, which prima vista appeared absurd, could generate very virtuous economic consequences in the end. Since the gas is supplied from Russian soil through the Baltic Sea, leading candidates would be Rosneft and Novatec.

5.6.2 Gerhard Schröder's Russian Energy Career

Schröder, born in 1944 and chancellor during 1998–2005, is a trained lawyer and not known to be an expert in energy economics.[77] Already in 2005, he was made to preside the board of trustees of Nord Stream 2, a project he had approved 10 days ahead of a federal election which he duly lost. His value for the Kremlin and for Gazprom consisted in his close links to senior Socialist politicians in Germany, like Sigmar Gabriel (Economic and later foreign minister during 2013-2018) and Walter Steinmeier (Foreign minister during 2005-2009, 2013-2017 and since then Federal President) and other Socialist worthies still in power. He had mentored their political careers in Lower Saxony and made sure that they did not forget and remained supportive for NS2.[78] Later he moved into the directorate of TNK-BP (which in 2013 was swallowed by Rosneft). In September 2017, his Russian energy career made another step forward: Nominated by the Russian government he was made head of the board of directors of Rosneft, a company of 280.000 employees, sitting on 40 billion barrels of oil reserves and paying € 20 billion of taxes in a good year. Apart from the Kremlin owning 50% of shares, other owners are BP, Qatar, Glencore and CEFC China energy. Rosneft also controls 12% of refinery capacity in Germany and is interested in moving into petrol retail, like Lukoil before. Also, Rosneft was interested to get into the LNG business, one leading technology supplier being Linde,[79] then still a German company. If there was any logic in his appointment, it was probably that Schröder's political connections could still be helpful in the age of a "grand coalition" in Germany. Apparently, his allowances per session

---

[77] In 2006 Schröder wrote a very a very bizarre ingratiating profile of Putin in der Spiegel 43/2006 in an article headlined: "Eines der schwersten Ämter": "His modesty is striking. He does not need luxury, nor splendors of glory…" Already earlier Schröder had called Putin an excemplary democrat.
[78] *Frankfurter Allgemeine* 25.8.2017, and 30.9.2017.
[79] *Frankfurter Allgemeine* 17.8.2017.

amount to € 580.000 per session, adding up to € 6 million per year.[80] Since Schröder since September 2017 (at least theoretically) is Igor Sechin's boss, the interesting question of his liability for Rosneft's recent misdeeds arises: Rosneft's billions of dollars sunk into Maduro's corrupt regime in Venezuela, the criminal shakeout of Vladimir Yevtushenko after the forcible take-over of Bashneft,[81] and the arrest of economics minister AlekseyUlyukaev trapped by Sechin a sting operation.[82] All of this happened under Schröder's "watch".

In 2021, also Karin Kneissl, a short-term foreign minister of Austria (2017-2019), a retired diplomat thought to be loosely affiliated with the pro-Russian Austrian Freedom Party, was also nominated to the Rosneft board.[83] She is not known for any expertise on the Russian energy sector (but rather on the Mid East), but was on spectacularly good terms with Putin, so as to invite him famously for a dance at her wedding in Styria in 2018 at the height of EU–Russian tensions.

5.6.3 Gas Pipelines in Asia

A lot of noise, memoranda of understanding have been signed by presidents Putin and Xi at annual rhythms with great fanfare for a decade and very little happened afterwards. First, all Russian pipelines follow an east–west structure. They cannot just be rerouted at will. Second, Russia does not want to become a raw material appendix to China, which is ten times stronger in terms of population and economic power. Third, the Chinese are brutal negotiators, even more so than the Russians. Like in Central Asia, they want the full control of the sources and of the pipelines from East Siberia to Xinjiang and Manchuria, finance, build and maintain them themselves, plus they want Siberian gas at a price based on cheap Chinese coal—unlike the Europeans who accept international oil prices as a benchmark. And Chinese giant state oil companies cannot simply be bullied around, like say, politically unprotected BP.[84] Putin since 2000 has thrown out most Western oil companies and smashed Yukos precisely for the reason to regain control, but surely not in order to hand Russian resources over the Chinese, so ceremonies apart, clearly no meeting of minds.

As the result, Russia builds the East-Siberia Pacific Ocean ("EPSO") from Tayshet in East Siberia along its long 2500 km Siberian border up to the

---

[80] *Frankfurter Allgemeine* 17.5.2017 and 30.9.2017.
[81] *Süddeutsche Zeitung* 21.7.2017.
[82] *Frankfurter Allgemeine* 16.12.2017.
[83] *Die Presse* 4.3.2021; Andre Ballin «Für Kneissl rollt der Rubel» *Der Standard* 5.3.2021.
[84] Pavel Baev « Asia–Pacific and LNG; The lure of new markets» in Barysch. Op.cit., 82–93, p. 89.

new terminal of Kozmics near Nakhodka (instead of the shorter and much cheaper route into Northern China), thus allowing exports also to Japan, Korea, Vietnam and other customers. Still a gas pipeline from Kovykta field (originally developed by TNK-BP, but taken over by Gazprom) North of Lake Baikal might still be built to China…

Needless to say that China has built its own pipeline networks to Central Asia, like CITIC, which already in 2006 for $6 billion constructed a line from the Western Kazakh oil fields to Xinjiang.

5.6.4 Policy Implications

Russia controls an estimated 27% of the world's known natural gas reserves, between 6 and 12% of oil reserves and 20% of coal reserves. It is the world leader in pipeline gas and as an oil exporter on a par with Saudi Arabia.[85] The EU imports 42% of its gas, 32% of its oil and 24% of its coal from Russia. Hence, it remains by far the single most important source of energy for the EU.[86] Yet the dependence cuts two ways. Two-thirds of Russian energy exports go into the EU and are mostly pipeline bound. That is, unlike oil or LNG they cannot simply be redirected and auctioned off at the world market. Plus Russian management has a strong risk-adverse affinity to long-term supply agreements like the ones which Gazprom concluded with E.ON and BASF in Germany, ENI and Enel in Italy, Gaz de France and Gasunie (Netherlands). And it adheres to them faithfully, as long as there are other potential suppliers…

Clearly not all is well in the Russian energy sector, on which the Kremlin depends for 60% of its revenue—financing, as mentioned previously, but cannot be stated often enough, anything from Putin's dachas to the wars in Syria and the Ukraine. The sector is certainly overtaxed with export tariffs, excise taxes, oil depletion taxes, value added taxes, profit taxes and any amount of "informal taxes" raging from bribes and kickbacks to "voluntary contributions" (like for instance for the Sochi Olympics 2014 or stadiums constructed for the world cup in 2018) organized by the "rent management" of the Kremlin, with the control of the rent flow as the key to Putin's long hold to power. But there are drawbacks: with lower taxes, companies could expand reserves and improve production capacities. The goose that lays golden eggs will not live forever, especially when mistreated.

---

[85] Konstantin Kosachev « Do we have a shared future in energy?» Ibid, 45–52, p. 50.
[86] Andris Piebalgs « Win–win cooperation is possible in energy» Ibid, 53–56, p. 53.

References

1. Barysch K (2008) Pipelines politics and power. Centre for European Policy Reform, London
2. Browder B (2014) Red notice. Hanser, Munich
3. Goldman M (2008) Oilopoly. Putin, Power and the Rise of the New Russia. One World. Oxford
4. Gustafson T (2012) Wheel of fortune. Harvard University Press, Cambridge, Mass
5. Grivach A, Simonov K (2019) The grand gas game. A 50-year-old Rivalry between the USA and Europe, Moscow
6. Hoevgaard J (2019) Gier gas und geld. Europaverlag, Munich
7. Popov D, Mistin I (2006) Julia Timoschenko. Die Zukunft der Ukraine nach der Orangenen Revolution. Dumont, Cologne

6

The Liberalization of Russia's Electricity Market

This is an interesting story that transcends a bit—but only a bit—our classical stereotypes about asset grabbing oligarchs and corrupt power-hungry siloviki. In fact, Putin and the Kremlin in large measures followed liberal recipes (advocated by Anatoli Chubais) for reasons of both power interests and of national industrial strategy. As a result, the Russian electricity market—in spite of all imperfections and distortions—is now more integrated and competitive than the one of the EU, of Japan and even of the USA. Since 2011, electricity, in principle, is sold freely at wholesale and spot markets, market imperfections described below notwithstanding.[1]

Foreign investors, courted during Yeltsin's days for capital and technology transfers, since 2003, have almost all been pushed out by Gazprom, except for some minor remaining capital participations by E.ON (Germany) and Enel (Italy). The EBRD in 2001 invested in the old state UES, insisted on the creation of a "UES Restructuring Committee" as a condition, and became one of the key drivers for reform. Already in the 1990s, the IMF had insisted on an end to energy subsidization, which had also been one of the core demands for Russia's accession to the WTO.

---

[1] Susanne A. Wengle. Post-Soviet Power. New York: Cambridge University Press. 2015.

6.1 The Soviet Heritage

Soon after the revolution in 1920, Lenin famously decreed: "Communism equals Soviet power plus the electrification of the entire country". Electrification was to lay the foundation of heavy industrialization and of reversing the economic backwardness of the country. For Soviet citizens, it became not only a symbol of progress but also an essential element to overcome the physical and climatic hardships of the country: to turn darkness into light, and cold into heat, and hence an important element of the legitimacy of Soviet rule. Thus, the electricity sector after the transformation played a much more salient political role than it does in the West—until our first policy-induced "black-outs" at least—so far.

Unsurprisingly, the first 5-year-plan formulated electrification as the political priority, with labour and resources allocated to dam building, coal extraction, the construction of power stations and grids. Essential to Soviet spatial and industrial planning was to locate metallurgical plants (steel and aluminium notably) close to these sources of power to constitute one mighty industrial complex. The workforce was then shifted into these newly created mono-industrial towns first into barracks in the middle of nowhere.

When the Soviet Union ended, one giant electricity holding United Energy Systems (UES), with a state bureaucracy operating like a ministry, controlled the regional fully integrated Energo "natural monopoly" networks. UES, in total, employed some 700,000 people, maintained 60 research institutes, 20 construction companies, plus the usual array of social facilities at all major production sites. It was also Russia's largest producer of central heat, on which most urban housings relied. Basically, European Russia was based on gas-fired power stations, Siberia on cheap hydropower generated from giant dams across the Yenissei and the Angara, and the Far East on expensively extracted local coal. The management consisted of electrical engineers who in this highly political sector were part of the trusted party nomenclature with the trappings of the typical apparatchik, interested in reliable plan fulfilment and the smooth production and delivery of the demanded quantities of electricity only, with little regard to conservation, the environment, innovation or profitability. By 1991, the entire system was in urgent need of repair, fresh capital and new technology as most of the old power stations and large parts of the grid predated the 1970s and had reached the end of their life spans.

6.2 The First Reforms

In the turbulent 1990s, electricity problems quickly became one of the core crisis areas of transition. Frequent power failures for factories or remote towns were seen as signs of state failure, as they stopped economic activity and plunged people into darkness and cold. With the state UES holding gone, governors basically acquired control of their regional Energo, which they used as a prime political tool for their personal power: for patronage and preferential tariffs to friendly companies, and a low tariff policy to consumers and to industry, in order to safeguard employment and to contain popular discontent in what essentially had become a barter economy. Non-payments by insolvent companies were not sanctioned with power cuts, with the predictable result that few felt obliged to pay any electricity bill. Regional oligarchs (who have almost disappeared since) negotiated favourable rates with the governors in return for political contributions. Obviously, the governors feared that high energy costs would force their energy and employment-intensive industries into bankruptcy and turn their settlements into ghost towns. Equally, they feared for social stability in their oblasts, if private consumers were cut off from power. In the absence of individual meters and thermostats, people had little means to control their energy consumption, let alone pay their aggregate housing bill (the infamous *kvart-plata* often amounting to one half of household income) in view of their own often unpaid wages and double-digit inflation.

Now it was the Energos turn to become insolvent with no funds left for repairs or fuel purchases, let alone for investments. Oligarchs like Deripaska, Potanin, Vekselberg and Khodorkovsky moved into the picture in order to acquire cheaply choice bits of the regional Energo, like modern power stations next to their processing plants. As neither the governors nor the oligarchs were interested in the liberalizing and unbundling ideas of the young reformers around Anatoli Chubais (who in 1998 became the chairman of UES), the reformers' concepts fell on deaf ears. Yeltsin's presidential decrees were simply ignored by the regional Energos, the governors and the oligarchs. Also, the Duma resisted effective liberalization until 2003 with a broad coalition, ranging from the Communists, the governors' party ("Fatherland-All Russia") and Yabloko, being opposed to Chubais and his young reformers, fearing yet another sell-out of national assets.

6.3 Electricity Under Putin

After Putin's ascent to power, his primary objective was first to break the power of the governors and to reestablish the primacy of national decision-making, second to end the independence of the oligarchs. In this context, the liberal ideas of Chubais and associates served him well. Seven federal *okrugs* as supra-regional authorities run by presidential envoys were created. As elections for governors were temporarily abolished in 2004 and dissident and too powerful governors one by one removed or sidelined, they were also stripped of their control of the regional Energo. The power failures during the cold winter of 2006 served as a convenient motive.

Putin and his former FSB colleagues pursued a vision of state capitalism, then with Gazprom as "arm of the government" concentrating all energy assets (oil, gas, electricity) and enjoying the monopoly for gas exports. The siloviki would be in control and channel its financial flows. Hence, there was an uneasy merger of two motives: state-building of the siloviki and market making of the young reformers.

By 2008, the Energos vertically integrated production systems were unbundled (into generation, transmission [high voltage], distribution [low voltage], and retail), and the power plants were privatized. The state in principle ended its subsidization of the sector and its control over the price of power, which was freely traded within the European Russia, and—at much cheaper rates—within Siberia (with the Far East remaining a regulated exception) and created new regulatory institutions. 21 new power companies were created, the old management, which had served the governors regional interests, replaced by a new breed of managers loyal to Moscow. Obviously, the question of asset valuation and tariff regulations were complex and took time, compromises and political bargaining with the oligarchs—this time in Moscow. Khodorkovsky's Yukos in 2004 very quickly lost Tomskenergo—and everything else. When approving electricity tariffs, the Kremlin also took regional objectives into account: to insist on more favourable rates to troubled remote areas in the North and East whose mono-industry towns remain threatened by depopulation. After 2000 also payment discipline was re-installed with the normalization of cash flows and the end of the barter economy. Energos were authorized to cut off non-paying customers. After minor protests and supportive media campaigns, this proved effective.

In the economically more significant European Russia, it was Gazprom which bought up the lion's share of the new 21 regional companies, the largest of them being the heavily indebted former Mosenergo (through debt-for-equity swaps), previously controlled by mayor Yuri Luzhkov, and Lenenergo in St. Petersburg. In 2011, it also acquired Viktor Vekselberg's KES, the owner of European Russia's largest power stations by means of a merger. By controlling domestic gas-powered stations and electricity delivery—in total at least 30% of European Russia's electricity assets—it could recoup its losses having to deliver gas cheaply to domestic industry and customers. By increasing the efficiency of the power plants, it could free quantities for more lucrative exports. Its business obviously relies on export sales at prices five times above domestic deliveries, electricity companies being its major customers (30–40% of sales). This dual pricing system constitutes a clear subsidy to domestic producers and customers in European Russia.

In regions unconnected to Gazprom's pipeline network, like resource-rich Tatarstan and Bashkortostan, the local electricity (Tatenergo and Bashkirenergo) and oil companies (Tatneft and Bashneft) for a long time remained the property of the ruling families, Shaimiev and Rakhimov respectively, whose ethnic republics during the 90s had enjoyed a contractually agreed semi-autonomy. In Sverdlovsk, gas continued to be supplied by Itera, Russia's largest independent gas company.

In Siberia, oligarchs like Deripaska pursued the old Soviet logic of territorial production complexes (TPK), that the hydroelectric power plants adjacent to their heavy industrial plants, like those of Irkutskenergo, should also be owned by them. As the overwhelming consumers of their electricity, they could live with low rates for the rest of the local population and the railways. In return, they were asked to finance and organize the upkeep and modernization of the hydroelectric dams and plants. Rusal also had to finish the construction of the giant Boguchansk hydroelectric dam at the Angara, abandoned in the late 1980s, in return for co-ownership, a "public-private partnership" of sorts. By 2008, already Rusal controlled 42% of Siberia's electricity production. Another 5% is controlled by Norilsk Nickel, co-owned by Potanin, Deripaska and Abramovich.

In the Far East, the story again remains different: In Primorye, in order to protect inefficient coal mines and coal-fired power stations, the market is sheltered against cheap Siberian electricity, with the loss-making regional Dalenergo remaining a state property, while in the remote North, territorial grids are isolated and not interconnected.

For the Kremlin (in line with Putin's doctoral dissertation), Gazprom and Rusal were national champions to be promoted to compete in global markets, but which at the same time at his behest had delivered in terms of "corporate social responsibility" by keeping employment stable and providing social services to their company towns and regions, like fulfilling investment and modernization targets, as defined by Moscow. Oligarchs were publicly set to task. Abramovich was forced to undertake modernizing investments, including public facilities, in Chukotka. Deripaska was forbidden to close his loss-making plant in the rundown town of Pikalevo (in Leningrad oblast), and told by Putin to continue to supply local energy and welfare services. In another aluminium company town, Sayanogorsk at the Yenissei in Khakassia, he had to continue to build roads, schools, new housing and even to run a former kolkhoz to assure the town's and his workers' food supply. The same story in Bratsk (Irkutsk oblast) at the Angara, built by Gulag labour in the 1950s, and in other mono-industrial towns built around Rusal smelters and hydro-dams.

According to estimates of the International Energy Agency (IEA) of 2011, however, the state continues to control some 60% of electricity generation: There remains the direct control of networks (as "natural monopolies"), of nuclear power stations and of dams and water power, plus cross-shareholdings in the 14 regional (OGK) and 6 trans-regional electricity companies. Again, according to the IEA, modernization and upgrade needs are huge, estimated at €470 billion, since most Soviet era electricity infrastructure, from dams to turbines and grid has outlived its life expectancy.[2]

Understandably, and since there is no integrated national grid given the distances, the main sources for electricity generation vary regionally: Water in Siberia, thermal energy: coal and natural gas in the West, and nuclear power in the South. The official interest in renewables in this fossil exporting country stands at zero.

As a more direct foreign electricity tool, the Kremlin created a state holding called Inter-RAO. It started purchasing power plants and transmission companies in CIS countries like Moldova, Georgia, Armenia, Kazakhstan, Kyrgyzstan and Tajikistan. The method of acquisition nolens volens was the same as Gazprom did domestically with the former Energos: Let them run up debts until they became unpayable and then settle for debt-for-equity swaps. As a result, by 2008, already Inter-RAO had become the largest owner of privatized electricity assets in the CIS countries, especially prominent in Armenia and in Georgia. In Armenia, it owned 50% of installed capacity and the Medzamor nuclear plant. As Armenia had a surplus production capacity and Georgia chronic shortages, Inter-RAO helped out by exporting to Georgia and further on through Georgia to Turkey and to Iran. Yet in total Russian electricity exports amount to only 2% of production and mostly go to Finland.

---

[2] Benjamin Triebe «Das größte Land der Welt braucht neue Energie» Frankfurter Allgemeine 27.7.2013.

In spite of nominal and partially effective price liberalization of the electricity market, the subsidization element shows up in various contexts:

First, Gazprom's requirement to run a dual pricing system between European Russia, selective client states, and the rest of the world.

Second, the separation of the Siberian market from the rest of Russia gives Rusal, Norilsk Nickel and the like access to unbeatably cheap energy. In 2002, it was estimated that the electricity costs for a ton of aluminium did cost Rusal US$120, while those of their US competitors Alcoa and Kaiser stood at $289 and $330 respectively. Also, Siberian railways benefit from these artificially low rates for their rail cargo and mineral exports.

Third, Tatarstan and Bashkortostan with their cheap oil and opaque low-cost price setting are less places of ethnic folklore (like the North Caucasus), but significant industrial sites.

Fourth, electricity prices to households and to companies remain set at low, below cost levels. This has two consequences. Innovation and modernization in investments in power generation are hardly profitable. Further, they give little incentive to save. Russian homes remain badly insulated and in the absence of thermostats, in case of overheating, the room temperature is regulated by opening the window, for instance, like during Soviet days.[3]

6.4 Conclusion

In sum, not unexpectedly we do not see a pure unified national electricity market with quantities going to the highest bidder. Yet the old bureaucratic UES and its regional Energo monopolies have been destroyed, as they were privatized often by tender in an unbundled form (with the state typically keeping ownership of the high voltage transmission lines and the power dams). Significant market elements were introduced. Yet central Kremlin control was reestablished at the expense of the regions with a system allowing for political interventions almost at will. Its electricity policy has become intrinsically linked with industrial, regional and even "near abroad" foreign policy objectives. Russia's varied policies of cheap energy for domestic producers as cross-subsidization surely could be a strong case for anti-dumping investigations by trading partners like the USA and the EU.

---

[3] Neue Zürcher Zeitung 18.10.2006.

Reference

1. Wengle SA (2015) Post-Soviet power. Cambridge University Press, New York

7

The State-Controlled Banks and the State-Owned Enterprises and Their Privileges

On the face of it, the Russian constitution prescribes a free market economy (Article 8), albeit with mixed ownership for land and natural resources (Article 9), with free competition (Article 34) and the protection of property (Article 35), further the rule of law, the division of powers and a democratic federal state. So far, so wonderful in theory. Yet Putin's presidential powers were expanded by sub-constitutional means, be they federal laws, presidential decrees (*ukazy*), or constitutional court decisions. Since 2003, there is a clear policy shift towards renationalization and state control of strategic sectors, usually done by presidential decree. Lists of companies were issued, which were prohibited for privatization (natural resources, finance, defence, high tech) and protected from bankruptcy.

An Agency for Strategic Initiatives (ASI) was set up at the same time to promote FDI in Russia's regions and facilitate government approvals, custom clearance and to support exports. Unsurprisingly, it showed little positive results. By 2014, a formal import substitution policy was adopted, first on procurement by State-Owned Enterprises (SOE)—foreign suppliers had to be at least 15% cheaper than domestic ones and also with tax breaks and direct grants to key sector companies worthy of the Kremlin's benefits. In October 2018, a grandiose plan was adopted for national goals until 2024: "a breakthrough in economy, infrastructure, technology and social matters", plus of course the quality of life and competitiveness, with private companies being obliged to participate in SOE projects. The World Bank[1] subsequently ranked the country down to 77 (out of 100) in 2019 in terms of business and investment climate in international comparison.

Since the early 2000s, there was an extreme centralization of decision-making towards the central government; economic involvement was either piecemeal by uncoordinated ministries (and their inherited "silo mentality") fighting incessantly amongst each other, or from the Kremlin. Understandably, their constant politico-bureaucratic interventions had a low professional quality. Yet during Putin's rule, there was a constant growth of power and economic involvement of the FSB, the Ministry of Defense and the Ministry of Emergencies, in other words, the "uniformed services", with the Ministry of Trade and Industry and the Justice Ministry having to play along.[2]

At the same time, the Ministry of Finance, the Ministry of Economic Development and the Central Bank played and continue to play a more technocratic and constructive role for macroeconomic stability. Yet the political game was somewhere else: state funding and lucrative procurement orders were available only to those with the best political connections. This showed the dominance of the incumbent players to all concerned.[3] Yet there is and remains a big a regional difference in terms of administrative qualities, depending on the Kremlin appointed governors, some of which at the time of writing in Kaluga and Tartastan were considered very positive. But this may not extend to their successors.

The rule of law has become very arbitrary, expeditious and unpredictable, depending on political connections and applied by the whims of more or less free-lancing officials. Presidential decrees are liberally used as quasi-judicial forms with presidential envoys (*polpredy*) like during Czarist days as implementers, creating legal insecurity and a massive capital flight at the rate of net $63 billion (2018), up from $25 billion (2017). As in the old Soviet days, instructions are given by phone to the judges, as obviously evident in the Yukos case among the many.[4]

Russia is not alone among countries in which underpaid officials, academics or judges seek private gain through corruption. But say, in comparison to Indonesia, Vietnam, Angola and Nigeria, where sometimes the wrong

---

[1] World Bank. Doing Business: Training for Reform. Russian Federation. Washington D.C. 2019.
[2] E. Huskey. "Elite Recruitment and state-society relations in technocratic authoritarian regimes: The Russian case". Communist and Post-communist Studies 2010, 43, 4, 363–372.
[3] M. Nistoskaya and L. Cingolani. "Bureaucratic structure, regulatory quality, and entrepreneurship in a comparative perspective" Journal of Public Administration Research and Theory 2015, 26, 3, 519–534.
[4] K. Hendley "'Telephone Law' and the 'rule of law'. The Russian case." Hague Journal on the Rule of Law 2009, 1, 2, 241–262.

hands are greased, it is more systemic. Thanks to the FSB, it serves as an organized system of rent extraction for the political power holders which in return co-opt the political and administrative for more flexible rules and their administration. According to Transparency International in their 2017 Index, Russia stood at 135 out of 180. Most problems were related to bribery, the fabrication of evidence in the legal system and corruption during public procurement.[5]

7.1 The Finance Sector

The Russian finance sector is clearly underdeveloped by any yardstick: 90% of assets are bank dominated in terms of GDP. Pension funds account for only 4%, investment funds for 3% and insurances and the rest for 3%. The banks' own capital corresponds to 10% of GDP (end 2017), with deposits being fairly limited: households supplying 28% of GDP and businesses 27% of GDP.

At the same, the sector has become quite concentrated: the five largest banks, led by Sberbank, control 60% of banking assets and 65% of household deposits (2017/18), which a growing gap to the rest of the other mostly private banks. Let us review the state-controlled banks (SCB) and their subsidiaries ("groups"). By 2018, they are by order of importance of all banks (public and private):

1. Sberbank: 50% owned by the Central Bank, 40% by foreign investors.
2. VTB (Vnestorgbank): 61% state owned by the Federal Property Management Agency.
3. Gazprombank: 46% Gazprom, 8% VEB.
4. Vnesheconombank (VEB): 100% state-owned, now termed Development Bank, but in reality slush fund for the Kremlin.
5. Otkrytie FC: 100% Central Bank owned.
7. Rosselkhozbank: 100% state owned.
9. Promsvyazbank: 100% owned by the Deposit Insurance Agency, a special purpose bank to serve the military-industrial complex.
15. All Russian Bank for Regional Development (VBRR): 100% owned by Rosneft.
17. Binbank: 100% owned by the Central Bank.

---

[5]A. Yakovlev and O. Demidova. "Access to firms to public procurement in Russia in the 2000s: Before and after radical reform of regulation" International Journal of Emerging Economies 2012, 5, 2, 140–152.

In contrast, the ranks of the remaining private banks:

6. Alfa Bank, with 4.3% of assets, owned by Mikhael Fridman and Petr Aven, two of the few surviving old oligarchs.
8. Moscow Credit Bank, with 2.7% of assets.
10. Rosbank (controlled by Societé Generale), with 1.7% of assets.
11. Unicredit, equally 1.7% of assets.
12. Sovcombank group.
13. Raiffeisenbank, with 1.4% of assets.
14. SMP Banking Group, with 1.4 of assets, owned by Putin's boyhood friends Arkandy and Boris Rotenberg.
16. Rossiya Banking Group (the "Kremlin bank"), owned by Putin's friends Yuri Kovalchuk (42%), Gennadi Tishenko (10%) and Nikolai Shamanov (10%).

Both banks are—not without reason—on the US sanctions list.

18. St. Petersburg Bank.
20. Uralsib.

These top 20 banks command 81.6% of all banking assets, with the state-controlled SCBs being in charge of 68% of all assets. This would constitute a unique concentration of the financial sector in a developed market economy. In fact, many small banks only operate as enterprise pocket banks, or as regionals banks are the only local banking providers.

From 1990 to 1998, there was a continuous decline of state influence until the financial crisis of 1998, originating in East Asia hit Russia belatedly and severely. This was reversed during 2008–2009 and 2014. This renationalization was basically first and foremost a banking rescue operation run by the Central Bank, which declared their ownership would only be a temporary one, and the banks would be sold after restructuring. Thus, the Bank of Moscow and Globex were rescued by the government in 2008, but in spite of public intentions to reprivatize them by 2015, they remained state controlled.

After 2009, there was strong government capital and liquidity support to stabilize mostly the state and a few private large banks. Shareholders were legally obliged to recapitalize and the banks forced to lend to the real economy (which, however, did not happen in reality). While this charade prevented a systemic banking crisis, support funds were rather funnelled out to offshore markets and channelled to the forex markets. The ruble went down by 40%. According to World Bank estimates, these operations did cost $45 billion to the Russian budget, which amounted to 4% of its GDP.

Once the crisis of 2014 struck, the Central Bank and the Ministry of Finance supported only systemic relevant banks, which meant two thirds of their funds supported the three largest state-owned banks. The total costs of this bail-out this time amounted to $46.3 billion, paid from the state budget and the Sovereign Wealth Fund, fed from oil export revenues. Banks now owed 12% of their assets to the monetary authority, representing 14% of GDP. The ruble declined again, as did foreign credits and household deposits reflecting the general crisis of confidence.

Basically, not only the state banks but also SMP Bank and Bank Rossiya have privileged access to government programmes and federal funds. SCBs also benefit from government guarantees and thus get cheaper funding and are more attractive to corporate and private clients. In 2015, it was estimated that this amounted to 1.5–2% lower interest costs. Sberbank and VTB are the only banks with a full nationally developed network, which can handle pensions, rents, utility payments and as a result of their retail business receive a large volume of low-cost funds, thus driving regional banks out of business. Hence, as duopoly, they are in the enviable position to pay low-interest rates on deposits while charging high rates for loans, which, no wonder, makes them highly profitable when things go right. As the Russian deposit insurance still does not cover deposits by businesses, also enterprises prefer SCBs.

In 2017, the Central Bank took over the distressed Otkrytie FC, the Promsvyazbank and the Bimbank, increasing the market shares of SCBs from 58.5 to 70.7%. The Deposit Insurance Agency reacted similarly. Thus, ultimately SCBs late in 2017 held 55% of private deposits, issued 78% % of corporate and 72% of private loans. This is similar to China and India, but surely not what was intended by the reformers during the 1990s.[6] There is clearly a conflict of interest between the supervisory functions of a Central Bank while being in charge of Sberbank as its largest subsidiary retail bank and largest creditor, while supervising the banking sector and being able to sanction the competition. With their market dominance SCBs have turned into an oligopolistic state instrument, creating the obvious moral hazard of abusing their privileged market position.

In sum, the dominance of SCBs is explained by their inherited infrastructure of Soviet industrial banks, by the financial needs of the government and SOEs, by their economies of scale which reduced costs, their low-cost access

---

[6] L. Bershidsky. "Putin's Creeping Nationalisation of Banks". Bloomberg Opinion 7 June 2018.

to international capital markets, the administrative support by the government, the financial support by the Central Bank, and last but not least by their image of stability for the general public.

7.2 Insurances

Accounting for only 2.8% of GDP, the sector is equally underdeveloped. With the ten largest players controlling 75% of the market (2017), measured by size of insurance premia, it is highly concentrated. The largest five stand for 51%. They are: Sogaz (13%), Rosgosstrakh (11%), Alpha Strahovanic (10%), Sberbank Strahovanic (9%) and VTB Strahovanic (8%). The Central Bank had revoked the licenses of smaller insurance companies, citing financial or regulatory problems. There was also a series of mergers and acquisitions. Again there is strong state influence via Gazprom and the SCBs (Sberbank, VTB and Otkrytie FC). Total insurance funds amount to 3% of GDP. Foreign investors play only a minor role, providing 12% of the capital of insurance companies.

Related non-banking financial institutions, like pension and investment funds, with combined assets of only 8% of GDP (2018) play an even more marginal role.

7.3 The Stock and Bond Market

Both peaked in the pre-crisis year of 2007 with a stock market capitalization at 100% of GDP, but by 2016 recovered only at 46%, meaning that more than 50% of value remained lost. Current values traded remain at 9.2% of GDP, which means that the stock market remains essentially illiquid. The reasons are: the end of the liberalization process, the state dominance over the economy, restrictions on FDI and also the fact that Russian companies prefer foreign stock markets for listings.

The bond market in 2018 had a total outstanding volume of 21% of GDP, growing in volume, but still far below potential. Government bonds accounted for 44%, corporate bonds for 53%, meaning mostly financial institutions and also oil, gas, mining, construction and real estate.

And who owns the Moscow stock exchange? The Central Bank at 12%, Sberbank at 10%, VEB at 8% and the EBRB, EU sanctions on Russian state financial institutions notwithstanding, at 6%.

7.4 The Capital Markets

One third of the capital markets are still nominally in private hands. Yet the state dominance is obvious. The private banks include the three foreign banks, UniCredit, Raiffeisen and Societe Generale in the second tier, almost along with micro and shadow banking. Obviously, a crackdown on undercapitalized and zombie banks with forced closures had been necessary by 2014, but it could have been done by transferring bad loans to the already existing Central Bank Consolidation Fund, to take care of them instead of sacrificing savers deposits.

The fundamental problem remains: How can Russia with such a reduced number of mostly state banks with their politically directed interests and bureaucratic mindset serve the financial needs of the population and of SMEs? The risk is that people and small businesses resort in despair to the "microfinance" of often usurious institutions. Ruling them illegal or placing interest caps will not help, if bureaucratic state banks are unavailable and arrogantly disinterested. In a World Bank survey conducted already in 2008, 28% of respondents among entrepreneurs replied that after tax problems access to finance was their second biggest problem. For SOEs and their politically appointed and well-connected managers, this problem does not exist. High-interest rates have enticed savers to invest into the formal banking sector. But as most banks and branches are located in Moscow and in European Russia, Siberia and the North, for instance, are becoming more and more underserviced. As a result of these market imperfections, private Russian companies always had to pay a premium on capital.

What we basically witness is a worrying trend like in China in the past: Big state banks squeeze out medium-sized private banks, and service SOEs and politically connected companies only, while leaving private people and small companies with their financial needs to a usurious informal and unregulated "micro" sector with all assorted risks and costs to the general economy.

7.5 State-Owned Enterprises (SOEs)

Let us recall that during the first stage of privatization (1992–1994), each Russian received a voucher with the nominal value of RUB 10.000 with the right to exchange it for shares in the company he worked at, buy shares in an intermediary organization, so-called check investment funds, or just sell the vouchers. Whatever its imperfections, the privatized economy had barely a decade to consolidate and to gentrify from its wild beginnings. The renationalization started with the crack-down on Yukos, the largest privately owned company, in 2003, whose assets were taken over by the state-owned Rosneft. In the oil and gas industry, this trend continued. It happened haphazardly and as "creeping renationalization" was not publicly announced nor discussed.[7]

Over the next 4 years, the government directly or through SOEs gained control over companies like Sibneft (oil), United Heavy Machineries and Power Machines (both engineering), AvtoVaz and major aircraft and helicopter plants. During the financial crisis of 2008/9, bail-outs were organized by state-owned banks, like by the VTB, followed by the Central Bank's policy to eliminate one-by-one more or less shaky private banks, gradually raising the state-controlled share in the banking sector to 70.7% by 2017.[8]

There are also so-called "unitary enterprises" controlled by federal, regional or municipal governments, like Rosoboronexport for the export of armaments, the Post of Russia, or Rosspiritprom for alcoholic beverages, the Air Traffic Management Corporation and the All-Russia State TV and Broadcasting Service. Local unitary examples are the Moscow Metro or Saint Petersburg Metro.

Finally, there are joint stock companies with the Russian acronyms OAO or ZAO, which are more or less in state ownership and whose shares cannot be publicly traded. Examples are Russian Railways, Sheremetyevo Airport and United Shipbuilding Corporation. But also there also those with a dominant state ownership like Gazprom, Rosneft, Sberbank, VTB, Aeroflot and Transneft, which at least are listed on Russian and foreign stock exchanges.

The IMF even went further to cover also the subsidiaries of the largest 20 non-financial conglomerates, which are Gazprom, Rosneft, Transneft, Inter RAO, Rushydro, Rosseti, Rostelekom, Aeroflot, Tatneft, Alrosa, United Aircraft Corporation, Helicopters of Russia, United Engines and United Shipbuilding. Then the formal state participation in the entire economy went up to 33% in 2016, dominant actually in all sectors except for agriculture and services.

Yet in comparison to other countries, the SOE share among the largest enterprises with 81% was still relatively moderate compared to China with 96%. According to these IMF estimates, the state's shares in value added were at 59% in finance, 52% in electricity and gas, 48% % in transport

---

[7] C. Sprenger. "State ownership in the Russian economy: Its magnitude, structure and governance problems" The Journal of the Institute of Public Enterprise 2010, 33 (1–2), p. 14 and: L. Chernykh "Profit or Politics? Understanding renationalisations in Russia" Journal of Corporate Finance 2011, 5, 1237–1253, p. 1241.
[8] IMF "Russian Federation. Selected Issues" IMF 2018 Country Report 18 18/ 276, p. 19.

and communications, 44% in mining and extraction and 21% in manufacturing. While being advantaged, still SOEs formally had to compete in the regulated markets of telecoms, transportation, banking and finance, postal services, and health and energy. The government clearly influences the key management decisions in large enterprises by issuing special directives.

Aeroflot for instance is the only recipient of royalties that foreign air carriers flying through Siberia pay for using Russian air space. These amount to $600 million each year, higher than its net profit of $395 million in 2017. Even EU airlines are still forced to make these payments ($3500 per flight, or €300 million for all of them all per year) even though a bilateral aviation agreement of 2007 foresaw their phasing out by 2013! Somehow in Brussels a few people in high places have been unable to follow up.

As mentioned previously, Gazprom and Rosneft are authorized to exploit deposits on the continental shelf, with Gazprom having an export monopoly on pipeline gas.

Certainly, SOEs are obliged to pay dividends to the federal budget. Unlike the taxes of private enterprises these are subject to negotiations at very high levels, and often are paltry amounts given their extra-budgetary "voluntary" contributions during the year.

In sum, SOEs remain significant in key sectors like finance, oil and gas, transport and communications and in mining. Yet there are not used in any instrumental way for a coherent industrial policy or for strategic economic goals. Rather the objective seems to be opportunistic rent-seeking through monopolization. This is not a recipe for industrial policy success. For them, there is very little public disclosure, and both the regional unitary enterprises and the SOEs are protected from bankruptcy. In short: This is corporate governance at its very worst.

7.6 Public Procurement

The public procurement market: the construction of roads and buildings, the repair and maintenance of locomotives and rolling stock, pipeline services, official cars and buses, the IT sector and also the supply of hospitals and schools in 2018 amounted to €108 billion, representing 7.7% of GDP. Among the top 50 suppliers were, surprise, surprise, 34 unitary, state-owned or state-controlled enterprises, supplying 70% of goods and services thus by far outstripping their weight in the overall economy. If there are tenders and auctions at all (they amounted to 4% of the total contracted volume in 2017!), for imported goods, there are both outright bans and price preferences for domestic producers depending on the sector. Some on defence equipment are justified with national security. Others on medical equipment, textiles, footwear, software, mechanical engineering, rubber, meat, fish (even foreign caviar!), wood, furniture, cars, buses, tractors, cranes, bulldozers, trucks, fire-fighting vehicles surely are not. All these cases of blatant import discrimination are entirely at variance with Russia's WTO obligations. But since they all are based on ad hoc presidential decrees without any strategic logic, we see a pattern of spontaneous, opportunistic implementation of Putin's import substitution policy, and be it the protection of Russia's caviar or forestry industry or its reindeer herders. 96% of public procurement was handled anyway by single-supplier contracts or other uncompetitive methods, where most foreign suppliers normally never have a chance.

Clearly, the public procurement market thus structured has the highest incidence of corruption, whether it is kickbacks, favouritism or outright bribes affecting the decision of government officials.[9] In 2017, 32% of Russian businesses reported corruption in municipal procurement processes, but expert estimates belief that nationwide in Russia they amount to 85–90%, while the OECD average stands at 3–10% (which includes countries like Mexico, Turkey and Korea). Basically, the Russian procurement market has become cartelized with suppliers from uncompetitive SOEs, relying on single-supplier contracts, overcharging the taxpayer for survival and greasing the palms of officialdom in the process. According to the fairly reliable Russian Federal Antimonopoly Service (FAS), the effects of this cartelization cost the Russian economy 2% of GDP per year. Had there been competitive bidding in public procurement, tender prices could have been 20–22% lower, the FAS conservatively estimated.

7.7 Trade Restrictions

In 2012, Russia became a WTO member, like China in 2001 beforehand, subscribing to the principles of free and unhindered world trade. But Putin soon became disinterested and pursued his idea of a post-Soviet customs union the shape of the Eurasian Economic Union (EEU) and by 2014 formally announced the pursuit of protectionist import substitution policies (even though it had already been practised beforehand, running counter to Russia's WTO obligations). The effects of various import bans dressed up as

---

[9]US Department of State. 2018 Investment Climate Russia, Washington D.C. 2018.

"countersanctions" were soon visible: the share of imported consumer goods in retail trade went down from 44% (2013) to 33% (2017); and those of imported foodstuffs from 36 to 21% during the same period, while retail price inflation shot up due to the absence of EU and US import competition. In pork and poultry, for instance, the share of imports fell from 57 and 33% (in 2008) to 10 and 4% (in 2017) respectively, the shares of imported cheese from 48% (2012) to 27% in 2017. Obviously, this cut-off of suppliers and competition offered neat windfall opportunities for domestic food processors at the expense of consumers (and at the expense of quality). According to an unpublished research paper,[10] the countersanctions that also applied to fish, fruits and vegetables, Russian consumers lost $7 billion per year (or 3000 rubles per person), hitting the poor, whose food expenditure is higher proportionally much harder than the rich. 84% of the benefits of import protection were redistributed to domestic producers.

Russian tariffs in line with the WTO accession agreement went down from 11.7% (1996) on average to 6.4% (2017). So far, so good. But there were always complaints about Russian custom procedures, non-tariff barriers and valuations, while the Russians had entirely eliminated custom duties on EEU members, like Belorus, Kazakhstan, Kyrgizstan and later Armenia and also reduced them considerably for favourite partners like Vietnam (2.9%) and Serbia (0.5%), with whom they had concluded Free Trade Agreements.

Yet Russia quickly used WTO instruments introducing 41 anti-dumping cases (against prohibited subsidies), of which 11 were directed against China. Safeguard clauses (emergency import protection) were introduced for porcelain table wear, harvesters, steel pipes and tubes, and flat-rolled steel. When Russia in turn was condemned in WTO settlement procedures, its implementation record remains decidedly mixed. Sometimes, like in the case of pork import bans, old sanitary restrictions were simply replaced by those based on national security.

In the services sectors, Russia is particularly restrictive in three areas: rail freight transport, cargo-handling and storage and warehouses, all related to the monopoly of Russian Railways, which is a country without a national motorway system is strategically placed, with freight rates and transportation costs given the huge distances being often a decisive cost factor.

---

[10] Natalya Volchkova and Polina Kuznetskova "Losers and winners of Russian countersanctions: welfare analysis" Moscov 2019.

7.8 Investments

Since the 2014 crisis, the perceived investment climate has deteriorated in Russia, coupled with negative macroeconomic expectations. The World Bank,[11] however, identified five areas where Russia ranked among the top five countries: obtaining construction permits, getting electricity, registering property, enforcing contracts and protecting minority investors. One may entertain doubts but not all seems bleak. In contrast, in the OECD's foreign direct investment index of 2017, Russia still ranks poorly compared to other OECD countries. Barriers include foreign equity limitations, discretionary screening of approval mechanisms, restrictions on the employment of foreigners, on branching, on capital repatriation and on land ownership. Sectoral restrictions on FDI go beyond traditional critical sectors like defence, national resources or finance. They also apply to insurances, air transport, legal services, the media (including TV and broadcasting), health care, telecommunications, surface transport, real estate investment, mining and transport equipment, and those sectors where SOEs enjoy their monopolies, like the domestic gas supply system of Gazprom. Here the government applies an investment control regime, which requires prior clearance, without as usual specifying any criteria for the assessment. The rest, notably in services and in primary sectors from agriculture to fisheries and forestry, has relatively low restrictions, again according to the OECD. All in all, it is estimated that the combined impact of sanctions and restrictions caused foreign investments to fall by 5%,[12] which, in my view, is an underestimate.

Sometimes, Chinese methods now also begin to apply: Bayer/Monsanto was obliged in 2018 to share its know-how and software regarding molecular selection tools and the germplasm for selected crops to produce highly productive seeds with Russian companies, so that they could compete on equal terms.

Russian capital is shy like a deer, and foreign capital even more so: During 2013–2015, the FDI stock declined from $471 billion to $263 billion. Even after subsequent increases, the stock of FDI in Russia represents only 2% of the world's FDI stock, while Russia's GDP stands at 3.1% of the world's GDP (2017), and thus continues to remain underinvested.

Interestingly, three quarters of Russian FDI hail from the EU, with by far the largest investor being Cyprus ($174 billion of total stock), followed by Luxemburg ($54 billion), the Netherlands ($47 billion) and Ireland ($31

---

[11] World Bank. Doing Business and Investing in the Russian Federation. Washington D.C. 2015.

[12] E. Gurvich and Ilya Prileppskiy. "The impact of financial sanctions on the Russian economy". Russian Journal of Economics .2015, 1, 359–385.

billion), and this is surely not mainly invested into EU-owned vineyards, tulip fields, breweries or cattle farms in Russia, but essentially represents repatriated laundered Russian offshore capital.

So where did this "EU" FDI go? Manufacturing ($99 billion), trade and retail ($78 billion), financial services ($56 billion), mining ($36 billion), real estate ($18 billion) and transportation ($16 billion), probably the same sectors where the money was gained and from where it was subsequently recycled.

References

1. IMF (2018) Russian Federation. Country report. IMF, Washington, D.C.
2. US Department of State (2018) Investment climate Russian Federation. Washington, D.C.
3. Volchkova N, Kuznetskova P (2019) Losers and winners of Russian countersanctions. A Welfare Analysis. Moscow
4. World Bank (2015) Doing Business and Investing in the Russian Federation. WB, Washington, D.C.
5. World Bank (2019) Doing business: training for reform. Russian Federation. WB, Washington, D.C.

8

Russian Industry

8.1 The Development

The quantitative achievements of Russia's heavy industrialization in the 1950s and 1960s are surely impressive; power generation increased from 2 billion kWh in 1913 to 49 bio kWh in 1940 and to 1240 bio kWh in 1979, oil extraction from 10 million tons (1913) to 31 million tons (1940) to 586 million tons in 1979. Coal went up from 29 million tons (1913) to 166 million tons (1940) and to 719 million tons (1979), steel from 4 million tons (1913) 18 million tons (1940) and 149 million tons (1979), cement from 1.8 million tons (1913) to 5.8 million tons (1940) and 123 million tons (1979), and so on across all industrial sectors. New industrial towns, like Magnitogorsk, Tchernogorsk ("Black city") and Kusbass, were set up in Siberia, or Karaganda in Kazakhstan, processing raw materials next to new dams supplying the energy, or melting steel next to coal mines. Huge industrial combinates like Krivoy Rog in the Ukrainian Donez, in Kunezk Alatau and in the Urals were built to combine the processing of iron ore and coal. Further metal processing plants were set nearby to produce metal containers or rail carriages for instance. The Soviet path of development clearly focused on heavy industrialization, while the Western capitalist and earlier Czarist approach started out with light industries, like textiles or the food industry for instance. The necessary work force was simply ordered to move (especially ruthlessly so, when in 1941 during the war, the 1500 plants of armament and engineering industry were shifted behind the Urals), their workers included.

Non-ferrous metals were scarcer in Russia. There was bauxite for aluminium production in Norilsk in the far North, first exploited by conscript forced labour and deportees, copper in the Urals, and also zinc, nickel, copper and lead findings in Siberia, thus motivating the construction "Baikal-Amur Magistrale" (BAM), as a second line north of the Transiberian in 1984. As transportation costs were high for these ores, processing was done on the spot in Norilsk, Bratsk and Sajanogorskin in their unhospitable climates.

Obviously, quantitative targets have outlived their usefulness, but they give an indication of the efforts and sacrifices undertaken (and remained determinants for the mindset of Gosplan planners and factory managers until the bitter end of the Soviet Union). Production was entirely planned for a division of labour within the Comecon. Exports to the rest of the world (oil and gas as foreign currency earners apart) or international competitiveness were not foreseen. As a result, the Russian manufacturing sector remained extremely wasteful as regards the human, capital and natural resources used, and except for the armament and aviation sectors, lost out in terms of innovation, quality, lean production, automatization, electronization and marketing compared to Western and emerging Asian competitors. Secretiveness prevented all technical spill over from the technologically advanced and privileged armament and space industries to the civilian sectors, which one should have expected.

In the late Soviet era under Brezhnev, in response, entire turnkey plants were imported from the West like the Fiat-plants in Togliatti, where 146.000 workers were supposed to produce one million Lada ("Shiguli") per year. Other turnkey imports were aluminium works and airports.

Other car production locations were in Moscow ("Moskvitch"), Gorki ("Volga") and Saproshe ("Saporoshez"). At the Kama with West German aid, Europe's largest truck maker was constructed in the 1970s.

In Russia's basic economic geography, there is a clear division of labour: the European part—including the metal-working centres of the Urals—is engaged in processing, while the East in a quasi-colonial pattern supplies the energy and the raw materials.[1] The centre of the processing industry is no doubt Moscow with its car, machine tools and aviation industry requiring higher engineering skills in its work force. Iron and steel are supplied from Tula and the Donbass. St. Petersburg is the second-largest processing centre with turbines, generators and diesel engines. The Ural finally is the centre of the armaments industry, in safe distance from any potentially hostile border, and for machinery for the mining, oil and metal processing industry. Siberia

---

[1] Wein. Op. cit., p. 187.

is less industrialized, with diverse machinery production in Novosibirsk, agricultural machinery and freight cars produced in Krasnoyarsk and Irkutsk, and shipyards and machine tools dominating Vladivostok.

The most dramatic was surely the development of the energy sector as the basis for all industrial production. Up to the war, Russia proper was considered energy poor, with most farm households in Europe burning peat for their heating needs. Since the postwar years, however, the discovery of fossil fuels in Siberia, of new coal deposits and the development of hydropower, have made Russia a world power in terms of energy generation (and of waste) as the world's largest individual producer of oil and gas since the late 1970s. Russia's problem once again is in logistics: 80% of energy is generated in the East, but 75% of consumption and demand is in the West. Transportation over thousands of kilometres by either rail or pipeline is obviously extremely costly. As industrial production remains very energy-intensive and insolation of apartments almost inexistent (in the absence of thermostats, windows are opened to regulate over-heating), in spite of abundance due to waste and transportation problems, energy shortages remain frequent.

According to Lenin, as mentioned before, communism meant Soviet power plus electrification. Hence in the 1920s, 10 giant water and 20 thermal power stations were built, over fulfilling—with US aid—the original plans by 200% in 1935. In the 1950s and 1960s again electrical power generation was multiplied by eight, since the mid-1970s increasingly also by nuclear power in the European part of Russia, like in Leningrad, Kursk and the North Ukrainian town of Chernobyl. Major Russian Rivers, like the Dnepr and the Volga, have been dammed with a cascade of water power stations, with the resulting lakes flooding fertile land and generating high evaporation levels of water, which is missing downstream for irrigation purposes. In Siberia, dam building is even more problematic as valleys are often the only ground suitable for agriculture. Coal production since mid-1970s has been starved of investments, obviously for the benefit of gas and oil extraction, which is more interesting for exports.[2]

Historically, the oil fields of Baku had fuelled Czarist Russia, were occupied briefly by the British in 1919–1920 and were the elusive objective of the German offensive in 1942. Yet as fields were exhausted and production had to move offshore into the Caspian Sea, Soviet extraction technology was unable to cope. By 1981, Baku fields delivered just 2.4% of Soviet oil needs. There were some oil discoveries in Central Asia in Uzbekistan and Kazakhstan, which then were not properly exploited either. The real discovery

---

[2]Ibid., p. 201.

happened in 1964 in the West Siberian Surgut, an oil province covered half by water and frozen swamps. Artificial islands had been constructed as well as all-weather roads to the sites and urban shelters for the work force. By 1982/1983, West Siberia accounted with 353 million tons of oil for 58% of the Soviet oil output and allowed it to be the world's largest producer ahead of the USA and Saudi Arabia. It was supplied to its Comecon partners at rates 40% below world market prices and sold at OPEC prices to the rest of the world.

The gas sector was only developed in the 1960s, notably after findings in Central Asia and Western Siberia. Earlier it was just flared. By 1985, already 32% of all consumed energy in the Soviet Union originated from gas. Obviously the construction of 170.000 kms of gas pipelines ("Brotherhood") through permafrost from Urengoi at the Polar Circle through the Urals up to the Russian centres of consumption and for export to Baumgarten (Austria) and central Europe as a planning priority required huge efforts and in spite of US sanctions the importation of the pipes from Germany up to its completion in 1983.

Russia's and the Soviet Union's enormous territory covering 11 time zones needed some spatial management and territorial subdivisions, if only for planning purposes. In 1921–1922, large economic areas were defined, each of which should supply its own labour and energy needs. Between 1944 and 1960, Gosplan merged them into 13 grander economic areas. Between 1960 and 1980 again, they were regrouped into 20 rayons, each of which from the Baltics to the Far East, should develop its own specific economic profile, yet at the same time become as autarchic as possible, as regards raw material, energy, labour and food supplies in order to reduce transport costs and losses.

In the 1960s, the concept of territorial production complexes (TPC) was developed and attempted to be implemented notably in Siberia for regional economic planning during the late 70s. Ideally, there should be abundant local sources of energy, like a dam with turbines or a coal-fired power station. Second, plenty of natural resources or food supplies. Third, good climatic condition for the work force to live and to secure local food through agriculture, and finally good transport infrastructure. While in places like Norilsk, Vorkuta and Magadan, obviously, the latter two conditions were not to be fulfilled, and hence slave and later contract labour were used, but the TPC Sajan at the Upper Yennissey was an example of a formerly agricultural area of the Chakassen autonomous region with husbandry products supposed becoming heavily industrialized.[3] Its industrial output was

---

[3] Wein; Op. cit., pp. 218.

supposed to surpass the one of Belgium by the year 2000.[4] A river dam would supply the electricity for industrial complex. Then there was plenty of coal and iron ore, plus non-ferrous metals and wood in the surrounding taiga forests. Along the Yennissey, there were black earth deposits and a sheltered microclimate, plus sufficient water supply, as well as rail access to the Transib railway. Industrial projects were rail containers, electrical engineering products in a new "Eletrograd", and the aluminium industry a new town called "Sajanogorsk", added with local heavy metal processing whose ores in the past had been shipped to the Donbass.

Further TPC were created in European Russia and in Central Asia, based on partly already existing industrial centres: Petchora (between Vorkuta and Uchta) based on its riches of coal, oil and gas; the Kursk Magnetanomalie (KMA) for iron ore extraction and steel making; TPC Orenburg based on regional gas extraction, TPC Mangyshlak along the Khazak Caspian shores with an industrial complex on the new town of Shevchenko based on regional and oil resources. Water will be supplied by a nuclear-powered desalination plant. Also along in the BAM ("Baikal-Amur Magistrale") region, with the newly gained railway access new mines and processing mega sites were supposed to be developed as TPK, based either on coal, wood, copper, iron ore or other metal extractions.

8.2 The Soviet Planning System

Since the early 1930s at the latest, private productive property had been prohibited. People could only own consumer goods, an apartment or a house. Centralized state planning as developed by Stalin contained four elements: (1) a central planning authority directs all elements of production; the initiative does not lie with individual factories or units of production; (2) Economic planning and direction is a bureaucratic administrative process; state organs direct production and distribution of products; (3) It is a system of command economy with a short time horizon. Annual administrative plans are authoritative for production units. Fulfilling the plans is their measure of success. Factory managers and their staff hence are extremely limited in the planning process; (4) the system operates in quantities, not in terms of prices—which are set arbitrarily—or of profitabilities.

The system of 5-year plans was introduced in 1928. After the chaos of WWI, the civil war and regional unrest, production and logistical dislocations

---
[4]Note that the entire GDP of Russia by 2018 is equivalent to the Benelux!

this seemed like a useful orientation, as private initiatives were impossible. From 1928 to 1932, the foundations for heavy industrialization were laid, like electrifying the country and industrializing the largely rural Siberia. Highlights were the construction of the steel mill Magnitogorsk, the TurkSib railway to Central Asia and the new industrial city Komsomolsk at the Amur. The second 5-year plan from 1933 to 1937 tripled the steel output to 17.7 million tons. A strong focus was the further expansion of the Ural-Kusnezk steel combinate, which led to the further construction of steel-producing cities in the East. The third 5-year plan was obviously shredded by the war. Planning in the enlarged and devastated Soviet union resumed with a fourth plan in 1946 until 1950 based on a reconstruction to reach the output back of 1940. The fifth 5-year plan (1951–1955) with its idea of virgin land development was disrupted by Stalin's death in 1953. The sixth 5-year plan, beginning in 1956, was aborted after 2 years and then in 1958 replaced by a 7-year plan, which again was made dysfunctional after a catastrophic harvest failure in 1963. The eighth 5-Year Plan of 1966–1970—masterminded by Prime Minister Kossygin aimed at the intensification of agriculture and started to offer material incentives to farmers and workers. These ideas were continued in the ninth 5-year-plan of 1971–1975, which aimed at increasing living standards by promoting consumer industries. The tenth 5-year plan (1976–1980) focused on efficiency, quality and productivity targets, none of which in spite of incessant propaganda exhortations could be reached; The 11th 5-year plan (1981–1985) after a downward correction of original objectives still envisaged significant agricultural and industrial output growth, none of which was reached, neither with unpredictable harvest nor in coal and steel production.[5]

The more complicated production processes became, the more cumbersome became planning processes. Growing potatoes or chopping trees by administrative order was easier than producing radio sets or brain scanners. In the mid-1980s, some six million planning bureaucrats were reportedly employed by various layers of the Gosplan administration and its sectoral and regional branches. Gosplan's twin brother "Gassnab" in charge of supplying factories with the necessary production materials, thus setting up their annual supply plans. Obviously, factory managers always ordered more than they would actually as hoarding for emergencies and supply shortfalls, there was systemic spillage and waste. As planning objectives were law, low quality and defective output proliferated. Factory directors were discouraged from taking

---

[5]Wein. Op. cit., p. 241.

innovative product or process initiatives of their own and had internalized over the decades that it was better to play safe than to be sorry.

With these structural dysfunctions, the resort to voluntarist exhortations, if not outright slave labour appeared imperative. One was a fake "socialist completion" of workers against workers, collectives against[6] collectives and factories against factories for higher out or less material losses, with medals, privileges and tables of honour for Stakhanovite model workers. Since the mid-1960s, the lure of medals and honours has declined. Subsequently, a supplementary monthly wage was offered per year for substantial norm over fulfilment and extra work.

8.3 Russian Defence Industries and Their Chinese Competitors

According to the ISS,[7] Russia's defence industries employ directly 1.3 million workers and indirectly a total workforce of 2.5 million, producing 20% of manufacturing output and 3.7% of GDP (2015). Four years later, the Finnish Defence Ministry arrived at slightly different figures: The Russian military-industrial complex employed some 2 million people and counted for 5–6% of industrial output, yet including inputs from machine-building, electrical, electronics and metal industries, this would add up to about 10% of industrial production.[8] Yet both highly informed guestimates imply the same: Like in the old Soviet days, Russia rather likes to produce tanks and fighter bombers rather than dishwashers, toothbrushes and hair dryers.

Domestic "sales", i.e. orders from the Defence Ministry, count for $61 bio and exports for around $15 bio annually. The mineral sector apart, the defence industrial complex is probably Russia most significant industrial segment, which during the Soviet era was massively privileged in terms of manpower, finance and material, and which even during the 1990s was able to modernize with Western know how. In Russian military doctrine, the ready availability of a large quantity of military equipment and ammunition is a must in all military districts for territorial defence ranging from the Far East to Karelia. This explains, why the costly built up of a blue water navy and

---

[6] Aleksej Stakhanov had overfulfilled his planning norm in coal mining by 14 times. In der GDR, this was followed by Adolf Henneke.
[7] Richard A. Bitzinger and Nico Popescu (eds.) *Defense Industries in Russia and China: Players and Strategies*. Paris: EU Institute for Strategic Studies. 2017.
[8] Christina Juola e.a. Resources of Russia's Defense industry» in: Ministry of Defense. *Russia of Power*. Helsinki 2019, 73–89, p. 83.

of long-distance bombers (which are the key to US military doctrine) so far have been neglected.

Given Russia's strategic preference to prepare for limited land warfare against its neighbours and to modernize its army and air force in its "New look" reform of 2007–2011, particular strengths lie in battle tanks, armoured vehicles, artillery, anti-aircraft and missile systems as well as in fighter planes. Already prior to 2014, import substitution policies were implemented in the defence industries aiming at autonomous production. Yet the interruption of Ukrainian supplies and of joint developments underway led to setbacks for missile developments and to the lack of helicopter engines, aircraft parts and gas turbines for frigates. Planned purchases of Eurocopters, Mistral assault ships (from STX yards at St. Nazaire) and Lynx armoured vehicles from Iveco, as well as most other production cooperation with Western suppliers underway since 2000, were cancelled as the result of EU sanctions in 2014. Local production could not yet fully make up for the deficiencies. Most affected is the navel sector, with Russian shipbuilding in crisis which is unable to produce the gas turbines (supplied in the past by Ukraine) for frigates and the diesel engines (formerly supplied by Germany) for submarines. Also Russia has difficulties to produce turbofan engines for jet aircraft.

Russian defence expenditure increases strongly since 2011, peaked in 2016 following the attack on Ukraine to 4.6% of GDP (which is more or less on a par with Israel), but then declined again to 2.8%[9] in 2020. Other estimates go as high up 4.3 to 4% in that year, the difficulty being that many provisions are secret and large parts of military procurement have become classified for fear of Western sanctions. State armament programmes run for 10 years, with a review after 5 years. They cover half of military spending with the objective of modernizing 70% of equipment. According to official figures, these objectives have been reached for the air force, air defences and the nuclear forces, but not for the navy (53%) and the ground forces (43%), presumably as mentioned, critical parts like turbines and ship engines, were no longer available from Western Europe and the Ukraine. Best successes have been the upgrades of Soviet era weapons, like the T-72 battle tank, Sukhoi fighter aircraft and S-400 anti-air defence systems.

Yet the industry failed to produce entirely new systems like the SU-57 fighter jet or the Armata tank platform for the ground forces from a few prototypes into serial production. Yet the Russian armed forces are better equipped today than 10 years ago—which is good enough for limited wars in Georgia, the Ukraine and in Syria. In 2018, Putin in his address to the Duma

---

[9] Ibid., p. 76.

demanded the production of new "wonder weapons".[10] One remembers to have heard this from someone else back in 1944/1945.

Russia is still one of the few countries which have the ambition to produce the entire line of military equipment themselves. According to military doctrine, the defence industry is a constituent part of the state's military organization.[11] It is organized in several state-controlled groups: aircraft (OAK), space (Roscosmos), shipbuilding (OSK), air defence (Almaz-Antei), nuclear weapons and also artillery, helicopters, small arms—Kalashnikovs, ammunition and radio electronics (mostly assembled in the Rostec state holding).

At the beginning of 2010s, the companies were deeply in debt—as the Ministry of Defence had and still has the habit of paying late until after delivery, so they had to borrow for their running costs. As state enterprises, they were burdened with obsolete machinery and poor productivity. With the growth of public procurement funds were available for some modernization, but due to the inevitable corruption, fraud and pilferage not all was put to good use. After all, they were monopolists with a monopsonic (single) buyer, showed in secrecy and protected from public scrutiny.[12] So low productivity and poor profitability continued compared to Western competitors.[13] Though the Kremlin ordered a write down the debts, this of course did not resolve the companies' managerial problems of productivity and profitability. In fact, this never works anywhere. But the Kremlin found a former corporate finance bank, Promswjasbank, which had collapsed in December 2017 and had just been rescued by the Central Bank with $3.5 billion of refinancing, and instead of re-privatizing it, appointed it to a new function as chief financer of the armaments sector, which thus be hopefully safe from US sanctions. The head of this recreated defence industry bank would be Peter Fradkov, son of Mikhael Fradkov, former PM and head of the SVR, the foreign secret service.[14]

Although the military-industrial sector lacks the necessary marketing and financial skills, after all, it needs to follow ministerial instructions, plans, directives and subsidies foremost, it is also asked to produce competitive products for civilian use, most famously a Sukhoi mid-sized aircraft. Yet the policy of import substitution adopted since 2012 has not helped, since key

---

[10] Ibid., p. 82.

[11] Tomas Malmloef and Johan Engvall "Russian armament deliveries" in: Frederik Westerlund and Susanne Oxenstierna (eds.) *Russian Military Capability in Ten-Year perspective*. Stockholm: Ministry of Defense. 2019, 115–136, p. 115.

[12] Ibid., p. 116.

[13] Juola. Op. cit., p. 83.

[14] *Frankfurter Allgemeine* 27.1.2018.

components could no longer be imported but had to be produced more expensively and in worse qualities at home—like in the rest of the economy; the secretive nature of the industry—like in China—does not help great R&D breakthroughs. Industrial spying, as practised by Putin in Dresden, is no longer good enough. The stock of knowledge inherited from Soviet times is nearing its end, and Russian universities do no longer supply the necessary skills. And if they do the private sector offers better pay and working conditions; On top of this there is this massive scientific brain drain, affecting all of Russian industry and business, of the best and brightest going West.

To no one's surprise, as mentioned before, like in all state enterprises and in public procurement, corruption is a major hindrance due to fraud, misuse of property and overcharging, all aided by secrecy, the absence of competition and poor control. Yet, again surprise, surprise, in the end deliveries are actually made, improving the fire power of Russian ground forces, air force and submarines with refurbished and modernized Soviet era equipment.

Exports are essential for the survival of the military-industrial sector, which due to better prices and foreign exchange count for up to 80% of its income. Bestsellers of the main governmental Rosoboronexport agency (which since 2011 is part of the Rostec conglomerate) are T 90 battle tanks, S-300 and S-400 air defence missiles (bought also by Turkey), Iskander missiles, Kilo submarines, Sukhoi helicopters, SU 35 fighter jets and SU 32 bombers. Main customers are China, India, Algeria, Vietnam, Indonesia, Venezuela, Azerbaijan, Kazakhstan, Serbia and recently again Iran. Half of the exports are military aircraft, some 30% is army material, some 20% air defence, and war ships just about 6–7%, clearly showing the current stepchild situation of Russian navy and their shipyards at home and abroad.

The war in Syria and the hybrid war leading to the occupation of Crimea and the build-up around Ukraine (deterring successfully Western intervention) served to showcase Russian hardware as well as a testing ground for prototypes. At the same time, Syria was used as a destocking exercise for surplus bombs and superannuated ammunition with plenty of collateral damage in Aleppo and elsewhere. Yet the excessive costs of the Russian intervention ate into the military budget, thus cutting future arms procurements.

As the world's second-largest arms exporter after the USA (with a world market share of 20–23%) sales during 2012–2016 stood at $15 billion per year, their share in total Russian exports accounting for around 5%. Yet future sales are expected to level off. This is due primarily to Chinese competition on products, prizes and markets and also due to greater Chinese self-reliance, cutting Russian arms imports (from a peak of $3 billion in 2005 down to $800 million in 2015). Also, Russia has been subjected to Chinese industrial espionage, procuring, for instance, the necessary know-how for attack helicopters. Also, the SU-27 has been "retro-engineered" as the Shenyang J-11 fighter, which is cheaper and easier to handle. China increasingly conquers traditional Russian markets in Asia and the Middle East like Algeria, Egypt, Cambodia, Indonesia, Morocco, Iran and Iraq. In Africa, where China has become the largest arms supplier, the Chinese main business model is politically discounted arms sales (assault rifles, mortars, drones, portable SAMs) in exchange for oil and mineral concessions in Nigeria, Tanzania, Kenya, Sudan, Zimbabwe, Ethiopia, Zambia and also in Venezuela and Turkmenistan. But China also offers "political loans" to Asian customers like Sri Lanka, Bangla Desh, Burma and Indonesia for arms purchases. For political reasons, China's strategic rivals India and Vietnam remain "safe" markets for Russia. Yet India in the long run will build up its own autonomous defence industry and reduce imports. If there is still a break on Chinese arms sales, it is their poor quality and doubts on their reliability, as complex systems like aircraft, air defence systems and naval ships often need to be refitted with Western technology.

At the moment (2017), 58% of Russian arms exports went to Asia (India, China and Vietnam foremost), 39% to the Middle East and North Africa (Iran, Syria, Iraq and Egypt mostly) and 3% to Europe (Serbia and Turkey). While as indicated above the export share to China decreased to 10% of total Russian arms exports, those to their Indian rivals increased to 25–30% during 2014–2016, with the country as usually insisting on formal technology transfers to develop her own arms industry, while the Chinese have stolen and adapted the designs already long ago successfully.

In the medium term, the Russian defence sector will be put before the strategic decision whether the Kremlin will continue its course for limited land warfare as in the past or opt for a more expensive expeditionary force (as needed in Syria and elsewhere, if wished, in the Third World), which would require a blue water navy, precision weapons, drones, airborne reconnaissance, military satellites, search and rescue, and long-distance bombers—all of which have been missing. Due to cost constraints, it cannot have both, as also NATO noticed during the last 25 years. Further problem areas are the high indebtedness levels of the sector, its commercial dependence on exports (in a sector with global overcapacities) and an ageing qualified work force suffering from the brain drain of younger scientists and engineers, and evident difficulties to put prototypes into serial production. Russia also dislikes the prospect of becoming a subcontractor to the Chinese military-industrial complex, given China's twice larger and rapidly growing defence budget.

In China, ten government-owned conglomerates operate in the armament industry. Although, they were recently given more operational autonomy, as SOEs they suffer from bureaucratism, secrecy, corruption and the lack of competition, with the PLA being its major and often only customer. R&D is weak, although the sector has begun to draw on resources of private companies as well. Jet engines, for instance, still need to be imported. In difference to Russia, the PLA has all but in name abandoned its Maoist doctrine of "People's War" of land-based warfare, and fully arms and trains to protect Chinese maritime interests in the Western Pacific and the Indian Ocean with a blue water navy and long-distance aircraft and missile deployment. Although Chinese arms exports have increased dramatically from $1 bio in the 1990s to $6 billion (2016), with joint developments notably undertaken with their Pakistani ally, in difference to Russia, for whose industry exports are a matter of survival, for China's armament producers, the volumes sold abroad are merely a "bonus". Yet the unscrupulous nature of China's export policy, flooding Africa and the Mid-East with cheap automatic infantry weapons and supplying terrorist groups like Hezbollah and Daesh with drones and man portables surface-air missiles, is a matter of international concern—but apparently not shared in Beijing.

Russia's military power in Europe will not recede, rather the opposite with more modern battle tanks delivered to combat ready troops in forward deployment. The Kremlin has successfully militarized Russian society with the general acceptance of the will to fight, in their propaganda in contrast to the "decadent" West. In their planning, Western command and control structures were to be blinded by electronic warfare and decapitated by cruise missiles, with key infrastructure paralyzed. 180 days were needed to reach the Oder and then to stop (?).

Given Europe's difficulties in joint defence developments, Russia's and China's technology gap, vis-vis EU producers, was narrowing. Clearly, the EU's checks on dual use "critical" technology exports and high tech corporate purchases by China were not working (or inexistent). Also, the Chinese used education and research cooperation (on jet engines for instance) effectively for their purposes. EU sanctions on both Russia (since the Crimean annexation of 2014) and China (since the Tiananmen massacre of 1989) had contributed to their greater self-sufficiency and industrial autonomy—albeit at a price. Also for arms marketing, both were happy to supply customers on whom the EU and the USA applied self-restraints (be they on political grounds or for corporate governance reasons) while pursuing their strategic interests in South Asia, Africa and the Middle East as well as on the lucrative open markets of South East Asia.

8.4 Russia's Car Industry and Its Cooperation with European Makers

In a nutshell, the Russian car sector demonstrates a typical case of a difficult industrial heritage, inefficient industrial policy interventions and market distortions with welfare losses and plenty of trade irritants in consequence.

Russia certainly has a historical tradition in car making. In 1896, the first petrol-powered car was built by Yakovlev and Freze. Three years later, Hyppolite Romanov developed the first electrical car and the first electrical bus. The First World War and the October revolution interrupted the development of an automobile industry. The civil war of 1917–1920 was fought with railways and the cavalry. Under Stalin, only the politburo was allowed to use cars: heavy black ZiL limousines, handmade in the former Stalin Auto works in Moscow until 2012. Only in 1966, Brezhnev decided to start producing cars for the mass market. In a Komsomol project in Togliatti at the Volga, the world's largest car plant AvtoVaz was built on 600 hectares, with the main plant having a length of 3 kms and a width of 2 kms. The technology and assembly tools were all purchased from Fiat, and for the next 40 years, the Fiat 124 was produced as Lada ("Zhiguli" in Russian) almost unchanged. Design and execution were so simple that any skilled driver could fix most of the frequent repairs by himself at the roadside. Due to the lack of suppliers, AvtoVaz had to produce most spare parts by itself as well. About 107.000 workers produced some 600.000 cars per year. There were yearlong waiting lines and a lucrative black market for new cars and spare parts. Like all Soviet combinates, AvtoVaz had its own clinic, cantines, sports clubs, sanatoria, employee housing and kindergartens. With the collapse of the Soviet Union, wages were no longer paid for months. The management reacted by setting up their own distribution channels, selling cars (which continued to be subsidized) for hefty profit margins. The work force also started black markets with stolen spare parts. Soon organized crime was attracted and fought violently over the control of the illegal car trade. In total, some 500 lives were lost in the "AvtoVaz wars" in the city of Togliatti with its 700.000 inhabitants during the 1990s until 2005.

In 2006, Putin had enough. He had defined AvtoVaz before as a strategic enterprise and had it taken over by the government-owned arms exporter Rosonboronexport. The previous dispersed owners, red directors mostly, were bought out by the siloviki controlled Novikom Bank, and the previous management was fired. A Putin colleague from his GDR days, Andrej Belianiov, took over the board of trustees, and a specialist for fighter aircraft, Vladimir Artyakov, the management board. Both had no expertise in car building, but were Putin loyalists and instilled discipline and a modicum of motivation among the frustrated work force. They also mobilized 5 bio € of fresh Kremlin subsidies for new model development. They also finished unceremoniously a joint venture with GM over public recriminations over prices and payments. Although the joint plant was modern and shiny, the jointly produced SUV Chevrolet Niwa flopped in its sales. Getting rid of US engineers did not solve the technological backwardness of the rest of the plant. Workers continued with hand held tools and muscle power. Whenever they felt the need they went for a cigarette or newspaper break. With monthly wages of around 500 euros, labour costs were not a decisive factor, amounting to barely 13% of the plant's cost structure.

The crisis year 2008 was important for the world's car industry to engage in Russia. With the world financing crisis hitting the demand for cars in particular, and GM and Ford becoming temporarily insolvent, Russia—which was hit later—seemed like the promised land of car consumption, which was hyped up by the usual suspects; PWC predicted 3.8 million sold cars and Ernst & Young even 5 million sold cars by 2012, which would have made Russia the largest individual car market in Europe, far ahead of Germany.

Indeed the purchasing power of Russia's middle class had made significant gains since 2000, following higher oil prices and state expenditure. And with only 200 cars per 1000 (EU average: 500), Russians were motorizing quickly. First with imported—often stolen—second hand cars, mostly from Japan and Germany. When the Kremlin introduced a 30% surcharge on imported used cars, customers and traders rioted in Vladivostok over the loss of the only lucrative business in town. Russian customers now switched to new imported cars. When buying cars Russian patriotism ends quickly.

Those who can afford it do not want a domestic small car, but a robust SUV of a foreign brand. It is important that the wheels are high and the lubricants freeze resistant. The demand for powerful cars is not only due to the bad state of Russian roads and their potholes, or the fact that many rural roads in the North and East are not paved, but also a question of prestige and muscular image. Often purchases are done with the help of consumer credits or when inflation threatens the value of the ruble. Hence in moments of crisis, such as in 2008, the market still showed signs of life.

The Kremlin now forced foreign importers with import duties of 30% to assemble locally. Unlike in China, they, however, were not forced to partner with a local manufacturer. In certain cluster areas, regional governors offered generous financial aid, tax exemptions and fully developed special economic zones. Red tape was promised to be centralized one-stop at a cooperative governor's office. These were the days under Yeltsin, when regional governors—especially in rich Tatarstan—could still decide independent development policies. Moscow offered duty-free part imports if an investor promised to produce at least 25.000 cars with 30% Russian value-added within 5 years. The problem was that reliable part producers hardly existed in Russia. Raw materials such as steel and aluminium existed in abundance but not thin special quality steels for chassis, for instance.

Renault–Nissan decided against greenfield investments in order to benefit from a trained work force and joined the small Moskvitch plant near Moscow, but also invested 1 bio Euro into AvtoVaz—with a share participation of 25%. Carlos Goshn announced the plan to double output to 1.5 million units, with Dacia models mainly based on Renault platforms. Volkswagen invested 500 million Euro in Kaluga, a former armament town southwest of Moscow to produce VW and Skoda models. Continental also produces tires there for the Russian market. General Motors bought a former tractor factory called Elaz in Elabuga in Eastern Tatarstan to produce Chevrolets and Opel Vectras, also in Elabuga Severstal-Auto manufactures vans in a joint venture with Fiat and Isuzu for the booming retail and home delivery sector. St. Petersburg with its excellent harbour and transport situation and its well-trained work force is another car cluster. The Austro-Canadian car parts supplier Magna produces plastic parts and bumpers there. Also Toyota, Nissan and Ford have assembly operations in St. Petersburg. Kaliningrad/Konigsberg at the Pregel (Pregolya) offers similarly good transport conditions for imports. Avtotor does the final assembly here for BMW, Kia and General Motors. Finally, in Nizhny Novgorod, the car producer GAZ of Oleg Deripaska does contract work for Daimler and VW, but in its main productions like vans and busses are the market leader in Russia.

After this short period of boom during 2007/2008, the world financial crisis belatedly also caught up with Russia, with demand collapsing in 2009. After a brief recovery, it again contracted during Russia's crisis of 2014/2015. All foreign investors stayed, even with very thin margins, except for Opel which in instruction by General Motors had to write off its $600 million investment in St. Petersburg during 2015.

The Russian car market peaked in 2012 with 3.1 million units sold (including all categories from passenger cars to trucks), declined steeply during the crisis of 2012, a decline from it never recovered. By 2018, the market had further shrunk to 1.5 million units. The market is thus still much smaller than the one of Germany. In this shrinking market, the share of cars manufactured in Russia—increased from 72% (2014) to 86% (2018). The rest are imports, mostly from Korea and China. Two thirds of the Russian made cars are actually made by foreign direct investment, that is, foreign-dominated joint ventures mostly. The total market share of cars sold by Russian-owned manufacturers stands roughly at 20%, even though they enjoy generous public guarantees, special credit conditions of state banks, tax breaks and are privileged in public procurement. In 2018, for instance, the government decided on the renewal of Russia's decrepit bus fleet, making buses the only growth sector of the industry. Subsidies are given to leasing and credit companies to support the purchase and preferential leasing of "family cars", "first cars" and "own business" cars, which were reserved for Russian made cars only, again in violation of WTO rules. Reportedly, this generated 125.000 extra sales (or 9% of total sales). Subsidies are equally paid to produce Russian made components like engines, gearboxes, control systems, chassis batteries, body parts, vehicles systems and interior equipment for localized production. Yet in sum, judged by its results the Kremlin's expensive industrial policies in this sector defined as "strategic", which accounts for 7% of Russia's GDP employs 600.000 people can hardly be judged as particularly successful.

Unlike her Chinese neighbour, Russia as a major producer and exporter of fossil fuels is not interested in electric cars, understandably also since distances are too long and many locations too remote to set up a network of loading stations. Rather it looks at traction powered by LNG, of which they have a lot.

If there is a bleak spot for Russian road transport, it is its appalling safety record. 20.000 people get killed every year in a population of 143 million. This is thrice as high as a ratio than in the EU where 25.000 get killed in a population of 540 million. The reasons are aggressive, reckless and drunk driving, poor and often icy roads and poor vehicle maintenance. It is a popular pastime to watch video-recorded Russian road accident clips with trucks smashing into the opposite lane, falling off the road side, motorcyclists or pedestrians being thrown into the air (and sometimes even getting up again alive), cars crashing into crowded crossings, into street signs, or houses without braking…

For the EU, as the world second-largest car producer after China, its importers and producers face a lengthy list of unresolved and opaque trade irritants. One is a "recycling fee" charged for all makers and importers, which only Russian producers get reimbursed. Then there are Russian anti-dumping duties on imports of mostly German and Italian vans, which is an issue pending in the WTO. Industrial assembly contracts concluded in the past were to be phased out by July 2018 to become WTO compatible. Yet there is still no clarity on a successor automobile regime. On the importation of car parts, their valuation and on local contents rules similar uncertainties reign, with Russian authorities often backdating claims and charging ex-post taxes and tariffs. An EU-Russia car parts agreement of 2015, which should resolve these issues, has never been implemented by them. In the absence of any significant progress in EU-Russia car talks, EU makers appear to have resorted to either taking matters into their own hands and to resolve their problems individually (or via their Russian JV partners) with the Russian authorities or to work through their national embassies and trade ministries.

9

Russia's Railways and Logistics

In difference to the USA, for whom historically, they played a similar role for development, Russia—like Canada—kept and maintained its transcontinental railways, a rare continuity from Czarism to modernity. The first railways of 27 km were built in 1835 and, after a long delay due to competitive views promoting waterways, by 1914, Imperial Russia operated 70,500 km of railways, two thirds of them state-owned, one third private,[1] with most bonds owned (and lost) by French investors.

As a heritage of the Soviet system of industrial concentrations with railway links still 80% of all industrial production is transported by rail. Already in its final decades, the Soviet Union was unable to keep up with the modernization needs of its overextended railway network. During the turmoil of transformation in 1991–1998 freight traffic was halved. Only in 2001, reforms started in earnest. The Ministry of Railways was divided up and dissolved in 2003. Russia's Railways became a state-owned private company (OAO RZhD) with 740,000 employees (2017) contributing 1.5% to the Russian GDP and controlling the world's third-largest rail network (after the USA and having recently been overtaken by China) with some 85,000 km of railways lines, on which however also private operators, prominent in the more profitable freight traffic (while passenger traffic remains in deficit), operate prominently. This is regulated by a Railway Transport Agency, overseeing tariffs and safety

---

[1] Freiherr von Röll «Russische Eisenbahnen» in: Enzyklopädie des Eisenbahnwesens, Band 8, Berlin, Wien 1917, p. 278.

© The Author(s), under exclusive license to Springer Nature Switzerland AG 2021
A. Rothacher, *Putinomics*,
https://doi.org/10.1007/978-3-030-74077-1_9

issues,[2] permitting a greater degree of economic liberalization in the sector, than, say, France.

During 2005–2015, Vladimir Yakunin, a trained engineer, previously working for the KGB as a First Secretary at the Russian Mission to the UN, and later a Deputy Minister for Transport who was considered close to Putin, was the powerful boss of the railways. His modernizing investment ambitions were usually grandiose, but the delivery of business results less so. Until 2030, investments of a total of €400 billion and 20,000 km of new tracks were planned and announced by Putin.[3] 120 billion Euros were to be spent on new locomotives and carriages. RZhD's main supplier is Transmash, a merger of 12 state-owned railway works, in which RZhD has acquired a 25% share. Transmash's 60,000 workers produce some 500 locomotives, 1000 carriages and 750 traction units and rail motor coaches per year, mostly for the Russian market (I.e. RZhD), and also for export to CIS countries, India and Iran. In 2006, Transmash purchased Fahrzeugtechnik Bahnen Dessau in the vain hope of technology transfers according to its CEO,[4] in order to let it slip into insolvency only 2 years later.

At least in 2009, Yakunin managed to get a high-speed link Moscow—St. Petersburg of 550 km with the help of Siemens made "Sapsan" (peregrine falcon) express trains underway—at total purchasing costs of US$260 million—successfully on the tracks which thanks to a speed at 230 km/h shortened the travel time to 3 h and 45 min. Yakunin in 2015 also started its 770 km extension from Moscow via Nizhny Novgorod to Kazan; a project budgeted at the modest US$19, 2 billion. With trains running up to 400 km/h, the travel time would be slashed from 14 h to 3½ h. Then, however—a fall-out from the 2014 sanctions which choked off Western finance to state-run projects—the design and engineering contract of US$400 million was already awarded to a Sino-Russian consortium, putting EU suppliers and bidders at a disadvantage.[5] Ultimately Yakunin planned an extension from Kazan via Yekaterinburg and Chelyabinsk, and further to Astana and Urumqi up to Beijing. The Russian stretch from Moscow would amount to 2080 km, the Kazakh to 1700 km and the Chinese to 4000 km. This grandiose construction scheme reminiscent of the 1930s would be part of the Chinese Silk Road belt initiative and obviously largely financed and subsequently built by them. Strangely enough, the Russian railways also took over the railways of Armenia as an unconnected subsidiary.

---

[2] Financial Times 7.3.2000.
[3] Vladimir Yakunin „Wir sind die Quelle neuer Fracht" Die Presse 6.12.2008.
[4] Dmitrij Komissarov "Europa ist kein offener Eisenbahnmarkt" Frankfurter Allgemeine 26.3.2008.
[5] Neil Buckley "Yakunin warns Europe missing out on Russian deals" Financial Times 8.7.2015.

In 2010, Yakunin also advocated a broad gauge rail link from the Ukrainian border to Bratislava and Vienna, a construction of 560 km of new tracks costing Euro 4, 7 bio.[6] Similar to the Chinese, understandably, Yakunin dreamt about the potential of the Eurasian land link compared to container shipping. Close to the Chinese border, he opened in 2008, the "Zaibakalskij" terminal with the capacity for 500,000 containers. With his investments along the 9000 km of the Transsib, he wanted to shorten the route Hamburg-Peking from 12–14 days to 9–10 days—while it took container ships 24–40 days. While this sounded wonderful, it overlooked the fact that modern container ships carry 20,000–30,000 containers each, while one transcontinental train pulls at most 40–60 containers each. Quite simply, it would need 500 smooth running trains (customs checks at border crossings and cows on tracks notwithstanding) to match the competitiveness of one modern container ship along the Eurasian route. It is hence attractive only for products (apples as perishables come to mind), for which long shipping along the tropics is unsuitable and air freight is too expensive.

In order to cement his partnership in transcontinental freight traffic, Yakunin proposed, in 2008, to purchase one fifth of Deutsche Bahn shares.[7] But nothing came out of it. The 2008 crisis hit Russian Railways hard. Not only did passenger and freight traffic decline by—12% and—19% respectively, the Russian state also ordered tariff increases to stay much below inflation in order to help troubled companies such as producers of metals, other raw materials and building materials relying on rail transport (of which RZhD still controlled 40%, including most commodity transport for export). Losses mounted rapidly. As a result, during 2009, half of the planned investments were postponed and all high-speed projects were frozen. 54,000 of the then 1.3 million railwaymen were fired, a rarity in a state-owned company.[8] In 1991, there had still been 2 million employees, the railways have been Russia's largest employer.

Russia unfortunately is not a stranger to terrorism. In 2009, terrorists bombed the Nevsky Express between Moscow and St. Petersburg, killing 26 people. Today, 30,000 armed guards are in operation protecting the Russian railway traffic.

When things went wrong, Putin had no hesitation to publicly blame Yakunin, when there were not sufficient rail cars for coal transport in Siberia.[9] Initially without consequence, yet in 2014, it became known that

---

[6]Frankfurter Allgemeine 28.5.2010.
[7]Frankfurter Allgemeine 26.9.2008.
[8]Frankfurter Allgemeine 11.4.2009.
[9]The Telegraph, 18.3.2012.

RZhD during 2007–2013 had paid a staggering total of US$3.5 billion to 11 letterbox companies with obscure owners and without employees, after having won-faked tenders. The money went to accounts of the soon defunct Capital Commercial Bank (STB), owned by an old Yakunin friend, named Andrei Krapivin, from where it quickly disappeared.[10] Yakunin, as a member of Putin's inner circle who was considered on a par with Igor Sechin, the chief of Rosneft, and one of the leading lights in Ozero, the cooperative that runs the datchas of the Putin entourage as a gated community at the Karelian Isthmus near St. Petersburg, in September 2015, was rumoured to become a senator to represent the Kaliningrad oblast (North East Prussia) at the Federation's Council. Speculation had it that he would be made head of this Council, a largely ceremonial post high in constitutional protocol, which would not have meant a demotion.[11] Yet the demotion happened which he accepted with good grace. Today, he is running a shadowy "Dialogue of Civilizations" foundation in Berlin and Vienna, with uncertain finances focusing on his orthodox conservative values.

As a successor, Mikhael Fradkov was first considered. But similar to Yakunin as a former foreign agency chief, he quickly appeared on the US sanctions list. This would have threatened RZhD's refinancing, with external debts running at currently up to US$ 10 billion, denominated mostly in US$, CHF, GBP, € and RUS. With a credit rating of BBB, current returns for mid-term bonds at 5.7% for US$ bonds and 3.4% for € bonds are not unattractive for institutional investors. Instead, a relatively non-descript former deputy transport minister, Oleg Belozerov, from St. Petersburg was appointed, and former Austrian chancellor Christian Kern, a Socialist former head of OeBB—a very well-run railway system—engaged for the board in 2019. For Moody's, the crucial issues for RZhD are its dependence on continued state support: subsidies, equity injections, low interest financing, and tariff rate setting.

The problems of the railway sector, with its still antiquated rolling stock, lack of proper management along the Transsib, and the lack of connecting tracks and trains to major transport centres—including overheated and low comfort departments for passengers—as well as the poor state of the roads especially in the East and North create major headaches for logistical companies. Not only Russia's 140 million consumers need to be supplied, Russia also remains the major logistical hub for most of the 280 million people of the CIS. The size of the country with 11 time zones where some goods have

---

[10] "Russian Rail pays billions in secret" Reuters 25.5.2014.
[11] Kathrin Hille "Leading Putin aid said to be facing demotion from rail job" Financial Times 18.8.2015.

to be shipped for some 10,000 km means that transport costs amount to 15–20% of production costs, while in the West, they only amount to 8%. The total volume of the logistics sector in Russia is estimated to comprise some 120 billion US$ per year. Russian companies as a rule will only ship products from A to B. It is often more costly to deal with the associated paperwork and to fulfil arbitrary decisions on incomprehensible regulations (and to grease the proper hands at the right addresses). With a distance of 1500 km, trucks lose their competitiveness to trains, also the strain on drivers becomes too strong. Yet there are too few road/rail transit terminals. While the size of the market continues to attract foreign operators with their stronger service sophistication, their main problems relate to legal insecurity, poor roads—as proper motorways and express roads only exist in European Russia—the lack of rail connections and the shortage of qualified local staff.[12] When in November 2015, an electronic road toll system of 4 cents per km was introduced for heavy trucks (which obviously do the most damage to road surfaces), protests were widespread with fears of ever-increasing transportation costs inflating retail prices as well.[13]

---

[12] Die Presse 20.9.2007.
[13] Rossiyskaya Gazeta 16.12.2015.

10

Russian Agriculture, Forestry and the Agrofood Business

With 1.2 million square kilometres of arable land agriculture accounts for 6% of Russia's GDP (2016), 16% of employment and as the second-largest item after oil and gas (and barely ahead of armaments) for 5.3% of her exports. In 2017, it proudly became the world's largest wheat exporter ahead of the USA, mostly supplying the North African and Mid-Eastern markets. The top crop by far is wheat, of which in an average year (2011), 56 million tons were harvested, followed by potatoes with 33 million tons, and plants for animal feed with 2.5 million tons. Russia is also the world's largest producer of sunflower oil. Farming at small private plots like during Soviet days continued to remain highly productive, in 2013 accounting for 42.6% of total agricultural production, worth US$34 billion. For the rest, small professional farmers accounted for 9.8%, and large commercial producers—the privatized successors of the old kolkhoz and sovkhoz farms—for 47.6% of output.

Like in the Western and East Asian experience, the agricultural sector and the farmers historically were ruthlessly exploited to support feudal rule and its courts and wars, and then in the nineteenth and early twentieth century to supply taxation, capital and surplus labour for industrialization. By the 1960s curiously—once the agricultural sector had shrunk to less than 20% of employment—in the Western democracies (but also in Japan, Korea and Taiwan), with ruling parties cultivating conservative rural voters, the rest of the economy, through state subsidies, high consumer prices and import protection began net transfers to the rural sector (which continued to shrink regardless). Czarist and Soviet Russia were no exemption, if only for different motives. In the 10th 5-year-plan of 1976–1980, for instance, when only 22% of Soviet citizens still worked in agriculture already 27% of all state investments flowed into the sector.[1] Or as Stephen Wegren put it: "Stalinist culture was a pro-urban, anti-kulak culture that viewed agriculture only as a sector from which resources could be exploited cheaply … During the post-Stalinist period coercive rural institutions were maintained … Agriculture was no longer a sector simply to exploit but instead benefitted from a large influx of state credit and investments".[2] Given their misallocation and waste, nonetheless, import needs remained high for cereals, and supply shortages severe for meat and dairy products,[3] leading to long waiting queues and occasional food rationing.

Yet also today, the Putin administration resorts to selective import bans for food, like fruit, wine, dairy and meat[4] in the name of self-sufficiency objectives in order to protect its agro-food interests at the expense of Russian urban consumers who experience higher prices and less choice and quality as a result. At the same time, it massively subsidies the agricultural sector, which like the EU's old common agricultural policy (CAP) helps to stimulate unprocessed agricultural output, like wheat, barley and soybeans, for export surpluses.

10.1 The Natural Conditions

Similar to Canada Russia faces extreme continental weather conditions, with the centre of polar cold around Yakutsk with an average temperature of − 43 °C in January. In the vast areas of East of the Urals where there are only 60–90 days frost-free, the growing period is too short for agriculture. Even areas north and east of Moscow with 105–120 frost-free days, late spring or early autumn freeze may affect harvests dramatically. The harshness of Russian winters explains why inter alia the Russian leadership and the people could not care less about "global warming".

---

[1] Norbert Wein. Die Sowjetunion. Paderborn: Schöningh. 1985, p. 50.
[2] Stephen K. Wegren "Rural Reform and Political Culture in Russia" Europe-Asia Studies 46, 2, 215–241, p. 215.
[3] Shortages were partly alleviated by the import of heavily subsidized EU surplus stocks shipped exclusively through "Interagra" of Jean-Baptist Doumeng, the "Red Billionaire" who with his profits also financed the French Communist Party. New York Times 7.4.1987.
[4] As "countersanctions" since 2014, they apply to EU, Norwegian, US, Canadian and Australian products. But also earlier food import bans were used with phytosanitary pretexts as a political tool against imports of fruit, vegetable, wine and mineral water against the Ukraine, Moldova and Georgia, who had been dependent on the Russian market as a result of the inherited Soviet division of labour.

10 Russian Agriculture, Forestry and the Agrofood Business

The extreme climatic zones of the North and the semi-arid areas of the South, stretching from the Southern Don, very visible for instance in the Kalmuck ASSR, through the Altai mountains up to the Amur river in Southern Siberia, can only be used for extensive nomadic husbandry, like for reindeers in the North and sheep in the South. The "Southern Taiga", an area of mixed forests covering the Moscow area and running from St. Petersburg to Kazan, is more densely populated with about 30% of the national territory used for agriculture (and utilized mostly for husbandry, potatoes and rye). The biggest problems for farming are high groundwater levels and swampy soil conditions, which make the construction of expensive drainage and its maintenance necessary. Further South, stretching from the Donbass and the middle Volga to the Lake Baikal and beyond, is the "forest steppe", which with rich top soils and sufficient rain remains Russia's most productive agricultural area. Here, in the classical surplus area of old and new Russia, wheat, sugar beet, sunflowers and husbandry prevail.

In Southern East Siberia and the Russian Far East islands of agricultural production were developed to supply the regional industrial towns with wheat, rye, soy, beef and dairy as much as possible locally.

Obviously Russian farmers during past centuries—a research priority during the Soviet era—have developed seeds for rye, summer and winter wheat, which were suited to the various harsh local conditions. A persistent problem remains soil erosion, which was worsened during 60 years of Soviet collectivization, destroying hedges, small forests and ponds in order to create industrial conditions for large-scale monocultures for doctrinal reasons and central planning objectives. Heavy rain eroded the top soil and through superficial outflows created deeply cratered valleys in the fields. Wind erosion was equally harmful, as strong storms blasted the unprotected deeply plowed dry top soil, including seeds and seedlings away as clouds of dust. As a result, 200 million hectares of fertile land were permanently damaged, not only in Russia but also in the Ukraine and Kazakhstan. The planners' reply was to increase the amount of mineral fertilizers for the lost top soil, but no solution.[5]

Apart from climatic and soil conditions, a third major problem during Soviet days concerned hydrology: While the soils of the North suffered from an excess of humidity, those in the South were excessively dry. The sorry fate of the Aral Sea is well known. By draining most waters from its tributary rivers Amudarya and Syrdarya—with most water lost in sloppily built irrigation channels—for cotton production in Uzbekistan, the over-dose of salt

---

[5]Wein. Op. cit., p. 69.

and of fertilizer residue first killed all sea and bird life, and then the absence of water ultimately the sea, which has become the main source of toxic sands blowing over central Asia since.

10.2 The Russian Farmers

Manpower is another headache of Russian agriculture. Biographically, farmers could not share the Western experience of centuries' generational free and independent professional farming, visible in old and large homes, barns and in professional pride, apart from the short period between Stolypin's reforms in 1861 and the forced collectivization of 1928. Consequently, the work-styles they experienced in their kolkhoz villages from early youth was one of carelessness towards the land, the facilities and the means of production. By the mid-nineteenth century, 38% of the total population of European Russia (statistically also including Finland and the Baltic provinces with their free farmers) had been serfs of large landowners or feudal lords, with their ancestors mostly for more than 200 years. On the fertile large holdings of the South, this took the shape of "batchina", forced labour of at least 3 days on their owners' land. In the wooded and less fertile north, it was "obrok", payment in cash to capitalize the serfs' labour. Sometimes both existed in combination. In any event, serfdom meant to be entirely tied to the soil and to the landlord's holding, to live at the bare minimum and entirely devoid of freedom. As we know from Russia's great realistic nineteenth-century writers from Gogol to Chechov, farmers could be sold, used as collateral or gambled away. The number of "souls" was the major indicator of the value of a landlord's holding. As land was worthless when not cultivated, banks required them as collateral for loans to landlords, regardless of whether these were used for agricultural modernization or to finance extravagant lifestyles at home or abroad. Indeed, there is great variance in the literature—as certainly also in real life—between well-run productive model landholdings, with the landlord's manor often being the only local centre for cultural and intellectual life on the one side, and of run-down estates of disinterested rent-seeking absentee landlords on the other, who as noble officers, senior civil servants or simply loafers were ignorant about farming and exploited their holdings to finance their luxury lifestyles in St. Petersburg, Moscow or in Western European residences. The average truth is probably somewhat in-between with the balance unresolved lying very much in the eye of the beholder. If we believe Alexander Pushkin's novella "Dubrovskij", written in 1833, then also in Czarist days legal titles to the land were not safe and could be expropriated by corrupt registry clerks and judges. Farm administrators and local officialdom almost without exception in the literature are portrayed as fraudulent, thieving, cruel and uncaring, and the local serfs, a few virtuous cases apart, as illiterate, ignorant, lazy, unreliable, superstitious, violent between themselves and against their wives, and drunk whenever possible.

As mentioned in Chap. 1 after Alexander II's liberation in 1861, farmers had to compensate their former owners with an amount representing 16 2/3 times the annual labour or cash rents, to be paid with interest over the next 49 years (that is until 1910). The village community mir allocated the land—between 3 and 8 ha at most) on a rotating basis by lottery. This meant little attention was given to proper crop rotation, fertilization, drainage or irrigation for land melioration. Productivity did not increase and crop failures were continued. The more entrepreneurial farmers moved to the virgin lands of the South or to Siberia. Richer farmers bought up the land from landlords tired of the countryside or feeling threatened by periodic rural riots.

With Stolypin's reforms during 1906–1911 (the year in which he was murdered), farmers could exit the "mir" and have their land (after a land reform ended the previous parcellization) registered as personal property. An agricultural bank would supply credits for modern equipment and the purchase of further land. Evidently, this differentiated rural society. By 1914, 65% were still poor farmers, 20% considered "medium-sized" and 15% large farmers,[6] the stratum of "kulaks" which Stalin would prosecute, send to the Gulag or simply murder. Agricultural production increased considerably. By 1913, 80 million tons of cereals were produced, which also allowed for considerable exports. According to Soviet statistics in 1917, poor farmers owned 135 million hectares of arable land, kulaks, using ("exploiting") partly hired help, 80 million hectares, and "some 4000" feudal landowners and the clergy 152 million ha..[7] Hence property relations do not seem to entirely out of balance and were probably more equitable than they are today.

During 1917, Richard von Stenitzer, a captured Austrian military doctor, gave a very vivid account of a typical farmers market in a small town East of Moscow, where in spite of the shortages of the war a lively and folkloric business atmosphere prevailed: not only plenty of local processed food was sold but also artisanal products made on farms or rural workshops, like wooden cutlery, colourfully painted pottery and earthenware, wooden toys, dried hides, clothing, agricultural implements, iron samovars, but also barrels of

---

[6]Wein. Op. cit., p. 81.
[7]Lev Voskresenski. «La agricultura. La Union Sovietica: hoy y manana». Moscow: Agencia de Prensa Novosti 1985, p. 14.

salted fish, sacks of wheat flour, bakery products, salt, matches, kerosene and tobacco.[8] All of this would be wiped out by the confiscations of war communism, driven to black markets and later destroyed by forced collectivization and industrialization.

10.3 After the Revolution

In November 1917, Lenin by decree expropriated all large landlords without compensation. What happened, in consequence, was a big land grab, including by 8 million urbanites and demobilized or deserting soldiers who all wanted their part of the expropriated land. The result was a mass of smallholders with on average no more than 0.5 ha of land, predictably unproductive and barely self-sufficient, while the surplus producing commercial farms had disappeared. Many new farmers were physically or professionally unable to cultivate their new land. Hence until 1922, the cultivated area was reduced effectively by 34%. In 1921, cereal production stood at half of its prewar levels, which it would not even reach by the end of the decade. The Soviets responded by sending armed thugs as workers militias into the villages to confiscate entire harvests. Local uprising and resistance were brutally suppressed as counterrevolutionary. When in 1921, a crop failure occurred, entire villages died of hunger, with a total of an estimated 10 million victims. It was US NGOs and volunteers, the Quakers in particular, who saved hundreds of thousands (not that the Soviets thanked them).

Lenin's NEP abolished forcible confiscations, which were replaced by a tax in kind of roughly half the crop while the other half could be sold freely. Within 5 years, the cereal production increased by 70%, while its cultivated area expanded by 40%. At the same time, land holdings were small and dispersed. Farms suffered from the lack of capital and technological backwardness. Productivity remained below prewar levels and bread remained rationed in the cities. Stalin as Lenin's successor began blaming the kulaks as hoarders of foodstuff in order to re-instigate class war in the villages and to prepare the ground for collectivization, which became part of the first 5-year plan of 1928.[9]

Collectivization started in 1928 in the fertile black earth zone in the South. By 1929, it was increasingly enforced nationwide. Squads of urban party activists were sent to villages. In order to fulfil their assigned quotas,

---

[8]Albert Pethoe (ed) «Belagerung und Gefangenschaft. Von Przemysl bis Russisch Turkestan. Das Kriegstagebuch von Dr; Richard Ritter von Stenitzer 1914/1917» Graz: Ares Verlag 2010, p. 199.
[9]Wein. Op. cit., p. 84.

they terrorized reticent farmers with arrests, deportations and murder. In the meantime also the Orthodox Church, in which the pious rural population had earlier found solace, had persecuted brutally with almost all churches and monasteries closed and desecrated. Most farmers rather butchered their animals than hand them free of charge to the kolkhoz. Central Asian nomads offered the most resistance. Their clan owned herds were their source of riches, identity and pride. Yet uncontrolled nomadism was equally unacceptable to Stalinism as were independent farmers, traders or craftsmen. Until 1941, there was armed resistance in the Tadjik high mountains. Many tribes sought refuge with their herds in neighbouring Afghanistan and in Xinjiang (East Turkestan) in the Chinese Republic (only to be forcibly incorporated there into Peoples' Communes after 1951).

10.4 The Holodomor

The history of Russian agriculture would not be complete without mentioning the Holodomor, during which in 1932–1934 in a policy-induced famine 5 million people died. 3.9 million victims were Ukrainians, the rest Russians in the Volga provinces, Ukrainians living in Kuban (Northern Caucasus), the German community and Kazakh nomads. Long after, the kulaks were expropriated, shot or deported and after the collectivization was well established, Stalin based on spurious secret police reports decided to end resistance, to break violently local riots against excessive production targets (unreachable with insufficient machinery and broken tools) and "sabotage" in the Ukrainian countryside by having his militia and party activists confiscating all foodstuff, seeds, animal fodder and livestock mercilessly over a 2-year period. The food collected, if it was not purposefully spoiled, was ruthlessly exported in order to pay for machinery imports. Ukraine's internal borders were closed and peasants were violently prevented from entering the somewhat better-supplied cities. Anne Applebaum has well documented the horrors of the unfolding drama,[10] during which international aid was refused and disinformation through gullible US correspondents and leftist fellow travellers prevailed (except for more accurate and honest German and Italian consular reports). Hardest hit was the West around Kiev and the North around Kharkiv with average death rates of 20%, where in the worst-affected districts, more than 50% died. Whole families were wiped out and entire villages were depopulated.

---

[10] Anne Applebaum. Red Famine. Stalin's War on Ukraine. Milton Keynes: Penguin 2018.

This was followed by attacks and large-scale purges of the Ukrainian (Communist) political and her intellectual elites. Stalin's intention was the destruction of Ukrainian national identity, its archives, libraries, language, newspapers, education, traditional village life, local traditions, churches, folk music, monuments, cultural life, historical memory and even of cemeteries with the objective to Russify and to Sovietize the country. Next to urban intellectuals, he saw farmers as reactionary upholders of national resistance. Hence, they had to be eliminated and broken in body and in mind. Clearly, the Holodomor was a precursor to the Great Terror of 1937/1938. In Ukraine, its dimensions had been equally horrific and bloody during the ethnocide 5 years earlier already.

10.5 The Kolkhoz and Sovkhoz Economy

The new kolkhoz eliminated all border hedges and strips between the erstwhile private fields, thus creating the vast monotonous spaces characteristic for Russian and large chunks of east European agriculture today. Once they were collectivized, the farmers (who in 1928 still counted for 75% of the Soviet population) lost their hardly gained independence and initiative and became listless and under motivated labourers on foreign soil again, this time not following their landlord's instructions but the orders of their kolkhoz boss. Only their small farmsteads remained their personal property and remained usually well maintained and clean. State planners—not always well aware of local climates and soil conditions—ordered the kolkhoz of what to produce and in which quantities. The state also had the monopoly for purchases and fixed the prices (at levels that allowed gains to be used for its ambitious industrialization, armament and infrastructure projects). Whatever the Kolkhoz received (and most remained very poor throughout the Soviet era) had to be spent on productive tools, the construction and maintenance of local infrastructure (a school, a kindergarten, a village clinic, a house of culture, a soccer ground etc.) as well as on meagre wages.

Over time, the kolkhoz size was increased massively. In the beginning, it was hamlet sized, with about 13 farms reflecting the size of typically small Russian villages. With progressing collectivization which by 1937 reached 99%, more and more village kolkhozes were merged, with an average size of 79 farm households. The political pressure for amalgamations (with the Soviet bureaucratic principle: the bigger, the better) continued in the postwar era. By 1982, 36% of kolkhoz comprised more than 500 households. Correspondingly, the total number of kolkhozes declined. At the beginning of 1950, there were still 254,000 them. Through forced mergers at the end of the year, 121,000 were left. By the mid-50s, there were some 80,000 of them whose average cultivating area had grown to above 4000 ha. Under Khrushchev, who favoured the model of agro-industrial cities, where farm workers would live happily under the same conditions as industrial workers (thus preparing for the advent of communism which he promised), there were forcible nationalizations of over-indebted kolkhozes into merged, even larger state farms (sovkhoz), where not even the fiction of collective property was maintained. Hence, by 1982, the number of kolkhozes had shrunk to 26,000.

Mechanization was relatively extensive. In the early 1980s, one tractor was used for 90 ha. Yet a lot of the agricultural machines in possession of the collective and state farms were not really usable, as they were overaged, badly maintained and had to survive the winters unprotected in the open for the lack of storage sheds. Only under Khrushchev, they were permitted to own their own machinery. In the first three decades of collectivization, all machinery belonged to 9000 state-owned machinery and tractor stations (MTS) employing a total of 3 million workers. The kolkhozes had to pay for their work: plowing, seed, harvesting and threshing, in kind, amounting in total to 31% of their harvest, thus skimming any surpluses left after forcible deliveries to the state. The state MTS also operated as political surveillance of the kolkhozes, which remained utterly dependent on their services and had virtually no managerial autonomy. Once the MTS equipment was sold to them and the MTS political role ended, a party secretary was appointed to supervise and to co-decide with the kolkhoz chief, much like the political commissars did with officers in the Red Army. Yet the technical problems of machinery maintenance and repair were not resolved. There were always too few "mechanizators" as trained mechanics and professional handlers of machinery. In spite of a nationwide network of 4000 repair stations, Brezhnev, in 1965, complained that they were able to put only 60% of defective machines back to working order. This obviously made itself felt during the spring planting and autumn harvest seasons—which under Russian climatic conditions remained always a race against time.

Originally, the MTS had been designed as being operated by mechanics defined as industrial workers, which were considered as politically more advanced and trustworthy and in consequence much better paid than the backward kolkhoz peasant. It soon transpired that this confidence was not matched by their behaviour. It was often arrogant, disrespectful and authoritarian towards the farmers (whom they were tasked also to control politically). They worked sloppily and were technically also often incompetent. Poorly maintained tractors and harvesters left in winter unprotected in the open frequently failed in harvest times and let crops rot in the fields. Originally, MTS workers were paid by the state per hours worked (or rather not worked). Then the kolkhoz had to pay them—as source for eternal tensions. In order to improve the situation, each MTS received a deputy director full time in charge of political education in the station and its collective farms, an obviously entirely unproductive and parasitic task. In Soviet doctrine, however, the right political attitudes mattered as much for productivity as did manpower and mechanical equipment. In reverse logic, when there were production failures (which were regularly numerous), the political attitudes of the workers and of their management had been wrong. Hence, they were potential political crimes to be punished by wage cuts, reeducation or worse as sabotage. In order to ensure surveillance and discipline, further "control commissions" travelled the countryside to inspect collective farms and the MTS—and to sanction mistakes and recalcitrants on the spot.[11] Since Nicolai Gogol's "Inspector general" (Revisor) of 1836, it remained much of the same.

The kolkhoz settlements consisted of five to ten old villages (called "brigades" for work purposes) and a new central settlement, which received revolutionary a name like: "Red Star", "Glorious revolution" or similar. The new village centre was given a pseudo-urban appearance with a cultural palace, a station, the kolkhoz office, the machine park, a sports stadium, a school, a kindergarten and a small clinic, plus a state-run sundry shop, petrol station, repair shop, silos, stables, and sheds for equipment. Under Khrushchev its ideological purpose was to end the difference between the towns and the countryside with the pretense that agricultural workers lived under equal conditions as industrial workers. In fact, they continued to live equally poorly, but under different conditions.

Kolkhoz chiefs were in theory and as a formality elected by all kolkhoz colleagues, but in reality were appointed by the party, which priced political loyalty over expertise. Most of them continued to have only elementary school education, whilst there were hundreds of thousands of agricultural technologists around with technical college and university education. These were rather employed in specialist functions in the kolkhoz, as agronomists, veterinarians, agricultural engineers, or as heads of brigades or of the husbandry department. Understandably, the dual leadership of the two parties appointed kolkhoz head and the party secretary, who had to control compliance with centrally set planning objectives, while both had to agree

---

[11] François Fejto. Histoire des démocraties populaires. Vol I. L'ére de Staline. Paris: Editions du Seuil 1952, pp. 322.

to all decisions jointly, frequently led to conflicts. On average, a kolkhoz in 1980 had 526 workers hailing from 495 farmsteads, representing a medium-sized enterprise cultivating 6500 ha, with 1800 cows, 1100 pigs and 1700 sheep. On average, it also possessed 42 tractors, 20 trucks and 42 combine harvesters.[12]

The state purchasing and tax system consisted of taxes in kinds, depending on the size of harvests, and compulsory deliveries of much the rest at state-set prices. Often these prices were set so low that they did not even cover the transportation costs to the government's collecting points. There were also "production contracts" with the state, the kolkhoz producing for him certain products at given quantities, which were somewhat better paid. Whatever was left as surplus, the kolkhoz could market more or less freely. The state agencies sold these cheaply acquired raw products at much higher prices to the processing industry or to the final consumers. The profits were invested into continued heavy industrialization.

The result of these exploitative conditions—which many African countries imitated with compulsory marketing boards from peanuts and sisal to cocoa and coffee after independence—led to an impoverishment and increasing indebtedness towards the state of the kolkhoz and to miserable living standards for its workers. On top of it, they gave no incentives whatsoever to increase let alone to improve the production.

Khrushchev, in 1958, ended forcible deliveries and relied entirely on contract farming. Purchasing prices were somewhat increased depending on production costs, which were linked to geographical production areas. Thus Latvian wheat was three times better paid than Moldavian wheat. Still, in 1965, one third of the 36,000 kolkhozes were loss making, as production costs exceeded purchasing prices, making them candidates to be merged into sovkhozes.

The wages of the kolkhoz labourers depended on the kolkhoz revenues and consequently varied from year to year. Until 1958, it happened that they were only "paid" in kind with almost no cash. Thus they carried the entire harvest risk, which as labourers they personally could hardly effect on their 4000 plus hectares. The basis for remuneration was the performance principle, based on the fulfilment of daily norms, which had to be set and controlled in a complex bureaucratic manner. Since wages were set so miserably low, none of this worked as an incentive to do better. It all depended on how the kolkhoz balanced its books at the end of the year. When it underperformed the kolkhoz worker at the end of the year received a handful of

---

[12] Wein. Op. cit., p. 88.

kopeks and a kilogram of wheat per working day, as Amalrik reported from his forcible working stay on a kolkhoz.[13] In 1968, a minimum wage of 60 rubles per month was decided for Kolkhoz workers. By 1982, their monthly wages had doubled. Certainly, families also lived on the produces and sales from their—highly productive—small garden economies, with poultry, pigs, potatoes, vegetables, fruits and collected mushrooms and berries resourcefully making up for supply shortages in the countryside and supplemented their miserable incomes with street side sales of pickled cucumbers and homemade fruit syrups. After 1969, they even got a miniscule public pension.

By 1980, in the Soviet Union, the earlier predominance of kolkhoz farmers had been reduced as such that there were 13.3 million Kolkhoz and 11.6 Sovkhoz workers, almost ex equo as agricultural hands. The political objective was to make their lives almost identical, i.e. to approximate the more "progressive" sovkhoz model for all.

The sovkhozes essentially were state property farms. Soil, means of production and farm houses were all state property. In terms of socialist ideology, they constituted a superior form of societal property than the kolkhoz as cooperatives. In consequence, as in the kolkhoz, the collective at least theoretically owned the means of production and the harvest, while in the sovkhoz, all belonged to the state. As the sovkhoz worker's incentives for productivity and for proper handling of equipment and inputs were nil, his proper stimulation became a major policy and propaganda issue. Hence there were endless exhortations and premia for the frugal and conscientious care of machinery, savings on fuel, fertilizers and feed—while increasing production. In a kolkhoz, workers were supposed to live in prefabricated high-rise buildings with no space for the intensive garden agriculture of his kolkhoz colleague. Hence, they were supposed to be less distracted by petit bourgeois private gains and more dedicated to the public good and to vodka.

In 1933, already the Soviet Union proudly announced that a sovkhoz had an average size of 19,400 ha, thus representing the largest agricultural holdings in the world (until Mao people's communes became larger by 1958). Kolkhoz' workers' conditions indeed had become almost as undistinguishable to those of an industrial worker and surely were similarly alienated. Most sovkhoz farms were fairly specialized, like for fruits and vegetables, dairy and meat, close to metropolitan centres of production, typically with pig and poultry industry sized facilities. In the newly gained Central Asian virgin lands, they were specialist "cereal factories" of up to 46,000 ha. On average, a sovkhoz had 2200 workers, every fifth of them was a technical

---

[13]Cited in: Wein. Op. cit., p. 95.

worker called "mechanizator", and 120 were engineers. In total, a kolkhoz settlement comprised about 8000 people. Being larger than the centre of kolkhoz, it is a prefabricated small town in the middle of nowhere with a silo, cereal sheds, food processing plants, central repair shops, a warehouse of sorts, a school, sports grounds, administrative facilities and similar.

Private agriculture in Soviet Russia for kolkhoz farmers was fixed at a maximum of 0.5 ha, the average in reality standing at 0.25 ha (2500 m^2). For other "agricultural specialists", the upper limit was 0.15 ha, and for urban workers 0.06 ha (600 m^2), that is for most in reality little more than a few vegetable, potato or herbal plots and some fruit trees in their datcha. Yet, in total, they constituted 4 million ha (representing 2% of the land area) of highly productive and intensively cultured agriculture, which essentially served the food needs of the rural population. They were self-sufficient even in eggs and milk. As a capitalist relict in times of need since the 1930s, they were partially promoted and then repressed again. In total, they amounted between 19.8 million (1955) and 12.8 million (1979) homesteads, reflecting also the steady move from villages to cities. By 1980, according to official figures, they produced about 30% of all milk, meat and eggs, half of all potatoes—in sum a quarter of all food—and 93% of all Soviet wool.[14] Statutes allowed one private cow, one calf, one pig plus piglets and ten sheep or goats per homestead. The land of course was not "private", but graciously lend by the state to the toiling masses to take care of their food needs in outlying areas by themselves, in total amounting to some 8 million hectares for 35 million Soviet families. Maximum acreage was 5000 m^2, but on irrigated land it was limited to 1250 m^2,[15] in other words, pure garden economy. Depending on shortages and availabilities, rules for "contract production" for the private fattening of kolkhoz animals were loosened or tightened again, often then kolkhoz feed and pasture was made available. Farmers then specialized in labour-intensive production, like potatoes, fruit and vegetable, often done by pensioners, while the kolkhoz concentrated on products in need of large acreage, like cereals and sunflowers. Private farmers then were allowed direct marketing on open market stalls or oriental bazaars in Central Asia—with better qualities, more choice and higher prices than the state shops.

Kolkhoz and sovkhoz, since 1973, were encouraged to cooperate on large-scale building, road construction and melioration projects where machinery, costs and equipment exceeded the needs and means of a single unit. Also,

---

[14] Wein. Op. cit., p. 107. Actually also the EU's public subsidies to the farm sector were estimated by the OECD to exceed to market value of agricultural production at the time. In the EU's case—in difference to the USSR—they created unsold food surpluses, not in chronic shortages.

[15] Voskresenski. Op. cit., p. 20.

there was pressure to specialize: one kolkhoz would focus on breeding calves, while others would do the fattening or milk production, or to supply feed only, all being liked with supply contracts. The purpose was to maximize output at an industrial scale, like having a 220 animal ratio per farm worker. In kolkhozes, specializing in fruit or vegetable production, industrial processing, like canning, were done on the spot in "agroindustrial complexes", thus employing farm labour also during winter. Voskresenski describes how one Kolchoz at the Kuban called "Kirov" ran a grain mill and feed combinate, and a repair shop, a sawmill and a brick factory for its own construction needs. Next to wheat, barley, watermelons, sugarbeet and sunflowers, the 4000 collective farmers of the former kosack village (stanitsa) also produced beef and pork, caught fish and produced a drinkable wine on 17,000 ha of arable black earth soil.[16] Calculated per capita this amounts to just 4.3 ha per agricultural worker, meaning in reality overmanned smallholding operations.

The same applies to the rest of the Soviet Union: 119.6 million hectares of arable land (including a lot of semi-arid or Swamy pastures) were cultivated by 24.7 million kolkhoz and sovchoz workers, in other words equally just 4.8 ha per worker. With 2.73 million tractors statistically in operation in 1984, this amounted to 1 per 43.8 ha. Any Central or Western European farm of a similar size would be equally mechanized and would need much less labour.

10.6 Soviet Agricultural Policies

Given the frequent food shortages, agriculture played a prominent role in socialist policies and propaganda as an ideological playground for unending experiments to prove the superiority of the collectivist Socialist system. "Volunteers" like students, soldiers and underemployed industrial workers were mobilized for harvest battles, regularly over fulfilling their assigned quotas with pre-organized publicity. Often, however, defective or missing machinery prevented crops to be harvested in time. But even bumper harvests were wasted, as storage, processing and transportation capacities were missing. Wheat was sometimes just covered by plastic sheets along railway lines, to be blown away in storms or eaten by mice. Losses were estimated at up to 40 million tons a year, or to one third of the crops in the Virgin territories.

Again looking at official Soviet statistics, the annual output of Russia's wheat production 1909/1913 stood at 72.5 million tons. During 1946–1950,

---

[16]Ibid., p. 9.

it was down to 64.8 million tons. Sugar beet during the same period went slightly up from 10.1 million to 13.5 million tons, as did milk output from 28.8 million ton to 32.3 million tons, while meat production went down from 4.8 million tons to 3.5 million tons.[17] In sum, then in spite of all technological progress that happened during these four decades, the period of 1917–1950 clearly was years of failure and policy-induced malnutrition and rural underdevelopment due to Leninist-Stalinist doctrinal blindness.

As agriculture was highly politicized, it was also subjected to the personal whims of the dictators. Khrushchev, for instance, was obsessed by maize, which he considered a miracle plant, which had to be planted excessively. Brezhnev's pet theme was the development of virgin lands to which major resources were allocated. 42 million hectares of Southern steppe were ploughed up in Northern Kazakhstan and Southern Siberia, with the construction of new settlements, roads, electricity grids, silos and machine parks. Quantitative objectives overruled ecological realities, like the erosion of these fragile soils and the strong and unpredictable variations of rainfall and draught. In the 1970s, gradually, US techniques of strip and dry farming were introduced to cope with regular harvest failures. Once the land reserves had been used, under Brezhnev intensified agriculture became the policy objective in order to reach the elusive self-sufficiency in foodstuffs: a higher degree of mechanization, more agroindustrial specialization, soil melioration (irrigation and drainage) and more use of chemical inputs. All of this required more public money to the farm sector, with public funds amounting to "up to one third" of the Soviet budget during 1981–1985 surpassing by far the value of agricultural production, which was estimated at barely 20% of the Soviet GDP at the time.[18] Plans to divert Siberian Rivers to the South luckily were never implemented.

Central planners in the Gosplan would define production objectives which then via the Ministry of Agriculture was allocated to individual union republics, oblasts and rayons until reaching the individual kolkhoz and sovkhoz. Correspondingly, their needs for seed, fertilizer, machinery, fuel and building materials were allocated. Procedures were excessively cumbersome, as machinery requests had to pass the entire planning chain upwards and (after approval) downwards again. As a result of planning mistakes and under-motivation, two thirds of collective farms by 1980 were loss making.

Living conditions in the villages remained tough and void of cultural and intellectual opportunities. Compared to the cities, kolkhoz shops were even

---

[17] Voskresenski. Op. cit., p. 40.
[18] Wein. Op. cit., p. 133.

worse off at the end of all supply chains. Medical care was similarly rudimentary. As a result, rural flight accelerated in the post-war era. In Russia itself, the share of rural population of 60% in 1951 was almost halved by 1982 (35%). The Soviet answer was to replace "backward" villages with their wooden houses with progressive small towns with prefabricated high rise apartments. Having lost their ancestral homes and gardens, rural workers would now also have to commute longer distances to their fields, while enjoying—perhaps—better access to local schools, shops and clinics. Much like in the Czarist days, rural workers were tied to their villages. During 1932–1992, the propiska internal passport prohibited them to move residence and to move to cities or elsewhere without official permission, usually by their kolkhoz chief. The purpose was to maintain an oversupply of labour to agriculture and to keep it cheap. By 1975, however, the labour shortages in the industry forced a loosening of the system.[19] In order to motivate rural workers subsequently, apart from complex premia for machinery maintenance and similar, non-monetary rewards were cultivated through socialist competitions between production units, medals, honorary titles as best sovkhoz worker distributed, and portraits of model workers displayed prominently.

Yet Soviet farms operated with high intensity of labour. There were 300 workers per 1000 ha on collective farms, while in the climatic and geographic comparable cases of the USA and Canada, there were roughly 36 workers. With an abundance of labour and a shortage of capital, it was a classical case study for an under-mechanized form of large-scale agriculture, which given the absurdity of the system with an extremely low labour productivity.[20]

Unsurprisingly, this did not prevent the huge and growing import needs, varying between 8 and 45 million tons per year of cereals alone to this erstwhile grain exporting fertile half-continent. The USA, Canada, Australia and the EU all competed to make up for this shortfall, and in the EU's case also with highly subsidized surpluses of butter, milk powder, beef, sugar, vegetable oil, tobacco and wine vinegar, to feed its class enemies properly.

Once yet another agricultural expert and reformer from Stavropol in the black earth area, Mikhail Gorbachev, came to power in 1987, the time-honoured practice of exhortations ran its course. Appeals to creative activity, initiative, independence and entrepreneurialism, which had been punished and discouraged for so long, simply did not match with the central planning apparatus and the kolkhoz and sovkhoz apparatchiks. After all, among

---

[19] Guenther Schmidt «Die Achillesferse der sowjetischen Landwirtschaft» Frankfurter Allgemeine 23.6.1990.
[20] Zvi Lerman, Csaba Csaki and Gershon Feder. Agriculture in transition: Land policies and evolving farm structures in Post-Soviet countries. New York. Rowman & Littlefield 2004, p. 36.

the 14 million "farm workers ", four million were apparently operating as bureaucrats pushing papers. His first attempt at reform was to merge six farm ministries into one giant ministry called Gosagroprom predictably did not work. An order issued by Gosagroprom took apparently 32 stages until it reached a kolkhoz in the field.[21] Meat and sugar remained rationed and long food queues even in privileged Moscow remained the rule, except at expensive private markets. Gorbachev's first real reform in 1988 was to allow individual farmers leases for land and equipment for up to 50 years. Yet uptake except for the Baltics was minimal. Bureaucratic obstruction of hardliners like the politburo's agricultural chief Yegor Ligachev and his people apart, who wanted to stick out his neck a new kulak? As in all transformation economies, it proved again that had been easy to drive out entrepreneurialism during the Bolshevik takeover by firing squads, but exceedingly difficult to reinsert it into apathetic societies. Gorbachev then allowed hard currency earnings for collective farms for production in excess of their plan allotment, and to permit work brigades to enter into contracts with their kolkhoz and to keep the extra profits from excess production for themselves—reflecting the Soviet experience that small private garden plots supplied 30% of agricultural produce took up only 3% of its arable land.[22]

10.7 The Reprivatization Process of Collectivized Land—And How It Failed in the Black Earth Region

Reformers in the early 1990s had hoped for and legislated for the dissolution of the collectivized land to individual farmers and their homesteads. The undoing of Stalin's dekulakization they hoped would lead to a class of independents family farmers and to a revival of entrepreneurialism and prosperity in Russia's neglected and deprived countryside. 700,000 ha in the Russian Federation in 1991 were scheduled to be privatized from state ownership. Thus the Russian Black Earth region, once Europe's breadbasket with top soils of 2 meters depth would soon outshine the US Midwest terms of productivity, rural income and progress.

This was not to happen, except isolated under very exceptional circumstances. First, local and regional elites, kolkhoz chiefs and agricultural bureaucrats fearing for their jobs, privileged positions and revenues did everything

---

[21] "Where's the beef?" The Economist 11.3.1989.
[22] "Farmers in USSR eligible to get dollars" The Japan Times 12.8.1989.

to sabotage the exercise. They continued to favour large-scale mechanized agriculture as a symbol of modernity and feared that smallholders with their lack of know-how, capital, implements and skills would represent a return to the nineteenth century. Giving up their control over the farms would deprive them of dispensing patronage (like selling land for dachas) and to forego rents due to the competition of independent commercial farms.[23]

Basically, a charade was set up, all collective farm workers, including retirees, nurses, teachers, shop keepers and clerks working at the kolkhoz, each would get a land entitlement certificate (which however did not specify the location), similar to the vouchers for the state-owned companies. Their fate was similar. The old collective farms as non-state enterprises would be turned into limited liability companies with the old kolkhoz or sovchoz chief—if he was still any good and had any brains—as the new chairman. The former kolkhoz chief would keep the certificates in his safe for safekeeping, exchange them for a few bottles of vodka, or usually force lease contracts on his employees: the use of their lands for a fixed amount of payment in kind: a pittance of a few sacks of grain, some beet sugar and vegetable oil and fertilizer and feed for their house garden and animals (depending on the whims of the chairman).[24]

For those few who insisted on real ownership, the obstacle race was almost unsurmountable. First, the land in question was not specified (and there was no restitution of old possessions expropriated during the collectivization) and there were no cadasters. The land was to be allocated by the assembly of the new "owners" of the village collective, which was usually hostile to any break up. Hence only the most infertile lands were approved if at all. It was usually located miles away from the farm houses, accessible only over fields and unreachable by road. Demarcation and cadaster work (if available at all) had to be done at own expense. Also, about ten permits had to be filled and stamped by regional officialdom in faraway towns that were mostly unhelpful or not available when a farmer would reach them after long journey on foot and by bus.[25]

Worse, when a farmer left the cooperative he was burdened with his share of the previous collective farms accumulated debt, which could amount to some US$400, while monthly cash incomes on average stood at US$20, if they were paid at all. He also lost access to cooperatives social services, like rudimentary health care or his children their places in the kindergarten.

---

[23] Jessica Allina-Pisano. The Post-Soviet Potemkin Village. Politics and Property rights in the Black Earth. New York: Cambridge University Press; 2008, p. 63.
[24] Ibid., p. 74.
[25] Ibid., p. 79.

Sometimes, he even lost his home. Socially ostracized, neighbours would refuse help, let alone the erstwhile colleges in the cooperative and their boss.

He had no cash, no access to credit (since land could not be used as collateral and banks would not lend to farmers, except via intermediaries at usurious rates), no implements except hoes and spades, no fertilizers, no machinery and little fuel. Unless living close to a big city, he had no access to markets and had to sell below costs at harvest time.[26]

Those few, who were not deterred, consisted of two groups. One were high-status people with access to resources, with capital to invest in machinery and labour. Large chunks of land—often around 1200 ha—using family, local and political connections ("blat", also often involving parliamentarians) given to district officials, to groups of professional agronomists or to retired officers with rural origins; Directors typically had their wives who worked as chief accountants on the cooperative register the land. Obviously, state officials approving these deals exacted their tributes. Often specialist farms like orchards or hog fattening were developed. The typical story goes as follows: The five godfathers of the cooperative: director, accountant, veterinarian, engineer and agronomist have accumulated the land. Then a "banker" arrives, offers them the right price and well-paid jobs for all and will get it for a larger operation,[27] often run by absentee landlords ("white farmers").

The other group were low-status villagers, refuges from Central Asia or the Caucasus, minorities like Tatars and Gypsies, single women or unemployed urban workers, who had felt that they had nothing to lose from subsistence farming for bare survival. By 2018, it was believed that every fourth smallholder was technically bankrupt, being unable to service his debts. In 2001, the state enacted a law repossessing land, which was not "properly used", targeting marginal farmers, which were accused of being lazy and unprofessional. Since 2002, the Russian state also the right of first refusal on land purchases. Regional and district authorities may refuse the sale of land and buy it for themselves,[28] thus further eroding its value.

Directors and local officials got away Russia-wide (the same story not only in the Ukraine but also in Bulgaria, Romania and in the former GDR), as the central state power with its chain of command had collapsed and allowed collusive officials in district administrations and directors control over the reorganization process which they with impunity could turn to their advantage. There was little local opposition to this. Poverty, isolation, long

---

[26] Ibid., p. 90.
[27] Ibid., p. 185.
[28] Ibid., p. 137.

distances, and the lack of information, communication and transportation prevented any regional or national farm workers organization.[29]

This did not mean that the newly acquired private cooperative started to prosper. As markets had collapsed and deliveries were often not paid, storage and trucks were insufficient the farm economy turned into a cashless barter economy, with dairy traded for sausages, and grain for household goods from nearby factories. Soon there was a lack a seeds, fertilizers, spare parts and packing materials. Often cooperative equipment was stolen—belonging to the "people" in Soviet days—like irrigation pipes or warehouse roofing sold as scrap metal. Since farm workers were unpaid for months they rather devoted their time, like in Soviet days, to their expanded kitchen gardens, where they used the cooperatives remaining seeds, fertilizer, feed and machinery. Hence the household's welfare depended on the director's discretion and patronage.[30]

As the result of the distorted de-collectivization process, the rural population became even more marginalized, impoverished and proletarized. Local bosses could deliver the votes of their farm workers and thus aid the coercive state.[31] In the absence of opportunities, the young and the more qualified began to leave the countryside in large numbers.

10.8 The Russian Land Market

As mentioned, the Russian law on land reform of 1990 and the Russian Constitution of 1993 which confirmed the right to private land for farming remained dead letters, since a moratorium on the sale remained effective until 2002, thus largely thwarting private landholding. Since state-owned land can be sold by auction or transferred to municipalities. Foreigners are banned from buying land in 380 ports and cities (like St. Petersburg). Farmland is subject to expensive and time-consuming land surveys prior to any sale.[32] Legally land is considered as a natural resource like water, the forests and the subsoil, hence no ordinary good but a national asset. 66% (1126 million hectares) of the national surface is covered by forests and 22.4% (383 million hectares) used for farming. The rest is settled land, used for industry, transportation and the military or designated as "protected" or "reserves". Among

---

[29] Ibid., p. 12.
[30] Ibid., p. 156.
[31] Ibid., p. 199.
[32] S. K. Wegren. "Land reform and the land market in Russia: Operation, constraints and prospects" Europe-Asia Studies 49, 1997, 959–987.

the 37 million land plots, some 4–5% are transacted every year, mostly small plots of a few hundred m², sold as state or municipal property. Still the amount of private owned land remains small with shares of 33% for agricultural land, 24% for urban ("settled") land and less than 10% of industrial land, while all forest land, protected territories and reserves remain in state property. The state usually sells at cadastral prices based on very rough mass appraisals averaging a section without consideration for individual parcels and with a tendency to over-estimate prices. Obviously, there is a great deal of variation between real estate prices in Moscow and St. Petersburg on the one hand and those of Siberia on the other. In Siberia, one m² of "unsettled land" is estimated at 36 kopeks (2012), which are roughly 0.5 Eurocents. One hectare would then amount to €50, and a landholding of 2000 ha of wilderness to €100,000. In the slightly warmer and more fertile, Far East one m² of unsettled land already fetches a steeper price at 79 kopeks. A modest land tax is levelled at 0.3% for agricultural and at 1.5% for industrial land.

10.9 Agriculture in a Market Economy of Sorts

The 1990s were less a decade of liberation than one of stagnation in the farm sector, when wages went unpaid for months, and the rural exodus intensified.[33] As mentioned, the marketing and supply systems for seed, fuel and tools and also for agricultural output had simply collapsed. The number of cattle was halved. The 150 million hectares still farmed collectively were littered with broken down tractors and farm machinery. Animal sheds stood empty with leaky roofs. As described above, during 1991–1993 by a decree from Yeltsin, all farmland was distributed to active and retired rural workers, up to 3–4 ha in the densely populated Moscow region, and up 20 ha along the Volga. Ownership for most however remained on paper, as no land registries were set up, and farmers were not even informed where their land actually was.[34] Restitution of collectivized land to their pre-1930 owners was never an issue, as records were claimed to be all destroyed. Collective management simply continued unchanged with the old kolkhoz chief in charge and kolkhoz relabeled as a joint stock company for better or for worse, even though their debts were sometimes forgiven by the state.[35] The kolkhozes continued employ their de facto landless labourers who lived on

---

[33] Rossiyskaya Gazeta 20.4.2016.
[34] Frankfurter Allgemeine 22.7.1997.
[35] Tatiana Nefedova «L'agriculture russe apres 10 ans de reformes: transformation et diversivite» Cairn Info 289–300.

subsistence wages, often paid in kind, and from the food they were allowed to produce. At the same time, they lacked the money for feed, fertilizers and equipment and due to the continued legal uncertainty had no access to capital and investments. Only in a few regions, like Tatarstan and Saratov at the Volga, governors dared to privatize farmland effectively or like in Zelinograd put it up for public auction. Overwhelmingly however public control over land—the most tangible asset of private property and to constitute a solid economic basis for middle class status—remained a source of political power patronage for Russia's rulers—as well as source of bribes for building permits. At the same time, the wide ranges of land owned the ministries, the presidential administration, the military and the security services could be handily exploited for private uses of the power holders.[36]

Hence, during the 1990s, Russia's agricultural crisis continued. Reasonably good harvests were followed by crop failures, as during Soviet day. During 1998, the cereal harvest had fallen to less than 50 million tons from 88 million tons the year earlier. With the concurrent fall of raw material prices, the ruble crisis and the collapse of many banks, Russia had no money for imports, of which it needed at least 7 million tons. As pensions and wages went unpaid also for factory workers and professionals, and 80% of the economy was estimated to be reduced to barter deals—and given scarcities food prices soaring 79 out of 150 million were believed to exist below the poverty line.[37] The USA now offered a food aid package worth US$950 million, and the EU 1.8 million tons worth 470 million Euros. The Russian state was supposed to deliver these shipments to hospitals, schools, orphanages and prisons, whose inmates had neither cash nor barter goods. Russian officialdom, whose vocabulary does not contain the word "Thank you", instantly responded by charging tariffs, complained about grain qualities, stopped shipments for inspection and charged a fee of $500 per truck.[38] Given their record for corruption and arbitrary obstruction, it is unknown which amounts of these well-intended donations actually reached their hungry recipients. The Red Cross, however, had its own more modest $17 million emergency appeal, and supplied under its own responsibility food packages to 1.7 million people in remote regions, elderly, sick, single mothers or multiple child families.[39]

It took this lost decade of legal uncertainty against yearlong traditionalist resistance of Communists, Nationalists and the Agrarian Party (representing

---

[36] The Economist 9.3.2000.
[37] Neue Zuercher Zeitung 19.2.1999, Financial Times 18.2.1999.
[38] Arkandy Ostrovsky "Russians hungry for food and way out of crisis" Financial Times 12.11.1998.
[39] Andrew Jack "Critics find food package hard to stomach" Financial Times 5.2.1999.

the interests of kolkhoz bosses) in the Duma, who argued criminals and foreigners would simply steal sacred, but cheap and abundant Russian land and dispossess the farmers[40]—to allow under Putin effective private property of farmland, including inheritance rights, and permanent and short-term leases by May 2001. Excepted are historical and cultural landmarks, natural park holidays resorts, forests and land for common use in villages.[41] Yet only few kolkhoz farmers were able to overcome bureaucratic obstacles and to re-establish viable private mid-sized farms (260,000 in 2000), like producing vegetables commercially for the urban markets. They cultivate 7% of arable land and account for 3% of agricultural production. Others survived as small-holders eking out a living from small patches, only marginally larger than their garden economy of the Communist era, to supplement their pensions or salaries typically with potatoes, cucumbers, cabbage and eggs. Yet all suffered from a shortage of capital (as land can rarely be used as a collateral for loans), most of the kolkhozes and sovkhozes were taken over by investment companies, cultivating 83% of national arable land, with farm labourers remaining as miserable and under-motivated as before, often only paid in kind, thus saving on taxation for both sides.

What did not happen, was the creation of a system of agricultural cooperatives among independent family farmers, worthy the name—like Raiffeisen in Germany and in Austria, the Danish, Dutch or Italian cooperatives, with joint purchasing of implements, joint marketing and processing of outputs and mutually owned specialist agricultural banks, like Credit Agricole, supplying the sector's unique financial needs. An EU Tacis report, which tried to propagate the concept, could list only a handful of new cooperatives in the district of Novosibirsk as best national practice, for instance: three meat coops of large and of private farms and meat factories for common meat processing; one for the milling and sale of wheat flour; five private farms which processed and packaged peas and buckwheat for retail; six farms which graded, packaged and sold potatoes and vegetables together, and finally four milk coops which produced and marketed fresh milk, cream and cheese. This is a fairly small order for a rich agricultural district. All of them had difficulties to get bank loans and had to pledge future harvest, assets or guarantees, as city banks had no confidence.[42]

---

[40] Wall Street Journal, 10.3.2000, Financial Times 15.9.2000.
[41] Viktor Pokhmelkin "Land reform" in: Russia on Russia, Issue 3. Moscow School of Political Studies and Social Market Foundation. 2000, p. 60.
[42] European Commission, Tacis. Today's co-operatives. A new form of agricultural organization in NIS. Luxembourg 1997, p. 9 and p. 22.

The depression of the countryside had predictable nefast demographic consequences. As Russia's population during 1991–2010 shrank from 148.3 million to 141.9 million, the number Moscow's inhabitants grew from 9.9 to 10.6 million (not counting hundreds of thousands of illegal workers and traders from Central Asia and the Southern Caucasus). But out of the 153,000 villages existing in 1989, today 20,000 are abandoned and 35,000 have fewer than 10 people, mostly pensioners or alcoholics, hence are likely to disappear within one decade as well. Also in small rural towns, which halved their population during the last 20 years, processing plants, schools and medical centres have closed, thus unravelling the public infrastructure and making life very difficult. Siberia apart, the worst affected regions in European Russia are those of Tula, Pskov, Komi and Bryansk.[43] According to Bullough in the regions in the Far North of Moscow, the local economy has vanished; Collective farms and processing facilities are closed. Farmland has turned into wilderness, livestock was invisible, farms and barns were abandoned and vandalized, stripped off electric circuits and copper.[44] Svetlana Alexiyevich received a similar testimony from a region 50 km East of Moscow: "In the countryside hardly any men are left. They drink themselves to death and start fighting. Those who do not drink are off to Moscow to make money.... Only the women don't give up and continue to dig in their vegetable patches" (my translation).[45]

10.10 The New Agrobusiness

The largest agricultural holding today is Prodimex, owned by Igor Khudokormov, Russia's sugar king, with 800,000 ha of arable land (representing the size of Corsica or of Crete), and who owns most of Russia's sugar refineries (benefitting handsomely from Import protection for which he lobbied hard). After the imposition of food import embargoes from EU, USA, Canadian and Norwegian foodstuffs in 2014 and food price inflation going through the roof, investments in large land holdings suddenly appeared as lucrative as those in the energy and metal sectors before. Land-grabbing was started by Cherkizovo, one of the largest meat producers, Rusagro, another big agricultural producer, companies, owned by the family of agricultural minister

---

[43] Oliver Bullough. The Last Man in Russia and the Struggle to Save a Dying Nation. London: Penguin 2014, p. 189.
[44] Ibid., p. 34.
[45] Swetlana Alexijewitsch. Secondhand-Zeit. Leben auf den Trümmern des Sozialismus. Berlin: Suhrkamp; 2015, p. 125.

Alexander Tkachev, and Sistema, the conglomerate controlled by the oligarch Vladimir Yevtushenko.[46]

Two of the better run giant enterprises are the Swedish owned "Across Invest" engaging in ecological cereal production and "Econiva Agro" owned by a German holding company called Ecosem Agrar. It started as an importer of US agricultural machinery in the mid-1990s. Two decades later, it is one of the largest dairy, seed and feed crop producers in Russia, cultivating 386,000 ha (50% larger than Luxembourg) and producing 290 million litres of milk from 50,000 cows. Unsurprisingly, Econiva welcomed the import ban on western dairy products, demonstrating its political loyalty and conveniently benefitted from reduced competition and higher milk prices.

Other examples of sizable European owned operations in the agrofood sector in Russia concern seed production by Bayer Crop Sciences, KWS (both Germany) and Limagrain (France), the local production of agricultural machinery by Claas (Germany) and John Deere (US), contract farming for locally produced vegetables, which are then canned by Bonduelle (France) in Krasnodar, and milk processing by Danone (France) in a joint venture with Unimilk near Moscow. For Pepsi, Russia is the largest market outside the USA, contributing some $5 billion in annual revenue (or 7% of the company's total). Mc Donald's also has more than 400 restaurants in Russia, generating around $2.5 billion per year (9% of the company's revenue in 2013)[47]—although it had difficulties to train its staff to smile and to be polite to customers.

Market convictions in the Kremlin did not run very deep. When there was an inflationary upturn of 17% prior to the parliamentary elections in December 2007 retails prices for basic commodities like bread, dairy, eggs, sugar, vegetable oil were simply frozen. Trade chains were instructed to keep "voluntarily" their margins at 10%. Failing this they would be face audits by the tax, sanitation and fire protection authorities. Import duties on dairy were reduced from 15 to 5% and export duties for cereals increased from 10 to 30%.[48] Yet at the same time, Putin publicly advocated policies of self-sufficiency and autarchy of food production to end the "humiliating dependency on foreign bread".[49]

By 2009, however, already Pyotr Stolypin's reforms seemed to be kicking again 100 years later, with Russia being a leading exporter of wheat, barley

---

[46] Kathrin Hille "Back to the land: Russia's farming transformation" Financial Times 11.8.2017.
[47] International New York Times 10.3.2014.
[48] Eduard Steiner «Rußland friert Brotpreis ein» Der Standard 23.10.2007. Neil Buckley "Russian food price controls before poll" Financial Times 24.10.2007.
[49] Isabel Gorst "Russia put to the test by grain shortage" Financial Times 5.10.2010.

and corn to North Africa and the Mid-East, with Kazakhstan and the Ukraine not far behind. The World Bank rightly believed that with proper technology, fertilizers and mobilizing fallow land again into production an export target of up to 50 million tons of wheat could be reached, provided also that storage and shipping bottlenecks at Black sea ports would be eased. Both private investors, like the Swedish "Black Earth Farming" with their 500,000 ha holdings and the state-owned "United Grain Company" have invested in grain silos and new export terminals to ease congestion.[50] One year later, however, a serious draught caused grain shortages and forest fires in Southern and Central Russia, from Krasnodar to Moscow, with the Kremlin ordering an export ban. Global grain prices shot up and doubts among Russia's traditional customers from Bangla Desh to Egypt resurfaced about the reliability of Russian supplies.[51]

Following the annexation of the Crimea in 2014, the Kremlin in a time-honoured manner—practised on Georgian and Moldovan food products, mineral water and wines before—struck food imports from the EU, Norway, Canada, Australia and the USA as "countersanctions".[52] Food as a weapon hit Russian consumers foremost, as retail prices for dairy, pork, fruit and vegetable shot up by 14% in 2015—no small matter in a country with consumers of limited purchasing powers, whose food bills account for 36% of disposable income.[53] For the Kremlin and its political friends in the food industry, the ban on French dairy, Baltic herrings, Polish fruits and Danish pork was once again a virtuous patriotic sacrifice in the name of food security and autarchy. For a while, these continued to be imported as re-labelled products from Belarus, Serbia and Kazakhstan and augmented conspicuously, until a certain crackdown. Then it became fashionable to invest into land and orchards, with the prime minister's cousin Andrej Medvedev, for instance, expanding his apple orchards in Krasnodar from 200 to 500 ha with the generous help of public subsidies.[54]

Already in 2013, Agricultural Minister Alexander Tkatchev (himself owner of Russia's fourth-largest agricultural holding) decreed a self-sufficiency target of 90%. The administrative squeeze on imports, from which his personal friends in the food industry soon benefitted—at variance with Russia's WTO obligations—had already started in 2012. Equally the depreciation of the

---

[50] Isabel Gorst "Kremlin attempts to double grain exports" Financial Times 13.11.2009.
[51] Javier Blas "Wheat price raises fear of food crisis" Financial Times 6.8.2010.
[52] Moscow Times 13.11.2014.
[53] Politico 7.11.2016.
[54] Frankfurter Allgemeine 10.8.2017.

ruble put a brake on imports and promoted exports. In December 2014, President Putin announced Russia would be fully self-sufficient in foodstuffs by 2020. An import substitution programme was launched with subsidized loans and tax incentives for investments in agriculture and food processing and state grants for the purchase of agricultural equipment, all of which however mysteriously eluded struggling small farmers. Prior to 2014, about 40% of Russia's food stuff were imported, mostly of the processed sort. By 2016, however, the balance still was negative: Food imports amounted to US$25 bio, while exports stood only at US$17 bio, consisting mostly of unprocessed wheat, corn, sunflower oil, vodka, caviar and some reindeer meat. A word is in order about the rationale of "food self-sufficiency" policies, which have been advocated by agricultural lobbies from continental Europe to Japan. They only make sense in a country threatened by a naval blockade, like the German and Austro-Hungarian empires back in 1914–1919. For a continental power with 1.3 million km^2 of arable land this policy objective unthreatened by any blockade is costly economic non-sense. It also ignores that the country would also have to be autarkic in downstream inputs like seeds, fertilizers, pesticides, insecticides, animal medicines, breeding animals, agricultural and processing machinery etc. In short, what in an open world economy, on which Russia needs to rely on for its much-needed export revenues, is an economically entirely idiotic concept, then clearly serves only one purpose: to satisfy vested power interests at the expense of mostly urban consumers. Once the Russian countersanctions were introduced, the share prices of the few listed agrofood companies like the meat processor Cherkizovo and the fertilizer companies PhosAgro and Acron shot up.[55]

Yet as affluent Moscow consumers and their favourite restaurants were suddenly deprived of French cheeses (unaffected neutral Swiss ones were considered a poor substitute), Italian prosciutto and pasta, German and Danish sausages, British jam, Polish apples and Florida oranges, local entrepreneurs managed to stimulate local homegrown food production in the accessible farm belts around the big cities, whose outputs suddenly became fashionable being sufficiently expensive. For the mass of urban consumers, however, affordable cheeses became rubbery in texture, as milk had been substituted by cheap palm oil.[56]

As a part of the state's oil and gas revenues were also converted into agricultural subsidies, amounting to 3.6–6.7 billion Euro per year, abandoned land was gradually brought back into production and the "agro-industrial

---

[55] Neil Buckley "Russian agriculture sector flourishes amid sanctions" Financial Times 19.4.2017.
[56] Hill. Loc. cit.

complex" modernized. With new capital investment into large-scale agriculture, the productivity of crops improved due to higher fertilizer use and more professional mechanization. According to Leonid Bershidsky, Russia also benefitted from global warming: Milder winters started to expand the growing season and allowed higher yields.[57] By 2016, Russian farmers could celebrate a major achievement. With 109 million tons of wheat, a record harvest was brought in, with 34 million tons available for exports. While wheat accounts for 70% of the crop, there were also 10 million tons of barley for malting and feed, and plentiful of oat, potatoes, flax and sugar beet, as well as soybeans in Southern Siberia for export to China. Agriculture had become Russia's second-largest export earner, behind the energy sector, but ahead of armaments. After three decades since 1970 of near permanent crop failures and as a major net importer, this was no small achievement.

The secret of successful commercial farming operations was not to copy capital intensive western models, but rather to opt for more extensive modes of production, given that costs for land, energy, labour and water are lower, the work force is less well trained and occasionally less reliable, machinery had to be robust and be repairable locally, climatic conditions were more severe and the logistical efforts with poor road, rail and storage conditions more demanding. In short, production conditions, plus the continued need for political protection and patronage, were more those of a developing country than those of the first world. Obviously, Russia still carries the burden of the 70 years of a demotivating collectivization and of Stalin's war against the Kulaks, the most skilled and entrepreneurial farmers, of whom he murdered 2 million in the Gulag.

Yet the question of demography strikes, invisible in the bright lights of Moscow and St. Petersburg, and equally much diminished in the darkness of outlying hamlets of the countryside. Among Russia's 155,000 villages, 20,000 are entirely abandoned. 35,000 have only ten or less inhabitants, mostly pensioners and will also be empty.[58] Often the last remaining aged villager cannibalizes his neighbours' abandoned property for firewood until he himself dies away. As during the war, only the brick-laid chimneys remain of the hamlet. Until the end, the public authorities sometimes still provide electricity and occasional snow-clearing.[59] Shops, schools, clinics and post offices are closed in the nearest village centres. What remains are stalls for the mere basics: sausage, bread, toothpaste and vodka. As villages are dying,

---

[57] "Russia as an emerging superpower in food supply" The Japan Times 15.9.2017.
[58] Oliver Bulllough. The Last Man in Russia and the Struggle to save a dying Nation. London: Penguin. 2014, p. 8.
[59] Seth Mydans "Migration empties Russian Villages" International Herald Tribune 6.4.2004.

they are still waiting for commands from higher up, which never materialize. Surely, local initiatives at reviving the self-governance of old are discouraged by regional apparatchiks, fearing for what little remains of their power.[60]

The question arises, after Alexander I.'s abolition of serfdom in 1861 and Stolypin's reforms of 1906, the continued hunger for land of Russia's peasants which fuelled the October revolution, and ultimately their rein-slavement during Stalinism after 1928, what does remain now for most Russian farmers? They are no longer formal serfs, free from corporal punishment and from the arbitrary justice of their former masters, free from food confiscations and from the terror against the kulaks, freed from the *propiska* and now are free to move.

But whether they performed 150 years ago, heavy physical labour on an estate of Count Y, or today do mechanized work for Prodimex, Econiva, Black Earth, United Grain Company or some other holding with their 500,000 ha, is not the alienation of the farmer from his land identical or worse? And are not these gigantomanic experiments by agrarian investors—similar to the absentee landlords of old (their contemporaries are now suitably called "white farmers")—as impressive as their current output recovery may seem, once again a road to disaster? And the most depressing question of all, why did Stalinist terror succeed to expunge almost all entrepreneurial spirit and their hunger for land from Russian farmers so brutally since 1928, with its system formally only ending by 1990, more successfully than Czarist absolutism and feudalism did between the seventeenth century and 1861? And why did the last three decades of relative freedom did so little of a positive difference to the Russian countryside?

10.11 Exports and Agricultural Protection

On average about 800 kg of grain, 70 kg of meat and 210 kg of milk are produced per inhabitant. While livestock products (except for some exports of reindeer meat and kaviar) are absorbed on the domestic market, agricultural exports essentially consist of cereals and oil seeds (sunflower oil mostly), all well as of fish processed on fish factories on the high seas, all amounting to 5.8% of total Russian exports in 2017. The main markets are Central Asia, China, Turkey, Brazil, Egypt and Korea.

---

[60] Arkandy Ostrovsky "An outsider strives to revive a hamlet's dead post-Soviet souls" Financial Times 1.9.2006.

Already during conflicts with Georgia and Moldova in the 2000s, The Kremlin used food import embargoes as a political weapon since both countries—fruit and vegetables for Moldova and wine and mineral water for Georgia—were highly dependent on the Russian markets. In August 2014, as countersanctions to the Western sanctions imposed after the annexation of the Crimea the Kremlin embargoed food imports from the EU, the USA, Norway, Canada, Australia and the Ukraine. For a while French camembert, Polish apples and Latvian canned fish still sneaked in after being repacked in Serbia, Belarus or Kazakhstan, until these loopholes were closed as well. In sum, a yearly total of €6 billion of EU food (meat, dairy, fish, fruit and vegetables) exports was lost. For some substitute markets (like pork to China) were found, but for traditional Baltic, Polish and Finnish suppliers of fresh fruit and vegetables to the St. Petersburg markets this meant hardship. Retail prices of sanctioned goods went up by 3% on average with Russian urban consumers paying the bill, notably hitting the poor who spend 53% of their income on food. In total consumer losses were estimated at US$7 billion per year (or 3000 rubbles per person).[61] The main winners were domestic producers who in the absence of import competition could increase prices and forget worries about quality, and to a much lesser extent due to trade diversion effects other importers, like Belarus on dairy products and Serbia for apples.

10.12 The Agricultural Policies of the Eurasian Economic Union (EEU)[62]

The political objectives are somewhat reminiscent of the EU's old Common Agricultural Policy (CAP) prior to its reform: "import substitution" (Putin), a "common self-sufficient market" and "able to resist any sanctions" (Alexander Lukashenko) and to "mitigate destructive consequences of global foreign economic trends" (Serzh Sargsyan). Even the terminology (export/import "balance sheets") is similar to Jean Monnet and the early CAP. Indeed policies are undertaken to increase output, to maximize exports and to reduce imports in the "common" EAEU agricultural market. During 2014–2017, self-sufficiency levels have increased to 91–99% for beef, poultry, dairy and

---

[61] Natalya Volchkova and Polina Kuznetsova "Losers and winners of Russian countersanctions: welfare analysis" Presentation, Moscow 2019.
[62] Source: Sergey S. Sidorskiy (ed.) "Three years of integration: Agreed agricultural policy of the Eurasian Economic Union" Moscow: EEC 2018.

sugar, probably in large measure due to the food import embargo on the Russian market, and to 146% for oil seeds.

The EEC agricultural department is headed by a "minister" and board member, Sergey Sidorskiy. It comprises four sections and organizes 12 working groups guided by an advisory board. Yet staffing levels are unclear, and there is no mentioning of any budget. It is claimed that "more the 50 decisions" have been taken during 2015–2018—according to EAEU rules necessarily by unanimity. Again it remains unclear in which fields and if and how they are implemented. The EEC simply lists the policy fields in which it claims to be active: export promotion (to China, Turkey, Iran, Vietnam, Korea and "some EU countries"), agricultural forecasts, price monitoring, import tariffs and customs clearance, sanitary, veterinary and phytosanitary measures, single technical regulations, unified rules on state support for agriculture, fair competition (and compensation in case of forbidden state support to other member states), analysis of taxation, agricultural credit, insurance and market state regulations, the promotion of storage and transportation, innovation and R&D ("with more than 150 research activities"), improved seeds and breeding animals (and a single registry for sorts) and international cooperation, like MoUs signed with the FAO and the Hungarian MAFF.

With an agricultural population ranging between 6.5% (Russia) and 35% (Armenia), the sector obviously is an important employer in the countryside. Yet the role of the EAEU is difficult to assess and distinguish fact from fiction. Are its declared mercantilist policies really effective, and not just the aggregate result of Russian protectionism and its import embargo of 2014? Can it really establish firm competition rules, given the Kremlin's tendency to privilege its favoured friends from sugar to apple and pork production? Could an export price cartel work when Russia and Kazakhstan compete with the same kind of cereals and oil seeds? Is it reasonable to speak of a common market when internal trade is almost marginal compared to third country exports? How can they speak of rural development objectives without an adequate budget and staff? Put positively, it could well be that common standards, single regulations and customs and transport facilitation could after all—against their stated policy objectives—also could aid European imports. Like the rest of the inter-governmentally organized EEU also their agricultural policies have to be decided by unanimity, which of course limits their scope and ambition. Whether and how common rules then are actually implemented, again very much remains to be seen.

If there is an organizational similarity of the EEC's Agricultural department, then it seems to be with the OECD's Committee for Agriculture which also deals with forecasting, monitoring and good policy advice—without actually executing anything.

10.13 The Tiraspol Kvint Distillery—A Case Study of Vicissitudes and Survival

To be sure the distillery is on Moldavan territory, but it operated and controlled by Russians, largely supplies the Russian market, with its corporate history reflecting Russian/Soviet economic history. Since I could find little similar case stories in English, I found it worthwhile to place a synthetic report here

Back in 2007, I was with an OSCE ambassadors mission in Transnistria in order to check ceasefire arrangements along the Dniester, to visit the EUBAM customs mission there, to talk with "president" Igor Smirnov and his men and to inspect the huge Colbasna ammunition depot maintained by the Russian military on Moldovan—de facto Transnistrian—soil further North. One of the highlights of the trip, however, was also the visit of the Kvint plant and the tasting of its products which left me quite impressed and not quite sober. At the time, we were also presented with a richly illustrated and well-documented fascinating corporate history written by its former chief engineer and director, on which the following synthesis largely draws.[63] In fact, I found such a Russian corporate history due to historical fate so entirely different from the classics which we know from the West: an entrepreneurial character produces prototypes in his garage, procures finance, against all odds and competitors strikes luck. The fledgling enterprise is developed and diversified by his sons and grandsons, until becoming a global conglomerate under professional management and worldwide investor base (see Siemens, Daimler, Thyssen, Nestle, Ford, Mars, Disney, Fiat, Sony, Honda, Toyota, Samsung et tanti quanti). It is also strikingly different from the fourth-generation plus family business histories from other liquor and cognac houses, like Hennessy, Camus, Monet, Martell, Courvoisier and Otard, which prospered without dramatic interruptions until they were bought up by international liquor giants like Bacardi-Martini, Dageo or Pernod-Ricard.

In sum, pars pro toto, the Kvint story appears as very instructive about the very singular ways in which a medium-sized consumer product company could survive in Russian and Soviet adverse conditions, and why even under

---

[63] Oleg Baev. *Century under the stork wing*. Tiraspol. 1997: Kvint.

today's market economy of sorts faces very different circumstances and challenges—difficult to imagine in a Harvard business school context. Hence, this story is both instructive to understand the unique experiences of Russian contemporary management and their seemingly often idiosyncratic ways of doing business, but it also helps to comprehend what the often traumatic political events of the twentieth and early twenty-first century in Russia and her near abroad meant for the economic realities on the ground.

It all began with a decree by Alexander I allowing distilleries in the newly gained government Kherson in 1809 to produce fruit vodka. Four of them were soon set up in Kherson and Dubossary by local capitalists and Greek and Armenian merchants, in addition to the winemaking distilleries already existing in the region and which were run by former general staff officers and large landlords (much like prewar regional sake brewers in Japan processing their landholdings production). Grapes were delivered from their estates and also by state farmers and free colonists and Cossacks settling along the Dniester. In 1829, Prince Piotr Wittgenstein, who commanded Russian troops during Napoleon's disastrous retreat from Moscow in 1813 and led the 1826–1828 Russian campaign successfully against the Turks, conquering the fortress of Brailov and crossed the Danube into Bulgaria, as a retired field marshal was given the huge Kamenka estate as gift by the Czar. The energetic war hero decided to use favourable local conditions to create vineyards on an industrial scale. For this purpose, he imported grapes from France and from the Rhine and recruited German viticulturists to plant them on cascaded slopes. The settlers received their land as long-term leases and as contract farmers were obliged to sell their harvest to Wittgenstein at a pre-set price. He had cellars constructed and imported the best winemaking equipment from Europe. Soon his wines were all over the empire from Warsaw to St. Petersburg and Moscow. Frequently distributors changed the labels and sold them as French wines without anyone noticing. Wittgenstein's scientific winemaking methods subsequently also spread to other estates.

With the liberation of the serfs, the quality of the grapes and the wines began to decline as smallholders tried to process them on their own. Soon there were 730 independent vineyards in the Tiraspol district run by Moldavian and Ukrainian peasants and German and Bulgarian settlers. By the end of the nineteenth century, Wittgenstein's tradition had died away. In Tiraspol, then a medium-sized country town with small factories and workshops processing agricultural products and supplying farmers' needs with mills and blacksmiths mainly, in 1896, a small distillery was founded. It had no electricity and workers were barefoot. During WWI, it was put under state control, while illegal distilleries in the region continued to work underground. Yet until March 1917, economic life continued largely undisturbed in this sleepy provincial backwater, albeit at somewhat reduced capacities.

In September 1917, the local Bolshevik organization was founded. They soon instigated food riots motivated by local shortages. While the town's stores were pillaged, the wineries were hit first with liquor from the barrels flooding the floors. Finally, Red guards were sent into suppress the wine riots in October 1917. Yet in the subsequent civil war in 1918, the warehouses were plundered again and burnt to the ground.

In 1921, the People's Commissars in Ukraine (to which the left bank of the Dnjster with Tiraspol now belonged—the rest of today's Moldova had become the Romanian province of Bessarabia) ordered to restore grape growing and winemaking on the former vineyards. In 1923, Lenin's NEP granted tax exemptions to vineyards and dispensed sellers of self-made wines from the sales tax. Yet these concessions did neither improve qualities nor help against the mildew plague. Thus by 1925, little was left of viticulture. 70% of the cultivating areas were lost due to revolution and war. Winemaking had remained an imported culture, which had not taken local roots. Also, plants had been cultivated in central Bessarabia and were often not suited to the local climate. Work in the vineyards was done unprofessionally as a side job of small farmers. For fear of theft, grapes were harvested prior to maturity, sorted only by the criterion "red" or "white" and processed in peasants' cellars. These poor—probably hardly drinkable—wines in 1928 were finally brought for distilling in the reconstructed Tiraspol collective winery, of which after 1918 only a chimney and a cellar had remained. A welcome by-product was instantly sellable vodka. After collectivization in 1934, grapes were delivered from state farms to be processed into fortified, dessert and sparkling wines. As there were no suppliers, workers of the distillery basically had to produce most of their equipment by themselves. The most popular product was then a strong and sweet Moldovan dessert wine called "Malaga" high in alcohol and sugar. Low proof wines were distilled into brandies called cognac. By 1936, a huge cellar was constructed and 1941 new work shops were opened. With the annexation of Bessarabia in 1940, supplies of grapes from its new collective farms flowed richly, allowing the production of grape juice, wine, grape vodka, wine concentrate, rectified spirit, champaign and cognac, with a fizzy wine "Moldavian sparkling" sold all over the USSR.

In 1941, the facilities were reportedly plundered by occupying Romanian troops (this is what victorious troops throughout the ages normally do when liberating wine cellars), but as thirsty occupants continued to use and to expand the distillery. With the return of the Red Army in 1944 either through fighting or wanton destruction, the distillery, however, was in ruins again. Pictures show burnt roofs at least. By the summer of 1945, production restarted anticipating Stalin's order of October 1945 to restore viticulture and horticulture in the re-annexed Moldavian SSR. The first post-war 5-year plan foresaw to restore production to prewar levels. By 1947 also cognac production was resumed with the blessing of the Moldavan Food ministry. Soon the distillery was awarded its "Red Banner" for the mass production of premium fine cognacs, and with the Stakhanov campaign some distillery workers laudably over fulfilled their plan objectives by 180%. Female workers' brigade was given medals for planting 80 trees around the factory and for constructing corporate housing. During the war, the Stalinist system was very generous with non-monetary rewards: Medals, titles, public announcements, publicity in party papers and banners which did cost very little. Yet grape supplies from state farms—it was quantity which counted—did not always have the sufficient quality. Incomplete machinery deliveries held up production and the planned mechanization of work. On 21st December 1949 to honour the 70th anniversary of Comrade Stalin the "collective" (i.e. the factory director) decided to finish the construction of the bottle shop (which they had to build by themselves). When in 1954, the director had the smart idea to let a befriended Red Army unit do renovation and rail laying work at the plant, this was unfortunately discovered and punished.

As a consumer industry, the distillery was surely no strategic priority in the Stalinist economy. In the absence of specialist industrial suppliers and repair services, the factory could only operate in an almost self-sufficient do-it-yourself mode with productivity progress depending on the ingenuity of its indispensable "worker-rationalizers", practically minded gifted handymen who were understandably cultivated and honoured by the management. Often they had worked their way up from an unskilled factory hand with learning on the job by doing and repairing to become innovator-tinkerers. Innovation was incremental and piecemeal on all of the plant's rudimentary machinery: on filtration, tanks, barrels, pipelines, pumps, boilers, bottling, labelling, packaging and the operations of the internal railway. Gradually, bottling was mechanized with filling machines (instead of being done manually), and transported by conveyor belt. A local inventor designed the automated corking labelling and sealing of the bottles. Also, empty bottles began to be cleaned and stabilized mechanically. Yet in-house production of equipment continued. Since too few copper supplies were received, old parts had to be recycled and substitute metals are used. Sometimes Stalinist paranoia struck. As barrels for the lack of proper storage cellars were kept in the open yard evaporation and losses through seeping were high. Then the plants' cognac specialists were purged and prosecuted on charges of embezzlement. Once the cognacs were left to mature for the necessary 7–10 years in oaks tanks properly stored in cellars by 1953, the losses went back to normal.

A recurrent problem was unreturned empty bottles and wooden cases. Most thirsty customers lived in Siberia and in the North. Possibly they had other uses for bottles and cases, or broke or burnt them happily. Yet the fact that 2.7 million bottles and 67,000 wooden cases annually never returned were not foreseen by the planners. Hence, there was always a shortage of bottle supply.

In order to celebrate the 300th anniversary of the Union of Russia and Ukraine 1954, 75 railway cars of wines and cognac were shipped to the Donbass. By now, a state "tasting commission" termed it "best in the USSR" against competition from Yerevan, Tbilisi and Odessa.

Yet in 1959, larger tanks reduced production losses and railroad access permitted to smooth dispatch of around 12 railway cars to all parts of the USSR. The Tiraspol Wines and Cognac Distillery with 30 brands of wine and five brands of cognac by now produced 95% of all cognacs and 20% of all bottled wines of Moldova.

By the 1960s, more than 100 brands were produced: sweet, dry table wines, port, dessert wines, still and sparkling wines, liqueurs with sugar added for alcoholic strength. Three million bottles of cognac by 1951 were produced annually. The distillery also collected dozens of herbs to reconstruct Italian recipes for vermouth like Cinzano—obviously with little regard to intellectual property rights.

Sometimes even suppliers over fulfilled their targets like the grapes from the state farm "Tsiganka" (gipsy) by 150% in 1956. By now also supplies arrived from Bulgaria, Yugoslavia and Romania by train or by barges.

With Khrushchev in power slogans of market relations, self-supporting and self-financing operations with economic stimuli were propagated, without however lessening the imperatives of centrally set planning targets and ministry approval for product introductions. Workers received only small symbolic premia for cost savings, quality improvements and greater efficiency. Exhortations to their collective spirit to improve production continued. After winning a competition for less production costs and better qualities with the Kishinev winery, the cognac shop was awarded the title "shop of communist labour". Factory directors were inevitably wine and distillery technologists appointed by the Tiraspol City Community of the Communist Party (CCCP). Roughly every decade the state organizations and commissions to which the distillery was subordinated were reorganized. In the 1960s, it was for instance the "Self-Financing Agroindustrial Association of Winemaking Industry of Moldvinprom of the Ministry of Food Industry of the MSSR". Decisions taken there were often bizarre. In 1959, for instance, a weaker and mellower cognac called "Nistru" was developed to suit female tastes. For a year, the male-dominated Central Tasting Commission would not approve of the brew. Yet when the 50th anniversary of International Women's day approached by March 1960 approached, it gave its blessings. In the mid-1960s, planners decided that ageing took too much time. The idea was to reduce stocks and to increase sales. Thus they insisted on high volumes of quickly aged 3 months "cognacs" to be shipped. Potential high-value drinks were thus wasted as cheap barely drinkable plonk—and sorely missing 7 years later, when they would have had the right qualities in their oak barrels.

1960 also saw a 7-year plan, which demanded the tripling of the wine-growing area in Moldova. This implied not only a corresponding increase in wineries and warehouses but also a massive expansion of the Tiraspol facilities for wines, dessert wines and cognac. The uneven quality of deliveries of grapes and "wine materials" from state farms, canning factories and primary wineries required some standardization, ultimately resulting in quality contracts with supplies. After mutual consultations, quality controls and regular training were established, notably on sanitary hygiene. Unfortunately, there was a lack of public funds to build the needed modernized new production facilities and the administrative and social centre in 1967. Own enterprise funds (i.e. retained profits) were mobilized as well as bank loans. Suddenly budgeting became important: Only equipment and material that were needed were ordered in the right quantities and not just maximum stuff to be hoarded for emergencies or for barter. Yet the usual mishaps of central planning continued: Unfortunately too small tanks for maturing were delivered, thus restraining future production. Also, the local fire department refused permission for liquor storage on three factory floors already under construction. The distillery had to mobilize the personal intervention of Soviet Interior Minister Shelekov to straighten out the stubborn chief of the Tiraspol fire brigade. By the mid-70s, Kvint had grown into not only into one of the most profitable companies of the Moldovan SSR but with 34 brands also into one of the largest cognac and wine producers of the USSR, but exports even to the GDR, as it was proudly announced in local newspapers, which regularly praised the factory and its model workers.

Modernization started by stealth in the 1980s. Pipelines were insulated to avoid leakage and to save energy. By 1984, bills and transportation documents were computerized. After an analysis of the Economic Institute of the Academy of Sciences of the MSSR—operating as a sort of management consultancy—the company was reorganized and its management reshuffled.

Like many Soviet enterprises, the distillery engaged in manifold social works for its workers. Given the shortage after the war, in 1949, company housing started and in 1954 a kindergarten was built—by the plant's construction crew. This was followed by a recreational dacha, a sauna and a sea side club at the Black sea, with recreation travel and cruises for meritous workers at company and trade union expense. In Tiraspol, trees and shrubs were planted along the roads and on public squares, and the plant itself beautified with greenery, quite in difference to the usually drab Soviet factory settings. Among the workers brass bands, chess tournaments and a drama theatre were organized. There were pet corners to breed singing birds and pheasants, a billiard room, a volleyball ground, a dance floor, a library (as well as campaigns against illiteracy among workers), a first aid station and a gym. At the same time, the company remained accessible for school excursions and for professional visits.

With the collapse of the Soviet Union and the brutal civil war between Moldavans and the Transnistrian Russians in 1990–1992, new turmoil occurred. The company had to cope with cut off supplies from right bank Moldova, with hyperinflation, the loss of all traditional state trading customers, constantly changing extortionate excise tax regimes and to live in an internationally unrecognized entity called Transniastria with the local dictator continuing Soviet habits and to have to balance its books with a Mickey Mouse rubble currency. 230 retirees and their families in the absence of pension payments had to be supplied with food and basic necessities.

At the same time, the domestic market of glorious Transnistria with its 475,000 impoverished inhabitants was simply too small to sustain this major distillery. Yet the newly found freedom allowed the company to finally purchase first rate up-date equipment from abroad, like bottling machines from West Germany, labelling equipment from France, Italy and the GDR. As Moldova was essentially economically cut off along the ceasefire lines, packaging was purchased in Bulgaria and spirits supplies from Western Europe from producers, who unlike CIS suppliers could guarantee the quality of their alcohols. "Kvint shops" with luxury cognac-based products were set up at the right places. Hardly had the Russian market been developed with 30–40 freight cars with wines and cognac rolling each month and with a representative office in Moscow supplying 1500 new wholesale, retail dealers and supermarkets—often naturally of dubious commercial repute and unable to pay in advance replacing the dissolved previous state trading associations—that Gorbatchev's prohibition decree in May 1985 struck, which aimed at the eradication of drunkenness and alcoholism. Unlike other decrees, its enforcement was merciless with inspectors coming from Moscow and Kishinev, from CP committees and public control. In addition, an 80% sales tax was struck on the "wine growing complex". Central planners now demanded to change production to fruit juices, candies and cookies.

Soon there was a nationwide overproduction of soft drinks and lemonades with often poor water quality (subsequently used as cattle fodder), while dubious home brews and moonlighting proliferated as serious health risks. By 1989, the political pressure for prohibition lessened. Yet the company had been forced to remove all references of alcohol production and to cut links to suppliers of grapes and bottles and machinery. Vineyards in Moldova were turned into orchards and vegetable fields. With the civil war starting late in 1990, wine supplies from the right Dniester bank were almost cut off anyway. Quality standards once again declined. The company responded by producing vodka which with the right filtration technology quickly produced the best qualities.

Interestingly enough management—some 30 people in total—now went to 1–3 month business courses to Duke University in North Carolina to acquire the skills needed to negotiate with foreign suppliers. As the traditional Moldovan suppliers were cut off, bottles were bought from Germany and Bulgaria, decanters from Austria, France and Germany. Transnistia was now developed as a wine growing and supplying region. Yet as the local regime was stuck to the very old ways, there were the traditional difficulties to implement the grandiose plans: the absence of fertilizers, the shortage of pesticides, herbicides, fuel and equipment, as well as of seedlings and material (like vine posts) for what in Transnistria remained state farms.

While Kishinev tried to build its own "Dacia-Phoenix" brand as a competitor, the Tiraspol plant took over the spirits plant at Doibany, which was then owned by the Association "Aroma" in Kishinev, but had apparently left wages and bills unpaid since months. Legal battles with the former owners followed. Worse was to come. In March 1996, Russia enacted a retroactive law on imported wines and liquor charging 5 Euros per litre, corresponding to (and hence roughly doubling) the retail price. At the same time with bankrupt banks and trade organizations and with a Transnistrian ruble, how could one settle bills and get foreign exchange? Debts simply accumulated. The Smirnov regime from 1996 until 2011 forced them for all such transactions to go through Transnistrian state trading organizations.

As they lost the Russian market, the Ukraine "Kvint" subsidiary had to make up for the losses. Yet suddenly a 280% import tax had to be paid in

Ukraine, thus destroying the market, which earlier had operated as barter of liquor against coal and other goods. Now fake Kvint cognacs appeared.

Back in Tiraspol, the distillery took over pig and cattle breeding plants and their meat processing facilities, which had gone bankrupt. At least they could now decently feed their own workers and pensioners.

Trademark legal battles followed with Kishinev. But the company noted proudly that not only Brezhnev had liked their "Yubileiny" top brand frequently but so also did apparently Jacques Chirac. Luxury bottles and packaging were delivered from France, labels from Bulgaria, screw caps from the Netherlands and glue from Spain. Prices and awards from international exhibitions and fairs came aplenty. A new laboratory and computerized quality control were established, a far cry of the do-it-yourself tinkering of the Soviet past. The same applies to the new method of marketing in flashy Kvint liquor shops.

By 2006, the distillery was finally privatized into the hands of Sheriff Ltd. Sheriff is Transnistria's second-largest company and owned by the two former secret service officers Viktor Gushan and Ilya Kazmaly. The conglomerate comprised a chain of petrol stations, supermarkets, a Daimler dealership, an advertising agent, a construction company, a TV channel, a publication house, a mobile phone company, bread factories and textile plants, plus the local FC Sheriff Tiraspol soccer club and the Sheriff Stadium. In their respective sectors, they often operate as the local monopoly. Naturally, they were first allied with Igor Smirnov with his two sons as silent partners and in executive positions. In return for Sheriff's political support, the company was exempted from customs duties and granted reduced tax rates. Gradually, however, the Sheriff owners became more powerful than the president and his clan. In 2000, they supported the "independence party" Renewal, which in 2005 obtained an absolute majority in parliament. By 2006, Sheriff was in open opposition to the Smirnov regime, which accused them of plotting his overthrow. When in 2011, Renewal leader Yevgeny Sherchuk beat Smirnov in the presidential elections, he subsequently abolished the tariff and tax privileges granted to Sheriff by Smirnov.

Hence was there finally a return to normalcy and to a regularly functioning market economy for the Kvint plant? Well, first with international rules on geographical indications, it could not name its "cognacs" as such any longer—though de facto it still does in Russia—but officially uses the Moldovan term "divin". It also has to state that the drinks are "made in Moldova". Transnistria clearly is too small of a home market both for the supplies and for sales. Hence the company remains extremely export dependent, with shipments also going to Italy and to China. From a Kremlin point of view, this external dependency of a major Transnistrian company, which produces 20 million bottles of alcohol per year and accounts for 5% of the Transnistrian GDP (2014) suits its geopolitical interests well. At the same time, the EU's EUBAM mission that facilitates customs and transit along the ceasefire line with Moldova has in no small measure helped to reestablish supplies and outward shipments in the interest of both affected populations and workers and thus contributed to a modicum of prosperity and confidence between two alienated populations.

Interestingly enough minor Russian oligarchs, in 2007, bought eight minor Cognac houses and two medium-sized reputable ones, Jenssen (by "MVZ") and Croizet-Eymard (by the "Russian Wine trust") to benefit from Russia's booming demand for cognacs, then running at 5 million bottles a year. This raised fears that purchasing a few hectares and a small bottling plant in France would allow them to benefit from the even stronger growth for imitation products which some of them already sold successfully as "Konyak".[64] The major quality houses like "Camus" for instance remained unconcerned. Camus had been a purveyor to the Court of Nicolas II, and since 2001 again been reappointed to the Kremlin.[65]

10.14 Russian Wine Production Today

With an annual wine consumption of wine of more than 7 l per capita Russia the ninth-largest consuming country and in 2017 imported wine worth 875 million Euros.

Russia had 77,000 ha of vineyards and produced 536,000 tons of grapes in 2017. The biggest producer of grapes is the rayon of Krasnodar followed by Dagestan. After the annexation of Crimea in 2014, its territory of vineyards increased by 38%, where, however, due to the draughts and the shortage of water for irrigation yields are very low.

Russia plans to increase the surface of vineyards up to 140,000 ha before 2020. To reach this figure, Russia would need to plant at least 10 000 ha of new vineyards every year. However, during the last 3 years, only 13,000 ha were planted, instead of 30 000 ha "planned". There is also a shortage of local vine propagating material. Currently, most of the vines are imported from Southern Europe.

In line with its policies of self-sufficiency, in September 2018, the Ministry of Agriculture tried to order to purchase only locally produced wines for state

---

[64] Die Welt 30.4.2007.
[65] «Russische Investoren entdecken Vorliebe fuer Cognac» Frankfurter Allgemeine 5.5.2007.

and municipal use,[66] but the proposal was criticized by the Antimonopoly service.

In 2019, a WHO report stated alcohol consumption in Russia had fallen by 43% during 2003–2016, to a level smaller than per adult than in France or Germany.[67] It is true that after 23 h, the sale of liquor has been prohibited in shops. But it is rare to see an even less credible UN agency report.

10.15 Forestry and Timber Exports

Russia's forests count with 1.2 billion hectares for 20% of the world's total. It is mostly coniferous trees (spruces, larches and pines), which protect the taiga and the snow forests and their ecosystem and rare species, like the Amur tiger. Yet there two major threats; one is illegal logging mostly by the Chinese, hiring locals with giant harvesting machines and mobile sawmills. In these remote areas, underfunded Russian forestry officials and rangers have little access, and to get the timber out of the country corrupt border patrols can be bought.[68] In China, itself large-scale logging for environmental reasons has been prohibited. So the craving for timber for construction, furniture and paper now comes at the expense of her neighbour. With illegal logging, of course nothing gets replanted. As a result, Russia, during 2000–2013, lost 10% of its remaining virgin forests, or 5.5 million hectares lost in a single year, representing 27 soccer fields every minute.[69]

Like in California, Australia and the Mediterranean continental heat conditions regularly trigger forest fires in Central Russia, which sadly consume entire villages. Yet the huge Siberian summer fires of 2019 were much worse than usual. Overwhelming the firefighters, they ravaged unchecked during July and August, destroying a total of 13 million hectares—an area larger than Greece—around Krasnoyarsk and Irkutsk.

Despite the shrinking demand for newsprint and letter paper, the overall demand for wood products in Europe is constantly increasing: Cardboard bags for internet sales, cellulose textiles for sanitary articles, paper bags and cake paper. For wood pellets and chips alone for heating purposes, demand

---

[66] Interestingly, the frugal Japanese Ministry of Finance for its annual reception uses only foreign wines, namely those confiscated by customs at the borders. Quite possibly those confiscated at the Russian borders don't reach Moscow.

[67] Metro 2.10.2019.

[68] *Russia Business Today.* 9.10.2018.

[69] *The Moscow Times* 30.9.2014; Helen Womack "Russia's forests in Retreat" *Financial Times* 30.12.1998.

has doubled in the last 15 years. Accordingly, import demand is high—currently 15% of the EU's total consumption, two thirds of which came from Russia, Belarus and Ukraine by 2016 with a value in 2016 of EUR 420 million. The flows were well established: Russian birch and conifer wood went to Poland, the Baltics and to Finland as the world champion for processing as paper and pulp.

However, for 3 years, Russia has been increasingly restricting her timber exports to the EU, The official justification: We no longer want to export raw materials, but to promote domestic processing and value creation, since currently, the forestry sector contributes only 1.3% to the GDP. Russia imposed temporary export bans on birch round wood and veneer wood, which are, however, constantly being extended. This is intended to lower their prices for the "wood clan" among local processors. Similar export bans also apply to Russian fur and animal skins.

There are export quotas for other timber exports (to the extent that they are legal), which are increasingly used for the booming Chinese demand. Exports of the banned birch round wood to China simply doubled between 2013 and 2016. In addition, there are the usual customs frauds at the border: Remove everything to measure the stem diameter or arbitrarily decide the wood grades. In addition, the Russian state railway increases its freight tariffs for timber exports at will. In 2007, Russia had already doubled its export taxes on timber overnight to 25% of the value. This has hit, for example, by Stora Enso's paper factory hard in the small town of Imatra, with its 2400 employees as the main employer of the town, which is dependent on the permanent rail deliveries of Russian wood, especially birch logs, for its special papers. A total of 200,000 people work in the woodworking industry in Finland, which generates 16% of industrial production.[70] In Russia, wood is not scarce (which could justify export barriers as an emergency measure), if it was properly managed and replanting incentives and controlled. It owns a quarter of the world's wood resources and could harvest 600 million cubic meters of wood each year, but only one third. Above all, forests in Siberia and the Far East are used only in winter, when the soil is frozen due to the lack of infrastructure and unpaved long transport routes. Due to the suppressed foreign demand and the lack of domestic processing capacity, the harvested wood is often just left to rot or used as firewood.

However, anyone who processes himself in Russia remains unmolested, like the Austrian company Hasslacher, which produces high-quality prefabricated components ("Norica") for earthquake-proof wooden houses in Novgorod

---

[70] David Ibson 'Finns fear that Russia aims to reduce their mills to pulp' *Financial Times* 12.4.2007.

and exports them to Japan. The same applies to the paper mill Syktywkar, owned by the South African group Mondi, a world-class paper and cardboard manufacturer based in Vienna. In 2002, it bought an underutilized, non-productive paper combinat in the Komi Republic, 1000 km north-east of Moscow. It was built at the beginning of the 60 s by Komsomol "volunteers" with gigantomanic dimensions on 1000 ha in the middle of the Taiga at party command. After investments of EUR 545 million, the 8 500 employees now produce one million tons of paper and cardboard to be profitable for the growing Russian market.[71] Mondi has cutting rights for 5 million cubic meters of wood per year on 2.1 million hectares of forest. In practice, however, this only happens in winter when the soils are frozen. In Svetogorsk (Finnish: Enso) in Karelia, the US Group International Paper participated half of the Russian Ilim Group as the largest pulp and paper producer in Russia. Close to Dmitry Medvedev, who is said to be a major shareholder, it mainly benefits from the Russian export embargo through cheaper supply of wood, which is no longer allowed to go to Finland.

The mono-industrial city of Baikalsk, on the other hand, was not lucky to find a foreign investor for its scraped pulp, which had previously poisoned the Baikal lake, after Oligarch Oleg Deripaska found the plant unprofitable and lost its majority shares after losses. At Soviet times, such industrial cities were stacked out of the ground with their slabs around a single combinat. For the 15 000 inhabitants of Baikalsk, in addition to tourism and strawberry cultivation, there is only an alternative between unemployment, alcoholism and emigration.[72]

The forest sector needs to think in generations. The Russian state forest awards concessions after the wild period of the "forest war", when the logging companies wanted to acquire their land between 2000 and 2004, only for a period of 49 years. Although both domestic and foreign sawmills have a duty to provide fire protection and do replanting for reforestation—and most often to comply with it a minimum of costs and care—the time limitation for the concession is simply too short to provide incentives for sustainable, cost-intensive forest management in the impasse of the Russian forest zone. The trees are ripen here only after at least 80 years. Thus, the Russian legislator is damaging the interests of future generation.[73] The Russian Forest Agency Rosleskhoz has set the fees for logging at EUR 50 cents per cubic meter at

---

[71] Hubert Kickinger "Das Taiga Project" *format* 29/2008, 18.7.2008.
[72] 'Mit der Fabrik stirbt auch die Stadt" *Frankfurter Allgemeine* 6.4.2010.
[73] Gerald Hosp "Russlands Wald waechst nicht in den Himmel" *Neue Zürcher Zeitung* 10.11.2010.

a very low level, a fraction compared to the fees charged in Finland. This reflects the Soviet and Marxian work value doctrine that natural resources have no monetary value and should not cost anything. Payments for the timber are made only after it has been processed.

11

Russian SMEs and Their Problems

The Russian economy does not only consist of oligarchs and state-controlled energy conglomerates. There are 3.2 million businesses operating as SMEs, employing 18 million people (less than 30% of the workforce; by comparison: Germany: 65%) and 4.7 million people are self-employed.[1] Together they account for 25% of Russia's GDP (2012), 7.6% of capital investments and for 32% of enterprise sales. Still, their spread is fairly low: there are 31 SMEs per 1000 inhabitants (while there are 102 in the USA and 146 in Korea, the OECD's most entrepreneurial country). There is great regional variation. In places with greater purchasing power and qualified workforces like Moscow, St. Petersburg, Kaliningrad, Novosibirsk and Jaroslav, SME frequency is denser per inhabitants than in thinly settled Tuva, Zaibaikalsk and the North Caucasus, for instance, where business conditions are more adverse and transportation problems abound. At the same time, the scale of Russian SMEs remains small. 80% are micro-enterprises with 1–9 employees, and 16% small enterprises with a workforce between 10 and 49.

They struggle against an impressive array of difficulties: be they regulatory (construction permits, export/import licenses), access to finance, the recruitment of skilled labour, getting electricity and water, being harassed by officialdom and bankers for bribes, subjected to non-competitive practices by established local businesses (often regional monopolies), perhaps unsurprising in a country where until 1991 almost all entrepreneurialism has

---

[1] All figures in this chapter are taken from: OECD «Russian Federation. Key issues and policies» *Studies on SMEs and Entrepreneurship*. Paris: OECD Publishing 2015.

been violently suppressed during three generations of state socialism. In fact, entrepreneurialism still has a poor public image, being frequently seen and portrayed in the media as exploitative and manipulative businessmen. There are no role models of successful established multi-generational family businesses around, and there is no generation of trained successors or inherited corporate wealth.

Understandably, one cannot expect a grown Mittelstand culture, where fourth-generation family companies produce and export industrial niche products worldwide, from confectionary and sports shoes to water filters, calendar binding machines, fire extinguishers, industrial scales, sleeping bags.....

Rather Russian SMEs operate in wholesaling and retailing (around 50%), and one third as hotels, restaurants, in transportation and communication, construction, real estate or offer business services. Only 7% operate in manufacturing. As a result, less than 20% of industrial employment happens in Russian SMEs, while the comparative figures stand at 49% in the USA and 76% in Italy, for instance. For the self-employed, typical professions are beekeeping, tailoring, repair of household appliances, computer repair, mushroom collection, hairdressing, carpentry and the renovation of apartments. The informal sector with an estimated 7.8 million irregular jobs (accounting for 12% of non-agricultural employment) is fairly large. Estimated at around 41% of GDP—by comparison: Italy and Greece: 15%, Germany and France: 10%—its productivity is low, working conditions are poor, and incomes low with no social protection. As things stand, neither the SME sector nor the self-employed or the informal sector can make a meaningful contribution to the generation of income and jobs, let alone help to diversify Russia's commodity-based industrial and export structure.

New business owners—fashionably called start-ups—are only 2.4% of the adult population. In China, their share stands at 10.2%. As a result, the share of new business startups is low at 5%—again compared to China with 16%. In surveys, 70% of Russians doubt their skills and competencies to run their own business. This self-doubt and fear of failure are particularly pronounced among women, even though women count for 47% of SME ownership and for 40% of start-ups—very high shares indeed.

11.1 R&D and Training

Russian SMEs typically stick to traditional products and services, perhaps unsurprising given their poor endowment with capital and labour. Only 5% undertake any form of innovation in terms of products, processes, marketing or organization, which compares to some 50% in OECD average. This reflects the Russian overall low R&D spending levels at 1.1% of GDP, which is less than half of the OECD average of 2.4% of GDP. The private sector in Russia undertakes only 28% of total R&D investments. SMEs themselves spend only 1.6% of their turnover on innovation. 88% of entrepreneurs admit that they offer no new products or services, and 94% do not use new technologies. But two thirds of them are at least visible and active on the internet.

Less than 4% of public sector scientists and researchers have any experience of commercializing their discoveries. Reasons are poor laboratory equipment and materials and insufficient and over-regulated grants.

Although labour markets are flexible with 30% of employees changing jobs every year, with low costs for hiring and firing and the wide use of non-standard labour contracts and adjustable work hours, there is a chronic shortage of skilled labour not exclusively but most acutely for SMEs. Pisa ratings for high school students in math, reading and science are on a par with low US ratings, but far behind the front runners Korea, Japan, Switzerland and the Netherlands. 34% of a generation enters into fairly theoretically orientated tertiary education, while there is low participation in the less prestigious secondary level vocational training and education. After graduation, Russian adults show very little interest in continued education. In 2012, only 20% of those aged 25–64 participated in any form of further training—which compares to 65% in virtuous Scandinavia or the Netherlands.

11.2 Governance Problems

Already the "false start" of the early stage of transition in the 1990s, when quick returns and capital flight were rewarded due to continued legal uncertainties notably over property rights, and long-term horizons needed for manufacturing investments were discouraged, led to an almost lost decade for productive SMEs.

Yet also all well-known Russian macro-economic, structural and governance problems understandably continue to affect SMEs, stunt their growth, increase business risks and reduce their profitability.

With low inward FDI and the domination of state-owned enterprises of 80% of the banking, energy and transport sectors, state control of the economy in Russia is on a par with Turkey and China, but less though than in India (2013). Incumbent firms—irrespective of whether state or oligarch-owned—tend to abuse their national, regional or local monopoly power—important given the size and distances of Russia—and engage in anti-competitive practices, which are rarely checked by the Federal Anti-Monopoly Services. All this squeezes SMEs, limits their opportunities and increases their costs. Russia's commodity-driven export economy with its cycle of boom and bust (the latter painfully felt in 1998, 2008 and 2014) also puts SMEs at the receiving end of this unpredictable pig cycle, which they cannot affect and from which—given the absence of financial reserves—there is a little shelter or escape. Continued capital outflows at the order of US$ 140 billion (2008) to US$ 45 billion (2013) also contribute to limit their access to finance.

Opening a new business in principle is not particularly difficult. The average time needed has been reduced from 43 days (2004) to 15 days (2015) and is now equal to Germany or the UK. The difficulties start afterwards. Export and import licenses need nine to ten procedures and take 3 weeks on average. Building permits require 36 procedures on average and 300 days. Also, the supply of electricity and water is usually difficult.

Although corporate income tax rates have been reduced to 20% (2010) and the total corporate tax rate to 50.7% of profits (2014)—down from 60% (2006), the remaining tax load with the added social security payments remain a significant barrier. The more complex, costly and ambivalent administrative regulations are, and the poorer paid officials with a wide room of discretion are, the higher is usually the incidence of corruption. Russia for the very same reasons is here in the good company of other post-Soviet states like Azerbaijan, Belarus, Kazakhstan and Ukraine. SMEs report that in 16% of their meetings with public officials bribes and gifts for public services (like licenses, customs clearance and utility supply) and for lenient tax and other inspections are expected.

There is little possibility of recourse against arbitrary administrative decisions and are hence little constraints of government powers, as the rule of law is generally considered worse than in Eastern Europe and even Central Asia (??—lumped together in the survey quoted in the OECD study). Fundamental rights, regulatory enforcement, civil justice and criminal justice all are overwhelmingly negatively affected by corruption and arbitrary judicial decisions according to a large majority of Russian respondents.

Yet there is regional variation. Smaller cities like Ulyanovsk, Saransk and Vladikavkaz, as the result of the efforts of reformist mayors or governors, have reduced regulatory and tax burdens and hence the incidence of corruption, while the metropoles of Moscow, St. Petersburg and Novosibirsk have not.

11.3 Access to Finance

Most SMEs continue to rely on internal finance for their investments and working capital. According to a World Bank study, only 22% of Russian companies had access to bank loans, which for SMEs remain nonetheless their most important source of external finance. The 20 largest banks—mostly state-controlled—grant 70% of loans, typically to large companies and public holdings. Most other banks have little expertise in corporate loans, to assess balance sheets, business plans and collateral and to evaluate credit histories and default risks. As a result, they act extremely conservative with high refusal rates, even though the record of non-performing loans remains low with 4.3% in 2013 (a normal year of recovery) and 5.8% in the crisis year of 2009. Nominal interest rates are high with 14–17%, and so are real interest rates with 7–10% (2012). Loans are usually short term, up to 3 years. There are also smaller institutions with an unsophisticated risk assessment—similar to the Chinese "shadow banks"—which grant small loans at high rates. Loan sharks even offer weekly consumer credits at usurious annualized rates of 2700%.

11.4 SME Policies

The problems of the SME sector somewhat surprisingly have not escaped the attention of the Kremlin. After President Putin announced his wish for a more entrepreneurial society, in which by 2020, 50% of the workforce would be employed by SMEs, in 2007, an SME law was enacted, which mainly focused on financial support. At least 15% of public procurement should be awarded to SMEs both nationally and locally. Tax accounting rules were simplified for SME. Under the auspices of the Ministry for Economic Development a Federal Credit Guarantee Agency, 21 regional loan funds and 21 venture capital funds were created, as were 104 state-supported business incubators (hosting a total of 1600 SMEs) and 34 export support centres covering

83 regions. Between 2007 and 2011, seven technology parks were opened. Subsidies of the Ministry of Agriculture were made available for coops and farm enterprises, as well as funds from the Ministries of Education and Science and of Health for business support in their remit. A State Commission for Competition and SME Development operates as cross-governmental working party for programme implementation and consults with "Business Russia" (the entrepreneurs association), the National Association of Farm Enterprises and Agricultural Cooperatives (the farm lobby), and the National Chamber of Commerce and Industry.

There was also a Small Privatization Law in 2008, due to which 33.000 SMEs could buy their premises. Also, municipal properties became available for lease.

The state-owned development bank (and former Soviet foreign trade bank) Vnesheconombank (VEB)—which since 2014 is on the EU and US sanctions lists—was endowed for SME credit lines and subsidies for plant and equipment. Through its arm, the SME bank, funds were channelled to 130 regional partner banks and 141 non-bank institutions. Until 2015, some 38.000 SMEs (1.2% of total SMEs) were assisted with guarantees and loans at rates of 11–12% for a duration of 2–10 years. It is estimated that the SME bank's microfinance facility in Moscow and St. Petersburg covered about 10% of needs.

11.5 Conclusion

SME finance needs stretch beyond simple credits and guarantees so far in focus but comprise a mix of loan products, factoring, equity instruments, trade credit and leasing, supplied not only by a state bank and its partners but by deposit banks, insurances, pension funds, investment banks and venture capital funds.

Needs beyond finance pertain to missing or insufficient consultation, training, advisory and information services, export centres and business incubators.

Federal SME policies since 2007 prima vista appear as well intended, but their means are insufficient, a proverbial drop in the bucket, and too narrowly focussed, while structural, human resource, finance and governance conditions remain overwhelmingly adverse.

There is obviously a great deal of regional variation. While SMEs and startups benefit from densely populated areas with a more skilled workforce and higher purchasing power, they are conversely at a disadvantage in rural areas, with a less-educated workforce and their handicap of underdeveloped roads, costly rail freight and poor communication and infrastructure.

Proper governance by reform-minded mayors and governors can sometimes redress these disadvantages in small towns and oblasts by simplifying local regulations, construction permits and tax administration, strengthening the rule of law, opening local procurement effectively, and establishing business-friendly "single windows" and regional business ombudsmen. Kirov, Smolensk and Kaluga are such examples. Unfortunately, most regions, big cities like Moscow, St. Petersburg, Rostov and Chelyabinsk as well as most mono-industry towns are disinterested in both local and federal SME support, as the business taxes they raise locally are all transferred to the federal level.

Reference

1. OECD (2015) Studies on SMEs and entrepreneurship, Russian federation: key issues and policies. OECD Publishing, Paris

12

External Trade: The Roles of the EU, of the Eurasian Economic Union and of China

12.1 EU–Russia Trade Relations

Despite the restrictive measures being in place, the EU and Russia still have very strong economic links. In 2017, bilateral trade expanded to e 254 billion, with the EU's exports remaining flat at €86 billion during 2018. Russia's trade surplus is clearly caused by her energy exports to the EU (and unlike Chinese manufacturers do not destroy any industrial jobs). The EU is Russia's largest trading partner, representing 45% of Russia's foreign trade, while in turn Russia after the USA, China and Switzerland is the EU fourth largest partner, accounting for 6% of foreign trade.

Russia remains a major commodity exporter to the EU with oil, gas ferrous metals, aluminium, platinum, vanadium, wheat, wood, vodka, caviar and even some reindeer meat. For a total of €168 billion (2018) in return, the EU mainly sells cars, trucks, machinery, chemicals, pharmaceuticals, medical equipment, alcoholic drinks and high-speed trains for a total of €86 billion, hence, with a cover ratio of barely 50%. Since one decade, this bilateral trade deficit varies between €60 billion and €80 billion per year, and as mentioned is essentially cause by Russian oil and gas exports, as many EU member states are unwilling or unable to diversify away from Russian gas supplies. Equally responsible are the openly protectionist policies adopted by the Kremlin already in 2012, which discriminate against EU manufactured exports and services.

There is an open but difficult dialogue on trade because of current Russian protectionist policies. EU–Russia trade was already decreasing before

Ukraine crisis with a sharp slump since 2014 mainly as a result of the decline in Russian purchasing power. This drop, however, has now started to reverse, with EU exports to Russia increasing by 19% in 2017 (and imports from Russia increased by 22%), also thanks to gradual recovery of Russian economy.

Since 2012, Russia has adopted clearly protectionist stance. EU launched four WTO cases against Russia and so far won two of them (another one is ongoing and one is on hold). In addition, we face a number of trade irritants (e.g. sanitary and phytosanitary, subsidies linked to local content; public procurement) and are looking at compatibility with WTO rules, inter alia, of massive Russian import substitution plan. Russia pushes not only for promoting contacts between the EU and the Eurasian Economic Union but also in view of the wider political context contacts remain limited to technical level.

Russia's import substitution policy uses different trade-restrictive instruments to protect and support domestic Russian producers. This affects most sectors of the economy (automotive, machinery, IT, textile, agriculture, pharmaceuticals, medical devices). These measures are also aimed at encouraging European and other foreign companies to invest and localise their production in Russia. Subsidies to domestic industries linked to local content requirements and restrictions for foreign operators in government procurement and in the purchases by state-owned enterprises are tools used in this respect. Some technology transfer and research and development activities are also requested. Other trade restrictive measures such as excessive and WTO inconsistent import duties as well as frequent unjustified phytosanitary bans are also part of the Russian protectionist toolbox.

EU restrictive measures have had only a limited impact on EU business. For instance, increased exports of sensitive goods to the world fully offset the losses from the Russian market. The total exports figures as to sensitive goods remained almost identical from 2014 to 2016, i.e. EUR ca. 16.6 billion annually. As to industrial products, the steep decline of EU exports has been caused by the economic recession in Russia and by the implementation of the import substitution policy. There are no Russian sanctions in place concerning foreign industrial imports.

The continued implementation of anti-competitive measures in Russian economy is aimed at isolating domestic producers from external competition and is supportive to ever stronger vested interests representing an obstacle for any attempt of market opening.

Economic Sanctions

The economic sanctions (related to access to capital markets, arms embargo, dual-use goods and sensitive technologies) were rolled-over regularly by the European Council for a period of 6 months and are linked to the full implementation of the Minsk agreement to reestablish full sovereignty of the Ukraine in the Donbass.

Travel ban/asset freeze listings targeting 150 people and 38 companies are also prolonged regularly. With regard to Russia's illegal annexation of Crimea, the EU continues to implement its non-recognition policy. The EU restrictions on economic relations with Crimea and Sevastopol were prolonged since 2014.

In addition to these measures, the European Council of July 2014 also requested the EIB to suspend the signature of new financing operations in Russia. Since then, EU Member States have also coordinated their positions in the EBRD to refuse the financing of new operations in Russia.

Since August 2014, Russia has banned the import of a large part of agricultural products from the EU. This comes on top of many protectionist measures that restrict EU's exports to Russia. The Russian countermeasures, affecting EU agro-food exports (cheese, meat, fruits, fish etc.) worth €6 billion per year were equally extended since 2014.

The EU's sanctions policy and, to a greater extent, the decrease in oil and gas prices had a significant effect on Russia's economy and on its longer term growth potential. After 2 years of recession, Russia's economy recovered in 2017 with an estimate growth of 1.7%, due to the improved macroeconomic environment. The economic sanctions will continue to affect the specific areas targeted.

On the other hand, sanctions have had only a marginal impact on the EU's economy. Commission estimates are that the sanctions against Russia and Russian counter-measures have reduced total EU GDP growth by around −0.1% in 2016 while their effect is expected to be neutral in 2017. Sanctions have had both an economic and political impact but perhaps their most important achievement has been to deter further escalation of the conflict.

12.2 Russia and the Eurasian Economic Union (EEU)[1]

In difference to other regional integration initiatives, like the EU, ASEAN, the African Union, Mercosur etc., the EEU appears as a special case, originating in the geostrategic interests of its by far largest member state with asymmetric policy-making permeating its membership structure. Thus, the Kremlin decides autonomously on new protectionist variants of its import and transit policies and its countersanctions with little regard for consultation of its four much smaller partners (Armenia, Belorus, Kyrgisia and Kazakhstan). They in turn attempt to maximize their autonomy in economic and trade decisions in order to safeguard their national sovereignty. Formal EEU decision-making of the five EEU members is by unanimity, and whatever little is decided, its secretariat, the Eurasian Economic Commission (EEC) and the EEU Court in Minsk are powerless for the lack of personnel, budget and legal resources to enforce implementation. When their customs union (starting already partially by 2010) was set up, tariffs were typically raised to higher Russian levels, thus putting EU exporters at a disadvantage in the other four EEU member states (notably Kazakhstan, Kyrgisia and Armenia).

While the EEU leadership and the Kremlin aspire to pair relations and its formal recognition by EU authorities, yet, thus, far EU consultations are held the EEC on technical subjects at "technical" levels only, on issues like toy standards, cement imports, alcoholic beverages, cosmetics, pharmaceutical testing, customs procedures, competition law, taxation and other trade irritants on which the RU authorities claim that the EEU has now competence. De facto the expertise on these issues continues to lie in the various capitals, with the result that the EEC's polite letterbox functions have yielded only very modest results on the EU's years-old technical requests. Rather the creation of the EEC has made the interaction with the RU economic and trade authorities more complex, allowing them to play ping-pong between their more or less uncooperative institutions. It is now a regular feature that RU authorities argue: "Well, it is now the EEU which is in charge. Talk to them". Once this is done, the EEC's reply will be: "We don't have the expertise here, but on this issue Minsk or Bishkek is tasked". There, they are often more helpful than their colleagues in Moscow, but in the end, the decisions are taken there…

What the EEU is not: It is not the Comecon. It is an intergovernmental body deciding with unanimity with an asymmetric membership

---

[1] Many of the facts are based on a very interesting and well researched, but strangely undated recent European Commission "Study on Eurasian Economic Union (EEU)".

(RU counting for 86% of GDP and trade, 89% of territory and 80% of population), in which four out of five members do not want to be forcibly integrated—and Kyrgistan and Armenia only joined after Russian arm twisting after threatening to introduce visa and work permit obligations for their nationals, as the countries depend on their remittances. Hence, it will not go anywhere politically, certainly not an ever closer union.

Secondly, it is not a functionalist instrument for positive spill-overs to impact positively on the Kremlin's protectionist policies and to resurrect the dreams of the Yeltsin years about a common space from Lisbon to Vladivostok,[2] as RU policies remain unpredictably unilateralist and mercantilist.

The EEU's shortcomings. Clearly and predictably it suffers from intergovernmentalism and Russian unilateralism (aka bullying). On trade issues, Kazakhstan has no access to the Russian oil and electricity market. The Gazprom pipeline monopoly continues to block Central Asian gas exports to the EU. When Kazakhstan and Belarus did not join the Russian food import embargo, Russia reintroduced border controls. Also, Kazakhstan and Belarus did not introduce the Russian "recycling fee" on cars (which Russian producers get reimbursed, but not importers). Export duties were maintained on oil exports to Belarus. On embargoed food stuff, Russia blocks transit from the EU to Central Asia and to China. On competition issues, in this declared "common market" the Russian dual pricing system on gas (high export prices, low domestic ones) gives a particular advantage to privileged domestic producers (steel and fertilizers, for instance). In public procurement, it also discriminates against EEU suppliers. In defence and space industries, state loans, guarantees and tax incentives work for Russian domestic industries only. EEU competition rules are essentially toothless. There is no discipline on industrial subsidies, and services are not covered. On legal issues, there are different regimes for foreign direct investment protection, disagreements over trademarks as well as no effective rules of origin.

So, what are the economic effects of this customs union, set up in 2012 (as a successor to the ill-fated CIS) in 2012 and formalized as the EEU in 2014? Just to put it into perspective: The entire EEU amounts to 13% of the EU's GDP (and RU's GDP is equal to the one of Spain or of the Benelux). In the EU, 61% is intra-EU trade, within the EEU, it is barely 15% (and amounts to only 6–7% of RU foreign trade). Put simply, they are all commodity producers and very uncompetitive in manufactures and services. Hence, there is little complementarity.

---

[2]Alexandra Valiseva "Engage ! Why the EU should talk with the EEU" Friedrich Ebert Stiftung. September 2017.

12.3 A Very Unequal Alliance

12.3.1 The Politics and Economics of China–Russian Relations

The relations of the bear and the dragon on the Eurasian landmass had always been ambivalent. After constructing the Transsiberian Railway, the Czarist empire pushed into Manchuria and built a huge land and sea fortress in Port Arthur (today: Dalian), where were ejected during the Russo-Japanese War in 1905, while their Baltic fleet was sunk near Tsushima. Outer Mongolia, which belonged to China's traditional tributary sphere of influence, was conquered by the Bolsheviks in 1923, the first foreign country to be forcefully Sovietized. East-Turkestan (today: Xinjiang) was ruled for a few years by white Russian officers. Later also thousands of Kazakh herders arrived, fleeing Soviet collectivization (only to be forced into people's communes after 1949). Russian military aid and captured Japanese weapons in Manchuria facilitated in 1948 the Communist victory in China's civil war over Chiang Kai Chek. Yet in 1964, Mao Tse Tung broke with Moscow and denounced China's humiliating treatment on the hands of the "social imperialists". In March 1969, a dispute over poorly marked swamps, some inhabited islands and the more strategic island of Damanski in the Ussuri in front of Khabarovsk erupted into a small border war, with more than 1000 killed, mostly on the Chinese side using mass attacks against superior Soviet troops. In 2004, Putin conceded 174 square kilometres of the disputed territory to China, ignoring the protests of local residents and Siberian Cossacks, the only territorial concession he has undertaken thus far.

In the meantime, the scales of power have shifted further. The economic might of China weights nine times the one of Russia, which is equivalent of the GDP of Spain or of the Benelux. Her population size with 1.4 billion is ten times larger. Under the regime of the Kremlin oligarchs, who prefer to plunder rather than to invest Russia for China (armaments apart), remained a backward supplier of raw materials with a decaying infrastructure. China, however, thanks to the ambitious and ruthless industrial policies of the CPCh using all means available—cheap state bank credits, export dumping, the use of the secret service and the massive theft of intellectual property—to from the status of a cheap mass producer to a high tech country that will reach and bypass the US by 2025 as targeted, while Russia stagnates as an "Upper Volta with missiles" (a bon mot dated 1977 by the late German Chancellor Helmut Schmidt). These imbalances will increase further. While China grows further at the rate of 6% per year, the Russian economy by 2030 will decline from world rank 10–15, while her population will shrink from 144 million to 139 and age further dramatically (except for men who for well-known reasons continue to die at 64 on average). It hardly fits the Kremlin's aspirations at super power status to be treated continuously at junior status, as Beijing hardly conceals its newly found feelings of superiority and its stronger bargaining power. However, since Putin has decided to play the anti-Western card for the purposes of enemy projection, which helps him for his aggressive policies vis-à-vis Georgia, the Ukraine up to Syria and Venezuela, for the use of short victorious wars and for internal repression to cement his rule, he can hardly choose his only largest remaining friend.

The bilateral economic data are hardly impressive. In terms of FDI, China in 2016 invested a total of US$185 billion abroad, out of which only US$350 million went to Russia. This increased in 2017 when CEFC bought a 14.2% in the state oil producer, Rosneft. Volumes of bilateral trade are at the whim of oil price variations. In 2016, they stood at US$70 billion (US$8 billion of which was Russian armament to China). By comparison, EU–Russia trade was at €225 billion and EU–China trade at €560 billion. 70% of Russia's trade continues to be handled with the EU, only 17% with China. The problems are striking on both sides. Both are extremely tough negotiators and at a loss to comprehend their neighbour's business cultures. Russian manufactures are not competitive (apart from guns, airplanes, caviar and vodka), and the Chinese, like the Europeans, are hurt by Russian protectionism, arbitrary red tape, lousy infrastructure and bizarre distribution.

Since a long time, China has thrust longing eyes on the resource riches of depopulating Siberia: oil, gas, precious metals like mangan and bauxite, anthracite, diamonds, gold, coal, wood, fish and water. Their deposits in places like Magadan and Kolyma were developed and exploited by millions of slave labourers of Stalin's gulag, deportees from occupied Europe and German and Japanese prisoners of war at horrendous human costs and sufferings during 1939–1953. Indeed, during their numerous summits—up to five per year—innumerable Memoranda of Understandings are regularly signed between Presidents Xi and Putin. Yet, out of all these magnificent pipeline and cooperation deals, only preciously few are actually implemented. In negotiations without end, one disputes over prices, credit conditions and project terms. The Chinese line is very clear. They pay the piper and hence want full control from inception, construction, maintenance up to the source (like in the rest of the world where they engage). For the Russians, this is fundamentally unacceptable. They did not kick out Western giants like BP, Shell and Exxon from their strategic resource sector in order to hand control over to the Chinese. Hence, in spite of all Putin talk about an "Eastern pivot" since 2014, all major oil and gas pipelines—Yamal, Drushba, Soyus, Brotherhood, Northstream—continue to run from West Siberia to East and Central Europe: In the past to supply the Soviet empire, today to finance the state budget and to fill the oligarchs' coffers. At least China participates in the Yamal LNG project, since tanker transports to the Far East are now possible through the North East Passage during the summer months.

There are acute Chinese desires for Siberian water, like the tributaries of the Ob river, the Balkash lake in Kazakhstan or drinking water from Lake Baikal in order to combat the scary desertification of Northern China with its dramatically sinking groundwater levels.[3] China wants to continue its water-intensive irrigation-based agriculture for rice, maize, soy and sugar beet. The ecological situation of the Amur River is worst, as Chinese drains of water threaten river navigation and its inflow of industrial waste has made fishing and the use of drinking water too hazardous.[4] China has rented millions of hectares of forests, which it will cut during the next 50 years. Whether it will reforest correctly, as legally prescribed, is uncertain. Precisely, 564 Chinese sawmills are currently in operation, since cutting trees has been heavily restricted in China.[5] The hunger for wood for construction and furniture, however, remains. Furthermore, hundred thousands of hectares of agricultural lands have fallen fallow in Southern Siberia, which China would dearly lease for its hard-working peasants. Yet there is political resistance on the Russian side.[6] Currently, in Russia's Far East, which covers 36% of its territory, there is a population of only 6.3 million. 20 years ago, it had still been 8.1 million, a decline of 15%. The region continues to be threatened by out-migration to metropolitan Russia and by ageing.[7] After the end of the Gulag, slave labour system workers had been lured by the promise of higher wages and early retirement. Yet, with the demise of the Soviet Union, many remain trapped in poverty, unable to move back. South of the Amur River the population of Manchuria, heavily industrialized by the Japanese in pre-war years and now China's "rustbelt", stands at 120 million, people who are eager, mobile and hungry for a better future. According to the more serious estimates, the number of documented and undocumented Chinese immigrants in entire Russia stands at roughly 2 million. They control the casinos, many hotels in

---

[3]Paul Goble "Russian Elite Profiteering Enables Growing Chinese Control of Baikal Region" Eurasia Daily Monitor 16, The Jamestown Foundation, 5.3.2019.

[4]Frederic Lasserre "The Amur River border. Once a symbol of conflict, could it turn into a water resource stake," Cybergo: European Journal of Geography. 242, 2003.

[5]Vita Spivak "The Bugbear of Chinese Deforestation: The real Threat to Russia's Forests" Carnegie Moscow Center 10.9.2018.

[6]Daniel Broessler. «Die Chinesen kommen» Süddeutsche Zeitung 3.8.2006.

[7]Anna Nemtsova "Shrinking Siberia" Newsweek 17.9.2012.

the Far East, work in road construction, in retail trade and in agriculture. The Russian government, however, tries to cure the shortage of labour in the Far East by recruiting North Korean slave labour. Their wages are lower and mostly captured by the Kim-Regime. Once their contracts are terminated, they are repatriated to North Korea.

China clearly does not consider Russia's territorial possessions as legitimate. Only in 1639, the first Cossack troops and fur hunters had reached the Sea of Okhotsk. And, in 1858 and 1860, the Czars forced the powerless Manchu emperors to accept their claims to the Amur plains and to the territories East of the Ussuri up to Vladivostok (Primorye). For the Chinese, these are the last of the hated "unequal treaties" to which they had been forced to submit in the nineteenth century, which are still in force.[8]

Officially there is still entente and harmony. With their Shanghai Organization for Cooperation (SOC), both managed successfully to eject US influence from Central Asia (in which already the Obama administration showed very little interest) and to establish a dual security hegemony.[9] Yet China with her Silk Road initiative acquires more and more economic leverage in Russia's erstwhile backyard. Motorways, railroad lines, energy grids, pipelines delivering gas and oil to China, warehouses and terminals for Chinese exports, airports, power stations and glass fibre grids: all constructed with Chinese funds, under Chinese control and in China's national interest; projects which Russia cannot possibly match. In short, the entire region up to the Caspian Sea will turn into a Chinese sphere of interest, apart from some residual European and Turkish interests. De facto Russia begins to play the unenviable role of an unpaid guardsman for Chinese economic interests, similar to NATO in Afghanistan. Indeed, already, during 2015 reports surfaced that Putin wished to diversify from the Chinese dominance in Russia's Asian policy by cultivating India, Japan, Pakistan, Vietnam and ASEAN,[10] so far with little systematic efforts and few tangible results.

China and Russia surely are no formal allies. China reacts with neutral caution and scarcely hidden reservations to Russia's policy of annexations and destabilization in Georgia and in the Ukraine. With her Tibetan and Taiwanese interests, territorial integrity remains a foreign policy dogma. Never would China be drawn into foreign policy disputes in which she does not see a national interest. Vice versa Russia is helping her arch-enemy

---

[8] Theo Sommer. China First. Die Welt auf dem Weg ins chinesische Jahrhundert. Munich. 2019, p. 319.
[9] Jamil Anderlini "Russia and China agree to boost military ties" Financial Times 20.11.2014.
[10] Bloomsbury 17.7.2015.

Vietnam to develop oil fields in disputed waters in the South China Sea.[11] Also, cooperation on arms sales is not unproblematic. Russia's most important export customers are China's rivals India and Vietnam. However, since 2014, Russia has resumed to supply China with S 400 air defence systems and with SU 35 fighter aircraft. Exports had been interrupted one decade earlier after china rebuilt Russian SU 27 fighters as the Shenyang J11 and sold them as a cheaper version to her friends in the Third World.[12] Obviously like any long-nosed barbarians, the Russian friends were not safe from technology theft either. The Russian military has few illusions. Relatively most of its troops are stationed in four armies along the 4300 km long common border in the eastern military district. Here also most of Russia's intermediate nuclear Iskandar missiles are located.[13] In fact, their development had been the reply to Chinese missile deployment—mostly directed against Taiwan. If someone has to be blamed for Russia's breach of the INF treaty—abrogated by the Trump administration—it should in all fairness be the Chinese—with Europe now footing the bill for the associated risks.

In September, Russia organized "Vostok" as the largest military exercise since the cold war along the Mongolian border and at the Pacific coast. 300,000 men, 36,000 armoured vehicles, 1000 aircraft and 8 warships were involved. This was a multiple of "Zapad", which took place in the West with 130,000 Russian and Belorussian troops, exercising a small victorious war against an unnamed Western neighbour (which one could identify as Poland or Lithuania). Surely it is more impressive than NATO infantry exercises in battalion strength with a few reconnaissance tanks in the Baltics. This time China participated with 3200 troops, 900 tanks and 30 fighter aircraft. Redland successfully defeated an invasion of Blueland, involving also a simulated tactical nuclear strike.[14]

It is unclear for how long Russia will accept her political and economic junior role with China, watch her foreseeable loss of a sphere of influence in Central Asia and face the risk of a geopolitical loss of Siberia, the main source of her resource riches. Post-Putin who exclusively operates according to short-term power interests and tactical whims, the cards will be remixed.

---

[11] Michal Makocki and Nicu Popescu. China and Russia: an Eastern partnership in the making? IIS Caillot Paper no 110, December 2016, p. 14.

[12] Cyrille Bret "Armaments exports" in: Richard A. Bitzinger and Nico Popescu (eds.) Defense industries in Russia and China. ISS Report No. 38, December 2017, p. 23.

[13] Sommer. Op. cit., p. 342.

[14] Brian G. Carlson "Vostok-2018: Another Sign of strengthening Russia-China Ties" SWP Comment No 47, November 2018.

After all, the West does not threaten Russia with an invasion or a political revolution. For China, in the end only one rival superpower counts: the one of the USA. In the long run, Russia for the Middle Kingdom is as expendable as her friends in North Korea, Myanmar or Pakistan.

Printed in the United States
by Baker & Taylor Publisher Services